3800 15 0
KU-001-219
High Life Highland

James **Gangland** series. He also worked for many years as a solicitor specializing in criminal work and was for a number of years editor of the *New Law Journal*.

HIGHLAND
LIBRARIES
WITHDRAWN

Also available

The Mammoth Book of Conspiracies
The Mammoth Book of Lost Symbols
The Mammoth Book of Shark Attacks
The Mammoth Book of Body Horror
The Mammoth Book of Steampunk
The Mammoth Book of New CSI
The Mammoth Book of Gangs
The Mammoth Book of One-Liners
The Mammoth Book of Ghost Romance
The Mammoth Book of Best New SF 27
The Mammoth Book of Pulp Fiction
The Mammoth Book of Horror 25
The Mammoth Book of Slasher Movies
The Mammoth Book of Street Art
The Mammoth Book of Angels and Demons
The Mammoth Book of Ghost Stories by Women
The Mammoth Book of Unexplained Phenomena
The Mammoth Book of Futuristic Romance
The Mammoth Book of Best British Crime 11
The Mammoth Book of Combat
The Mammoth Book of Dark Magic
The Mammoth Book of Zombies
The Mammoth Book of Hollywood Scandals
The Mammoth Book of Losers
The Mammoth Book of Warriors and Wizardry
The Mammoth Book of SF Stories by Women
The Mammoth Book of Southern Gothic Romance
The Mammoth Book of the Vietnam War
The Mammoth Book of Air Disasters and Near Misses

Justice Denied

James Morton

HIGH LIFE HIGHLAND	
3800 15 0028754 9	
Askews & Holts	Jul-2015
345.0122	£10.99

ROBINSON

First published in Great Britain in 2015 by Robinson
1 3 5 7 9 8 6 4 2

Copyright © James Morton, 2015

The moral right of the author has been asserted.

All rights reserved.
No part of this publication may be reproduced, stored in a retrieval system, or
transmitted, in any form, or by any means, without the prior permission in writing of
the publisher, nor be otherwise circulated in any form of binding or cover other than
that in which it is published and without a similar condition including this condition
being imposed on the subsequent purchaser.

A CIP catalogue record for this book
is available from the British Library.

ISBN 978-1-47211-131-9 (paperback)
ISBN 978-1-47211-941-4 (ebook)

Typeset in Plantin by Hewer Text UK Ltd, Edinburgh
Printed and bound in Great Britain by Clays Ltd, St Ives plc

Papers used by Robinson are from well-managed forests and other responsible sources

MIX
Paper from
responsible sources
FSC® C104740

Robinson
is an imprint of
Constable & Robinson Ltd
100 Victoria Embankment
London EC4Y 0DY

An Hachette UK Company
www.hachette.co.uk

www.constablerobinson.com

Contents

Introduction

1 No Bodies   1

The Campden Wonder   2

Michael Onufrejczyk; Jesse and Stephen Boorn   6

Louise Butler and George Yelder; Leon Sanchez
and Gregorio Valero   9

Guillaume Seznec; Leonard Fraser   13

2 Folk-Devils and Moral Panics   19

Devils and Witches: Margot de la Barre and
Marion la Droiturière; Jehenne de Brigue and
Macette de Ruilly; Urbain Grandier;
Alice Samuel; the Bideford Three;
Jane Wenham; Mary and Elizabeth Hicks;
Janet Horne; Anna Göldi   20

The Witches of Salem   29

Helen Duncan   33

Ethel Rosenberg   41

The West Memphis Three   53

3 The Road to the Court of Appeal 67
  Edmund Galley 68
  William Habron 82
  Florence Maybrick 91
  Samuel Clowes and Henry Johnson;
  Joseph Hodgson, Joseph Lowson and
  William Siddle; Henry Hardwick and
  Richard Walford; Michael Brannagan and
  Peter Murphy 103
  George Edalji 116
  Adolf Beck 130

4 Poison Pen 139
  Mary Johnson; Rose Emma Gooding 140

5 Mistaken Identity 145
  Oscar Slater 146
  Joe Hill 152
  Walter Rowland 169
  Mahmood Mattan 178
  Patrick Meehan 186
  Rubin Carter and John Artis; David McCallum 192

6 Race Hate 203
  The Scottsboro Boys 204
  The Scooba Three 225

7 Incompetent Lawyers 231
  James Fisher; Richard Glossip; Russell Tucker;
  Reginald Love Powell; Ann Marie Boodram 232

8 The Power of the Press   239
    Joseph Majczek   240
    Dr Sam Sheppard   246

9 Three Who Got Away   257
    John Bodle   258
    Harold Loughans   262
    Tony Mancini   272

10 Fit-ups and False Confessions   285
    Alfred Dreyfus   286
    Ameer Ben Ali 'Frenchy'   296
    Reggie Dudley and Bobby Maynard   302
    The Darvell Brothers; the Cardiff Three;
    Idris Ali   315
    The Mickelberg Brothers   326
    Arthur Allan Thomas   332
    The Maxwell Confait Case   341
    Warren Billings and Tom Mooney   348
    Colin Ross and the Gun Alley Tragedy   358
    James Finch and John Stuart   372

11 The Road to Abolition   389
    Derek Bentley   390
    Ruth Ellis   402

12 Expert Evidence?   415
    Charles Stielow; Sacco and Vanzetti; Stephen
    Witherell; William Lancaster; Manny Strewl   416
    Bill Dillon; Juan Ramos   426

13 False Forensics?   433

    Lindy Chamberlain   434

    James Hooten; Darwin Haselhuhn;

    Donald Lee Shirley; Eddie Browning;

    Glen Woodall; Jeffery Todd Pierce;

    David Gibson; Randall Dale Adams   441

    Ray Krone; Levon Brooks and Kennedy

    Brewer; William Richards   456

    David Wayne Kunze; Mark Dallagher   464

    The Narborough Murders; Kirk

    Bloodsworth; John Kogut, Dennis Halstead

    and John Restivo; John Schneeberger   472

14 The Future   483

Introduction

'On that evidence he is entitled to be acquitted. That will not help him now. He is dead. That is the iniquity of the death penalty: its hopeless, ineluctable finality.'
  Sidney Silverman MP on the hanging of Walter Rowland,
  Hanged or Innocent?, England 1947.

What have Derek Bentley of England, Colin Ross of Australia, Mahmood Mattan of Wales, Joe Hill of America and many, many others in common? The answer is they were all wrongly executed. What have Oscar Slater of Scotland, Alfred Dreyfus of France, the West Memphis Three and many, many others in common? They all served lengthy sentences following wrongful convictions. And what have the Englishmen Harold Loughans and Tony Mancini and many, many others in common? They were all wrongly acquitted.

What is a miscarriage of justice? Part of the answer is easy. It occurs where an innocent person is convicted. And, many people would say, when a person who has committed the offence is acquitted. But what if the acquittal is simply because there is not sufficient evidence against him? Does that make it a miscarriage? Then what about the situation when a guilty person is convicted only because of trickery and dishonesty by the prosecution? Isn't that a miscarriage of justice in the strict sense of the word?

Years ago I defended three men on a charge of safebreaking. They all pleaded not guilty and were convicted mainly because dust from the turn-ups of their trousers matched that from the floor of the bank. Afterwards I went to see them in the cells and one said, 'You know that was a right fit-up. The coppers planted that dust. We burned our trousers after the job.' Over the years it has become generally accepted in criminal and legal circles that in 1953 the Scotland Yard detective Herbert Sparkes planted evidence on the safebreaker Alfie Hinds to secure a conviction when the Maples store in London's Tottenham Court Road had been robbed. It is also accepted that Hinds did the job. Were those miscarriages of justice?

How do miscarriages of justice occur? In his book *Getting Justice Wrong*, Nicholas Cowdery, the former New South Wales Director of Public Prosecutions, argues that the periodic exposures of police misbehaviour show that if there are not strong controls in place over bodies like police forces, there will be improper conduct and corruption. Unprofessional police will always be quick to exploit any loophole in procedures to achieve what they regard as the 'right' result. For a police force under pressure for results and immune from genuine scrutiny, Machiavellian cynicism must be a constant temptation. Provided the victims of injustice are unpopular and without means – skells in American police lingo, while dingoes is the Australian word – the rewards for solving cases are great, and the risks to the individual police officer are small.

Another Australian, Paul Wilson, in his essay 'Miscarriages of justice in serious cases in Australia', identifies several different factors that contribute to miscarriages of justice. They include overzealousness by police, police taking 'short cuts' to secure convictions against a 'guilty' person, evidence from experts who are in reality acting as 'propagandists' for the prosecution and confessions that have been either fabricated or extracted through pressure. Often, he believes, there is no conscious decision to convict the innocent. The police adopt tunnel vision and will not look at evidence that might exculpate the suspect. Any illegal means is justified by the end result of obtaining a conviction. And, once charges are laid, prosecutors will collaborate with the police to do everything possible to make them stick.

The Oscar Slater trial, wrote John Mortimer in his introduction to *Famous Criminal Cases*:

> ... provides us with a manual of injustice, from the incompetent defence to the police who refused to admit their mistakes, from the passionately convinced prosecutor, to the unfair judge, no one emerges well from the proceedings except the prisoner.

Another good example is in paragraph 339 of the Report of the New Zealand Royal Commission in the case of Arthur Allan Thomas:

> We consider that by now the Police were exhibiting a readily understandable desire to bring to a successful end a long and difficult homicide investigation by ensuring the conviction of the one suspect against whom there seemed to be any evidence at all, weak as that evidence has now been shown to be.

It is the same the whole world over. The *New York Times* had been similarly critical of Inspector Thomas Byrne in the case of Ameer Ben Ali in 1891:

> 'The head of our detective force is undoubtedly a keen and energetic officer but he has shown more than once that success in catching and convicting somebody is more to him than the demands of exact justice.'

There are the biased district attorneys:

> [Bob] Macy's persistent misconduct ... has without doubt harmed the reputation of Oklahoma's criminal justice system and left the unenviable legacy of an indelibly tarnished legal career.

... said the Tenth US Circuit Court of Appeals in 2002 of his lengthy time in office.

And then there are the hopelessly biased judges, such as Mr Justice Stephen in the Maybrick case, and Lord Goddard in the Bentley case, both in England; Judge Kaufman in Ethel Rosenberg's trial in New York; the tribunal in the Dreyfus case and the judges in a number of other American cases. The line stretches on. Given a system of election and re-election in many American states and a public that is keen on law and order, defendants cannot expect much help from the bench. Nor, although the Court of Appeal has said the judge is there to protect a defendant, can they always expect it from an English judge. Too many acquittals do not sit well with those monitoring a judicial career. In the past, barristers who have alleged police misconduct when defending suddenly find themselves protecting it on appointment to the judiciary.

In the case of the Birmingham Six there was a notable reluctance even at Appeal level to accept the police might not have behaved as well as they should. Indeed, the so-called 'people's judge' Lord Denning, shutting down a civil action brought by the men, pontificated:

> If they won, it would mean that the police were guilty of perjury; that they were guilty of violence and threats; that the confessions were involuntary and improperly admitted in evidence; and that the convictions were erroneous . . . That was such an appalling vista that every sensible person would say, 'It cannot be right that these actions should go any further.'

Some cases, such as the Birmingham Six and the Rosenbergs, are bedevilled by a baying public and a hostile press. Dr Sam Sheppard was convicted as much by the efforts of the local newspaper editor as anything else. There again Joseph Majczek and many others have been released only after prolonged campaigns by newspaper editors and journalists.

Then there are bribed juries and, perish the thought, there are bribed judges, such as Judge Frank Wilson in the case of the Chicago contract killer Harry Aleman in 1972. When Aleman was on trial for the murder of Willie Logan who had been beating his wife – Aleman's cousin – lawyer Robert

Cooney approached Wilson who was to sit without a jury. His fee for an acquittal was a modest $10,000. During the late 1980s, investigators started Operation GamBat, into years of corruption and mob ties inside the Chicago court system with a now penitent Cooney working for them. In February 1990, after threats of a prosecution, Wilson killed himself at his Arizona retirement home. There was no double jeopardy for the previously acquitted Aleman, ruled the court, because the first trial in front of Wilson had been a sham. The second time around in 1997 Aleman was convicted and sentenced to 300 years. He died in prison in 2010.

That was bad enough, but on the other side of the coin two Wilkes-Barre, Pennsylvania judges, the presiding judge Mark Ciavarella and Michael Conahan, pleaded guilty to accepting money from a contractor in return for imposing long sentences on juveniles to increase the numbers in the detention centres run by him. The judges were sentenced to twenty-eight and seventeen-and-a-half years respectively.

Then, in 2014 a San Antonio, Texas, lawyer pleaded guilty to bribing judge Angus McGinty on a regular basis to get favourable rulings, including one that kept a drunk driver out of prison. McGinty has entered a plea of not guilty but resigned on 14 February 2014.

In England, with the prosecution in serious difficulty about proving their case in a December 2008 rape trial at Birmingham Crown Court, the senior judge at the court Judge Frank Chapman offered a helping hand. He telephoned the prosecuting counsel, leaving a message on his answering machine advising him that he needed an expert witness to help him out. The prosecutor reported the call to the defending barrister and both went to see the judge, who later issued a statement:

At the end of a long and stressful week, I left a message on the voicemail of a prosecution counsel.

The matter was brought to my attention before the end of the case and as I felt I had made a serious error of judgement, I immediately recused myself from the case and reported what had happened.

Having had the opportunity to consider the situation fully, I decided the most appropriate course for me to take was to resign from my judicial office, which I did on 19 December.

The trial collapsed at a cost of £50,000

One estimate is that in US felony cases 2 per cent result in wrongful convictions. Obviously the greatest miscarriages of justice occur when the unfortunate defendant is either hanged or serves a lengthy prison sentence, but they occur even more frequently in cases that fall under the public radar and therefore go unreported and unnoticed. Probably they occur mostly at a lower level when there are pro-police magistrates or judges and inexperienced or simply inept defending lawyers.

Of course many miscarriages result from a combination of circumstances. In his essay Paul Wilson lists ten Australian cases, including Lindy Chamberlain, of proven miscarriages and a further ten, including the Mickelberg brothers and James Finch, in which he believes there was a reasonable doubt. Only four, the cases of Raymond Geesing and Bernie Matthews, which relied on a prison and police informer respectively, Reg Varley convicted on the evidence of the corrupt New South Wales detective Fred Krahe, and Frederick McDermott convicted of murder on unreliable scientific evidence, can be attributed to a single cause. All the others have up to six contributing factors including four involving media pressure.

Then again many defendants do not help themselves. They – Mahmood Mattan, Joe Hill and the Australian David Eastman, recently released after serving a lengthy sentence for the murder of a police officer, are good examples – can, unsurprisingly, be truculent and uncooperative. Publicly sacking their lawyers and quarrelling with the judge are factors that do not appeal to juries. Given they have been wrongly accused of murder it is hardly surprising they have behaved in this way, but it does not win friends and influence the people who matter. They can also be caught lying and still be innocent. In 1911 Steinie Morrison, the man convicted of the murder of

Leon Beron on London's Clapham Common, called a patently false alibi and, despite the trial judge Mr Justice Darling telling the jury that this did not mean he was guilty, they convicted him. Darling was not convinced of Morrison's guilt and he was reprieved, only to die in Parkhurst prison ten years later.

Sometimes they occur because of a fad in forensic science such as the discovery of the so-called 'earprint' before it has properly been tested. Then there are the 'expert forensic scientists' who, through their advocacy, ability in the witness box and sometimes sheer chicanery, have brought about both wrongful convictions and acquittals.

This then is a book about unqualified forensic scientists, forensic blunders, overzealous police, faulty police work, dishonest and incompetent lawyers, lying witnesses, biased judges, a baying public, a rabid press and vapid politicians. Everything, in fact, that helps make for a flawed criminal justice system worldwide. I have also, where possible, tried to include an account of what happened to these victims of miscarriages. As with all groups of people, while some prospered many others never really recovered from the experience.

My thanks are due to many people including Amanda Corlett of the American Civil Liberties Union, Sunil Badami, J. P. Bean, Paul Donnelley, Tony Gee, Jeffrey Gordon, Barbara Levy, Susanna Lobez, Michael Heap, Duncan Proudfoot, John Rigbey, the staff of the British Library, the National Archives, Kew, the Radzinowicz Library, Cambridge, the Bibliothèque Historique de la Ville de Paris, the Bibliothèque des Littératures Policières, Paris, the New York Public Library, the National Library of Australia and the State Libraries of New South Wales, Queensland, South Australia, Victoria and Western Australia. Wikipedia has been indispensable.

The book could not even have been considered, let alone completed, without the endless support, help, research and advice of Dock Bateson.

CHAPTER 1

No Bodies

The Campden Wonder

Michael Onufrejczyk; Jesse and Stephen Boorn

Louise Butler and George Yelder; Leon Sanchez
and Gregorio Valero

Guillaume Seznec; Leonard Fraser

The Campden Wonder

One of the most difficult aspects of a criminal trial – for the prosecution that is – comes when there is no body. The principal danger is that the defending counsel will tell the jury, 'I now call my last witness Mr(s) X' and into court will walk the missing person. In England in 1953 just such a fear earned a murderer a reprieve, and the situation was narrowly averted in Australia in 2000.

For centuries in England there was a mistaken view that if there was no body then there could be no trial for murder. This misconception arose after the case known as The Campden Wonder.

On Thursday, 16 August 1660, William Harrison, seventy-year-old steward to the Dowager Lady Campden in the English village in the Cotswolds of the same name, disappeared after he went to Charrington, about two miles away, to collect rents. When he had not returned by the evening, sometime after eight o'clock she (or her husband the Viscount) sent Harrison's servant John Perry to find him. Neither he nor Harrison reappeared that night and the next morning Harrison's son Edward went to search for his father. Just outside Charrington he met John Perry, who told him he was not in the village, and the pair then went to nearby Ebrington. A man there told them Harrison Snr had called at his house the evening before but had not stayed. It was then on to Paxford, half a mile away, and, when there was no news of him there either, they returned to Campden.

On the way back home they were told that a woman gathering waste grain had found a hat, collar band and comb. They went to see her and recognized the possessions as being William Harrison's. The collar band was bloodstained. A bank of gorse where she said she had found the objects was searched but, despite more or less the whole village turning out to help, nothing else was found and of Harrison there was no sign.

Now began a story that John Perry had robbed and killed him. He was taken before a justice of the peace and questioned. His story was that he had started off to look for Harrison but it had become dark (although it would normally be light until around 10 p.m. at that time of year) and he had been afraid to go on. He returned and stayed in Harrison's hen roost until the clock struck twelve, when he began to walk towards Charrington. It had turned misty and he slept under a hedge. Four men who had seen him on the road at various times confirmed his story so far as it concerned them. He explained the claim that he was too scared to continue the search after 9 p.m. but brave enough at midnight by saying the moon was then up. The Justice declined to release him and he was detained in the local inn and then in prison for the next week. He was questioned again and repeated his story. There was still no sign of Harrison or a body.

At this point the rumours multiplied, and the gossip was that Perry had told a man that Harrison had been killed by a tinker, and told another that a gentleman's servant had robbed and killed him, hiding the body in a beanrick in Campden. But when it was searched there was still no trace.

On Friday, 24 August he was again brought before the justice who urged him to confess what he knew. Now he changed his story completely. He personally had had nothing to do with Harrison's death, but his mother Joan and brother Richard had robbed and killed him. Ever since he had gone to work for Harrison the pair had been pestering him for money and they had wanted him to tell them in advance when Harrison was going to collect the rents. On the day Harrison vanished, Perry met his brother and told him it was rent collection day. Richard met him again around eight that evening and told him to follow Harrison into a piece of land known locally as 'The Rabbit Warren'. Meanwhile he walked around the fields and, when he came back, there was his brother standing over a strangled Harrison with his mother nearby. He, John, had been the one who had planted the hat and collar (after cutting it) so it would seem Harrison had been robbed.

Joan and Richard were promptly arrested and the cesspool and other fishpools were dragged but still no body was found. Then it was suggested that the body might have been hidden in the ruins of Campden House, which had been destroyed in the Civil War. It could not be found there either.

On 25 August, when Richard Perry and his mother were brought before the Justice of the Peace, John repeated his story and they denied it. The previous year there had been a burglary at Harrison's home while he and his wife were in church and John Perry admitted he had told his brother that Harrison had the considerable sum of around £140 in the house. They had agreed to hide the money in the garden. Again when it was searched there was no trace of it.

When their cases were heard at the September Assizes, John, as an accessory before the fact, Richard and Joan pleaded not guilty to a count of breaking into Harrison's house and stealing £140 and secondly to a count of robbing and murdering Harrison. The judge refused to try them on the murder count because the body had not been found and they changed their plea on the first count to guilty because, as first offenders, they were entitled to a Free Pardon. John further compounded the troubles of his brother and mother by saying they had tried to poison him.

They all appeared at the Spring Assizes of 1661 before Sir Robert Hyde and now John retracted his confession, saying he had been mad at the time of making it. All were convicted in short order and executed on Campden Hill. Joan was hanged first as it was believed she was a witch and had so bewitched her sons they could not confess to anything while she was alive. Richard climbed the ladder saying that he was innocent, begging his brother to say what he knew about Harrison. John told the crowd he was not obliged to confess to them but added he knew nothing about Harrison's death. His body was left to hang in chains.

Sometime before 2 August 1662 Harrison reappeared in the village with the wildly improbable story that he had been kidnapped by three men in white robes and taken to Turkey where he had been sold for £7 as a slave to a local elderly doctor who had once been to England. When the doctor died he escaped, taking a silver gilt bowl with him. He paid for his passage to Lisbon with the bowl, where he was put ashore. There he approached some men who, by chance, he heard speaking English; one of the men put him on a ship to Dover. From there he made his way to Campden. Harrison ended his story with the following flourish:

> So, honoured Sir, I have given you a true account of my great sufferings and fortunate deliverance, by the mercy and goodness of God, my most gracious Father in Jesus Christ, my Saviour and Redeemer, to whose name be ascribed all honour, praise and glory.

Not everyone believed the story, while others thought that the witch Joan Perry had used her powers to transport him to Turkey. Harrison died before 1676 never having changed his story nor, it seems, having expanded upon it.

What was the truth about Harrison's disappearance and subsequent return? And why did John Perry lie about his part in the murder and falsely implicate his mother and brother? It is impossible to be certain, but one suggestion is that Harrison had embezzled Lady Campden's money and had hidden himself away until he could obtain a pardon under the Act of Indemnity for crimes committed before the Restoration of King Charles II. His wife, who seems to have committed suicide shortly after his return, knew this but was prepared to let the Perrys go to the gibbet. John Perry can be explained away as a schizophrenic. From then on, however, no trial without a body took place in England and Wales until the late 1930s.

Michael Onufrejczyk; Jesse and Stephen Boorn

The last time former Polish soldier Stanislaw Sykut, then in his late fifties, was seen alive was by the village blacksmith at Cwmdu near Llandeilo in Carmarthenshire on 14 December 1953. Sykut had paid £600 for a half-share in the pig farm of another Polish ex-soldier Michael Onufrejczyk in March that year. Two months later the men had fallen out, with Sykut calling the police about being bullied and Onufrejczyk complaining that his partner would not do his share of the work but finally promising not to hit him again. From 14 December Sykut never collected his mail from the village post office, nor was any money drawn from his post office account. When the local police officer went to the farm to make a routine check on alien registration, he found Sykut's razor and other belongings in the house and the kitchen wall covered in bloodspots. Onufrejczyk explained them away saying the spots came from dead rabbits. He claimed his partner had left on 18 December and the blacksmith had been mistaken.

Onufrejczyk was not arrested and charged with murder for a year, at which time the body had still not been found. Now he said the blood spatter on the wall had come about after Sykut had cut his finger. Convicted, he was sentenced to death and reprieved. In between, Onufrejczyk had appealed and the Lord Chief Justice had set out the requirements for a conviction in a no-body case:

> The fact of death can be proved by circumstantial evidence, that is to say by evidence of facts which lead to one conclusion, provided that the jury are satisfied and are warned that the evidence must lead to one conclusion only.

Onufrejczyk, who spent much of his time in prison playing and teaching chess, was released in 1965. The next year he died in a car accident in Bradford where he was then living. It was said his reprieve was principally because the government had a lingering fear that Sykut might still be alive and that to everyone's embarrassment he might appear from behind the Iron Curtain after Onyfrejczyk had been hanged.

There was no such ninny-like squeamishness in America, where in 1812 farm worker Russell Colvin disappeared from Manchester, Vermont. He had been working on his father-in-law's farm and Jesse and Stephen Boorn, his brothers-in-law, made no secret of their dislike of him. His vanishing was in line with his previous behaviour. Colvin would disappear for days at a time but previously he had always returned to his wife Sally. When he did not reappear this time, suspicion fell on the Boorn brothers, although no action was taken until some seven years later when their uncle Amos had a dream in which Colvin appeared saying he had been murdered and his remains had been dumped in a cellar hole in a potato field on the Boorn farm. There was no body in the cellar but there were pieces of broken crockery, a button, a penknife and a jackknife identified by Sally Colvin as her husband's. She did have an incentive to make her identification. After Russell disappeared she had given birth to a child well outside the gestation period, but because the law presumed that any child born to a married woman was fathered by her husband she could not get support from the actual father. It would suit her well for Colvin to be proved dead.

Shortly after, a barn was burned down and, when a dog unearthed some pieces of bone that doctors said were human, a scenario was developed that the brothers had killed Colvin, moved his body to the barn, moved it a second time to where the dog found the bones and torched the barn to cover their tracks. Jesse Boorn was arrested and a warrant went out for Stephen, who had moved to New York. A jailhouse snitch then said Jesse had confessed to him. Jesse, presumably believing Stephen was safely out of the state, now confessed, laying the blame on his brother. However, when Stephen duly returned from New York 'to clear his name' Jesse promptly withdrew his confession. Stephen now confessed, claiming self-defence, and to complicate matters further the largest of the bones found was compared with a human bone, and the doctors decided it had come from an animal. What was left by way of evidence was Jesse's repudiated confession and some eyewitness evidence that the brothers had been seen arguing with Colvin the day he disappeared. Both were sentenced to death although Jesse was reprieved.

Then there was what could almost be called divine intervention. James Whepley, once from Manchester but now in New York, read an article in the *New York Post* about the case and recalled he knew a Russell Colvin who had said he had once worked as a farmhand in Vermont. Whepley contacted Colvin, who was lured back to Manchester where he was recognized by some of his former neighbours. Pardons followed.

There have been suggestions, based on more jailhouse conversation, when some years later Stephen was awaiting trial for counterfeiting in Illinois, that the new Colvin was a ringer, but the better view is that he was genuine. All in all, however, it is a cautionary tale of the dangers of accepting the evidence of jailhouse informers, dreamers and unscientific examinations.

Louise Butler and George Yelder;
Leon Sanchez and Gregorio Valero

Even into the 1920s there were a surprising number of no-body cases in the United States, particularly in rural areas and in the Deep South. One came in 1928 in Lowndes County, Alabama, when Louise Butler and George Yelder, with whom she had been conducting a paid affair, were convicted of the murder of her fourteen-year-old niece Topsy Warren. Butler found that in her absence Yelder had given Topsy a silver half-dollar for services rendered and in turn she gave the child a whipping. Shortly after, Topsy disappeared and when investigations were made as to her whereabouts, Louise Butler's twelve-year-old daughter Julia and another niece gave a graphic account to Deputy Sheriff Buck Meadows of seeing Butler kill Topsy and then watching as she and Yelder cut off her arms and threw the body, tied to the chassis of a car, into the river. Butler was arrested and made a confession, which she retracted immediately. She was kept in custody and when Julia began crying, asking why her mother wasn't coming home, she was told that if she had been lying she should admit it. She replied, 'She sure done it.' Both she and her cousin told their story at the trial with some skill. Despite trying to establish alibis, on 26 April both Butler and Yelder were sentenced to life imprisonment.

Within a week Topsy was found living with relatives some twenty miles away. A Joseph Bell, who later wrote an unpublished manuscript on the case, said there was 'evidence of a beating but no evidence that she had ever been deprived of her arms'. The pair were pardoned in June that year. It was thought the girls had been coached by a man with a grudge against Yelder.

Other jurisdictions have had their own no-body cases, with very mixed results. In August 1910 a shepherd, Jose Maria Lopez Grimaldos, nicknamed Cepa or 'The Stump' – he was just five foot tall – from Tresjuncos, a village in Cuenca, some 300 miles from Madrid, sold some sheep and then disappeared. He had been constantly ridiculed over his height by two locals, Leon Sanchez and Gregorio Valero. A few weeks after Grimaldos went missing his family lodged a complaint alleging murder against the pair. In September 1911 the case was dismissed for lack of evidence.

With the arrival in the locality in 1913 of a new judge, Emilio Isasa Echenique, Grimaldos' family pressed for the case to be reopened and Valero and Sanchez were rearrested. Officers of the Civil Guard began torturing the men, both to obtain confessions and to find out what they had done with the body. The pair were beaten, their fingernails pulled out and they were fed meals of salt cod without water. Finally they confessed to murdering and dismembering Grimaldos.

They said they had been intending to steal from Cepa, so Gregorio had taken him to the dovecote and hit him with a heavy stick. Then they managed to stuff the corpse into a pigsty, but this was not big enough so they had to dismember him. Later they broke up the bones and burned them; Gregorio said Leon took the head away in a handkerchief.

Grimaldos' death was registered in the civil register of Osa de la Vega on 11 November 1913, stating that death occurred between 8.30 and 9 p.m. on 21 August 1910 in Palomar Virgen de la Vega as a result of his being killed by Gregorio Valero and Leon Sanchez. In the register there is a note stating that the corpse had not been identified because it had not been found.

Like so many jurisdictions, the Spanish criminal process can be very slow and it was not until 1918 that a trial began. After a retirement of only thirty minutes by the twelve-man jury it ended with the men being sentenced to eighteen years.

They had at least avoided being garroted. Valero was sent to prison in Valencia and Sanchez to Cartagena.

On 8 February 1926, the priest of Tresjuncos received a letter from the priest of Miro, 150 miles away, asking him to send Grimaldos' baptismal certificate as he wished to marry. Afraid of a scandal, he did not and Grimaldos, impatient to get married, returned to Tresjuncos on 19 February where, unsurprisingly, the villagers mobbed him. The judge in Belamonte was contacted and he set in motion proceedings for a judicial review. The Minister of Grace and Justice then ordered a retrial for both men and for the prosecutor of the Supreme Court to commence a judicial review against the decision of the hearing in Cuenca. Valero and Sanchez were released on 'provisional liberty'.

On 26 March 1926 the minister issued a statement saying he had sufficient grounds for believing that the confessions had been 'extracted by force using violent means and that there had been a lack of care and procedural mistakes during the case'.

Releasing the men the High Court ruled that:

> Although the condemned men should be in prison to await the judgement it was repugnant to common decency to deny those who had served an unjust term the personal satisfaction of hearing themselves rehabilitated. In a case of such evident errors a revision is even more human, more necessary and more suitable to the aims of society and justice.

During the retrial Grimaldos told the Supreme Court, 'The truth of the matter is that I went off to take the waters [healing baths] at the La Celadilla country house.' He had intended to return to work but then changed his mind. Over the years he had worked in the vineyards and as a shepherd. He also said that seven or eight years previously he had written a letter to his sister, who had not bothered to reply.

The Supreme Court quashed the decision in Cuenca of eight years earlier, cleared Valero and Sanchez, nullified the death certificate of Jose Maria Grimaldos and ruled that the state must now pay appropriate compensation to Valero and Sanchez.

Officially it seems the priest in Tresjuncos drowned accidentally and the magistrate Echenique died from angina at his home in Seville, but suicide was suspected in both cases. The official who had been present when the confessions had been made was put on trial along with three of the Guardia Civil. They were all acquitted.

After their release Sanchez and Valero went to live in Madrid where they worked as security guards. In July 1935 they were given a 3,000-pesetas-a-year pension backdated for five years. On 28 August Valero told the *Mundo Grafico*:

> After so many years faced with the irreparable damage we suffered and after our innocence has finally been properly proved, neither I nor my companion wanted to be the cause of anyone else being punished ... As far as I'm concerned I accept the pesetas they are giving us with alacrity because they serve to alleviate the economic circumstances of my home.

The case was used by the liberal press to attack the criminal justice system as well as the Guardia Civil. The right-wing press took a more detached view. In 1979 the director Pilar Miro made a controversial film of the case, *El Crimen de Cuenca*.

Guillaume Seznec; Leonard Fraser

In France at five o'clock on the morning of 25 May 1923 Guillaume Seznec, owner of a sawmill at Morlaix, and his friend, wood merchant Pierre Quéméneur from Landerneau in Brittany, left the Hotel Parisien at Rennes where they had stayed the previous night and drove towards Paris in their Cadillac.

There, according to Seznec, Quéméneur had an eight o'clock meeting with a man, variously described as an American named Sherdy, Chardy or Charley L'American, but in reality called Boudjema Gherdi, who lived in boulevard Malesherbes, to arrange a black-market sale of second-hand Cadillacs left behind by Americans after World War One. The idea was they should be sold to Russia. Seznec returned to Brittany on 27 May but Quéméneur, who had told his sister he would be back on 28 May, was never seen again.

By 4 June Quéméneur's family were beginning to worry and contacted Seznec asking if he knew where he was. Seznec told them they had broken down twice on the way to Paris and he had left Quéméneur at the railway station in Dreux to catch the Paris train. He thought Quéméneur had stood to make a great deal of money from the deal and that he might even have gone to America to complete it. On 10 June Louis Quéméneur and Jean Pouliquen, Quéméneur's brother and brother-in-law, along with Seznec, reported him missing at Rennes police station and were told not to worry; after all, he was a forty-four-year-old bachelor in Paris. Three days later Quéméneur's family received a telegram from Le Havre, saying all was well and he would be back in a few days' time. As a result they asked the police to suspend their inquiry, but by 16 June, with still no sign of Quéméneur, they began to worry that the telegram was not genuine.

On 20 June a station employee at Le Havre found a suitcase with papers in Quéméneur's name and a message was sent to the family. Two days later the inquiry was officially reopened. In the suitcase was a typed sale agreement of land near Paimpol in Brittany from Quéméneur to Seznec for a sum of 35,000 francs. Quéméneur had bought the land a year earlier for 25,000 francs. Two years later, in 1925, it would be sold for five times that amount. There was also a notebook showing Quéméneur had bought train tickets from Dreux to Paris and from Paris to Le Havre, although there was considerable doubt as to whether this was in Quéméneur's handwriting. In the absence of a body there were a number of possible lines of inquiry but Seznec was arrested during the investigation in which the dubious police officer Pierre Bonny took part. Bonny claimed that he had found a Royal typewriter, whose print matched that on the sale agreement, hidden in a barn on Seznec's property. None of Seznec's family nor his lawyer nor the examining magistrate were present when Bonny produced the machine.

Seznec was charged with murder and his trial lasted eight days during which nearly 120 witnesses were heard. The trial began explosively when on the first day a telegram arrived at court apparently from the dead man, which read, 'Returned from Russia. Shocked. Will appear as soon as possible.' He never did.

The prosecution's case was that Boudjema Gherdi did not exist and that Seznec had planned Quéméneur's murder to take over his land. In fact Gherdi did exist. He was a car trader and an informer for Pierre Bonny. Years later Colette Noll, a Resistance member deported on Bonny's orders, gave evidence that Gherdi had informed on her and smashed her network, and the Algerian-born go-between was a 'very frequent visitor' to the French Gestapo's headquarters in Paris. Witnesses who claimed they had seen Quéméneur after his disappearance were disregarded. Witnesses who later withdrew their statements identified him as the purchaser of the typewriter.

On 4 November 1924 Seznec was found guilty but, since the prosecution could not prove premeditation, he was sentenced to life imprisonment with hard labour instead of the guillotine. Later, six members of the jury said they believed they had made the wrong decision. He was taken to the transportation camp from where he sent a note to his wife Marie-Jeanne – 'I tell you once more I am innocent. Goodbye, goodbye and Goodbye. To Heaven' – before being transferred to the prison of the Iles du Salut in French Guiana in 1928. His eldest daughter Marie became a nun, hoping to be sent to the penal leper colony in Guiana so she could meet her father, but she died in 1930, aged twenty, without reaching him. Seznec's wife died in poverty the following year.

One alternative theory for Quéméneur's disappearance was that he had been trying to muscle in on the black market and had upset the Minister for the Interior, Camille Chautemps; as a result he had been killed by a Jean Quemin. One witness claimed he had seen Quemin throw a body into a river; however, no body was found and when he was interviewed in July 1928 Quemin denied any involvement. The next year he successfully sued for libel.

Another suggestion is that Seznec did pay 35,000 francs for the property but, as was common, there was an under-the-table arrangement and he had paid an additional 65,000 francs, which would make a sensible price. Quéméneur was in tax difficulties, strapped for cash and wanted quick money to buy the black-market cars. Seznec was never going to admit the under-the-table deal.

Seznec was released in May 1947 and died on 13 February 1954. His death itself raised considerable suspicion. On 14 November 1953 a lorry driver, who claimed not to have realized what happened, had backed into him and crushed him. Seznec died of his injuries.

Throughout his life, and after his death, Seznec and his family, particularly his mother and grandson Denis Her-Seznec, maintained his innocence. One strand of their claim was that he had been framed by Inspector Pierre Bonny, who in 1935 received a three-year sentence for corruption and during the

Second World War became the assistant of Henri Lafont, head of the Gestapo in France. Bonny was executed by the Resistance on 26 December 1944. Before he died he told his son he had sent an innocent man to the 'bagnes', as the French penal colonies were known.

A total of fourteen attempts were made to quash the conviction until in 2005 the Public Prosecutor accepted that it was unsafe. On 11 April, Denis Seznec came within a whisker of clearing his grandfather's name when a *commission de révision des condamnations pénales* agreed to reopen the case.

His hopes were, however, short-lived and on 14 December 2006 the *Cour de révision* refused to annul Seznec's conviction, ruling there was no new evidence to call doubt on his guilt. It thought the implication of Bonny, although an interesting element, was not sufficiently new. After the decision the Seznec family intended to take the case to the European Court of Human Rights but, on legal advice, they finally gave up the struggle.

By 1911 Australia, and in particular the state of Victoria, had proved itself far ahead of Britain so far as no-body cases were concerned. On 10 August that year twenty-seven-year-old Mary Davies, under the name Mrs Nelson, went for an abortion to be carried out by Dr Samuel Peacock at his private hospital in Melbourne. She was visited by a man, posing as Mr Nelson – but unfortunately named Poke – on three occasions, the last on 22 August when he was told she was dead. Her body was never found but there was some evidence it had been burned. Peacock was charged with her murder and after the jury convicted him, since there was no body the trial judge stated a case for the High Court to determine whether there could be a conviction. There, Chief Justice Griffith said the law had been clear since 1842 and, 'I think it is now settled law that the fact of death may be proved by circumstantial evidence as well as any other part of the case.' Peacock's conviction was quashed on other grounds. In February 1912 a second jury disagreed, and at a third trial in March 1912 he was found not guilty. The case evidently did his practice no harm. When he died in June 1932 he left real estate including vast tracts of land and substantial properties in downtown Melbourne.

Some other states were more reluctant to prosecute in no-body cases and on 16 November 1971, Alex Duncan Carstens became the first man to be tried in Queensland in a no-body case.

Carstens was found guilty of the murder of Peter Francis Colburn, who disappeared after work one evening at Dinmore Meatworks, twenty miles outside Brisbane, on 13 March 1970. Carstens, later found in possession of Colburn's airgun, had advertised in the papers for skin-divers to work in Indonesia and Bruce Peters and Kerry Rowan, who had replied, also disappeared. Witnesses told the court they had bought property from Carstens that actually belonged to the youths. He claimed that he had merely been recruiting divers for a lugger, the *Cutty Sark*, and that once hired the boys must have become involved in drugs, gun smuggling or pilfering wrecked boats in the area. The prosecution maintained the *Cutty Sark* did not exist. The jury was out for less than three hours after a seventeen-day trial and Carstens was sentenced to life imprisonment with hard labour.

Although there was no miscarriage of justice in Carstens' case, Queensland was perhaps right to look at no-body cases with some scepticism. In 2000 sexual predator Leonard John Fraser who, said a jailhouse snitch, had confessed to him in prison, was charged with the murder of teenager Natasha Ryan; she had been missing for about five years. Fraser was said to have admitted smashing her head and dumping her body in a pond. To the embarrassment of the prosecution she turned up alive and well shortly before Fraser's trial. She had been living with her boyfriend in Rockhampton.

CHAPTER 2

Folk-Devils and Moral Panics

Devils and Witches: Margot de la Barre and
Marion la Droiturière; Jehenne de Brigue and
Macette de Ruilly; Urbain Grandier;
Alice Samuel; the Bideford Three; Jane Wenham;
Mary and Elizabeth Hicks; Janet Horne;
Anna Göldi

The Witches of Salem

Helen Duncan

Ethel Rosenberg

The West Memphis Three

Devils and Witches: Margot de la Barre and Marion la Droiturière; Jehenne de Brigue and Macette de Ruilly; Urbain Grandier; Alice Samuel; the Bideford Three; Jane Wenham; Mary and Elizabeth Hicks; Janet Horne; Anna Göldi

'Societies', wrote Stanley Cohen in his *Folk-Devils and Moral Panics:*

> . . . appear to be subject, every now and then, to periods of moral panic. A condition, episode, person or group of persons emerges to become defined as the threat to societal values and interests; its nature is presented in a stylized and stereotypical fashion by the mass media; the moral barricades are manned by editors, bishops, politicians, and other right-thinking people; socially accredited experts pronounce their diagnoses and solutions; ways of coping are evolved or (more often) resorted to; the condition then disappears, submerges or deteriorates and becomes more visible . . . Sometimes the panic passes over and is forgotten except in folk lore and collective memory . . .

Cohen was writing about the 'moral panic' caused by the emergence of the teenage gangs, the Mods and Rockers, in Britain in the 1960s – Australia had a similar problem with

Bodgies and Widgies – but he might well have been writing about the witchcraft trials that surged through Europe and America from the thirteenth to the eighteenth centuries.

Until then witches and wizards had been treated reasonably well. Penance and reparation were required but, unless a person died, there was little prospect of the death penalty. Then, coinciding with the beginning of the Inquisition and the rise of the Cathars, towards the end of the Middle Ages there was a strong belief, fostered by the Church, that the Devil could give certain people power to harm others in return for their loyalty. As a result a 'witchcraft craze' spread through Europe from the 1300s to the end of the 1600s.

The circumstances of the witchcraft trials were all depressingly similar. A community turns on its most vulnerable members – the poor, the elderly, the mentally unstable – and makes them the scapegoat for some misfortune, perceived or real. Very often there is an element of hysteria.

The accused were overwhelmingly female – only about 15 per cent were male – and often they were unmarried women or widows with no family to protect them. Some were herbalists or healers, practices opposed by the Church, and some probably did try to practise the so-called dark arts; most were innocent.

Sorcerers – again predominantly women – who had long been a traditional part of the social fabric of their communities, were marginalized and targeted by both the Church and the judicial system. Herbalists and fortune-tellers who compiled magic love philtres were arrested and taken to the torture chamber, where on the rack they soon confessed their worship of the devil and participation in Witches' Sabbaths. Tens of thousands of supposed witches were executed by hanging, strangulation, burning or drowning. In 1579 a council in Melun in France, long deemed to be a hotbed of witchcraft, ruled that all witches and consulters with them should be executed and so should fortune-tellers and conjurers.*

---

* Before the recent crop of cases of defendants from Africa the last actual trial in Europe in which witchcraft was alleged was in Melun in 1926, when two men and ten women from the sect Notre Dame des Pleurs

An early example came in France on 9 August 1390 when two women, an itinerant prostitute named Margot de la Barre and Marion la Droiturière, were sentenced by the judges of the Châtelet in Paris to the pillory and then to be burned at the stake. The pair were first interrogated at the end of July when the accusation against them was the casting of a spell on Ainselin, the former lover of Marion, and his wife Agnesot. To regain her lover's interest, Marion had been advised by a friend to share a drink, made of a few drops of her menstrual blood mixed with red wine, with Ainselin. She had also obtained two recipes from Margot de la Barre, the first based on herbs gathered during the magical eve of Saint John on 23 June. The intention was twofold. First, to make Ainselin lose any sexual interest in his wife, and secondly to rekindle his desire for Marion. This love potion involved roasting the testicles of a white rooster, grinding them into powder and putting the result into Ainselin's pillow for nine days before mixing it in his food and drink. Quite how this last one was to be accomplished goes unrecorded.

On its own their behaviour, however unhealthy, and which was immediately accepted by the women at their first questioning, did not merit the death penalty. But after sessions in the torture chamber, it was a short step to their admitting their rejection of Christ and adherence to the Devil, crimes which, if suitably confessed, could lead to spiritual redemption, but which still required capital punishment in the temporal world.

---

were put on trial for having flogged the Abbé Desnoyers after Mass on 3 January that year. The Abbé had had to be rescued by gendarmes. He had earlier performed an exorcism of Mme Marie Meslin who claimed to be the mystical heiress of Mélanie Calvet. Because she had fainted in church the next year, she claimed the exorcism failed. Now they alleged he was an agent of the Devil. Part of his devilment had been to arrange for canaries and sparrows to circle over the victims' homes. The birds' droppings formed fantastic shapes and gave off odours which spread disease. The women were unrepentant, saying that they had saved the honour of 'Maman Marie'. In 1927 the two men received eight months' imprisonment and eight of the women were imprisoned for six months.

A few months later, at the end of October that year, two other women similarly fell foul of the judiciary. Jehenne de Brigue, described as a soothsayer, specialized in the recovery of lost objects, a respectable enough vocation in the Middle Ages. Some six years earlier, she had been approached by the priest of a neighbouring village for aid in recovering a sum of money and a silver cross stolen from his church. It was not uncommon for a parish priest of the time to share his parishioners' beliefs in such a woman's gifts.

In 1391 Jehenne de Brigue, now married to Hennequin Le Cordier, was tried at the Châtelet in Paris with Macette de Ruilly over an exchange of recipes of love and disenchantment. Jehenne had shown Macette how to cast a spell on her husband, using three toads fed with breast milk and then tormented with pins, as well as a puppet made of wax and including some of her husband's hair, all melted in a copper pan. Macette, in return, was accused of helping Jehenne, who wanted to marry the father of her children. In this case, for nine nights the melted wax was to be rubbed between the man's shoulders while he slept. Stretched on the rack, both soon confessed and they were taken to the Châtelet-Les Halles wearing the conical hat decorated with devils signifying heresy. They were burned at the stake on 17 August 1391.

The most famous of the so-called possession trials in France was that in 1634 of the handsome, well-educated and probably sexually promiscuous priest, Urbain Grandier, in Loudun, some seventy kilometres from Poitiers. He had already been in difficulties and was thought to be the father of a child with the daughter of the King's solicitor, as well as having a long-term mistress. Following an accusation by the Bishop of Poitiers he had been found guilty of immorality in 1630 but, with friends in high places, he was restored to the priesthood within a year. Four years later Grandier was again on trial when, most likely, the Bishop of Poitiers arranged for allegations of witchcraft to be fabricated by Jeanne des Anges, the Mother Superior of the local convent of Ursuline nuns, who claimed she had been bewitched by Grandier. She then complained she had been possessed by no fewer than three devils. Grandier was arrested, imprisoned and comprehensively tortured.

The trial was, of course, a farce. Seventy-two witnesses were called against Grandier, but the defence witnesses were told that if they gave evidence for him they would be arrested as traitors to the King and have their possessions confiscated. Many left the region and even France.

However, some did give evidence in Grandier's defence, even including some of the possessed nuns. The prosecutor explained that this was a ploy by Satan to save Grandier. Jeanne des Anges appeared in court with a noose tied around her neck, swearing that she would hang herself if she could not recant her earlier lies. She need not have bothered. Grandier was convicted and was burned alive at the stake.

Various explanations have been offered for Grandier's trial. One was that he had upset the powerful Cardinal Richlieu, and another that it was part of a plan by the Catholic Church to demonstrate its power and so drive the Huguenots from the region.

In England nearly half a century earlier, the first allegations against Alice Samuel had been made in November 1589 by Jane, the ten-year-old daughter of Robert Throckmorton, the Squire of Warboys in Cambridgeshire, after she began suffering from fits. Jane accused the seventy-six-year-old woman of being the cause, and the child's claim was backed by her four sisters and some household servants who also began exhibiting similar symptoms.

Throckmorton was a close friend of Sir Henry Cromwell, one of the wealthiest commoners in England, and in March 1590, when Lady Cromwell, grandmother of Oliver Cromwell, came to Warboys she also accused Alice Samuel of being a witch. She took the elderly woman aside and cut off a lock of her hair, which she gave to Mrs Throckmorton to burn – a standard folk remedy to weaken a witch's power. Unfortunately for Alice Samuel she asked, 'Madam, why do you use me thus? I never did you any harm as yet.' The hair-cutting did not seem to have had any great effect. That night Lady Cromwell had nightmares, became ill and died two years later.

In December that year Alice Samuel begged the Throckmorton sisters to stop their accusations and they did. However, the local parson persuaded her to confess to witchcraft, something she recanted the next day. She was taken before the Bishop of Lincoln to whom she confessed again, after which she was taken to Huntingdon where she was imprisoned with her daughter Agnes and husband John. All three were tried on 5 April 1593 for the murder by witchcraft of Lady Cromwell. Apart from her confession, the crucial evidence was her remark to Lady Cromwell, 'I never did you any harm as yet.' The trio were found guilty and hanged.

Sir Henry Cromwell confiscated the Samuels' small amount of property and used it to pay for an annual sermon against witchcraft to be preached in Huntingdon in perpetuity. This continued until 1812, by which time it was being given against a simple belief in witchcraft.

George Kittredge, Professor of English Literature at Harvard, considered that the Warboys trial influenced the passage of the Witchcraft Act of 1604 calling it '. . . the most momentous witch-trial that had ever occurred in England', partially because it had '. . . demonstrably produced a deep and lasting impression on the class that made laws'.

In 1604 James I issued a statute against witchcraft, and as a result witch-hunts reached their peak in the seventeenth century, when the church viewed witches as devil-worshipping heretics. Numerous trials followed, many instigated by Matthew Hopkins, self-appointed witchfinder general, from 1644 to 1647. Hopkins, who was paid up to £1 for each witch he exposed, travelled the south-east seeking them out, using torture to secure confessions and well-tried methods such as swimming – throwing the accused into a river and judging them innocent if they sank – to determine guilt. He is thought to have executed 200 to 400 'witches'. In the village of Manningtree, Essex, alone, he accused thirty-six women, nineteen of whom were executed; a further nine died in prison.

Devon was a hotbed of witchcraft and, in August 1682, Temperance Lloyd, Susannah Edwards and Mary Trembles, all of Bideford – the Bideford Three as they have come to be known – were arrested and charged with sorcery or witchcraft. Lloyd was accused of causing the death of several people through the black arts, to which she confessed. The other two were accused of causing sickness through witchcraft. It is not surprising that, in an effort to save herself, Trembles blamed Edwards for leading her astray and in turn Edwards blamed Lloyd. They were tried at the Assizes in Exeter on 14 August and hanged on the twenty-fifth. For some years it was suggested that these were the last executions for witchcraft in the county, but this probably occurred in 1684 when Alice Molland was hanged, also in Exeter.

In fact trials for witchcraft continued sporadically in the eigthteenth century. One was that of Jane Wenham, convicted at Hertford Assizes. She had married twice and her first husband had died in suspicious circumstances. In 1712 she was accused of bewitching Matthew Gilston, a farmhand, into giving her some straw. She was also accused of flying, something the trial judge Sir John Powell said was not a crime. The Revd Godfrey Gardiner, the Revd Robert Strutt (the vicar of Ardeley) and the Revd Francis Bragge all gave evidence against her. Bragge, the newly appointed curate of Biggleswade, was the son of the fanatical rector of Hitchin, and appeared to want to live up to his father's reputation. Evidence was given of Jane's bewitching of Gilston and Anne Thorn, as well as two infants who had subsequently died, sheep that had died, and others that 'behaved strangely, skipping about and standing on their heads'. The jury were told that 'innumerable' cats appeared in the village and haunted the rectory. Bragge gave evidence that the feathers in Anne Thorn's pillow were gathered into round 'cakes', which seemed to be stuck together with what might be grease from a dead man's bones.

After considering the indictment and evidence for two hours, the jury found her guilty of 'conversing with the Devil in the shape of a cat'. She was convicted, but the humane and very sceptical Powell respited the sentence, asking for a Royal Pardon from Queen Anne. Wenham was released and given refuge, first on the estate of Colonel Plummer at Gilston Park and then, when he died in 1720, in a cottage on the

Hertingfordbury estate of the Whig William Cowper, where she lived until her death aged nearly ninety in 1730. Bishop Francis Hutchinson, the author of 'An Historical essay concerning witchcraft', visited her late in her life, and found her to be 'a simple, pious woman'.

Another case, and probably the last in which the death penalty was imposed in England, involved Mary Hicks and her nine-year-old daughter Elizabeth, who were condemned to death by the Assize Court and were hanged in Huntingdon on Saturday, 28 July 1716. They were believed to have taken off their stockings in order to summon a rainstorm. James I's statute was repealed in 1736 by George II.*

In Scotland, the Church outlawed witchcraft in 1563 and over the years some 1,500 people were executed. Although a stone in a garden in Dornoch in the Highlands gives the year of her execution as 1722, it was in 1727 that Janet Horne, a generic Scots name for a witch, and her daughter were arrested in Dornoch and imprisoned on the accusations of her neighbours. Horne was showing signs of senility, and her unnamed daughter had deformed hands and feet that resembled hooves. As a result, her kindly neighbours accused Horne of having turned her daughter into a pony for the Devil to ride. The deformation showed that she had failed to turn her back into a human. Both were taken to the local tollbooth, from where it seems the daughter managed to escape. The trial was

---

* Extrajudicial executions of wizards and witches continued until the end of the nineteenth century. In 1863 an elderly Frenchman living in Castle Hedingham in Essex died of pneumonia after being ducked – a traditional test for witches – by villagers. He had been accused of casting a spell on Emma Smith. Smith and Samuel Stammers were charged with his death and tried at Chelmsford Assizes where they were sentenced to six months' imprisonment on 8 March 1864. In March 1895 'the last witch burned in Ireland' Bridget Cleary was burned as a changeling in County Tipperary. Her husband Michael received fifteen years for manslaughter. The trial judge treated it as a simple wife-murder case. An Irish nursery rhyme runs, 'Are you a witch, or are you a fairy? Or are you the wife of Michael Cleary?'

conducted by the undersheriff and when Janet failed to recite the Lord's Prayer correctly in Gaelic, misquoting the opening line, this was taken as proof that she was worshipping the Devil. She was tarred and feathered and paraded round the village in a barrel, before being taken to a fire that had been lit for her. Upon seeing the flames, she is reputed to have held out her hands and said, 'Oh, what a bonny blaze.'

In Europe the last woman to be executed for witchcraft was probably Anna Göldi in Glarus, Switzerland in 1782, during the so-called Age of Enlightenment. She had been employed as a maid by the doctor and magistrate Jakob Tschudi, with whom this apparently handsome woman began an affair.

One morning in 1782 one of the Tschudi children found a needle in her milk. Two days later more needles were found, this time in bread as well as the milk, and suspicion fell upon Anna. She was sacked by the Tschudis. Adultery was a crime, and when she threatened to disclose her affair with her employer, to protect himself Tschudi accused her of witch-craft. Initially the illiterate woman was questioned day and night by the religious and political leaders of Glarus. And when she maintained her innocence, she was tortured, hanged by her thumbs with weights strapped to her feet. Her confes-sion followed the usual patterns of the Devil as a black dog and the Devil having given her the needles. She withdrew her confession and, for her pains, she was tortured again until she confessed once more.

She was tried for poisoning and, although non-fatal poison-ing did not carry the death penalty, two weeks later she was led out to the public square, where she was beheaded. Other accounts have her convicted of killing her child by Tschudi.

On 20 September 2007, the Swiss parliament acknowledged her case as a miscarriage of justice. She was finally exonerated on 27 August 2008, 226 years after her death, on the grounds that she had been subjected to an 'illegal trial'.

The Witches of Salem

Although the Salem witchcraft trials, which took place in Massachusetts between 1692 and 1693, lasted less than two years, more than 200 people were accused of practising witchcraft and twenty were executed. Part of the reason for the trials was an influx of strangers into a rural and tight-knit community. Many were refugees from the war begun in 1689 between England and France over the American colonies. They fled from upstate New York, Nova Scotia and Quebec to the county of Essex and particularly to the straggling rural community of Salem Village in the Massachusetts Bay. As a result, as is so often the case, the refugees placed a strain on Salem's resources. This aggravated the existing rivalry between families with ties to the old established port of Salem and those who still depended on agriculture for a living.

In 1688 there was a trial for witchcraft when, following an argument with laundress Goody Glover, thirteen-year-old Martha Goodwin began to exhibit bizarre behaviour. Days later her younger brother and two sisters followed suit. Glover was arrested and tried for bewitching the Goodwin children. Revd Cotton Mather saw Goody twice but she refused to recant and was hanged. The kindly Mather took the girl Martha Goodwin into his house, but her behaviour simply worsened.

There was also discontent with the English-born Revd Samuel Parris, the minister of Salem Village, who was appointed the next year. Parris was disliked because his wife was so beautiful and therefore he was thought to be lustful and, with more reason, over his extravagance in purchasing a pair of gold candlesticks for the meeting house. The Puritan villagers believed all of the ensuing quarrelling was the work of the Devil.

In January of 1692, Parris's daughter Elizabeth, aged nine, and his niece Abigail Williams, aged eleven, began to have 'fits'. After they screamed, threw things, uttered peculiar sounds and contorted themselves into strange positions, the local physician Dr Griggs suggested that witchcraft might be the reason for their behaviour.

The next month a villager, Mary Sibley, asked Tituba, Parris's West Indian-born servant, to bake a 'witch cake' and feed it to a dog. According to an old English folk remedy, feeding a dog this kind of cake, which contained the urine of the afflicted, would counteract the spell put on Elizabeth and Abigail. The reason the cake is fed to a dog is because the animal is believed to be a 'familiar' of the Devil. By the end of the month, under pressure from magistrates Jonathan Corwin and John Hathorne, the girls blamed three women for afflicting them. All of them fitted nicely into the category of suitable victim: Tituba, who was alleged to have taught the girls the principles of voodoo; Sarah Good, the wife of a labourer; and Sarah Osborne, an elderly and impoverished woman.

The women were brought before the local magistrates for questioning over a number of days. Osborne and Good maintained they were innocent but, after a good beating from Parris, Tituba confessed, 'The Devil came to me and bid me serve him.' She described elaborate images of black dogs, red cats, yellow birds and a 'black man' who wanted her to sign his book. She admitted that she signed the book and said there were several other witches looking to destroy the Puritans. Magistrates even questioned Sarah Good's four-year-old daughter, Dorothy, and her childish answers were deemed to be a confession. All three women were put in jail and, although Tituba survived, Sarah Good was executed. Sarah Osborne never confessed to witchcraft nor attempted to accuse anyone else. In a spirited defence, she was the first defendant to assert the theological claim that the Devil could take the shape of another person without their compliance – a view that eventually prevailed and brought the Salem trials to a halt, although not before a great deal of further damage had been done. Osborne never came to trial because she died in shackles in prison on 10 May. She was forty-nine.

In the March another girl, eleven-year-old Ann Putnam, had experienced similar episodes and she blamed Martha Corey. Now began a stream of allegations and the charge against Corey, regarded as a loyal member of the Church in Salem Village, seriously worried the community. If she could be a witch, then anyone could. The questioning became even more serious in April when Deputy Governor Thomas Danforth and his assistants began to attend the hearings. Now, dozens of people from Salem and other Massachusetts villages were brought in for questioning.

On 27 May William Phipps, governor of the colony, ordered the establishment of a Special Court of Oyer and Terminer for Suffolk, Essex and Middlesex counties. The first case brought to the special court was Bridget Bishop, an older woman and allegedly a promiscuous gossip. When asked if she had committed witchcraft, Bishop replied, 'I am as innocent as the child unborn.' The defence must have been unconvincing, because she was found guilty and, on 10 June, became the first person hanged on what was later called Gallows Hill.

It was all very well to convict and execute the poor and illiterate, but doubts began to be raised in the community after Rebecca Nurse was first acquitted and then convicted. George Burroughs recited the Lord's Prayer perfectly on the scaffold and eighty-one-year-old Giles Corey was pressed to death. He lasted two days under the weights. They had all been well thought of in the area. In addition, allegations of witchcraft were now made against the wife of Governor Phipps and other prominent locals.

Now the ministers Cotton Mather and his son, Increase Mather, began to doubt the value of the trials and Phipps banned 'spectral' evidence. Increase Mather tried to oust Parris from Salem and, although he did not succeed, he greatly reduced the minister's influence and Parris resigned in 1697.

Five years later Ann Putnam apologized for her behaviour. In 1711 a bill was passed restoring the rights and good names of those accused of witchcraft and awarding £600 as restitution for their heirs.

Helen Duncan

There was something of a moral panic about the penultimate British trial under the Witchcraft Act 1735, which took place at the Old Bailey in 1944 when the Scots-born medium Helen Duncan was prosecuted.

Born in 1897, she began, it is claimed, to exhibit signs of a psychic gift when she was a child. By 1926 she had progressed from clairvoyant to medium by offering séances, in which she claimed to summon the spirits of recently deceased persons by emitting ectoplasm from her mouth. A mother of six, she also worked part-time in a bleach factory.

Two years later photographer Harvey Metcalfe attended a series of séances at her house during one of which he took various flash photographs of Duncan and her alleged 'materialization' spirits, including one of her spirit guides 'Peggy' who spoke with a broad Scots accent. Peggy's speciality was to sing 'Baa Baa Black Sheep', but she could on occasion be persuaded to give a verse of 'Loch Lomond'. The photographs reveal the 'spirits' to have been fraudulently produced and included a doll made from a painted papier-mâché mask draped in an old sheet.

In 1931 the London Spiritualist Alliance examined Duncan's methods. Pieces of Duncan's ectoplasm revealed it was made of cheesecloth, along with lavatory paper mixed with white of egg. One of Duncan's tricks was to swallow and, with her exceptionally strong stomach muscles, regurgitate some of her ectoplasm and she was persuaded by the London Spiritualist

Alliance to swallow a tablet of methylene blue before one of her séances to rule out any chance of this trick being performed. On this occasion no ectoplasm appeared. That year she was denounced as a fraud by both the *Morning Post* and the London Psychic Laboratory.

At a séance on 6 January 1933 in Edinburgh, as soon as the child spirit Peggy emerged in the room a sitter, Esson Maule, grabbed her. When the lights were turned on, Duncan was found to be trying to hide Peggy, in the form of a woman's undervest, under her clothes. 'I'll brain you, you bloody bugger,' Duncan shouted. The police were called and she was prosecuted and fined £10 at the Edinburgh Sheriff Court on 11 May. Duncan's husband was also suspected of regularly acting as her accomplice, hiding her fake ectoplasm. She would frequently have nosebleeds during séances and another suggestion was that her nasal passage was one of her hiding places for the fake ectoplasm.

In 1936 Hungarian-born journalist Nandor Fodor wrote to her offering £20 and 50 per cent of the receipts of the film if she agreed to 'cinematographic evidence being taken by infra-red film'. She declined.

Harry Price, director of the National Laboratory of Psychical Research, was also sceptical of Duncan and had her perform a number of test séances. Suspecting her once more of swallowing cheesecloth to be regurgitated as ectoplasm, Price attempted to X-ray her. She reacted violently, running from the laboratory and making a scene in the street where her husband had to restrain her, so destroying the controlled nature of the test.

At the end of 1941 Duncan, then living in the naval town of Portsmouth, held a séance at which she claimed the spirit materialization of a sailor told her the HMS *Barham* had been sunk. Because the sinking on 25 November 1941 had been disclosed in strict confidence only to the relatives of casualties, and was not announced to the public until late January 1942, the navy started to take an interest in her activities.

Researcher Graeme Donald wrote that Duncan could have easily found out about the HMS *Barham* and her séance did not prove she had genuine psychic powers. Apart from anything else 300 men had survived. According to Donald:

> There was no shroud of secrecy ... The loss of HMS *Barham*, torpedoed off the coast of Egypt on 25 November 1941, had been hushed up, but letters of condolence were sent out to families of the 861 dead, asking them to keep the secret until the official announcement. So, allowing for perhaps ten people in each family, there were about 9,000 people who knew of the sinking; if each of them told only one other person, there were 20,000 people in the country aware of the sinking, and so on; hardly a closely guarded secret. In short, news of the sinking spread like wildfire; Duncan simply picked up the gossip and decided to turn it into profit.

This was not the only leak concerning the sinking of the *Barham*. A secretary of the First Lord had been indiscreet in a conversation with Professor Michael Postan of the Ministry of Economic Warfare. Postan escaped prosecution by insisting that he had made a mistake by believing the information had been imparted on an official basis.

Duncan was also found to be in possession of a mocked-up HMS *Barham* hatband. This apparently related to an alleged manifestation of the spirit of a dead sailor although Duncan appeared unaware that after 1939 sailors did not wear hatbands identifying their ship.

On 14 January 1944 naval lieutenant Stanley Worth was among her audience at a séance in a room known as the Master Temple Psychic Centre. The room was over a chemist shop in Connor Street, Portsmouth, owned by an Ernest Homer who charged an admission fee of 12/6d. At the séance Peggy declined to sing 'Baa Baa Black Sheep' but instead sang 'Loch Lomond' and everyone present sang 'You are my Sunshine'.

Duncan produced both an ectoplasmic parrot and a policeman, who appeared without his helmet and had to be sent back to the spirit world to find it. Unfortunately she also told Worth about his dead sister when the woman was actually driving an ambulance in London. When challenged, she said this had been an unborn dead sister but Worth's mother confirmed there had been no miscarriages.

Worth asked Homer's wife, Elizabeth, if next time he could bring along a naval doctor Surgeon Lieutenant Fowler, who was sceptical about séances. She agreed, telling him the doctor would have a seat in the front row and Duncan would 'scare him stiff'. She added that if the doctor touched the ectoplasm it would likely disappear into Mrs Duncan's body and possibly kill her. In fact it kept billowing until it was snatched by an assistant who disappeared with it. Mrs Duncan apparently produced a spirit guide named Albert who, in a husky voice, told Worth that she was his dead aunt. All Worth's aunts were alive. When the Surgeon Lieutenant asked a further question, Albert answered in a cultured Australian voice, 'Trying to ask strange, aren't you?'

On 17 January, War Reserve Constable Cross arrested her at another séance when a white-shrouded manifestation appeared which proved to be Duncan herself in a white cheesecloth, which she attempted to conceal when discovered.

She was initially arrested under Section 4 of the Vagrancy Act 1824, a minor offence triable only by magistrates, but the Director of Public Prosecutions regarded the case as more serious and she was prosecuted under Section 4 of the Witchcraft Act 1735, covering fraudulent 'spiritual' activity, triable only before a jury. There were also charges of obtaining money by false pretences and creating a public mischief. Charged alongside her with conspiracy to contravene this Act were Ernest and Elizabeth Homer and Duncan's agent, Frances Brown, who went with her to set up séances.

Duncan would normally have been committed to stand her trial at Quarter Sessions but the Portsmouth Magistrates committed her to the Central Criminal Court saying there were 'Special circumstances which make the case an unusually grave and difficult one and that delay and inconvenience would be occasioned by committal to Quarter Sessions.'

The DPP instructed the elegant if languid John Maude to appear for the Crown and the defence was funded by the

Spiritualists' National Union. To this extent Duncan and her co-defendants were doubly unlucky. With the D-Day landings in the offing, the authorities wanted to make sure that, however she might obtain the information, there would be no further public leaks. For the defence, the Union wanted to demonstrate that spiritualism was a genuine belief and there were such things as mediums in touch with the spirit world.

The trial began on 23 March 1944 at the Old Bailey in front of the Recorder of London, Sir Gerald Dodson. There were seven counts in total on the indictment; two of conspiracy to contravene the Witchcraft Act, two of obtaining money by false pretences and three of public mischief.

John Maude set the tone of the trial before a wartime jury of seven: 'The price of admission might have been reasonable if one were going to see the Ghost of Napoleon or the Duke of Wellington but not of much value if you were going to see a bogus conjuring trick.' And later he told the jury a psychic cat had miaowed during the session:

> What the cat was doing before it was summoned to make its appearance in Portsmouth one can only imagine; whether it was hunting pink mice in the Elysian Fields one does not know. All one knows is that a miaow came from behind the curtain; so I suppose, if one is a cat, one does not make much progress.

C. E. Loseby, who appeared for the defendants, was also in a bind. He could not call Duncan to say she was a genuine medium because, had he done so, Maude would have lovingly put her conviction in Edinburgh in evidence. Loseby then tried the tactic of asking whether she would be allowed to give a demonstration in court. This was smartly refused by Dodson, who said it was bad enough that they were having to try a case from Portsmouth and he was not having the jury waste further time on an investigation that might not help. They were there to try something that had happened in the past. Nor would he generally allow witnesses from earlier séances to be called to say they believed her to be genuine. Earlier séances might have been genuine, but what the jury was considering was the 17 January demonstration. All Loseby could do was to call witnesses who had been in the Temple that afternoon and who believed the séance was genuine. A number of prominent people, among them Alfred Dodd, an historian and senior Freemason, along with the journalist Hannen Swaffer, gave evidence they were convinced she was authentic.

Loseby did however call Homer, who said Mrs Duncan was paid £8 a time and had made £113 over six days. So far as he was concerned the ectoplasm was genuine. Some of his takings were donated to the British Wireless for the Blind Fund and he produced a receipt.

Summing up to the jury, Dodson said the case was not an attack on spiritualism; Duncan's behaviour was nothing more or less than a commonplace fraud. The jury was sure it was and convicted all the defendants on the first count in less than half an hour. Duncan was imprisoned for nine months. Brown, who had convictions for shoplifting, received four months and the Homers were bound over to be of good behaviour for two years in the sum of £5 each.

It was a triumphant week for Maude. Not only was he prosecuting Duncan, he was also appearing in another court at the Bailey obtaining the acquittal of Harold Loughnan for the murder of a publican, also in Portsmouth.

The prosecution may be explained by the mood of suspicion prevailing at the time; the authorities were afraid that she could continue to reveal classified information, whatever her source was. There were also concerns that she was exploiting the recently bereaved, Dodson noted when passing sentence.

Their appeals were dismissed on 19 June. On her release in 1945, Duncan promised to stop conducting séances. However, she was arrested during another one, this time in Nottingham in 1956. Three months later, with the case still outstanding, she died during a séance at her home in Edinburgh in what her supporters have called 'her premature promotion to the next world on 6 December 1956, shortly after yet another mischievous police raid'.

Duncan's trial for fraudulent witchcraft was a minor *cause célèbre* in wartime London, and after the 1944 verdict Winston Churchill wrote a memorandum to the Home Secretary Herbert Morrison, complaining about the misuse of court resources on the 'obsolete tomfoolery' of the charge. Her trial almost certainly contributed to the repeal of the Witchcraft Act, which was contained in the Fraudulent Mediums Act 1951. The campaign to repeal the Act had largely been led by Thomas Brooks, a Labour MP, who was a spiritualist.

Although Duncan's supporters have also claimed that she was the last person to be convicted under the Witchcraft Act, this is not correct. That dubious distinction goes to Jane Rebecca Yorke from Forest Gate in East London, who appeared at the Old Bailey in the same year. Yorke's alleged spirit guide was a Zulu and she also frequently claimed to summon Queen Victoria to help things along.

During séances with Yorke, undercover police were told to ask about non-existent family members. She offered elaborate details on them, which she claimed had been provided by her spirit guides, telling an officer that his non-existent brother had been burned alive on a bombing mission. She also terrified a woman who said she had seen the spirit of her dead brother. Now Yorke warned her that her husband might also be killed. However, on a more optimistic note, Yorke predicted that the Second World War would end in October 1944. She did not charge for admission but money was dropped into a suitably placed bowl.

She was arrested in July 1944 and at her trial in the September she was found guilty on seven counts under the Witchcraft Act. In evidence she claimed she had no knowledge of what she said when in a trance. After promising she would hold no more séances, Yorke was fined £5 and placed on a good behaviour bond for three years. The light sentence was due to her age of seventy-two.

Duncan's supporters still claim she was made a scapegoat because of official paranoia surrounding the forthcoming D-Day Normandy landings, and the fear that she might reveal the date and other details. The authorities were also furious there was a high admission charge and that she and the others were making money out of people's grief. Her supporters said that she charged only a nominal amount for holding séances and that she spent much of the money on discreetly providing medical services for her clientele, but over that two-week period in Portsmouth she received more than £110, the equivalent of roughly £2,900 today.

Efforts to have her posthumously pardoned on the basis that the trial was a miscarriage of justice, first because she was not allowed to demonstrate her art and secondly that the Recorder would not allow evidence of previous successful séances, have continued into the twenty-first century. In 2007, more than 500 pages of legal arguments were submitted to the Criminal Cases Review Commission. The Commission stated that it did not consider her case to be 'in the public interest', and declined to consider the application. In 2008, the Scottish Parliament rejected a petition to pardon her.

Ethel Rosenberg

A classic example of a moral panic occurred when the only spies to be executed post-war in America were New Yorkers Julius and Ethel Rosenberg, convicted in 1951 of spying for Russia during World War Two. Given the extreme anti-Soviet feeling at the time it was always likely to be their fate. Julius Rosenberg was born on 12 May 1918 in New York City, the son of Russian immigrants. He had one brother and three sisters. His wife, born Ethel Greenglass and three years older, was born on 28 September 1915, also in New York City and also the daughter of immigrants. Her father, who ran a sewing machine repair shop, had been born in Russia and her mother in Austria. Other members of her family, who lived in what has been described as grinding poverty, included her brothers David and Bernard, and a half-brother.

Julius and Ethel both lived on the lower east side of Manhattan for most of their lives and both attended the same high school, Seward Park, just below the Bowery. Ethel graduated in 1931 and became a clerk in a shipping firm from which she was sacked for organizing a strike. Julius graduated three years later. He then attended the school of engineering at New York's City College from September 1934 until February 1939, when he graduated with a bachelor's degree in electrical engineering. He was secretary of the Young Communist League while in college and later took various courses at other New York universities.

Around 1932 Rosenberg began stepping out with Ethel. From the start he was disliked by her parents and was not allowed to visit their home until 1935. During that time she and her two younger brothers had a flat on a floor above the home of their parents; the flat was littered with copies of Communist Party literature and the *Daily Worker*.

Sometime between 1932 and 1935 the pair became committed communists after which, the FBI would allege, they maintained that nothing was more important to them than the cause. They were members of the International Workers Order (IWO), founded in 1930 and which, at its height in the years immediately following World War Two, had almost 200,000 members and provided low-cost health and life insurance, medical and dental clinics. It also supported foreign-language newspapers, cultural and educational activities and ran a summer camp and cemeteries for its members. In 1947 the US attorney general placed the IWO on its list of subversive organizations. Although the IWO was financially solvent and well managed, the New York State Insurance Department contended that, since the IWO was engaged in political activity, something which was prohibited to insurance organizations, this placed its members' interests in jeopardy. It was disbanded in 1954.

Julius and Ethel married on 18 June 1939 in New York City and had two sons, Michael Allen, born in March 1943, and Robert Harry, born in May four years later. Ethel's brother David Greenglass married eighteen-year-old Ruth Printz in 1942 and the pair joined the Young Communist League shortly before Greenglass entered the US Army in 1943. Initially a machinist at the army base in Jackson, Mississippi, Greenglass was promoted to sergeant and assigned to the secret Manhattan Project, the wartime project to develop the first atomic weapons. At first Greenglass was stationed at the uranium enrichment facility at Oak Ridge, Tennessee, but later he worked at the Los Alamos laboratory in New Mexico.

In May 1940, after Ethel Rosenberg became an employee of the Census Bureau in Washington, D.C., the FBI's New York Field Office learned that she was a devout communist. She and another woman, alleged to have been a communist sympathizer, had distributed communist literature and had signed nominating petitions of the Communist Party.

The Government's case was that on 7 September 1942 at a Labor Day rally in New York City, Semen Semenov, an officer of the NKVD (later the KGB), the law enforcement agency of the Soviet Union, recruited Julius Rosenberg to spy for the Soviet Union. After Rosenberg suggested to his NKVD superior, Alexandre Feklissov of the Soviet consulate in New York, that he use his sister-in-law Ruth Greenglass's apartment as a safe house for photography, the NKVD discovered that her husband was working on the Manhattan Project. Prompted by Rosenberg, Ruth Greenglass then recruited him. Feklissov met the couple and on 21 September, he reported to Moscow: 'They are young, intelligent, capable, and politically developed people, strongly believing in the cause of communism and wishing to do their best to help our country as much as possible. They are undoubtedly devoted to us [the Soviet Union].'

In turn David Greenglass wrote to his wife, 'My darling, I most certainly will be glad to be part of the community project [espionage] that Julius and his friends [the Russians] have in mind.'

Now David began to pass nuclear secrets to the Soviet Union via the Soviet courier Brooklyn-based Harry Gold, who in a separate trial received thirty years, and more directly with a Soviet official in New York City. He was a spy for about two years, from November 1944 until he left the army in 1946. According to the counter-intelligence Venona project, intercepts decrypted by the National Security Agency (NSA), David and Ruth were given the code names 'KALIBR' and 'OSA' respectively.

In December 1945, after United States government officials discovered his membership in the Communist Party, Julius Rosenberg was relieved of his duties by the NKVD.

After the war Greenglass, his brother Bernie and Julius Rosenberg ran a small machine shop located in Manhattan but by 1947 it had failed, something that caused ill-feeling in the family. Now Greenglass continued his contact with the Soviets independently of Rosenberg.

In 1950, British and American intelligence agencies

discovered that a Los Alamos theoretical physicist, Klaus Fuchs, had spied for the USSR during the war. Through Fuchs' confession, they found that one of his American contacts had been the laboratory chemist Harry Gold. Through Gold, the FBI's trail led to Greenglass and on to the Rosenbergs, who had also used Gold as a courier. When Fuchs was first arrested, Julius allegedly gave the Greenglasses $5,000 to finance an escape to Mexico. Instead, they went to the Catskills and used the money to seek legal advice.

At a Grand Jury hearing in August 1950 to hear the Justice Department's case for indictments against the Rosenbergs and Greenglasses, Ethel Rosenberg took the opportunity to plead the Fifth Amendment designed to prevent her incriminating herself, and at the subsequent trial a good deal was made of this despite her going on to answer the questions she had previously declined to answer.

On 17 August the Grand Jury handed down indictments alleging espionage against Julius and Ethel Rosenberg along with Morton Sobell, another member of their ring, as well as David and Ruth Greenglass. Their trial began on 6 March 1951 in Part 110 of the courts at Foley Street, Manhattan. David Greenglass pleaded guilty and no evidence was offered against Ruth. Both became prosecution witnesses.

With the forty-year-old Judge Irving Kaufman, described by Julius Rosenberg as 'looking like a cross between a rabbinical student and an army sergeant', presiding and a non-Jewish jury of eleven men and one woman, all the other principals in the case were Jewish. The charges were bitterly contested, with the Rosenbergs' lawyers challenging every point they could and with Kaufman overruling almost every one of their objections.

The prosecution was represented by United States Attorney Irving Saypol and Roy Cohn, son of a Supreme Court judge, who conducted the examination of Ruth Greenglass, which would prove fatal to Ethel. Ruth Greenglass was an impressive prosecution witness. Well groomed, calm, evidently well-rehearsed, she confirmed her husband's account of Ethel's typing of the Los Alamos information. She added two more incidents that showed Ethel was wholly involved in the spying. One was her admission to Ruth that she did not find David's handwriting difficult to decipher as she was getting used to it. She also said that Ethel had told her by letter that a meeting that Ruth was to have with her courier, Harry Gold, had been rescheduled. Efforts by Bloch to shake her during cross-examination failed.

In his memoirs Cohn would boast that he had been instrumental in arranging the appointment of Kaufman as the judge and influencing him over imposing the death penalty. During the trial, without telling the defence lawyers, Kaufman, a known anti-communist, discussed the case with the prosecution and officials in the Justice Department during the trial and after during the appeals process.

Many miscarriages of justice arise when the defendants' lawyers are disinterested or incompetent but, although many have questioned his trial strategies, no one could say that their lawyer Emanuel Hirsch Bloch did not do his best for them in what amounted to hopeless circumstances. Here he is talking to the jury about David Greenglass who gave his evidence on the fourth day of the trial:

Now, let us take Dave Greenglass. This didn't come out of my mouth. This came out of his mouth. Is he a self-confessed spy? Is there any doubt in any of your minds that Dave Greenglass is a self-confessed espionage agent? He characterized himself that way. What did this man do? He took an oath when he entered the Army of the United States. He didn't even remember what the oath was. That is how seriously he took it. But, in substance, he swore to support our country. Is there any doubt in your mind that he violated that oath? Is there any doubt in your mind that he disgraced the uniform of every soldier in the United States by his actions? Do you know what that man did? He was assigned to one of the most important secret projects in this country, and by his own statements, by his own admissions, he told you that he stole information out of there and gave it to strangers, and that it was going to the Soviet Government.

Now, that is undisputed. I would like Mr Saypol or anybody who is going to sum up on the part of the Government to refute that. Is there any doubt in your mind about that?

You know, before I summed up, I wanted to go to a dictionary and I wanted to find a word that could describe a Dave Greenglass. I couldn't find it, because I don't think that there is a word in the English vocabulary or in the dictionary of any civilization which can describe a character like Dave Greenglass.

But one thing I think you do know, that any man who will testify against his own blood and flesh, his own sister, is repulsive, is revolting, who violates every code that any civilization has ever lived by. He is the lowest of the lowest animals that I have ever seen, and if you are honest with yourself, you will admit that he is lower than the lowest animal that you have ever seen.

This is not a man; this is an animal . . . Did you look at him? I know you did; you watched him; all your eyes were fastened on him, just as people are fascinated by horror; and he smirked and he smiled and I asked him a question, so that it would be in the cold printed record, 'Are you aware of your smile?' And do you know the answer I got? Do you remember it? 'Not very.' Listen to that answer, 'Not very.'

Well, maybe some people enjoy funerals; maybe some people enjoy lynchings, but I wonder whether in anything that you have read or in anything that you have experienced you have ever come across a man, who comes round to bury his own sister and smiles.

Tell me, is this the kind of a man you are going to believe? God Almighty, if ever a witness discredited himself on a stand, he did. What kind of a man can be disbelieved if we are going to believe Dave Greenglass? What is the sense of having witness chairs? What is the sense of having juries subject witnesses' testimony to scrutiny and analysis? Is that the kind of a man that you would believe in your own life or would you punch him in the nose and throw him out and have nothing to do with him because he is a low rebel?

> Come on, be honest with yourselves, ladies and gentlemen, is that the kind of testimony that you are going to accept?

But believe it they did. The jury retired on 29 March and returned their verdicts of guilty against all three defendants within twenty-four hours.

Morton Sobell was sentenced to thirty years and served seventeen, mainly in Alcatraz, before he was paroled. In the political climate of the time the Rosenbergs could expect no sympathy from the trial judge and on 6 April Justice Kaufman did not disappoint them. Sentencing them to death he told them:

> I consider your crime worse than murder . . . I believe your conduct in putting into the hands of the Russians the A-Bomb years before our best scientists predicted Russia would perfect the bomb has already caused, in my opinion, the Communist aggression in Korea, with the resultant casualties exceeding 50,000 and who knows but that millions more of innocent people may pay the price of your treason. Indeed, by your betrayal you undoubtedly have altered the course of history to the disadvantage of our country. No one can say that we do not live in a constant state of tension. We have evidence of your treachery all around us every day for the civilian defense activities throughout the nation are aimed at preparing us for an atom bomb attack.

Commenting on the sentence given to them, Julius Rosenberg claimed the case was a political frame-up:

> This death sentence is not surprising. It had to be. There had to be a Rosenberg case, because there had to be an intensification of the hysteria in America to make the Korean War acceptable to the American people. There had to be hysteria and a fear sent through America in order to get increased war budgets. And there had to be a dagger thrust in the heart of the left to tell them that you are no

longer gonna get five years for a Smith Act prosecution or
one year for contempt of court, but we're gonna kill ya!

Now, when a series of appeals were lodged and rejected,
support for the Rosenbergs grew and a Committee to Secure
Justice in the Rosenberg Case was formed. Much of the
evidence was circumstantial and in 1951 anti-Russian feeling
had been so extreme doubts about the death sentence were
raised worldwide. The convictions were upheld seven times by
the US Circuit Court of Appeals and six times the Supreme
Court found no reason to review the decision.

When the case was first presented the government was
convinced that Ethel's arrest would be sufficient to pressure
Julius to cooperate with them. Curt Gentry, the author of *J.
Edgar Hoover, The Man and the Secrets*, wrote:

> The FBI arrested Ethel Rosenberg. Despite the lack of
> evidence, her incarceration was an essential part of Hoover's
> plan. With both Rosenbergs jailed – bail for each was set at
> $100,000, an unmeetable amount – the couple's two young
> sons were passed from relative to relative, none of whom
> wanted them, until they were placed in the Jewish Children's
> Home in the Bronx. According to matrons at the Women's
> House of Detention, Ethel missed the children terribly,
> suffered severe migraines, and cried herself to sleep at night.
> But Julius didn't break.

Now the FBI thought the imposition of the death sentence
would concentrate his mind, and when that failed, in May
1953 they let it be known that if he confessed and provided
information about the spy ring their lives would be spared. It
had no effect. In a joint statement the Rosenbergs stood firm:
'[We will] not be coerced even under pain of death to bear
false witness . . . Our respect for truth, conscience and human
dignity is not for sale. Justice is not some bauble to be sold to
the highest bidder.'

With the prospect of the executions looming large, in early
June 1953 the Polish Embassy said it would grant asylum to

the Rosenbergs. The State Department said the offer was 'impertinent'.

Because the United States Federal Bureau of Prisons did not operate an electric chair at the time, the Rosenbergs were transferred to the New York State-run Sing Sing Correctional Facility in Ossining for execution. The day before the execution, fixed for 18 June, the Supreme Court Associate Justice William O. Douglas granted a stay. It had resulted from the intervention in the case by Fyke Farmer, a Tennessee lawyer whose efforts had previously been met with scorn from the Rosenbergs' attorney. Now he raised an interesting and ingenious argument. The pair had been tried under the Atomic Energy Act, which required a jury verdict to impose the death sentence, but they had not done so. Kaufman could not do this unilaterally. Did he have the right to sentence under the old Espionage Act 1917? Douglas thought there was something in the argument.

On 18 June the Court was called back into special session to dispose of Douglas's stay rather than let the execution be delayed for months while the appeal worked its way through the lower courts. The Court, by a six-votes-to-two majority with Justice Frankfurter abstaining, did not vacate Douglas's stay until noon on Friday, 19 June and as a result the execution was then scheduled for the regular time of 11 that evening. This was after the start of the Jewish Sabbath and, desperately playing for more time, their lawyer, Emanuel Bloch, filed a complaint that this offended their Jewish heritage. As a result, the execution was rescheduled to take place at 8 p.m., before sunset.

A final petition for clemency was rejected by President Eisenhower:

> The only conclusion to be drawn from the history of the case is that the Rosenbergs have received the benefit of every safeguard which American justice can provide. There is no question in my mind that the original trial and the long series of appeals constitute the fullest measure of justice and due process of law. Throughout the innumerable

complications and technicalities of this case, no judge has ever expressed any doubts that they committed most serious acts of espionage . . . I can only say by immeasurably increasing the chances of an atomic war the Rosenbergs may have condemned to death tens of millions of innocent people all over the world. The execution of two human beings is a grave matter. But even graver is the thought of millions of dead whose death may be directly attributable to what these spies have done.

Supreme Court judge Justice Frankfurter filed a ten-page dissenting judgement against the refusal to stay the execution, saying it had been a valid point to be argued properly and should not have been dismissed out of hand.

There was one last effort, this time made by lawyer Daniel Marshall, who tried again to get Judge Kaufman to stay the execution by arguing that the court had not vacated the portion of Douglas' decision which referred the legal issue back to the District Court. Kaufman would have none of it.

Eyewitness evidence shown on a newsreel in the 1982 documentary film *The Atomic Cafe* describes the circumstances of the Rosenbergs' deaths. While Julius Rosenberg died after the first electric shock, the supposedly frailer Ethel did not. After the normal course of three electric shocks, attendants removed the strapping only for doctors to find that her heart was still beating. Two more electric shocks were applied, and at the end there were reports that smoke rose from her. The executions produced protests worldwide, if not in America. In Rome fire hoses were used to quell demonstrators and in Paris there were 386 arrests.

The Rosenbergs were buried at Wellwood Cemetery, an annex to the Beth David Cemetery in Pinelawn, Nassau County. Anti-Rosenberg protestors demonstrated outside the cemetery claiming the bodies should be buried in Russia. Bloch delivered the eulogy at the funeral, saying, 'I place the murder of the Rosenbergs at the door of President Eisenhower, Mr Brownell and J. Edgar Hoover.' Earlier he had taken a final plea written by Ethel in her cell to the White House, but he was

turned away by guards. Bloch acted as guardian to their two
sons until they were adopted. He died in 1954 following a
heart attack.

In July 1954, the House of Representatives with no
dissentients voted that peacetime espionage should be made
a capital offence.

In 2008 Morton Sobell, who had not given evidence at the
trial, finally admitted that he had spied for the Soviet Union
and so the Rosenberg sons reluctantly accepted their father
had been a spy. Grand Jury testimony released in 2008 suggests
that the Greenglasses may have lied when they gave the crucial
evidence that Ethel Rosenberg had typed up the secret information provided to the Soviets. In her earlier evidence to the
Grand Jury Ruth Greenglass had said she wrote the secret
information in longhand, evidence that is consistent with
decoded Soviet cables indicating that the material came to
them in longhand form.

The same year Rosenberg's spymaster Alexandre Feklissov
wrote, 'He [Julius] didn't understand anything about the
atomic bomb and he couldn't help us.' However, he claimed
that Rosenberg had passed him a wealth of extremely useful
information on US electronic systems. Feklissov died in 2007
at the age of ninety-three.

Greenglass served ten years of a fifteen-year sentence for
espionage. After his release he lived with his family in anonym-
ity as controversy over the Rosenberg case flowed and ebbed
over the decades. He remained estranged for the rest of his life
from the Rosenbergs' sons and died unremorseful, aged
ninety-two, on 1 July 2014. He took the view, 'As long as they
had something over my head about my wife and family, they
could probably get me to do anything that would preserve
them . . . and most men would do that.' Alternatively he will be
remembered by history as 'the man that put his sister and
brother-in-law to death'.

Judge Irving Kaufman died in February 1992. He had
hoped, against the odds, that he would be remembered not for
his role in the Rosenberg case but as an innovative judge who
was the first to rule that a public school in the north should be

desegregated. The lead prosecutor Irving Saypol was appointed to the New York Supreme Court within months of the trial. Assistant Prosecutor Roy Cohn went on to assist Senator Joe McCarthy in the anti-Communist campaign, and when the Senator fell from grace Cohn fell with him. Federal investigations during the 1970s and 1980s charged Cohn three times with professional misconduct, including perjury and witness tampering, and he was accused in New York of financial improprieties related to city contracts and private investments. He was acquitted of all charges.

In 1986, the Appellate Division of the New York State Supreme Court disbarred Cohn for unethical and unprofessional conduct, including misappropriation of clients' funds, lying on a bar application and pressuring a client to amend his will. He died of an AIDS-related illness in 1986. Two years later, in June 1988, he was described in the American Bar Association Journal as 'a man so altogether loathsome that his opponents would settle cases just to avoid dealing with him'.

Fifty years after their executions a remembrance of the Rosenbergs was held at City Center, on West 55th Street in Manhattan. The proceeds went to the Rosenberg Fund for Children, a foundation headed by their son Robert Meeropol. The Foundation provides for the needs of children of targeted progressive activists, and youths who are targeted activists themselves. In ways that are often small – piano lessons, for example – it helps children who suffer because of their parents' political activities.

The West Memphis Three

On 6 May 1993 three cub scouts, Steven Branch, Michael Moore and Christopher Byers, were found dead in a creek in Robin Hood Hills, a wooded area in West Memphis, Arkansas. The eight-year-olds were naked and had been hogtied with shoelaces. The underwear of two of the boys was never found and Byers had apparently been sexually assaulted and castrated. As a result, among the blue-collar Southern Baptist community there was talk of satanic rituals.

The previous afternoon Michael and Steve had been seen riding their bicycles after school, while Chris was skateboarding. Then Deborah O'Tinger saw the three boys walking through her yard between 5.45 and 6.00 that afternoon. Her recollection was that they were pushing a bicycle. A little later Dana Moore, Michael's mother, saw the three boys together and at that time Michael was riding his bicycle. Between 6.30 and 6.45 Brian Woody saw four boys going into some woods known as the Robin Hood woods. He noticed that two of the boys were pushing bicycles, one had a skateboard, and the fourth one was just walking behind them. Around 7 p.m. John Mark Byers, Christopher's adoptive father, reported they had gone missing.

The next morning, members of the Crittenden County Search and Rescue Unit discovered a tennis shoe floating in a ditch just north of Ten Mile Bayou. The Robin Hood woods drain into Ten Mile Bayou, and the members of the search unit knew the boys were last seen in that area. When Detective Mike Allen walked along the ditch bank to the place where the tennis shoe had been found, he noticed that one area of the ditch bank was cleared of leaves, while the rest of the bank was covered with leaves and sticks. He got into the water, reached down to get the shoe and felt Michael Moore's body. The bodies of Christopher Byers and Steve Branch were subsequently found about twenty-five feet downstream. Another officer at the scene, policeman John Moore, noticed there was blood in the water, but none on the bank.

All three bodies had their right hands tied to their right feet, and their left hands tied to their left feet with black and white shoelaces. Michael Moore's body had wounds to the neck, chest and abdominal regions that appeared to have been caused by a serrated knife. There were abrasions over his scalp that could have been caused by a stick. Dr Frank Peretti, a state medical examiner, found that there was bruising and discolouring comparable to that frequently seen in children who have been forced to have oral sex. He thought that there were defensive wounds to the hands and arms. Moore's rectum was dilated and reddened, and Peretti thought that this injury could have come from an object being inserted. His opinion was that Moore was still alive when he went in the water.

Steve Branch's body had head, chest, genital-anal and back injuries. Wounds on the body suggested he was moving when he was stabbed. The anus was dilated. Penile injuries indicated that oral sex had been performed on him. There was also evidence that he, too, had drowned.

Christopher Byers' body also had injuries indicating that he had been forced to perform oral sex. The inner thighs had diagonal cuts on them and it appeared the back of the skull had been struck with a stick-like, broomstick-size, object. The skin of the penis had been removed, and the scrotal sac and testes were missing. There were cuts around the anus, and the haemorrhaging from those cuts indicated he was still alive when they were made, probably with a serrated blade knife. He had bled to death. The boys' bicycles were found nearby.

Two of the three came from dysfunctional families. In particular Steve Branch's stepfather had a long history of theft and drug offences and was an informant for the West Memphis police. He later admitted having whipped Steve shortly before the boy had disappeared. His offence was trying to break into his own home – he was not allowed a key and the house was locked when he returned from school.

The police looked at several men as potential suspects; one of them was John Mark Byers, and others included two West Memphis teenagers, both of whom had histories of drug-taking and who left for Oceanside, California four days after the bodies were found. On 17 May the youths were arrested in Oceanside and were given lie detector tests which, according to examiners, indicated 'deception'. One claimed he suffered from blackouts and admitted he 'might' have killed the boys. Almost immediately he withdrew the confession.

Another suspect was an unidentified black man, who came to be known as Mr Bojangles. Around 8.45 p.m. on the day the boys disappeared, he went to the female restroom at the Bojangles restaurant and defecated on the floor. Workers in the restaurant said he appeared dazed and confused. The police were called, but by the time an officer arrived three-quarters of an hour later he was gone. After the boys' bodies were discovered the restaurant manager, Marty King, again telephoned the police. After yet another call from King officers arrived, but unfortunately they were still dressed in the same clothes and footwear they had worn at the murder site and this may have contaminated the restroom. Blood scrapings were lost.

So far as the forensic evidence is concerned, the West Memphis police do not appear to have had the resources or skills to investigate the crime scene properly. The bodies were removed from the water before the coroner arrived. Forensic samples were stored in supermarket bags rather than in controlled containers. It was left to old-fashioned police work to 'solve' the crime. It was his probation officer, Jerry Driver, who suggested the police should look at Damien Wayne Echols. First, he thought Echols was 'capable' of the crime, a view he then upgraded by saying, 'It looks like Damien Echols finally killed someone.'

In a curious throwback to the witchcrafts trials four centuries earlier, eighteen-year-old Echols was an ideal scapegoat. A relationship with an early girlfriend ended when the pair ran away and were arrested after breaking into a trailer in a rainstorm. There were stories that the pair had planned to have a child, which they would then sacrifice. True or not, it was certainly sufficient for Echols to have been sent to an Arkansas psychiatric hospital.

Echols was interviewed two days after the bodies were found, and again the polygraph examiner claimed the chart showed 'deception' but there were no records to back this up. Two days after that Detective Bryn Ridge invited Echols to speculate on what might have happened. The conversation went unrecorded but Ridge's evidence was that Echols thought that the boys had died of mutilation; he had heard they were in the water and one had been more cut up than the others. The killings were to prevent squealing, in the sense of informing.

Other local teenagers were regularly questioned and they complained that they had been bullied by the police and yelled at if they did not give the answers expected from them.

On the day the bodies were discovered, a young woman, Vicki Hutcheson, was interviewed by Detective Don Bray over a possible theft from her employer. With her was her eight-year-old son Aaron, who was such a nuisance that Bray was unable to conduct a polygraph test on his mother. However, the child, who said he was a friend of the dead boys, told the detective that they had been killed at 'the playhouse'. Aaron went on to say that he had seen the killings committed by Spanish-speaking satanists, but when he was shown photographs of the boys he was unable to identify them. When he was taken to the place where he said he had seen the boys killed, there was no 'playhouse'. It was the leaking of Aaron's story into the community that added to the satanist theory. Nevertheless, the police persuaded Hutcheson that there was a great deal of help she could give them. Possibly in return for a go-slow into the theft investigation, she agreed to allow the police to put microphones in her home when another local youth, her friend seventeen-year-old Jesse Lloyd Misskelley, agreed to introduce her to Echols. She later said he made no incriminating statements, while the police said the recordings were inaudible, something she contradicted.

Next day she told the police that two weeks after the murders she, Misskelley and Echols had been to an esbat, a Wicca (pagan) ceremony on the night of a full moon. Echols, who was drunk, boasted about killing the boys but she could not recall the exact location or who else had been present. She was never charged with the theft.

At the time of his arrest Echols was living in a trailer park. Already on probation, conveniently he dressed in black, liked heavy metal, the novels of Stephen King, had read the British satanist Aleister Crowley and collected animal skulls. He was also a Wiccan.

A month after the deaths of the cub scouts Jesse Misskelley, who had an IQ of seventy-two, was arrested. After twelve hours of questioning, of which less than fifty minutes was recorded, and without a responsible person with him, Misskelley made a confession detailing how he had seen Echols and Jesse Baldwin take the boys into the woods where they raped and mutilated them before throwing the bodies into the creek. He retracted it almost immediately, but it proved to be a cornerstone of the prosecution's case at their trials in early January 1994. Echols and Baldwin were promptly arrested.

The trials were split. The police hoped Misskelley would give evidence against the other two but, represented by David Stidham who later became a municipal judge, when he would not, he was the first to be put on trial. First, Stidham tried to have the confession excluded. He claimed that Misskelley had not understood his Miranda rights about not having to say anything when he was questioned by the police, and Misskelley told the court he was scared of the officers. Richard Ofshe, professor of sociology at University of California Berkeley, called on his behalf, said that his interrogation was a classic of police coercion. The confession was in many places inconsistent. In a crucial passage Misskelley said he had seen Echols rape one of the boys. However an examination showed that their dilated anuses were a normal post-mortem condition.

But, over objections by Stidham, Judge David Burnett admitted the confession.

On 5 February 1994 Misskelley was found guilty of one count of first-degree murder and two counts of second-degree murder and was sentenced to life in prison plus forty years. However, on 17 February he gave another statement to the police, this time in the presence of Stidham who continually advised him to remain silent. Now he went into some detail about how he had watched Echols and Baldwin abuse the boys until he had decided to leave. However, once again he refused to give evidence against the other defendants.

Such was the local hostility that Echols and Baldwin were given bulletproof vests to wear when their trial opened. Once under way, the prosecution called Dale W. Griffis, a graduate of Columbia Pacific University, as an expert in the occult to testify the murders were a satanic ritual.

What evidence was there against the three youths? Anthony and Narlene Hollingsworth, who were well acquainted with Echols, gave evidence that they saw him and his girlfriend, Domini Teer, walking after 9.30 on the night of the murders near the Blue Beacon Truck Stop, close to Robin Hood woods where the bodies were found. They said that Echols was wearing a dark-coloured shirt and that his clothes were dirty. This evidence placed Echols in dirty clothes near the scene at a time close to the murders. Other evidence suggested that Domini Teer could be confused with Baldwin as both had long hair and were of slight build.

Twelve-year-old Christy Van Vickle told the jury that she heard Echols say he 'killed the three boys', while fifteen-year-old Jackie Medford said that she heard Echols say, 'I killed the three little boys and before I turn myself in, I'm going to kill two more, and I already have one of them picked out.' Echols denied making these remarks. Lisa Sakevicius, a criminalist from the State Crime Laboratory, said that she compared fibres found on the victims' clothes with clothing found in Echols' home, and the fibres were microscopically similar.

Dr Frank Peretti gave evidence that there were serrated

wound patterns on the three victims. Much of the evidence against Baldwin was that of association, but on 17 November 1993 a diver had found a knife in a lake behind the home of Baldwin's parents. The large knife had a serrated edge and had the words 'Special Forces Survival II' on the blade. So far as Peretti was concerned many of the wounds on the victims were consistent with, and could have been caused by, that knife. He believed that some of the head wounds to the boys were consistent with the size of two sticks that had been recovered by the police.

Deanna Holcomb claimed that she had seen Echols carrying a similar knife, except that the one she saw had a compass on the end. James Parker, owner of Parker's Knife Collector Service in Chattanooga, Tennessee, was called to say that a company distributed this type of knife from 1985 to 1987. A 1987 catalogue from the company was shown to the jury, and it had a picture of a knife similar to the knife found behind the Baldwins' home. The knife in the catalogue had a compass on the end, and it had the words 'Special Forces Survival II' on the blade. The jury could have made a determination whether the compass had been unscrewed, and, in assessing the value to them of the location of the knife introduced at trial, they heard ample evidence that Echols and Baldwin spent much time together. Therefore, it could have reasonably concluded that Echols or Baldwin disposed of the knife in the lake.

The state's theory of motive was that the killings were done in a satanic ritual. Various items, including a funeral register upon which Echols had drawn a pentagram and upside-down crosses and spells he had copied out, were found in his room. A magazine he had there contained images of and references to dead children. On cross-examination, Echols admitted that he had read a great deal about the occult and was familiar with its practices. He accepted that he wore a long black trench coat even when it was warm. One witness had seen Echols, Baldwin and Misskelley together six months before the murders, wearing long black coats and carrying long staffs.

The occult expert Dale Griffis gave evidence that the

killings had the 'trappings of occultism'. The date of the killings, near a pagan holiday as well as the fact that there was a
full moon was, he said, highly significant. He claimed that
young children were often sought for sacrifice because 'the
younger, the more innocent, the better the life force'. There
were three victims, and the number three, the first perfect
number and symbolic of the pagan trilogy, had significance in
occultism. Also, the victims were all eight years old, and eight
is a witches' number. Sacrifices are often done near water for
a baptism-type rite or simply to wash the blood away. The fact
that the victims were tied ankle to wrist was significant because
this was done to display the genitalia, and the removal of Byers'
testicles was significant because testicles are removed for the
semen. The absence of blood at the scene could be significant
because cult members store blood for future services in which
they would drink it or bathe in it. The 'overkill' or multiple cuts
could reflect occult overtones. He thought that there was
significance in injuries to the left side of the victims as opposed
to the right side. People who practice occultism will use the
midline theory, drawing straight down through the body. The
right side is related to those things synonymous with
Christianity while the left side is that of the practitioners of the
satanic occult. He thought that the clear place on the bank
could be consistent with a ceremony.

Lisa Sakevicius, the criminalist who gave evidence about the
fibres, stated that Byers' white polka-dot shirt had blue wax on
it and that the wax was consistent with candle wax.

Detective Bryn Ridge told the court that Echols said he
understood the victims had been mutilated, with one being cut
up more than the others, and that they had drowned. When
Echols made the statement, the fact that Christopher Byers
had been mutilated more than the other two victims was not
known by the public.

It is always a difficult point for lawyers to decide whether
their client should give evidence. In murder cases in America
it is generally thought that if the defendant does not have serious criminal convictions they should. So Echols gave evidence,
but he did not do well. When asked about his statement that

one victim was mutilated more than the others, he said he learned the fact from newspaper accounts. His lawyer showed him the newspaper articles about the murders. Under cross-examination, he admitted that they did not mention one victim being mutilated more than the others, and he admitted that he had not read it in a newspaper.

For Echols there was evidence that he had a 'serious mental illness characterized by grandiose and persecutory delusions, auditory and visual hallucinations, disordered thought processes, substantial lack of insight, and chronic, incapacitating mood swings'.

A suggestion by the defence that Mr Bojangles might have been involved was ridiculed by the prosecutor John Fogleman who claimed that it was 'a complete absurdity' to think the criminals who took pains to hide bodies, clothing and bicycles would, immediately thereafter, go 'into a public place all covered in blood'. Critics of the Bojangles theory also point out that the bleeding man may have worn a cast on one arm, something which, they argue, would have made it very difficult to tie up and murder the three boys.

On 19 March the pair were found guilty on three counts of first-degree murder and sentenced to life imprisonment for Baldwin and to death in the case of Echols:

> ... you are hereby adjudicated guilty of capital murder, three counts, and you are remanded to the custody of the sheriff to be immediately transported to the Arkansas Department of Corrections where the director of the Arkansas Department of Corrections or his duly appointed and designated representative will on the fifth day of May 1994, be directed to cause to be administered a continuous intravenous injection of a lethal quantity of an ultra-short acting barbituate in combination with a chemical paralytic agent into your body until you are dead.

In May that year their first appeals were dismissed. The appeal court thought that 'the foregoing, together, constitutes substantial evidence of the guilt of Damien Echols'. As for

Baldwin, the appeal court ruled, 'Jason Baldwin does not contend that there was insufficient evidence of his guilt.' This was, perhaps, in part, because of the testimony of Michael Carson, who testified that he talked to Baldwin about the murders. Carson's evidence had been:

> I said, just between me and you, did you do it. I won't say a word. He said yes and he went into detail about it. It was just me and Jason [Baldwin]. He told me he dismembered the kids, or I don't know exactly how many kids. He just said he dismembered them. He sucked the blood from the penis and scrotum and put the balls in his mouth.

Two years later as their appeals wound on, an independent film about the case, *Paradise Lost*, directed by Joe Berlinger and Bruce Sinofsky, went into production. During the making of the film John Mark Byers, Christopher's adoptive father, gave the directors a pocketknife that had some blood on the hinge. Tests showed it matched both his and Christopher's blood type. Byers gave various explanations, first saying it had never been used and then that he had used it to cut deer meat. A third explanation was that he might have cut his thumb.

In 2003 it was the turn of Vicki Hutcheson to cast some more doubt on the trials. In an interview with the *Arkansas Times* she said that everything she had told the police was wrong. Although she did not give evidence in the Echols–Baldwin trial she had made her statement because officers had implied that if she did not help out then her son Aaron would be put in care. She also claimed that photographs of Echols and the others had been pinned on a station wall and used by officers as a dartboard.

In 2007 Echols petitioned for a retrial based on an Arkansas statute, which allowed that, because of the advances in DNA testing, post-conviction evidence might be admitted to show the innocence of the appellant. 'Although most of the genetic material recovered from the scene was attributable to the victims of the offences, some of it cannot be attributed to either the victims or the defendants.' On 29 October, the defence filed a Second Amended Writ of Habeas Corpus, outlining the new evidence. The suspected knife marks on the bodies were, an expert said, caused by animals. The trial judge Judge David Burnett refused the petition.

In July 2008, it was disclosed that Kent Arnold, the jury foreman on the Echols–Baldwin trial, had discussed the case with a lawyer prior to the beginning of deliberations. During the retirement he had argued for the conviction of the pair based on the inadmissible Jesse Misskelley statements. Legal experts agreed that this issue had the strong potential to result in the reversal of their convictions. It did not.

In September 2008, Misskelley's lawyer David Stidham, giving evidence at a post-conviction relief hearing, said that Judge Burnett had erred during the trial by making an improper communication with the jury during its deliberations. Stidham had overheard Burnett discuss taking a lunch break with the jury foreman and the foreman's reply that the jury was almost finished. He said that Burnett had then said, 'You'll need food for when you come back for sentencing.' When the foreman then asked what would happen if the defendant was acquitted, Stidham said the judge closed the door without answering. He also argued that his own failure to put this incident on the court record, and his failure to meet the minimum requirements in state law to represent a defendant in a capital murder case, was evidence of ineffective assistance of counsel and that Misskelley's conviction should therefore be quashed. It was not.

By 2010 Echols was more fortunate. Burnett had been appointed to another judicial position and now the Arkansas Supreme Court allowed new appeals by the three. It was at that hearing the Arkansas attorney general had suggested that the justices reject Echols' appeal against the death penalty because 'we all need closure on the West Memphis Three case'.

On 19 August 2011, the trio entered what were called Alford pleas, a curious legal device which allowed them to maintain their innocence while acknowledging that prosecutors had enough evidence to convict them.* Apart from anything else such a plea effectively eliminates any possible civil suit against the state. Judge David Laser accepted the pleas and sentenced the three to time served. They were released with ten-year suspended sentences, having served eighteen years and seventy-eight days in prison.

In 2000 Rick Murray, the biological father of Christopher Byers, had described his doubts about the guilty verdicts on the West Memphis Three website. In 2007, Pamela Hobbs, the mother of victim Steven Branch, joined those publicly questioning the verdicts, calling for further investigation of the evidence. In late 2007, John Mark Byers also announced that he now believed that the three were innocent, saying 'I had made the comment if it were ever proven the three were innocent, I'd be the first to lead the charge for their freedom.'

In 2010, District Judge Brian S. Miller ordered Terry Hobbs,

---

* The Alford plea came about after Henry Alford was indicted on a charge of first-degree murder in 1963. Witnesses said that he and the victim argued at the victim's house. Alford left, and later the victim had been shot and killed when he opened the door in answer to a knock. Another witness said Alford had told him that he had killed the man.

At the time if two conditions were satisfied in a case, the death penalty was the automatic sentence in North Carolina. The defendant had to have pleaded not guilty, and the jury did not instead recommend a life sentence. Had he pleaded guilty to first-degree murder, Alford would have had the possibility of a life sentence, but would have avoided the death penalty. Alford did not want to admit guilt, but pleaded guilty to second-degree murder saying he was doing so to avoid the death sentence. He was sentenced to thirty years in prison, after the trial judge in the case accepted the plea bargain and ruled that the defendant had been adequately informed by his lawyer.

He appealed claiming his plea was involuntary, but in 1970 the United States Supreme Court ruled there was nothing to stop a judge accepting a guilty plea from a properly advised defendant who wanted to plead guilty but still maintained he was innocent. This sort of admission became known as an Alford plea and differs slightly from the *nolo contendere* plea in which the defendant agrees to being sentenced for the crime, but does not admit his guilt. *North Carolina v. Alford*, 400 U.S. 25 (1970).

Steven Branch's stepfather, to pay $17,590 to Dixie Chicks singer Natalie Maines for her legal costs in a defamation lawsuit he had brought against the band. He alleged that she had implied at a 2007 Little Rock rally that he was involved in killing his stepson. The judge said Hobbs had 'voluntarily injected' himself into a public controversy over whether the three teenagers had been wrongfully convicted.

Echols' legal team had commissioned a report from John E. Douglas, the FBI Unit Chief of the Investigative Support Unit of the National Center for the Analysis of Violent Crime for twenty-five years. Douglas, who had interviewed the country's most prolific serial killers, was now working as a profiler to help police in their searches for violent criminals. In his report he said the killing of the three West Memphis boys was not the work of three unsophisticated teenage killers, but rather that of a single person who set out to degrade and punish the victims. Douglas went on to say that there was no evidence of satanic ritual involvement in the killings and agreed that post-mortem animal involvement explained the alleged knife injuries. Douglas believed that the perpetrator had a violent history and was familiar with the boys and with local geography. He stated that the victims had died from a combination of blunt force trauma and drowning in a crime driven by personal cause.

In 2013 Pam Hobbs filed papers naming four men as possible suspects. The new documents claim that they killed Steven and two of his friends after they caught the boys spying on them while they were taking drugs. A variation on this came the same year when separate affidavits signed by Billy Wayne Stewart and Bennie Guy suggested that the three boys had come across two men and two teenagers from a local trailer park indulging in homosexual activities on a dirt road by the Blue Beacon Wood. As a result the boys were attacked and killed. Both men claimed they contacted the authorities to tell them what they had seen and believed but they had received no response.

CHAPTER 3

The Road to the Court of Appeal

Edmund Galley

William Habron

Florence Maybrick

Samuel Clowes and Henry Johnson; Joseph
Hodgson, Joseph Lowson and William Siddle;
Henry Hardwick and Richard Walford;
Michael Brannagan and Peter Murphy

George Edalji

Adolf Beck

Edmund Galley

Worldwide there cannot be too many instances when a future Lord Chief Justice takes up the cudgels on behalf of a man he believes to be innocent. One instance was in the case of Edmund Galley.

On 16 July 1835, wealthy farmer Jonathan May rode from Sowton Barton near Dunsford, Devon, now in Dartmoor National Park, to the fair at Moretonhampstead to sell some cattle. In the evening he bought some provisions from a local shopkeeper and went for supper at the White Hart Inn, leaving around 10 p.m. to ride to his home about six miles away. It was a light night and according to the landlord, Samuel Caunt, May was perfectly sober. A little after ten o'clock he rode past James Norsworthy, who was the tollhouse keeper, and wished him goodnight.

Around half past eleven Nicholas Taverner was going home with his wife and some friends when he found a horse saddled and bridled, but without a rider. Later he told the Assize Court:

> I went in search of the rider. I rode into Moreton, and then returned on another road. When I got near Jacob's Well I found a person lying in the road on his back. I lifted his head up, and the blood came bubbling out of his nose and mouth. It was Mr May. I called out 'Murder,' and then got on the horse and rode homewards, when I met my party. I left them there, and I rode for a doctor and alarmed the people of the town. I got a cart and put Mr May into it and took him to Moreton.

He also said that May's waistcoat and underwear were unbuttoned. The next witness was Taverner's wife, Grace: 'After my husband found the horse I went home, and then I returned in search of my husband. I heard my husband call murder; I went up and saw Mr May lying in the road in a gore of blood; his pockets were turned inside out.'

Taverner's friend John Tallamy told the court, 'I went with other persons to the body. I searched his pockets; there was nothing in them. There were two £5 notes in a concealed pocket in the waistcoat. There was no pocketbook nor watch. It was two o'clock in the morning.' A surgeon, John Ponsford, examined the body:

> I was called up about two in the morning. I went to the White Hart Inn, and found Mr May; he was in bed. He had a wound over his left eye, three others on the upper part of the head, two others on the back part of the head, another by the left ear. He died about ten minutes before nine that night. He did not recover any consciousness. I had a post-mortem examination; the skull was fractured; the injury on the head was the cause of death; it could not well have been caused by accident; a stick or kick might have occasioned it. There was no mark of violence except on the head.

He believed it was impossible the injury could have been caused by a fall or indeed a kick from a horse, and another surgeon Alfred Puddicombe told the court, 'I agree with Mr Ponsford; the fracture extended ten inches in length. I think it impossible that a fall from a horse could have occasioned such extensive injury.'

Another man had found a stick with blood on it and a second, Backwell, completed the chain of evidence:

> I found part of a stick which had been broken from the stick produced by the last witness; there were marks of bloody fingers on it. I also found the frill of a shirt which was completely covered with wet blood. There was blood on the hedge bank. It appeared to me as if the murdered man had

crept some fifty or sixty yards. The hedge was sprinkled
with blood for seven or eight yards. It was about four o'clock
in the morning.

As with most fairs at the time, there were a number of itinerant
pedlars, vagrants, card sharps and other riff-raff. It was a question of rounding up the usual suspects, and among those
arrested the next morning were George Avery and his companion Elizabeth Harris. At one time Avery had been apprenticed
to May but had become a wrestler touring the fairs. Harris had
been in service but had taken up with Avery and went with
him selling trinkets. She was released, but Avery was remanded
in custody and charged with the murder and also with an
attempt to rob a John Hill on 18 March the previous year.

Harris was soon rearrested for theft, and it was some four
months later while she was in Exeter Gaol awaiting transportation that she asked to see the prison governor to tell him about
the May murder.

Meanwhile Thomas Oliver, who was known as Buckingham
Joe, was in Dorchester Gaol awaiting transportation for a
burglary in Chipstead in September 1835 when Captain
Ranken shot and killed James Hill, another of the burglars.
Oliver became friendly with a trusty prisoner John Hiscox and,
naturally under promise of silence, foolishly confided in him
that he and his friend Dick Turpin (of whom there were many
at the time), had robbed and killed May. When he had enough
details Hiscox went to the governor.

As a result a notice was placed in the police journal *Hue &
Cry* in March 1836 giving details of Turpin who, according to
Hiscox, had a 'cage full of teeth' with a front tooth missing.
Turpin, whose real name was Edmund Galley and who had
few teeth at all, was found in Coldbath Fields gaol and taken to
Bow Street Court. There, before he was sent to Devon, he told
the magistrate he was innocent of the murder. Once in Devon,
Galley and Oliver were charged with robbery and murder and
committed to the Assizes.

Avery's girlfriend Elizabeth Harris had a very self-serving
– and serving Avery for that matter – story to tell the court.

During her travels with Avery at a variety of West Country fairs she had seen Thomas Oliver and the man Turpin together. They had been at the Moretonhampstead fair where she had heard them discussing potential victims:

> Buckingham Joe [Oliver] said to Turpin, 'It's a fine looking gaff, and there's some quisty [or crusty] looking-blocks; we must have some gilt in the rot.' I knew what it meant; 'gaff' meant 'fair'; 'blocks' meant 'farmers'; the gilt is money; 'rot' means 'evening'. I then lost sight of them. I was close to them. I saw them again in three or four hours.

She had, she said, later quarrelled with Avery and had decided to leave him and catch the cart going to Exeter.

> In the evening, about nine or ten o'clock, I went out of the town to go to Exeter. I went as far as the first milestone. Not being able to overtake the cart, I returned back to Moreton. I met the two prisoners [Oliver and Galley] not a great distance from the turnpike gate. They passed close to me. I saw them quite plain. They had smock frocks on. They were walking a stiff pace down the hill. I stooped down to slack my bootlace, and I heard someone at the tollgate say 'Good night.' I then met a farmer on horseback coming from the tollgate, riding a very slow pace. I returned after him, and followed him on the road. I kept sight of him. I followed him till he came within a few yards of the first milestone. I had on a dark dress. He had not got quite to the top of the hill when Buckingham Joe then came over the right hand hedge, and laid hold of the horse's head. Something was said. Turpin then came from the same hedge behind the farmer. He had a stick with a head as big as my fist, and he gave the farmer two blows with it on the left side of his head. The farmer did not quite fall off his horse. Buckingham Joe then pulled him off, and in doing so Mr May and he fell together. Turpin was standing close by. Many blows then passed. They were struggling on the ground five minutes. I heard one say to the other, 'Have you got it?' The other said, 'I

have' and at that time I saw Buckingham Joe give Turpin what appeared to be a book. I heard something rattle like a watchchain. I heard the farmer say, 'If you rob me, for God's sake don't take my life.' It appeared to me as if Turpin give him two kicks to the head. They then got over a gate into a field, where there was some kind of corn growing. I never saw them after. I stopped about ten minutes before I could get myself to go back, I was so much frightened. I heard the farmer groan once or twice, but I did not observe him move. I was standing close by the hedge all the time. I went back to Moreton; the next morning I was apprehended, but afterwards discharged. I said nothing about it till I was in Exeter Gaol the last time, about four months afterwards. I was in custody upon another charge. I was tried and convicted, and it was after my conviction that I mentioned this affair.

As she said, she did not tell Avery, although she had slept with him that night, nor anyone else until in the March she had asked to see the governor of the gaol she was in because she said she 'could not rest or sleep'. At Exeter Gaol she identified Galley as Turpin but said, nevertheless, she thought he was 'much changed'.

One problem for the prosecution was that as a convicted felon she could not give evidence and this was resolved by giving her a pardon. Giving evidence, she denied she had even wished for one, but it also meant that Avery was saved from the gallows on the murder charge.

At least five other women maintained that they had seen Galley with Oliver. Avery was produced and, very decently, said he had never seen Galley/Turpin before in his life. There had, he said, been another man at the last Assizes who had been transported and who also went by the name Turpin.

There was, however, one witness, Charlotte Clarke, who supported Galley:

I sell lace caps. I was at Moreton fair in July 1835, I went from Exeter. I went into the Lamb Inn on the road. Oliver came into the Lamb and another man called Turpin. The

Edmund Galley 73

prisoner Galley is not the man; it appeared to me a different man altogether. I talked to the one called Turpin. I had seen these two men before at Taunton. Black Nance was at the Lamb with Oliver. We all went out together towards Moreton. As we were going along the road I saw Oliver take a pistol out of his pocket. We arrived at Moreton between five and six o'clock. The man that was with Joe had not any teeth out, but had a nice mouth of teeth, and was a respectable looking man. I am sure it was another man; he had large dark whiskers that met.

The trial judge, Mr Justice John Williams, was regarded as an excellent scholar who wrote Greek epigrams, but he was not a strong judge. His summing-up was described as weak. It was very much a question of 'If you believe Elizabeth Harris then they must be guilty', giving no reasons why they might not believe the girl.

Williams summed up the case for four hours and the jury discussed the matter in the jury box for about ten minutes before finding the pair guilty. Galley burst into tears and turned to Oliver and pleaded, 'If you know anything about it, my good friend, do for God's sake tell the truth for you know I am innocent.' Oliver replied, 'It is all over now; it is no use telling a lie about it, you are innocent, and know nothing about it.'

The officer of the court then asked the prisoners to say why the court should not give judgement upon them according to the law. Once again Galley loudly protested his innocence, asking why he should suffer on account of his having gone by the name of Turpin; that the witnesses had sworn falsely, and that the Almighty knew his innocence and would punish them for it.

Oliver then chipped in, 'Indeed, my Lord, they are mistaken; don't let me ascend the scaffold with this man, for he knows nothing about it and I wish I may instantly be hurled into eternity, if that is not the truth.'

The judge then put on his black cap:

Edmund Galley and Thomas Oliver, you have been convicted of the crime laid to your charge, after a long, I trust a patient, and I am sure I may add, a most impartial inquiry, in which every circumstance, omitting nothing that could be supposed in any degree to bear in your favour, has been most zealously and industriously presented to the jury, who are the judges of the fact of the crime. The jury, who, as I said before, are the judges of the fact have come to the conclusion that you are guilty on grounds I think too strong to be doubted. They are satisfied of the credibility of the witnesses who have been examined. They have had full opportunity of witnessing the manner in which those witnesses have given their evidence, particularly the female witness, Elizabeth Harris – they are, I repeat, satisfied of the truth of her statement, confirmed, as they consider, and doubtless very rightly consider, by the other circumstances which have been brought forward, and which it was impossible to say were not most powerful in establishing the truth of her evidence. With respect to the nature of the offence, it is not my intention to aggravate your feelings by any observations on what the feeling of men have been ever since history recorded them, in regard to the circumstances of the trial or temptation that offence has been committed. Assuredly there is nothing present in this case which distinguishes it from others of the same class, or offers any circumstances to mitigate the sentence.

At which point, much to the amazement of the spectators, Oliver interrupted the judge saying:

My Lord, I have a statement to make, and I hope your Lordship will hear me. I am innocent of the murder, but I know who did it; it was not this man, and he knows nothing about it; he was never with me in the county; it was a man who goes by the name of the Kentish Youth [sometimes given as Hero or Hugh], with a full mouth of teeth, and as clever looking man as you will see.

Then Galley added:

> My Lord, would you not think it hard to be condemned when you were innocent? I am sure you would not sentence an innocent man to have his life taken away. God knows I am innocent, and I thank God for it, and I hope he will receive my soul. I know that if a man commits murder he ought to die, and if I was guilty I should expect to die; but, my Lord, I am innocent; and I never was in the county before May.

Oliver agreed, saying, 'My Lord, he never was. He is mistaken for another man.'

Williams had let them have their say before continuing with his sanctimonious sentencing:

> I can now only strongly recommend you to employ the short time you have remaining to live in earnest and anxious endeavour to obtain forgiveness in that quarter to which you have so frequently appealed, to obtain that mercy which in this world cannot be extended to you, and which you must not expect. I would earnestly recommend you, forego-ing every other consideration, and abandoning every other idea and hope, to resign yourself to that express and single purpose – that of obtaining forgiveness in that quarter where alone it may be obtained. The duty – the very painful duty, now devolves upon me – and God knows how will-ingly, how gladly I would at any expense and any sacrifice, have avoided this duty. It is now my bounden duty to pronounce that sentence.

Oliver tried again, 'I hope your Lordship will not hang an innocent man – I hope you will not. He [Galley] was not with me in the county. I never knew him before we met here.'

The judge was in no way convinced:

> The evidence that you were together is accumulated to such a degree as to leave no doubt on the minds of the jury. I

never in the whole course of my experience saw such a quantity brought forward. The sentence of the court, therefore, on you Edmund Galley, and you Thomas Oliver, is, that for this offence you be taken to the place from whence you came, and thence to the place of execution, and there you be severally hanged by the neck until you are dead, and that your bodies be interred within the precincts of the prison in which you have been confined; and may the Lord have mercy on your souls.

The immediate general opinion of the spectators was that Oliver was just trying to row Galley out and his statements were simply made in bravado, but when he was returned to prison he tried again, telling a warder: 'It was a hard fight, for we had a long struggle with farmer May. As to Turpin [Galley] – he was not near the place but it was Kentish Hero who was with me: I protest before God that Turpin is innocent. I am guilty and I'll die like a man.'

He went on to say that the Kentish Hero or Kentish Youth had already been sentenced to transportation for fourteen years and that Elizabeth Harris could not have seen the murder because she had made no mention of the trouble they had with May's horse kicking and rearing. He maintained that the other 'Turpin' who was with him when May was murdered was a good three-and-a-quarter inches taller than Galley.

A number of junior barristers who had watched the trial, including the future Lord Chief Justice Alexander Cockburn, were seriously worried about the verdict. They saw Galley in the cells and on his behalf commissioned a shorthand writer who had also been at the trial to investigate the man's alibi that he had been in Kent and Surrey. Along with solicitors John Carew and Ralph Saunders, respectively the County Under Sheriff and Clerk to the County Justices, they also met with Mr Justice Williams and persuaded him that instead of the usual two days which then passed between sentence and execution, he would respite the case to 12 August for further inquiries. In the event he respited Galley until 26 August. Meanwhile Oliver continued to maintain that Galley was not the man who had been with him. Now he named the man as John Longley who had, fortunately for him, indeed already been transported.

On 15 August 1836 Oliver, allegedly wearing a red handkerchief to show he would 'die game', was executed, still maintaining on the scaffold that Galley was innocent. By the September there were stories circulating that Galley had been hanged, however it turned out that the balladeers who sold sheets after executions had not been able to get rid of the ones naming Oliver and had simply substituted the name Turpin.

The respite was continued and the money given to the court reporter was well spent. His findings were sufficient for the Home Secretary to appoint Sir Frederick Roe, then Chief Magistrate at Bow Street, to make further inquiries. Montague Smith, who had represented Oliver, went with him to Kent.

On 22 August Roe began his inquiries. Galley had remembered that at around the time he was supposed to have been in Devon with Oliver he had been to a fair in Dartford, Kent – and a fairly memorable day it seems to have been. First, in some brawl, a stall was overturned and he helped the stall owner to pick up the ginger biscuits that had been scattered. Then he had had a fight over a 2/6d bet that he had lost and had been obliged to pay up. Finally he had swindled the winner of the fight out of the 2/6d. Those at the fair confirmed this. One problem for Galley was that when Roe took statements he did so on a strictly legal basis, excluding speculation and hearsay, which would not have been admissible at a trial.

Meanwhile the prisoner governor of the Devon county gaol wrote to the Home Office suggesting that the men who had been in custody with Oliver and Galley be asked about the pair. Although his gaol operated a silent system under which the men could not speak to each other, he had no doubt they did communicate. The upshot was that the men said Galley and Oliver did not know each other before they were in the gaol together. Later when Galley was on the hulk *Ganymede* at Woolwich awaiting transportation, witnesses from the fair were brought to identify him and they all did so correctly.

The statements taken by Roe were sent to the then Lord Chief Justice Baron Denman. His opinion was, 'If William or John Longley ever be found, the whole case may assume a new aspect and require a new discussion. In the meantime the preponderance of proof appears to be decidedly in favour of the verdict.'

Lord John Russell, the Home Secretary, announced that the death sentence would be commuted to transportation for life. Another reason for not granting a pardon was, it seems, that Mr Justice Williams would not accept the jury had been wrong. A reprieve could be granted on the basis that there was some doubt it was Galley who had struck the fatal blow. Off to Australia he went.

The year after Galley's case, J. W. Smith, editor of *Smith's Leading Cases*, wrote a poem satirizing the judicial system of the time:

> The speedy arm of Justice
> Was never known to fail
> The gaol supplied the gallows
> The gallows thinned the gaol.
> And sundry wise precautions
> The sages of the law
> Decently framed, whereby they aimed
> To keep the rogue in awe.
> For, lest some sturdy criminal
> False witnesses should bring –
> His witnesses were not allowed
> To swear to anything.
> And lest his wily advocate
> The Court should overreach
> His advocate was not allowed
> The privilege of speech.
> Yet, such was the humanity
> And wisdom of the law,
> That if in his indictment there
> Appeared to be a flaw
> The court allowed him counsellers

> To argue on the doubt
> Provided he himself had first
> Contrived to point it out.
> Yet, lest this mildness should, perchance,
> Be craftily abused
> To show him the indictment
> They sturdily refused.
> But still, that he might understand,
> The nature of the charge
> The same was in the Latin tongue
> Read out to him at large.
> 'Twas thus the law kept at awe
> Gave honest men protection
> And justly gamed by all was named
> 'Of wisdom the perfection'.

And there for over forty years the matter ended. Galley disappeared into rural New South Wales, first working on the roads in a chain gang and then for 'private masters'. He did well, was given a conditional pardon and a ticket of leave in 1839 and became a shepherd. Then, on 12 May 1877, supported by the editor of the *Yass Tribune*, he wrote to the Home Secretary petitioning that he should have a full pardon. The letter also appeared in the *Western Mail* and was seen by Alexander Cockburn, now the Lord Chief Justice. Cockburn wrote a long letter to the Home Secretary saying that he had been in court to see the case, and how he and other members of the Bar had been seriously worried about the verdict, that Williams had not properly directed the jury about the evidence of Elizabeth Harris, not pointing out how she had every reason to lie, and finally that Roe and Montague Smith had been completely satisfied with Galley's alibi. In turn, a man named Seccombe, the last surviving juror, wrote in support saying how troubled he had been when he had heard the full facts.

It took the Home Office a year to send Cockburn a dusty reply. It might be that the present incumbent would have taken a different view but that was no reason to overrule his predecessors. The next step was for Sir John Eardley-Wilmot, the former Recorder of Warwick, to take the matter up in the House of Commons on 9 May 1879, complaining how shabbily the Lord Chief Justice had been treated by the Home Office. Had the Home Secretary any objections to the publication of the 1836 papers? Yes, he had. The papers were 'confidential and I would be the last person to break the rule and publish them'.

The Times was rather worried that Galley's case was being championed by a bleeding heart liberal who wanted to see the abolition of capital punishment, but it was heartened that Wilmot's seconder, Bulmer, was 'a lawyer of a different type – dispassionate and calm in temperament'. At first it was not plain sailing for Wilmot and Bulmer. One MP said that by his life as a card sharp and petty thief Galley had assisted very much in his own conviction by the irregular and improper life he had led. It was something like contributory negligence. Another thought that Galley had done rather better for himself by being transported than by continuing his life as a 'thimble-rigger'.

The papers were sent again to the law officers, Lord Bramwell, then a Court of Appeal judge, Sir Adolphus Liddell, the Undersecretary of State, and Lord Justice Brett. All except Brett thought he should be given a free pardon, and with Parliament now unanimously in Galley's favour, on 26 July 1879 the Homesecretary, making clear that this was not an admission of Galley's innocence, rather reluctantly announced there would be a free pardon. Galley wrote thanking everyone who had assisted him but wondered why nothing was being done about Longley, who was now living in the colony under the name French. 'He ought to have been executed instead of my being here.'

It took another two years of wrangling before the Home Office agreed to give Galley £1,000 compensation, identical to the sum paid to William Habron, wrongly convicted of murder. At first it was suggested that the money should be invested and paid as a form of pension but it was pointed out that since Galley was now well into his eighties it might not do him much good. Finally, in November 1881 the Home Office gave in, still less than graciously. Galley would have the £1,000 to buy land or do whatever else he wanted with the money. A trust was set up and Galley took £100, leaving the remainder with his trustee for his children.

Over the years more romantic versions of the story have transposed Galley into a hard-working local baker who leaves behind a sweetheart. Elizabeth Harris becomes the beautiful, if wild, village girl Mary or Molly Smith whose romantic overtures he has rejected and who revenges herself on him.

William Habron

Twenty-year-old PC Nicholas Cock of the Lancashire police was a new and keen recruit to the force. Known as 'Little Bobby' because of his size, he was shot and killed at West Point, Whalley Range just outside Manchester on the evening of 2 August 1876. On patrol he and PC James Beanland had noticed a suspicious character lurking in the area. The pair became separated and, when trying to arrest the potential burglar, Cock was shot in the chest. The man escaped.

In charge of the murder hunt was Superintendent James Bent. When giving evidence later he said he had immediately suspected the Habron brothers, John, Frederick and William – Irish labourers who lived in a hut on the land of their employer, a local nurseryman William Deakin, about 100 yards from the murder scene. Apart from convictions for drunkenness they were all of good character. Bent based his suspicions on threats they had been making in the local public houses. Cock had apparently arrested one or more of them for drunkenness and they were threatening that if they were arrested again, they would get their employer to have Cock 'shunted' (have him removed). John Habron was due in court and he was heard to say, 'If he does me today, I'll do him on Wednesday.' Witnesses said the brothers had not been drinking at the time of the remark. A factor that may also have influenced Bent was that, at the time, Manchester was a hotbed of Fenian activity and an Irish Republican stronghold.

Bent, with other officers and William Deakin, went to the

brothers' hut, where they were in bed, and arrested them all. John said he had been in bed 'at the time', a comment that the police said meant he knew Cock had been shot. No firearms were found. The local magistrates ruled that Frederick had no case to answer and refused to commit him to the Assizes. There was mere suspicion against John but a case was built against William and both were committed for trial. First, the threats; secondly PC Beanland thought the appearance of the man he had seen resembled William; thirdly, a man, possibly William, had tried to buy ball cartridges from a local iron-monger. Fourthly, caps were found in his waistcoat pocket. Fifth, Bent said he had measured boot prints in the lane where Cock had been shot and these matched William's. Despite plaster casts of boot prints having been taken as early as the 1820s by the French detective Vidocq, Bent did not have one made of the boot. Finally, William had also told the police he was in bed by 9 p.m., but there was evidence he was still drinking at eleven.

The trial took place at Manchester Assizes in November that year with Mr Justice Lindley presiding. Before the trial a Grand Jury had to agree to a bill of indictment being preferred and Mr Justice Lopes, in charge of the Grand Jury, rather indi-cated they should not do so. However, as William Habron remarked later, 'It was a police affair altogether. A policeman had been killed and they meant to hang somebody for it.' Under the rules of evidence at the time defendants could not give evidence in murder trials in English courts but, piece by piece, the prosecution's case was undermined.

As for the threats, the threat to shoot Cock had been made by John, and William had not been there at the time. In any event he had only said that he would 'shunt' the officer. Deakin said that it was highly likely the caps in the waistcoat were already there when he gave it to William. None of the other shop staff would say it was William who had been in the iron-mongers, and Deakin confirmed William had been at work when he was said to be enquiring about bullets.

As for the footprints, it was by no means an exact science and even if Bent was right and they were William's, he could

have made them on his way home from work. The identification by Beanland was contradicted by a lay witness, J. M.
Simpson, who described the man as elderly, walking with a
stooping gait. What is so extraordinary is that it must have
been apparent Cock was shot by a burglar, and there was
nothing to suggest that any of the Habrons were thieves.

On 27 November John Habron was acquitted, but after a
two-and-a-half-hour retirement William was found guilty
with the jury adding a recommendation to mercy because of
his age. In sentencing him to death Mr Justice Lindley notably
did not add that he agreed with the jury's verdict. To an
extent Habron was fortunate. There had been a recent surge
in the movement for the abolition of capital punishment. In
1867 the abolitionists had succeeded in their campaign to
stop public executions and now they sensed they could do
even better. Petitions were presented for a reprieve and were
supported by the trial judge. Habron and William Flanagan,
who had cut his common-law wife's throat and who was due
to be hanged with him, had already been measured for size
and weight by the public executioner William Marwood when
a respite was granted on 19 December, two days before
Habron's execution.

The *Manchester Guardian* thought it had been on the
grounds that the evidence did not conclusively fix the guilt on
Habron. A reprieve came in the following February.

Off Habron went, first to Millbank Prison picking oakum,
which involved unravelling old ropes covered in tar for
which the required amount to avoid punishment was two
pounds weight a day. It was then to the stone quarries of
Portland Prison in Dorset. Throughout he continued to
protest his innocence.

His rescue came from an unlikely source – the Sheffield-
based burglar and murderer Charlie Peace who had, in fact,
watched his trial at Manchester Assizes the day before he killed
Arthur Dyson, after whose wife he lusted. Now Peace and his
mistress Susan Bailey, along with his wife Hannah, moved to
Blackheath, south-east London where, as Mr and Mrs John
Thompson, they seemingly lived a respectable life attending

the local church and with Peace playing the violin at musical evenings. It was a double life for Peace who was caught on 10 October 1878 just after burgling a house on Blackheath Common. The police had been waiting for him and he shot PC Edward Robinson in the arm before he was overpowered. The following month, on 19 November, he was sentenced to penal servitude for life for the attempted murder of Robinson. He was taken back to Sheffield to stand trial for the murder of Dyson. There the jury retired for a bare ten minutes before finding him guilty.

It was while he was in the condemned cell that he made a detailed confession to the Revd Littlewood, admitting the murder of PC Cock:

> But the policeman like all Manchester policemen was a determined man. They are a very obstinate lot these Manchester policemen. After I fired wide at him – and it was all the work of a few moments, sir – indeed he had seized his staff, which was in his pocket, and was rushing at me and about to strike me. I saw I had no time to lose if I wanted to get away at all that night. I then fired the second time and I assure you again that I had no intention of hitting him. All I wanted to do was to disable the arm that carried the staff and in order that I might get away. But instead of that he came on to seize me, and we had a scuffle together. I could not take as careful an aim as I would have done and the bullet missed the arm, struck him in the breast and he fell. I know no more. I got away which is all I wanted.

He went on, 'If they will take the bullet which they extracted from his body and examine it and weigh it, they will find it was such a one as I was in the habit of using and would fit my revolver. I shot him with the same revolver that I shot Mr Dyson.'

At first Peace's confession to the Cock murder was greeted with scepticism. On 23 February 1879 the Chief Constable of Lancashire C. G. Legge wrote to the Undersecretary of State

saying that while a plan that Peace had provided of the area
was substantially correct, there were mistakes and it was nothing that a burglar well acquainted with the area would not
know. He wished he could have met with Peace and asked him
some detailed questions. On the credit side, he wrote, was the
fact that Peace was about the same size as Habron. He had
been around Lancashire at the time and his was the name in
the frame for the murder among local criminals.

On 24 February *The Times*' Manchester correspondent
thought:

> It is a curious proof of the deep conviction of Habron's guilt
> that [after the reprieve] the very persons who had memori-
> alised the Home Secretary on the ground of his innocence
> made no further effort in his favour when the sentence was
> commuted to penal servitude for life.
>
> 'It is believed that in his written confession Peace is
> considerably at issue with the evidence of more than one
> witness . . . Peace says there were two officers and two civil-
> ians which is most decidedly not the fact.

He then went on to dissect Peace's confession, questioning
why he had made it and concluding that he was buying time:

> The only motive which can be attributed to Peace, and it is
> a very plausible one, is that he hopes to obtain a respite to
> give time for further investigation by the police and for the
> investigation of similar charges against him. The trial for the
> murder of Cock would be necessary in order that the inno-
> cence of Habron might be established.

On the gallows before he was hanged by Marwood at Armley
Gaol on 25 February, Peace made a pretty, if sanctimonious,
speech:

> Tell all my friends that I feel sure they have sincerely forgiven
> me and that I am going to the Kingdom of Heaven, or else
> to that place prepared for us to rest in until the great

Judgement Day. I have no enemies that I feel to have on earth. I wish all my enemies or those would-be enemies I wish them well and I wish them to come to the Kingdom of Heaven at last. And now to one and all I say Goodbye. Goodbye, Heaven bless you and may you come to the Kingdom of Heaven at last . . .

And much, much more before Marwood dropped the trapdoor.

On 26 February another column appeared in *The Times*, which showed that 'The Thunderer' at least was unconvinced: 'To the clergyman who heard the confession, Peace declared that it was absolutely true with all the glib unction which often springs from the theological ministrations of the condemned cell.'

But the next day the matter was raised in the House of Commons by Dr Keneally MP, who wanted to know if it was true Peace had confessed and, if so, what did the Home Secretary propose to do about Habron? And, if indeed there had been a case of mistaken identity, might not the same apply to the Tichborne Claimant and that case also be reopened? The reply was guarded so far as Habron was concerned. He had been reprieved not because there was any doubt of his involvement in PC Cock's murder but because it could not be definitely established that he was the one who had fired the fatal shot. As for the Australian fraudster Arthur Castro who had masqueraded as the Tichborne Claimant to obtain an inheritance, there was no question of any doubt.

On 5 March Joseph Lomas presented a memorial petitioning the Home Secretary for Habron's immediate release. The judge had summed up for an acquittal; the visit to the Manchester shop about cartridges was a mistake; the caps found were explained by his employer; Habron's boot marks were not properly identified, but if they were his they might have been made when he was on his way from work; the bullet had been the same kind as that used by Peace, and Peace had confessed. The inquiry was concluded by 14 March and three days later the Home Secretary Richard Cross told the House of Commons:

> After the confession of the man Peace it was necessary to consider very carefully all the circumstances again and I stated to the House that owing to the confession the question would receive the most anxious consideration of the Secretary of State how far the sentence should be allowed to stand. At the same time the confession was one which would undoubtedly require the most rigid scrutiny that could be applied to it. I, of course, had every assistance from the learned judge and I thought it only right to lay the whole matter before the law officer. The result to which certainly I myself have come is that the statement made by the man Peace has been so entirely corroborated in the important points that I shall feel it to be my duty to advise the Crown to grant a free pardon to Habron. [Cheers.] It may be satisfactory to the House to know that in that conclusion I have the entire concurrence of the learned judge and the law officer of the Crown. [Hear, hear.] Although it has not been the practice in such cases, however unfortunate, to make compensation, I may be allowed to state that I can see my way to make certain arrangements by which care will be taken of the future of this most unfortunate unhappy man. [Cheers.]

Compensation was certainly unusual. When Charles Frost and Edward Smith, sentenced to fifteen years penal servitude in November 1878 for burglary, were released after it was found the police evidence was perjured, they received nothing. Four years later the Home Secretary, passing it off as an unfortunate case of mistaken identity, was able to tell Parliament that one of them had been found employment 'for which he had expressed himself grateful'. The other man had simply disappeared.

Habron was brought from Portland Prison in handcuffs to Millbank Prison, and released the next day. Cross accepted that he was responsible for this last humiliation and apologized.

There had been suggestions that Habron would go on a tour of the music halls but the authorities arranged for his former employer William Deakin to meet him and ensure he did not 'fall into the hands of agitators', that is, abolitionists. There would be a substantial fund set up with the Roman Catholic Bishop of Salford and Deakin as trustees. Habron was put on the five o'clock express from St Pancras to Manchester but the news of his release had leaked out and cheering crowds appeared at all the stations where the train stopped. At Bedford one man gave him £5 and at Leicester another gave him half a sovereign.

Habron's father had died while he was in prison. The trial had cost the family £140, their entire savings, and this was refunded by the government. A public subscription was also set up for the family. The Home Office authorized Deakin to buy Habron new clothes and pay his fare to wherever he wanted to go. He wanted to go to Ireland and he and John left Manchester for Dublin. From there it was on to Ballyhannis, County Mayo, where the local brass band welcomed them.

On 24 March the *Manchester Guardian* suggested the compensation would be £250 to enable him to buy a farm but the Home Secretary said this was speculation. On 3 April it was announced the figure would be £1,000. There was to be no criticism of the Lancashire police, whom the Home Secretary said had given their evidence 'with an absence of zeal and eagerness'. Habron put part of the money into a beer shop, which he ran for some years.

It was a time for questions over other miscarriages of justice. The Lord Chief Justice said that between 1800 and 1843 he had known of twenty-two capital and non-capital cases and now the cases of Edward Smith and Charles Frost, Henry Johnson, Samuel Clowes, Sweeney and Edmund Galley, who forty years earlier had been convicted of murder, reprieved and transported, were again raised in Parliament. What the House of Commons particularly wanted to know was why in the case of a property dispute there could be an appeal but in the case of a man convicted of murder there was none. The Home Secretary said he was certainly in favour of an appeal mechanism. However it would be another thirty years before yet another series of cases led to the foundation of the Court of Criminal Appeal.

Over the years Nicholas Cock's grave fell into disrepair and on 29 November 1956 the headstone was taken to the Lancashire Constabulary's headquarters near Preston.

Florence Maybrick

Travelling alone to England, eighteen-year-old Florence Elizabeth Chandler, born in Mobile, Alabama, met wealthy middle-aged Liverpool cotton broker James Maybrick on board the White Star Liner *Britannic* soon after it left New York. Shortly before it docked in Liverpool the captain asked the first class passengers to drink to the health of the newly engaged couple. On 27 July 1881 they were married at St James's Church, Piccadilly, in London. Unfortunately Maybrick did not tell his bride that he already had several illegitimate children by the same woman. From there it was downhill all the way and the story of Maybrick and Florence Chandler is a compelling argument against turning shipboard and holiday romances into long-term relationships. Eight years later Florence, said at the time to be the most beautiful woman in Liverpool, stood trial for her husband's murder.

The press in the form of the *Liverpool Daily Post* was implacably hostile towards Florence Maybrick, the daughter of banker and former mayor of Mobile William G. Chandler – the nephew of a United States Supreme Court judge – and Caroline Chandler Du Barry, née Holbrook. They made much of the fact that when Florence was a baby her father had died suddenly and mysteriously in Mobile. Her first stepfather had also apparently died suddenly and mysteriously at sea during the Civil War while on a mission for the Confederate government.

The ship's captain had been suspicious and had wanted to

bring the body back to America but her mother had insisted on a burial at sea. She was now separated from her third husband, Baron Adolph von Roques, a German cavalry officer of the Eighth Cuirassier Regiment. Like mother like daughter, thought the newspapers. To compound things, Florence's first child had been born a mere eight months after the wedding. No mention seems to have been made of Maybrick's mistress and their five children.

Back in 1881 the honeymoon had been spent in Brazil and the pair lived in Liverpool until, after their son James Chandler Maybrick was born on 24 March 1882, they went to America to live in Norfolk, Virginia for a time. When they returned to England they settled in Battlecrease House, Aigburth, a fashionable suburb of Liverpool, where their daughter Grace was born on 20 June 1886.

Quite apart from failing to mention his illegitimate children, Maybrick had also omitted to tell her that he was a chronic arsenic and drug taker, and had been for some years. By 1888 she was sufficiently concerned to speak to Maybrick's doctor and ask him to advise her husband of the dangers of continual drug taking. In March that year she wrote to her brother-in-law Michael Maybrick saying how worried she was about his drug taking. When Michael Maybrick spoke to his brother about it James told him it was 'damned lies'.

When Florence eventually learned that her husband had a mistress with five children to whom he was paying £1,000 a year support, she discontinued sexual relations with him, but unfortunately in 1888 began a short and ill-fated affair with a frequent visitor to the Maybrick home, the handsome, debonair and amusing Alfred Brierley.

It was Florence who made the arrangements for them to meet as Mr and Mrs Maybrick on 21 March at Flatman's Hotel, near Oxford Street in London. Brierley would not be able to arrive until late in the evening and she compounded her bad behaviour by asking her young cousin, John Baillie Knight, to take her out to dinner earlier. It was clearly a lengthy one because the hotel porter and room service waiter, Alfred Schweisso, had gone to bed before she returned. But he saw Brierley in a dressing gown in her room the next morning.

After Brierley headed back to Liverpool she went to stay with her cousins, shopping for a parasol and bag to take with her to the Grand National Meeting at Aintree racecourse. This was one of the great social occasions of the north-west and the Maybricks hired an omnibus to take them and their friends to the meeting which the Prince of Wales was to attend.

A violent row ensued between the Maybricks after Brierley, who had bought grandstand tickets for the party, had taken Florence to the paddock before the race was won by amateur jockey Tommy Beasley on Frigate. That night Maybrick tore her dress, blackened her eye and threatened to turn her out of the house there and then, announcing he would sue for a divorce. He was persuaded by their servants to allow her to at least remain that night at Battlecrease. Both she and Brierley thought he had not learned of their night together; it was their conduct at the race meeting about which he had taken umbrage.

It was the family doctor Arthur Hopper who seems to have effected some sort of temporary reconciliation suggesting she ask for forgiveness, but in addition to his matrimonial difficulties Maybrick was fretting about his health, fearing he might become paralyzed. He was still not, however, admitting the full extent of his drug taking.

On 25 April Maybrick signed a will leaving everything to his brothers in trust for the children. Florence was to have the benefit of two life policies, which, coupled with her own money, would produce an income of £125, 'a sum which although small, will yet be the means of keeping her respectable. It is also my desire that my widow shall live under the same roof with the children so long as she remains my widow.'

That week on 22 or 23 April and again on the twenty-eighth, Florence purchased some flypapers which would become a crucial point in her trial. The prosecution alleged she was obtaining arsenic from them to use as poison. She claimed that flypapers were used in America and on the continent as a cosmetic aid to improve the skin and she certainly does not seem to have tried to hide them. They were soaking in the washbasin in her room. Since Edwin Maybrick, another brother whom she liked best of them all, had just arrived in Liverpool and was coming for dinner, no doubt she wished to look her best. There was also a grand *bal masqué* the Maybricks were soon to attend.

On the Saturday James Maybrick rode to the Wirral races across the Mersey in torrential rain. While he was there he spoke with his brother Edwin and also a friend, William Thomson, who remarked he did not seem to be able to keep on his horse. Maybrick replied he had taken 'a double dose' that morning. Dining with friends that night he could not hold his wine glass steady.

He became seriously ill on 27 April 1889. His doctors treated him for acute dyspepsia, but his condition deteriorated. On 8 May Florence Maybrick wrote a hopelessly compromising letter to Brierley, which she gave to the nanny, Alice Yapp, to post. At the trial Yapp claimed that when she had taken Gladys to post it, the child had dropped it in the mud. Instead of posting it Yapp opened the envelope with the intention, she said, of putting it in a new clean one. However, when she saw the words 'my own darling' she brought it back to the house and passed it on to Michael Maybrick. It read:

Dearest -- Your letter under cover to John K. came to hand just after I had written to you on Monday. I did not expect to hear from you so soon, and had delayed in giving him the necessary instructions. Since my return I have been nursing M. day and night. He is sick unto death. The doctors held a consultation yesterday, and now all depends upon how long his strength will hold out. Both my brothers-in-law are here, and we are terribly anxious. I cannot answer your letter fully to-day, my darling, but relieve your mind of all fear of discovery now and in the future. M. has been delirious since Sunday, and I know now that he is perfectly ignorant of everything, even of the name of the street, and also that he has not been making any inquiries whatever. The tale he told me was a pure fabrication, and only intended to frighten the truth out of me. In fact he believes my statement, although he will not admit it. You need not therefore go abroad on that account, dearest; but, in any case, please don't leave England until I have seen you once again. You must feel that those two letters of mine were written under circumstances which must even excuse their injustice in your eyes. Do you suppose that I could act as I am doing if I really felt and meant what I inferred then? If you wish to write to me about anything do so now, as all the letters pass through my hands at present. Excuse this scrawl, my own darling, but I dare not leave the room for a moment, and I do not know when I shall be able to write to you again. In haste, yours ever.

   Florie

By Michael's orders Florence was immediately deposed as mistress of her house and effectively held under house arrest. On 9 May a nurse reported that she had seen Mrs Maybrick outside her room surreptitiously tampering with a bottle of Valentine's meat-juice. It was afterwards found to contain a half-grain of arsenic. Mrs Maybrick later claimed that her husband had begged her to administer it as a pick-me-up. However, he never drank its contents.

James Maybrick died at his home at about 8.40 p.m. on 11 May 1889. His brothers, suspicious as to the cause of death, had his body examined. It was found to contain slight traces of arsenic, but not enough to be considered fatal. A search of the house and in particular of Maybrick's clothes and hatboxes turned up bottle after bottle of poison.

After a series of forensic tests and faced with the compromising letter, Florence Maybrick, charged with his murder, was committed for trial at the next Assizes to be held at St George's Hall, Liverpool. Because of the hostility of the local press there was the question of an application for the trial to be moved to London. She wanted it, writing to her mother, 'I shall receive an impartial verdict there which I cannot expect from a jury in Liverpool, whose minds have come to a "moral conviction" *en attendant* which must influence their decision to a certain extent.'

The next thing was to find her leading counsel and the formidable Sir Charles Russell, at the time probably the best known member of the English Bar, and earning around £16,000 a year, (the rough equivalent today of £1.5 million), was approached and agreed to take the case. His fee would be £500 with a £100 daily refresher. But he was not a noted defence lawyer.

The trial judge was Mr Justice James Fitzjames Stephen. Although Stephen is remembered for his *Commentaries on the Laws of England*, a textbook for law students until well into the second half of the twentieth century, he was not generally regarded as having a brilliant mind. He had not been academically distinguished at school, college or at the Bar. In 1885 he had suffered a slight stroke at the Derby Assizes. He was thought to have recovered, but in the 1887 trial of Israel Lipski at the Old Bailey for the murder of a young woman, Stephen had already shown signs of mental deterioration and prejudice.

He began the Assizes by telling the Grand Jury, which was there to decide if there was what was called a True Bill, something which would lead to the trial itself: 'The next case I will mention to you is a case which has excited very great attention in this country, and certainly if the prisoner is guilty of the crime alleged to her in the charge, it is the most cruel and horrible murder that could be committed.' He read out the allegations, adding, about her visit to meet Brierley in London: 'But certainly if a woman does carry on an adulterous intrigue with another man it may quite supply – I won't go further – a very strong motive why she should wish to get rid of her husband.'

The Grand Jury duly found it was a True Bill and the Liverpool papers enthusiastically printed His Lordship's words. Then, when an application was made to him for a fraud case to be stood down until after the Maybrick trial, the barrister asked when he should have his witnesses ready. Stephen told him he must make the decision for himself adding, to the required sycophantic laughter, 'And you know Sir Charles Russell may very likely wish to plead guilty.' The *Liverpool*

Daily Post duly headlined, 'The Judge and the Maybrick Case. Extraordinary Judicial Joke.'

The trial began on 31 July 1889 at St George's Hall with a crowd still striving to get seats, most of which had been allocated to Liverpool's lawyers and the great and good. Outside the building the crowd whistled and booed Florence Maybrick as she was driven in a black van to the court.

But as the trial continued through four days the atmosphere changed. Sir Charles Russell gradually eroded the medical evidence against her, and at the end of the second day was cheered as he left the courthouse. He called both Dr Charles Tidy, Examiner of Forensic Medicine at the London Hospital and Dr Rawdon Macnamara, professor of *Materia Medica* at the Royal College of Surgeons of Ireland, both of whom said that it was clear to them the cause of death was gastroenteritis and not arsenic poisoning at all. He called a string of witnesses from America and England, including the Lord Mayor of Liverpool, to say they all knew of Maybrick's more or less life-long penchant for arsenic. He also called a chemist to explain that flypapers were used for cosmetic purposes.

At the time there were only certain crimes about which the accused could give evidence in court. They could in a rape case, for example, or on a charge of housebreaking; amazingly not so in a trial for murder. Florence made a statement from the dock. The newspapers and public were now wholly behind her and an acquittal was confidently expected.

Stephen began his summing-up to the jury on Tuesday, 6 August. That morning his fellow judge on the Assize had advised him to keep it to within a day, but the warning fell on deaf ears. As the hours went by Stephen rambled on, confusing dates, mixing evidence, reading from letters from Florence that had not been put in evidence. Part of his rambling included:

> The next date after that took place is the Grand National something. I don't know whether it is a race or a steeple-chase or what it is – but it is something which is called the Grand National, as if everybody knew what the substantive

was – but the Grand National took place on the twenty-
ninth of March.

Much of the blame for the summing-up can be laid at the door
of the absent Sir Charles who had left the court that day to
take another case. As the leading silk at the Bar, Russell was a
man of such stature that he could continually have corrected
the judge. His junior William Pickford had no such status. He
did what he could to try to correct the judge over the dates of
the purchase of the flypapers, but was firmly put in his place
by Stephen who replied, 'I said April. There is no disputing
whether I used one word or another.' That night the jurymen,
quite improperly, had a three-and-a-half-hour discussion
about the case despite the fact that Stephen had not finished.

An acquittal was still confidently expected and a group of
women had brought bouquets to give to Florence on her
discharge. Now Stephen's summing-up became totally hostile.
It included an anecdote about a dog and ended with an attack
on why Mrs Maybrick had not disclosed her defence when she
was charged. Pickford made an ineffectual attempt to explain
that the decision was his and should not be laid on his client.

By that point, however, the jurymen had already agreed on
their guilty verdict. At their discussion the night before they
had decided that one of the defence witnesses had been so
shaken they were convinced of her guilt. She was sentenced
to death.

Now began a sustained campaign for her reprieve. A crowd
of 5,000 attended a meeting in front of St George's Hall. The
Northern Bar presented a petition and thought the medical
profession would do so as well. There were suggestions that a
technical or scientific expert should be appointed as an asses-
sor to assist the court and jury.

In fact there had been a recent precedent for a reprieve.
After the death in 1877 of Harriet, the wife of the art dealer
Louis Staunton, he and other members of his family were
convicted before 'hanging' judge Henry Hawkins and a jury,
with society ladies watching the proceedings through opera
glasses, reading the latest edition of *Punch* and sipping

champagne in the lunch adjournment. Hawkins, never known for his sympathy towards defendants, had been hostile to the accused throughout, suggesting they had committed another murder with which they had not been charged. The verdicts of guilty and the death sentences were well received by a cheering crowd outside the court, but the cause of the defendants was successfully taken up by both the popular novelist Charles Reade, author of *The Cloister and the Hearth*, and the medical profession.

Now nothing less than a pardon would do for the supporters of Mrs Maybrick. The meetings and demonstrations in her support continued countrywide. Members of the Liverpool Exchange and the Liverpool Produce Exchange petitioned for a reprieve, as did merchants in Cardiff, and now the *Liverpool Post* also supported a reprieve. More than 100,000 signatures were obtained by her solicitors. A group of Liverpool doctors, some of whom had been in court, concluded their petition: 'Lastly, your memorialists agree with the evidence given by Dr Tidy, Dr Macnamara and Mr Paul on behalf of the defence, that the medical evidence had entirely failed to prove that the death was due to arsenical poisoning at all.'

After the public outcry, in a typically British spirit of compromise Henry Matthews, the Home Secretary, and the Lord Chancellor Lord Halsbury produced a fudged decision concluding that 'The evidence clearly establishes that Mrs Maybrick administered poison to her husband with intent to murder; but that there is ground for reasonable doubt whether the arsenic so administered was in fact the cause of his death.'

On 22 August the death sentence was commuted to life imprisonment as punishment for a crime with which she was never charged. During the 1890s new evidence was published by her supporters, but there was no possibility of an appeal, and the Home Office was not inclined to release her in spite of the strenuous efforts of Sir Charles Russell, now the Lord Chief Justice, who visited her in prison. One version of the reason behind the refusal to release her was that Queen Victoria had taken a personal interest in the case and, since her own dear Albert had been taken from her, albeit forty years earlier, she would not contemplate any clemency for a husband-poisoner.

Florence Maybrick was a model prisoner throughout her fifteen years in prison. Her cell was kept sparkling clean and was shown to trainee warders as an example of how a cell should look. After her release in 1904 she returned to America where she undertook a tour of prisons and began lecturing on her case and on prison reform generally. She is credited with being instrumental in having the water cure and the ducking pool banned in Oklahoma. In 1905, her autobiography *Mrs Maybrick's Own Story: My Fifteen Lost Years* was published in New York. At the end of her life, and by then in serious financial difficulties, she lived as a recluse with up to a hundred cats in a cottage on property owned by the South Kent School, Connecticut. She was found dead there on 23 October 1941 and was buried in the school grounds. The story is that among her possessions was a tattered family bible. Between its pages were instructions on how to soak flypapers for use as a beauty treatment.

Florence Maybrick never saw her children from the time of her arrest; they were raised by the family's doctor. Her son, who became a mining engineer, died in 1911 of accidental poisoning when he mistook a cyanide solution for a glass of water.

After the verdict, amazingly Mr Justice Stephen is said to have supported a reprieve. This may not be true, but what is certain is that his mental health deteriorated sharply. His summings-up became more and more rambling and full of mistakes.

On 23 February 1891 the question of his ability to continue as a judge was raised in a veiled question in the House of Commons when the First Lord of the Treasury was asked whether he was aware of the great dissatisfaction among members of the Bar about the way the Queen's Bench business was being conducted and whether early changes were proposed. Replying, W. H. Smith said that he would make enquiries but no representations had so far been made to the Lord Chancellor. However in April that year, after speaking with the Lord Chancellor and the Lord Chief Justice, Stephen issued a statement:

> Not very long ago I was made acquainted, suddenly, and to my great surprise, that I was regarded by some as no longer physically capable of discharging my duties. I made every inquiry to ascertain what grounds there were for this impression, and I certainly rejoice to say that no single instance was brought to my notice in which any alleged failure of justice could be ascribed to any defect of mine. I consulted physicians of the highest eminence, and they told me that they could detect no sign whatsoever of decay in my faculties, and therefore it was not a matter of immediate necessity in the public interest that I should retire.

Nevertheless he did so. Within a matter of weeks he was confined in a mental asylum. He died at Red House Park, a nursing home near Ipswich, of chronic renal failure on 11 March 1894.

On no hard evidence whatsoever, in 1972 in his biography of the Duke of Clarence, Michael Harrison suggested that Stephen's son, James Kenneth, tutor to Prince Albert Victor, the Duke of Clarence, might be worthy of an entry in the race to name the Whitechapel murderer, Jack the Ripper. The principal grounds for his inclusion as an outsider seem to be that he was a known misogynist and a lunatic.

Then in 1992 Michael Barrett, a former Liverpool scrap metal merchant, produced a diary that identified James Maybrick as Jack the Ripper. Scientific tests appear to show that the diary is a forgery. Barrett admitted this, although he withdrew the admission. His estranged wife then claimed the diary had been in her family's possession for many years.

What motive was there for Florence Maybrick to poison her husband? Certainly not money. The financial provision he had made for her and his children in his will was paltry and she might have been far better off with him alive but legally separated from her. Possibly it was because he was threatening to divorce her, which would have seen her ruined in English provincial society, but she could easily have gone to the continent with her mother. If there was any motive at all, and given the evidence of Dr Hopper about the reconciliation this seems most unlikely a motive for killing him, it would be that with a divorce she would almost certainly have lost the custody of her children.

It was not until the Criminal Justice Act 1898 that defendants in all cases were allowed to give evidence on their own behalf.

Samuel Clowes and Henry Johnson; Joseph Hodgson, Joseph Lawson and William Siddle; Henry Hardwick and Richard Walford; Michael Brannagan and Peter Murphy

The end of the 1870s and the 1880s were not good years for the English criminal justice system. There were sporadic demands for a Court of Criminal Appeal but no one had any real inclination to pursue it. As a result there was a series of high-profile miscarriages of justice, which had to be cleared up with Royal Pardons. Two of the miscarriages took place at the same Newcastle Assizes.

However the first, known as the Penge Mystery or the Penge Tragedy, took place just outside London in 1877 when members of the Staunton family were convicted of the murder of Harriet, the wife of art dealer Louis Staunton. At first the doctors who examined her body believed she had been poisoned, but when they found no evidence they changed their opinion to one that she had been starved to death by the defendants. Staunton, his brother Patrick, Patrick's wife Elizabeth and Louis Staunton's young mistress Alice Rhodes, were all sentenced to death. There was conflicting medical evidence, however, that Harriet had died from meningitis or tuberculosis. More than 700 doctors signed a memorial complaining that this evidence had been ignored. The Stauntons were reprieved and Alice Rhodes, against whom the worst that could be said was that she had stood back and done nothing to help the woman, was given a pardon.

Three years later, in January 1880, two Staffordshire farmers, Samuel Clowes and Henry Johnson, men of good character, each received ten years for what the judge called 'a very barbarous and brutal crime', an unprovoked assault on another farmer Isaac Brooks, who had been attacked and partially castrated in what was called the Rushton Mutilation case. In the previous December the men had quarrelled over the sale of some geese in which Brooks had been outbid. Along with Enoch Sherratt, they had met on the road near the Fox Inn, Rushton Spencer near Macclesfield, the same evening and, realising Brooks was still angry, left him there. Another version of the story has all four of them attending a rent dinner and walking home together before separating.

According to Brooks, three men, and he later identified Clowes and Johnson but not Sherratt, leaped out of a hedge and cut him. When he first saw a surgeon the next day he had said he could not identify any of the men but he then changed his mind.

On New Year's Eve 1881 a dying Brooks said he wanted to see a parson. Instead, his friend William Harrison was called to the bedside; Brooks told him that the evidence he had given was false and that he had cut himself with the object of extorting a large sum from Clowes and Johnson or their friends. Fortunately Harrison wrote down the confession and had Brooks sign it. Harrison went to find a magistrate, but by the time they returned Brooks was dead.

So strong was the feeling in Rushton that it was hard to find men who, even for money, were prepared to carry Brooks to the grave. On their release the accused men were critical of the way their defence, or lack of it, had been conducted and which, as a result, had reduced their families to poverty. Clowes' wife, for example, had been evicted from their farm and now ran a shop. The men were awarded £500 apiece.

In 1884 three men, Joseph Hodgson, Joseph Lowson and William Siddle, were charged with the murder of a Police Sergeant William Smith at Butterknowle, Bishop Auckland. They had been to a pigeon shooting match and stopped at an inn on the way back. Sergeant Smith was outside and Lowson made some remark to him. After they walked away he said, 'Let's go back and rib him.' A fight ensued and Smith was beaten to death. Hodgson was acquitted while Siddle and Lowson were sentenced to death. In the condemned cell, Lowson claimed that Siddle was innocent, and on the gallows he is said to have remarked, 'Siddle is perfectly innocent. I hope the Crown and country will look after this and see Siddle safe home again.' Lowson said that he had been with Hodgson, who had struck the first blow, but under the double jeopardy rule Hodgson could not be tried again. Siddle was pardoned but soon afterwards was sent to an asylum where he died.

Before that, the Newcastle Winter Assizes of 1879 brought with them no fewer than five miscarriages of justice. On 13 January 1879 came the Duddo Hill shooting, not far from Morpeth. At half past five in the evening, three men, one of them armed with a gun, appeared at the Duddo Hill farm. The farmer, John Robson, his brother, and brother's son, his servant-girl plus several children were standing in a group – nine in all – some twenty yards from the men, when one of the men said, 'If you come any nearer, I'll fire.' On the basis that actions speak louder than words, he raised his gun and fired at the Robsons. Several of the group were wounded, but none seriously.

The next day three miners, Henry Hardwick, Richard Walford and a man named Morgan who lived at Seghill, were arrested by the police. Robson identified them all. The evidence against all three was precisely the same. Nevertheless, at the Assizes, for some inscrutable reason the jury convicted Hardwick and Walford and yet acquitted Morgan. They were sentenced by Mr Justice Manisty, one to twenty, and the other to fifteen years' penal servitude. It was subsequently proved that on the evening in question they had never left the village of Seghill, eight miles from where the shooting took place. In March 1883 they were released on licence, with the Home Secretary saying he had examined this case to which others in Chatham Gaol had now confessed but he could not say whether the men were innocent or guilty. As a result he could not recommend a pardon.

Literally preceding Hardwick, Walford and Morgan in the dock had been Michael Brannagan and Peter Murphy, charged with burglary and attempted murder at Edlingham Rectory.

The Lancashire police may have had things wrong in the case of William Habron but, as the Home Secretary pointed out and therefore it must be so, they had not acted with excessive zeal. The same cannot be said about the Northumbrian police dealing with Michael Brannagan and Peter Murphy in 1879.

In effect, the case had started six years earlier when Constable George Grey was killed in a fight with three poachers at Edlingham in Northumberland. By this time a constabulary had been established with each officer having a regular beat to patrol. At 3 a.m. on 18 January 1873, PC Grey was walking his beat along the lane just outside the village. It seems that he saw something suspicious in a nearby field as he climbed the fence and began walking, then running, over the ploughed ground – at which point he was shot at close range with a shotgun. The sound of the gunshot brought men running from the village, one of whom saw three men running off towards some nearby woods. There was some evidence that Grey had called out 'Schofield'.

When the police arrived they found the boot marks of three different men in the field, together with some discarded game. Clearly Grey had come across poachers, given chase and been killed to ensure their escape. One of the boot marks showed a clear split or cut along the heel. All the known poachers of the area were rounded up and their boots inspected. One, Charles Richardson, was found to have a boot with a cut along the heel. He was promptly arrested along with his friends George Edgell and Schofield. Edgell and Schofield produced alibis that they were out of the village and were released. Schofield promptly left the district.

Richardson was held on the basis he would not tell the police what had happened to his gun. He was in custody for around six weeks until in March the local magistrates refused to commit him for trial and he was discharged to great applause in the courtroom.

Both Edgell and Richardson had convictions for poaching. Edgell, a spare, thin man, about five foot eight in height, with a slight moustache, was also a well-known runner, and had won a good deal of money in bets on local foot racing. On one occasion when he was summoned for poaching in Earl Grey's woods at Howick, some six or seven miles to the north-east of Alnwick, the defence he had set up was an alibi. He had been seen in Alnwick so soon after the keepers alleged they had seen him on the moors that it was impossible for him to have been at Howick at the time alleged by them. However, the keepers said they had plenty more evidence if the magistrates would remand the case for a week. This was done, but when the case came on again for hearing, no Edgell appeared. He knew he must be convicted, and he knew also that all the Howick keepers would be at Alnwick to give evidence. So he spent the day poaching in their absence to pay his fine.

According to the Revd Jevon Perry, the vicar of Alnwick, Charles Richardson was a totally different proposition:

> Nearly six feet high, and broad in proportion, he had all the massive strength of a bull. In one poaching affray he had had his leg gnawed by a large retriever dog so that it presented the appearance of a shin of beef, and his head split open by a keeper with his own gun, which was broken clean off between the stock and the barrel by the force of the blow.
>
> When caught with hares in his possession by a policeman as he came into Alnwick, he raised his gun and threatened to do for him as he had done for 'the other damned brute'. For many years he had done no work, but lived at other people's expense, either by depredations on society when at large, or by the contributions of the rate-payers when in jail. It is doubtful whether at any time during this century the town of Alnwick had seen his equal for strength, ferocity, and desperation.

In the early hours of 7 February 1879, twenty-nine-year-old Michael Brannagan and his brother-in-law, nineteen-year-old Peter Murphy from Alnwick, happened to be in the wrong place at the wrong time when they were caught after poaching rabbits at Jenny's Lantern with Brannagan's dog Matt. The men were described later by a London newspaper as having 'indifferent morals'. Murphy had a rabbit spade and on their way Brannagan had stolen another one.

They netted four rabbits, burying them to be retrieved later, and around 7 a.m. returned to the village where they were stopped by PC Buglas and PC Gibson, questioned and released. Then an Inspector Harrison arrived at Brannagan's home to say that Superintendent George Harkes wanted to see them. Harrison told them to change coats.

The reason the police wanted to see them was that earlier that night there had been a burglary a few miles away at Edlingham Rectory. The seventy-seven-year-old vicar, the Revd Buckle, and his daughter Georgina had bravely confronted the burglars and both were shot, he in the arm and she in the stomach. She persuaded her father not to chase after the men, one of whom he thought he had cut with his sabre. Although badly bleeding she ran to a nearby cottage for help.

Superintendent Harkes, in charge of the case, was determined to nail the pair. Although he had not been in charge of the inquiry into the murder of PC Grey he was still smarting from his force's failure to solve that case. He had also recently lost a case in which Murphy had given evidence for the defence. The pair were examined by Dr Wilson and neither had any sign of a sword wound. When the men were taken to the rectory, neither Buckle nor his daughter could identify them. Georgina Buckle said the man who had worn a dark coat was squarer in the shoulders, and the man who ran past her was slighter than Brannagan.

However, a week later a piece of newspaper found in Murphy's jacket, which had been in the possession of the police the whole time, was said to match one found at the rectory. The police also claimed that the men's boot prints matched tracks from the rectory. A chisel had been left behind at the burglary and now the police persuaded the elderly half-blind John Redpath to say it was his. Murphy lodged with Redpath and the chisel tied him in nicely. Brannagan and Murphy were now charged with attempted murder.

They were brought before the magistrates on 8 February, remanded until the fifteenth and then until the twenty-eighth when the committal took place. In the meantime Mary Ann Murphy, Peter's sister, sold her bedding and his girlfriend sold her umbrella and other objects to raise a total of £4 to instruct a solicitor, Webb of Morpeth, to defend them.

For reasons that were never made public, their committal for trial was conducted behind closed doors. The trial itself took place on 23 April at the Moot Hall, Newcastle and, sharing the £4 with Webb, was the barrister he instructed, Thomas Milvain.

Brannagan and Murphy had value for their money. Milvain did what he could, claiming the police had planted the newspaper and that a button had been taken from Brannagan's trousers and dropped outside the rectory. There had been no button missing when he was first searched. Harkes admitted he had not taken plaster casts of the footprints when he had Brannagan and Murphy's boots and clogs with him at the rectory. Murphy's landlord John Redpath had been taken to the workhouse and was too ill to attend, so the evidence that it was his chisel was admitted in evidence by the judge. Thomas Milvain, who could not call his clients, called two witnesses to say they had never seen the chisel in Redpath's home. He compared the case with that of William Habron, reminding the jury it was all circumstantial evidence and that Buckle was convinced he had wounded one of the burglars. The police were, he said, paid on results and their evidence must always be regarded with suspicion. If his clients had been involved in the burglary in which two people had been shot and possibly killed it might be thought they would have disposed of all their poaching equipment and changed their boots and clothes.

It was all in vain. The jury convicted in three hours. Buckle asked that there be some clemency shown but that went unheeded and both men were sentenced to penal servitude for life. Not everyone, however, was convinced they were guilty. In an act of charity Buckle gave Brannagan's wife money for her fare home.

Georgina Buckle particularly wanted her watch returned, but when the men were interviewed separately by the prison governor at Morpeth, they both reiterated they had not got it and were innocent. On 20 November the Newcastle *Daily Chronicle* printed a story 'Important statement by a prison warder'. William Rose had called at their offices and voluntarily made a statement:

> At the time of the committal of Murphy and Brannagan to penal servitude for life, I was warder at Morpeth prison. I, along with chief warder Nichol, escorted the men to London after their conviction. Previous to my going I was offered £10 if I could get out of the two prisoners where the watch had been hidden. I believe the watch was an heirloom, and as such the owners wished to get it back again. On the journey I said to Murphy, 'Will you tell me where you put the watch? Mr Buckle has been very kind, for he has written to the Home Secretary about you, and I think you will be doing good to yourself by acknowledging where you put it.' Murphy then began to cry and said, 'Mr. Rose, I was never near the place.'
>
> I turned to Brannagan and said, 'Now, Brannagan, you have a wife and two children, I have been offered £10 and I will give it to your wife and family, if you will tell me where the watch is placed.' Brannagan replied, 'I was never near the place.'

Murphy and Brannagan went from Morpeth to Pentonville, but as they were Catholics they were transferred to Millbank where they consistently maintained they were innocent.

One man who did come to believe they were innocent was local solicitor Charles Percy. He arranged a meeting with Jevon Perry, the vicar of St Paul's, Alnwick. Murphy's sisters had been to see him about a quarrel they had overheard between Edgell and his niece. She had said she could put him 'away in a place from which he would never come back'. There was also some evidence that a man called White, who worked on the roads, had seen Edgell out and about on the morning after the burglary when the police said he had been at home all night. Then a chimney sweep named John Allen told him that before Superintendent Harkes had died in 1882 he had come to see him in his kitchen and said that he now agreed with what Allen had told him before the trial, that there had been a mistake over the burglary but that it could not now be put right. The only thing that would help the men was for the watch to be found.

Now it seemed that Edgell's small daughter Maria was dying from consumption and that Edgell himself was in poor health, too. His wife had been dropping hints that she would not let him die without confessing everything. Would the clergyman delicately raise the subject of the burglary when he met Edgell, to see what, if anything, he had to say?

Perry seems to have been a disciple of the Moody and Sankey form of evangelism, putting bread in stomachs before giving a sermon, and he arranged for food and medicine for the girl. As a result gradually he acquired Edgell's confidence.

By October 1886 Murphy was in Portsmouth Prison from where he wrote to his sister:

> I am sorry to tell you that I am very unhappy here. In fact it would be a great blessing to me if Almighty God would release me from this dreadful punishment, and close my eyes in death. For what is life to me here, but a slow, lingering death? I cannot find words to express the sufferings I have undergone here; but I believe I am the most unfortunate being upon the face of this earth. And why, dear sister, should this bitter chalice pass with me? What evil have I done that this should be my bitter lot in life?

Perry, furnished with the information he had received from Edgell, now firmly believed that Murphy and Brannagan were innocent and went to see Buckle and his daughter. She was still convinced they were the men but conceded that there was one point that only she and the men who actually stole her property would know about, and if they could describe that then she might believe there was something in it. She told Perry and Percy that the seal to a chain on the watch was a little bird.

It took Perry a whole year before he persuaded Edgell to confess, and he was only able to do this because Edgell's daughter Maria had died in February 1887 saying that she would see her father in heaven. According to Perry, Edgell had been having fits of conscience and was becoming ever more religious with tracts and pictures on the walls of his cottage. Finally the man agreed that he had been on the burglary but that he was not the one who had fired the shot. Perry's other problem was Charles Richardson who, unsurprisingly, was opposed to the idea of owning up. Ultimately on 17 November 1887 he went to the vicarage and made a long and detailed confession written down by Percy. They had stolen a watch but, although he could say it had a chain with a seal on it, he could not give any further description. They had failed to sell or pawn it and had thrown it in the river Tyne. He did not know what had happened to the chain. Perry then went to the vicarage but found that Buckle and his daughter were recalcitrant and Buckle resented his interference.

Perry and Percy now had some good fortune. Their barrister Thomas Milvain had become a QC and also the MP for Durham. They sent him a copy of Edgell's confession and, with the members for Morpeth and North Northumberland in support, he took up the cause. At first, he received nothing but replies that the Home Secretary 'saw no sufficient grounds for reconsidering this case'. On 6 August 1888 he put a question in the House of Commons asking whether the Home Secretary had received a confession. He had, and the Home Secretary had directed the Solicitor to the Treasury to hold an inquiry.

George Dransfield, a Newcastle solicitor, was appointed to conduct the inquiry but when he told Edgell that his name would be published and he would doubtless be punished he refused to say anything more. Dransfield, however, continued to make enquiries and took a series of statements that backed up Edgell's unsigned statement. Eventually Edgell came round and Perry and Percy tried to obtain an indemnity from the Home Secretary under the Charges and Allegations Act, which had been passed that year, but they were told that this was impossible.

In the middle of October Edgell agreed that he would make

an unconditional confession. There had been a local belief that a George Bamburgh had been involved but Edgell specifically cleared him, declining to say who the other man was. Finally, Charles Richardson joined Edgell in admitting his involvement.

On 9 November Milvain asked whether the Home Secretary had received a report that showed Murphy and Brannagan to be innocent. The following Wednesday the Home Secretary announced there had been a careful inquiry and report made on the subject of the burglary. 'The circumstances elicited by the inquiry were most singular and unprecedented.' After careful consideration he had directed criminal proceedings to be taken against two other men; and, while these were pending, Brannagan and Murphy would be released on licence.

On their arrival at Alnwick station on 16 November 1888 the pair were carried shoulder high through the town while a Salvation Army band played 'Home, Sweet Home'.

Brannagan made a statement:

> I feel very thankful to be released, and I do hope the judge will deal leniently with the men who have confessed. From the time I was convicted until now, I have never seen either my wife, sisters or any of my children. Two of my children have died since I have been away, and this morning I actually did not know my children. I left the youngest a girl of two years of age, and she is now twelve. I would never have known that it was my daughter. I am free now, and I know well enough that if either Mr or Miss Buckle had died, I would not have been here now. I would have been hanged, and so would Murphy too, for the judge said he could see no difference between us. But I can say this, that if I had known what I had to go through, I would rather have been hanged at the first.

The *Newcastle Chronicle* thought the pair as poachers had only themselves to blame: 'If, as alleged, their painful experience has taught them a lesson amounting to reformation of character, they have not been wholly losers nor has society by their being punished for other men's misdeeds.'

Richardson and Edgell were arrested on 15 November and a week later were committed for trial amid a great deal of local speculation that they would withdraw their confessions. Their defence was organized by Perry and Percy, and a petition signed by some 2,600 people was then submitted asking that the pair should receive the lightest possible sentence. Firstly, a heavy one would never encourage felons to come forward; secondly, Richardson and Edgell had not given evidence against Murphy and Brannagan; thirdly, the pair had now confessed, which had allowed the release of Murphy and Brannagan; and finally, they were deeply penitent.

Unfortunately for the prosecution, Revd Buckle was adamant that neither Richardson nor Edgell were the men at the rectory. The magistrates decided however there was just sufficient evidence to corroborate their confessions and committed them for trial.

At the Assizes there was an ingenious 'special plea' put forward. Since Brannagan and Murphy had not yet been pardoned, the Crown should be prevented from proceeding against Edgell and Richardson. The trial judge, Baron Pollock, rejected this and the pair then pleaded not guilty to the shooting but guilty to the burglary. The prosecution offered no evidence and, as a result, on the attempted murder charge the judge said he felt they were in a very different position from Murphy and Brannagan and so he could pass a five-year sentence on them.

Perry at once got up a petition to have the sentence reduced. There was also the question of whether the police had deliberately concocted a case against Brannagan and Murphy in planting pieces of newspaper matching those at the vicarage.

Unfortunately the Revd Buckle was not displaying any form of graciousness by admitting he had been wrong in his identification of the men. He thought perhaps the four men had been involved in the burglary.

In January 1889 it was announced there would be a prosecution against four police officers. The trial took place at the end of February when Edward Besley, for the defence, lambasted the prosecution witnesses, and the prosecutor himself said the case against Brannagan and Murphy was stronger than it was ten years previously and that Edgell and Richardson were not guilty of the burglary. With Mr Justice Denman in his summing-up agreeing with him, it took only half an hour for the jury to acquit the officers, something described by the judge as a 'very right verdict'.

Finally Brannagan and Murphy were awarded £800 each in compensation. On 31 May that year the *Auckland Star* reported rather sanctimoniously that:

> Brannagan and Murphy, you will be glad to learn, are doing well. Murphy, whose sweetheart deserted him and married another whilst he was in gaol, has found consolation and opened a bakers' shop in Alnwick. Brannagan emigrated with his family to the River Plate [Argentina] and obtained remunerative work there at once. Both are staunch teetotalers and consequently likely to keep straight.

Murphy died in June 1934 aged seventy-seven.

George Edalji

Solicitors, when they are convicted, usually go down for fraud and swindling, and perhaps occasionally for murder. Very few are accused of writing poison pen letters and maiming animals.

George Ernest Thompson Edalji was the eldest of three children. He had a brother, Horace, and a sister Maud, who suffered from ill-health throughout her life. His mother was Charlotte Stoneham, daughter of a Shropshire vicar, and his father was Revd Shapurji Edalji, a convert from a Bombay Parsi family. He had paid for his passage to England and for his studies by writing a *Dictionary of Gujerati*. Edalji Snr served as the curate in several parishes before, in 1875, he was presented with the living of vicar of St Mark's, Great Wyrley, near Walsall in south Staffordshire. The right to make this appointment lay with the bishop, and Edalji obtained the position through the previous incumbent, his wife's uncle, who arranged it as a wedding present. He was probably the first South Asian incumbent in an English parish.

Livings were highly prized, but it was a strange appointment, certainly as far as the locals were concerned, a mixed mining and rural community. Late-nineteenth-century rural English society was not one that generally had foreigners, let alone Indians in their midst, and this would have been particularly true of a village such as Great Wyrley. On his appointment Edalji and his wife moved into the Great Wyrley vicarage, a large house with its own grounds, and George was born there soon after.

Unsurprisingly, the Edalji family was viewed with some suspicion by the local community. The Reverend was more assertive than his predecessor and involved himself in the parish business, allowing the Liberal party the use of the church hall for election meetings, something that engendered bad feeling. There would, without doubt, have been gossip in the village about the 'mixed marriage' and particularly about the sleeping arrangements in the household. Through much of his life the vicar, who was said to suffer from lumbago, slept in the same locked bedroom as George. Charlotte slept in the same room as her daughter Maud. The vicar said it was a matter of economy since they only had one housemaid, but there were rumours that the vicar had an incestuous homosexual relationship with George. Later there was a suggestion that George had always been a night wanderer and that was why the Reverend slept with him in a locked bedroom.

In 1888, when George Edalji was twelve-and-a-half, anonymous threatening letters were sent to the vicarage demanding the Reverend order a particular newspaper and threatening to break windows if this was not done. He ignored them. Now unordered goods arrived and vicars from across the country came scurrying to help after receiving apparently urgent letters from him. After the windows were broken and a threat to shoot the Reverend was made, he became alarmed and called in the police. Graffiti slandering the Edaljis was written on both the outside and inside walls of the vicarage.

Pseudonymous letters were sent to the Edaljis' maid-of-all-work, seventeen-year-old Elizabeth Foster, threatening to shoot her when her 'Black master' was out. One written on pages from the exercise books of the Edalji children was found inside the hall with the envelope wet, making it seem that either Elizabeth Foster or George was responsible. Now the Reverend and his wife, along with Police Sergeant Upton, claimed the handwriting of the girl was similar to that in the threatening letters, something she denied.

As a result the Reverend prosecuted her. Triable only by jury, the case would have had to go to the Assizes. Ironically, in view of later letters, there was no scientific evidence produced

that Foster was responsible, and the Reverend agreed to drop
the case if she confessed. She refused and went to live with an
aunt. However, unable to pay for a defence at her trial, she
pleaded guilty to a lesser charge in front of the magistrates and
was bound over to keep the peace. The Reverend congratu-
lated Upton on his diligence in solving the case. Throughout
the remainder of her life Elizabeth Foster continually maintained her innocence.

Then four years later in 1892 a series of poison pen letters
was sent to a local parish council member, W. H. Brookes,
some of which included detailed allegations of his adult daughter sexually abusing her ten-year-old sister. Other poison pen
letters mentioned Edalji among others, but later ones concen-
trated on George and his father, who was sometimes referred
to as the 'blackman', a description used in the 1888 letters
attributed to Elizabeth Foster. One letter was written in two
distinctly different 'hands' of writing. The letters to Brookes
also accused his son of writing the 1888 letters to the vicarage
and giving them to George Edalji to post.

Others of the 1892 letters sent to Revd Edalji and a vicarage
servant accused him of 'gross immorality with persons using
Vaseline in the same way as did Oscar Wilde'. Letters purporting to be from Revd Edalji were also sent to other vicars.
Brookes and the Reverend called in the police and Sergeant
Upton again investigated. Attempts to get the post office to
identify the sender failed when the mailed letters ceased. Now
notes began appearing at the vicarage, and various objects,
including a bag of dung, were left on the doorstep. Police kept
watch and claimed to have established that a key stolen from
Walsall Grammar School six miles away had appeared on the
doorstep when only George Edalji had used the entrance.
Following this, excrement was smeared on the outside of
upstairs windows, and now the Chief Constable of
Staffordshire, the Honourable G. A. Anson, a former army
officer, decided George had been responsible for the letters.

At that time a chief constable of a local constabulary was not
required, nor even expected, to have any police experience
and George Edalji was unfortunate that Anson took an openly

hostile attitude towards him, writing on 23 January 1893 to his father, 'I may say at once that I shall not pretend to believe any protestations of ignorance which your son may make about this key.' If George would admit it was a practical joke, 'I should not be inclined to allow any police proceedings to be taken in regard to it.' George did not.

A police ploy clearly aimed at getting George Edalji to incriminate himself as the note writer was unsuccessful, and brought protests from his mother at the way the investigation was focusing on him. Responding to her complaint, Anson told Mrs Edalji that if she wanted his men to spend more time on the matter she should make a serious effort to help catch the culprit, who was obviously either her husband or son. The Reverend Edalji threatened to complain to higher authority about Anson's conduct who, on 25 July 1895, in turn wrote, 'I trust to be able to obtain a dose of penal servitude for the offender.' She and her husband demanded that Foster again be arrested. The campaign of hoax ordering of goods and services for the vicarage lasted for three years, by which time the police had largely ceased investigating the incidents.

Brookes had also come to believe George Edalji was the author of the 1892 letters, claiming that after he returned a smile from Edalji in the railway station with a disagreeable look, the letters began to refer to him as 'sour face'. He also said the letters to him stopped after he got out of a train and swung punches at Edalji on the platform, because he was peering in the compartments. And then suddenly the notes and hoaxes ended.

Academically George Edalji was exceptionally bright. He was taken on by King and Ludlow, a Birmingham firm of solicitors, as an articled clerk and he qualified in December 1898, receiving second-class honours and a bronze medal in the Law Society's Final examination. Only one candidate received first-class honours. The next year his family helped him set up on his own as a solicitor, working out of an office in Birmingham and from the vicarage. In 1901 he published a small book, *Railway Law for the 'Man in the train'*.

George was described as looking younger than his age. He

had very poor eyesight and as a result a rather peculiar goggle-eyed appearance. He began taking evening strolls by himself, and in 1900 two men were fined for hitting him one night while he was walking three miles away from his house. His attackers were not from Great Wyrley nor known to Edalji. The next year a solicitor and clerk to the local justices, C. A. Loxton, accused Edalji of writing 'immoral and offensive' allegations about him and his fiancée on walls. Curiously, Edalji's younger brother, Horace, does not seem to have had any problems either with locals or the authorities.

Then, in 1903, when Edalji was twenty-seven years old, things took a more serious turn when a series of slashings of horses and other livestock, known as the 'Great Wyrley Outrages', occurred. From 1 February, when a horse was maimed, to 29 June, when two horses were similarly wounded, a number of animals received injuries that resulted in them being put down. Isolated cases of livestock maiming are not unheard of as a way of settling scores in farming communities, but this series of attacks provoked a public outcry far beyond the area.

Pseudonymous letters were sent to the police purporting to be from one of a gang of culprits, fifteen-year-old Wilfred Greatorex, who named people as members of the gang, including Edalji. Several others named in the letters were schoolboys with whom Edalji regularly commuted to Birmingham in the same train compartment. Questioned, Greatorex denied being either a member of the gang or the writer of the letters.

Again Chief Constable Anson believed Edalji was the author but that, because of his professional status, he had had no actual involvement in the maimings. An Inspector Campbell headed enquiries into the attacks and, although there were a number of suspects, from an early stage considered Edalji a person of particular interest because most of the attacks had occurred within a half-mile radius of the vicarage. Now Edalji was seen 'prowling' the area at night and on two occasions trails of footprints from attack locations seemed to lead to the vicarage.

When, on 29 June, two horses were mutilated in a seventh

attack, based on a sighting of him in the field, Campbell felt sure Edalji was responsible and as a result began to focus on him. Things became even more serious when a letter posted on 10 July 1903, addressed to The Sergeant, Police Station, Hednesford, Staffordshire, and with a Walsall postmark, suggested that 'little girls' would be the target of the next attacks. It concluded, 'You bloated blackguard, I will shoot you with Father's gun through your thick head, if you come in my way or go sneaking to any of my pals.'

Now Anson agreed to a watch being kept on the vicarage and nearby countryside. When there were rumours that Edalji was going to be arrested for the attacks, he placed an advertisement in a local paper offering a £25 reward for information about who was spreading them. Perhaps inadvisedly, he continued his habit of taking long evening walks and he returned from one at around 9 p.m. on 17 August.

Early the next morning a wounded roan pony was discovered half a mile from the scene of the first attack. Inspector Campbell sent a constable to the railway station where Edalji was waiting to catch his train, to ask him to help with inquiries. He declined and left for his office in Birmingham. Along with a sergeant and constable, Campbell duly went to the vicarage and asked to see any weapons in the house; a small trowel was the only thing shown to them. The police also looked at Edalji's clothing, which included muddy boots as well as mud-stained serge trousers and a housecoat – both of which the police said were damp. The inspector said there was a hair on the housecoat, and a dispute followed between him and the Reverend over whether it was a hair or a loose thread.

The next day police searched the vicarage and found a case with four razors in the bedroom that Edalji shared with his father. The Reverend said the razors were old ones not in use but, according to the police, when it was pointed out that one razor was wet, the Reverend took it and wiped the blade with his thumb; he later said this was not true. The police also said a heel on the boots was worn down in an unusual way, and left a distinctive pattern on the ground that matched heel impressions in an alleged trail of footprints between the vicarage and the scene of the crime. A Dr Butler who examined a waistcoat for the police said it was bloodstained. The doctor said that twenty-nine hairs on it, although they were small and difficult to see, were in fact similar to ones near the pony's wound. The handwriting expert Thomas Gurrin inspected the various letters, one of which had been written on the back of an enve- lope addressed to Edalji at his Birmingham office. He said he had no doubt the handwriting was that of George Edalji.

Edalji was arrested and charged under the Malicious Damage Act 1861 with maiming the pony and sending a threatening letter to a police officer. He declined to ask for bail, saying that he could not then be accused of further attacks, and was committed for trial at Staffordshire Assizes. After Edalji's arrest and when he was in custody awaiting his trial there had been another maiming in the area when a Henry Green slashed his own mare's stomach. Green claimed that it was a sick animal and the police took no action.

Unfortunately for Edalji the case was then remitted to Staffordshire Quarter Sessions where he appeared in the second court. A legally qualified Chairman of Quarter Sessions conducted trials in the first court but the second had only a local dignitary, Deputy Chairman Sir Reginald Hardy, who was not legally qualified.

Now the prosecution shifted its ground on two points. First, that Edalji was not alone in the maimings but was part of a local gang. Secondly, a vet gave evidence that the pony had been attacked no earlier than six hours before it was found. This meant Edalji was alleged to have got up in the middle of the night to carry out the attack rather than to have committed the crime during his evening walk.

Edalji consistently maintained he was innocent of all charges. He pleaded not guilty to injuring the pony. The indictment for sending a letter threatening to kill a policeman was not tried but evidence of the letter was brought into the maiming trial.

He was defended by C. F. Vachell and, with hindsight, prob- ably not very well defended. Vachell appears not to have mentioned his defective eyesight. Edalji later said he had been told by his lawyers that the prosecution case was so weak he was sure to be acquitted, and so it was unnecessary to bring up how poor his sight really was. Nor was any real effort made to exploit the change in the prosecution's theory of a one-man maimer to Edalji being part of a band. Nine witnesses were called on Edalji's behalf including five who said they had seen him between 8.30 and 9.30 nowhere near Great Wyrley. The Reverend said he had hardly slept that night and knew that his son could not have left the bedroom they shared. He had locked the door as usual. Unfortunately it appears his pedantic family were not good witnesses.

On 23 October 1903 Edalji was convicted in less than an hour with the chairman saying he agreed with the verdict. Despite a recommendation for mercy by the jury because of his position, Hardy sentenced him to seven years hard labour, which he served in Lewes and later Portland Prisons. On 2 November another horse was maimed in the area and on 24 March 1904 yet another. Now petitions were drafted with some 10,000 signatories, including hundreds from lawyers, protesting at the conviction. Some legal figures thought that it was improper that the threatening letters had been used against him on the maiming charge and the chairman of the Law Society made a post-trial contribution to Edalji's costs.

Writing in his book *Miscarriages of Justice*, criminal defence barrister C. G. L. Du Cann thought that:

> His prosecution was fairly conducted; the judge directed the jury with care and fairness. To a degree the local jury may not have been exempt from prejudice, for the happenings had been much canvassed locally long before the trial. Neither was the police theory that George Edalji was guilty, on which the prosecution was based, anything but a reasonable and tenable one.

Those who claim they have been wrongly convicted need a spokesman, preferably someone well known to the public and authorities, to campaign on their behalf. Edalji's first great champion was Roger Dawson Yelverton, a former Chief Justice in the Bahamas, who thought the case for the prosecution had been conclusively disproved. He asked, perhaps naively, 'How could a gentleman in the position and of the education of Mr Edalji, be supposed to write the following, put by the Prosecution before the Jury, as written by him. "You great hulking blackguard and coward I have got you fixed you dirty Cad – bloody monkey!"'

Senior civil servants at the Home Office reviewed the case and reported that there were no serious flaws in the trial and conviction. On 5 May 1904 the Home Secretary Ackers-Douglas wrote to Edalji Snr saying he would not interfere with the conviction. On 21 May he refused to disclose documents that Anson had sent to him. Somebody, however, must have had doubts because in October 1905 it was announced Edalji was to be released on ticket of leave on 19 October the following year. The Home Secretary later explained that this was because he considered the sentence to be too long. For a time Edalji was required to report to the police but this was eventually reduced to reporting by letter.

Edalji's second champion was Sir Arthur Conan Doyle. After his release either he wrote to him or Conan Doyle saw an article in the *Umpire* (accounts vary) but a meeting was arranged at a London hotel. When Conan Doyle arrived Edalji was reading a newspaper in the lobby, the pages held close to his face, and he was convinced that Edalji was innocent, believing it impossible for someone with eyesight as bad as Edalji's to have moved through the countryside at night attacking animals while successfully evading the police. The night of the attack on the roan had been a particularly dark one. Now, beginning with letters to the *Daily Telegraph*, Conan Doyle joined Yelverton in a campaign for a pardon.

On 19 January 1907 Yelverton and Conan Doyle issued a statement asking the public to call for an inquiry. That month Conan Doyle prepared a memorial arguing the grounds of his innocence and, taking things a stage further, sent a second document arguing that the outrages had been committed by a Royston Sharp with some help from his brothers and friends. On 29 January *The Times,* which had not been a champion of Edalji, joined in, saying that while not all Conan Doyle's points were good they were sufficient to justify the Home Secretary reopening the case.

On 10 February the Home Secretary, now William Gladstone, announced he had appointed a committee to be chaired by Sir Robert Romer. They had only newspaper reports on which to work because unfortunately there was no transcript taken of the trial and Hardy had merely pencilled some abbreviated notes for himself. Things got off to a bad start when Romer, realizing the committee would have no power to call witnesses or take evidence on oath, resigned, writing that he was not willing to sit as judge and jury. He was replaced by Chief Magistrate Sir Albert de Rutzen who, most unfortunately, was Captain Anson's second cousin.

Anson had corresponded with Conan Doyle and met with him to discuss the case, but relations between them quickly soured. Anson was under the impression that the writer was still considering all the evidence and when, two days later, Conan Doyle told him of his intention to campaign for a pardon, Anson thought he had obtained his cooperation and an interview by misrepresenting himself as having no settled opinion about the case. Conan Doyle wrote to the Home Office saying Anson had implied homosexual incest between the Reverend and Edalji. Anson insisted he did no such thing.

When the Committee reported, it considered it highly unlikely that the police would have fabricated evidence by planting the hairs after the Edaljis had vehemently drawn attention to the absence of hairs on the housecoat when it was handed over.

Conan Doyle became an active investigator, going to the crime scenes, interviewing participants and critiquing the reliability of handwriting expert Thomas Gurrin who had given wrong evidence in the 1896 Adolf Beck case. Peculiarities found in the handwriting of Edalji also occurred in the 1903 pseudonymous 'Greatorex' letters to police naming Edalji as a culprit in the animal mutilations. Legal technicalities made the evidence about the letters being used to convict Edalji controversial, because he had not been tried on the charge of sending a threatening letter. Opinion within the Home Office was split on the matter, but Conan Doyle persisted in his belief that the perpetrator was a local man, Royston Sharp.

Sharp was born in 1879 and his academic career was the antithesis of that of Edalji. At the age of twelve Sharp set fire to a hayrick, for which his father paid to avoid a charge being brought. He did not do well at school. In late 1891 he was caught cheating. Things did not improve the next term when he was found to have falsified his schoolmates' marks. His conduct was 'unsatisfactory, often untruthful'. Sharp was removed in the summer of 1882 after forging letters and initials. It seems that if left alone on a train he would cut the leather window sashes and slit the undersides of the cushioned seats.

Over the years there has been a variety of opinions about whether Conan Doyle was justified in his belief. One writer, Michael Harley, researching for the publisher John Murray, believed that George Edalji was far more devious than Conan Doyle imagined, and the man who had been duped over photographs of fairies by two schoolgirls had been duped again.

Newspapers suggested visual impairment would have made it impossible for Edalji to have committed the crime. Captain Anson told the Home Office he thought Edalji was physically more than capable of the nocturnal maiming, asserting that Edalji had a panther-like gait and eyes that 'came out with a strange sort of glow, like a cat's eyes, in a low light'.

According to Anson's communications with the Home Office an assertion Edalji made that he was not abroad after nightfall was 'indisputably false'. Anson said several people remembered coming across Edalji very late at night and miles from his house during 1903.

Nevertheless Edalji was granted a pardon for the maiming conviction in May 1907, though the Committee did not recommend he receive any compensation, which was now available to the wrongly convicted. The Committee found there had been an unsatisfactory conviction in Edalji's case but that was not the same thing as innocence. They specifically said they did not disagree with the jury findings over the letters and that he had brought prosecution upon himself by sending the pseudonymous 'Greatorex' letters to police during the summer of 1903. They had not called Thomas Gurrin before them, even though by now his evidence in the Adolf Beck case had been discredited.

Eighty years later, a June 1907 memo by the then Home Secretary Herbert Gladstone was discovered. It contained details of a conversation Gladstone had had with Alfred Hazel, by then MP for West Bromwich. At the trial Horace Edalji had brought Hazel and Vachell a letter which was meant to show a difference in handwriting from the earlier letters. In fact it was in the same writing and contained a series of obscenities similar to ones Edalji was accused of sending. Vachell and Hazel thought it would be fatal to the case to introduce it. When the 1907 letters started, Vachell had remarked to Hazel, 'He is at it again.'

He was referring to an incident on 27 August 1907 when two more mares were mutilated in the area. Revd Edalji told reporters that his son had been in Great Yarmouth at the time and that he himself had received a postcard postmarked Margate saying, 'Be cheerful your son will be proved all right. I will see you soon, Yours A.L.' He said that this was in the same handwriting as the anonymous letters. In November that year, after a campaign by lawyers, Edalji was restored to the roll of solicitors.

In the autumn of 1912 there was another outbreak of letters from 'Captain Darby' and attacks on horses. A warning was received in July and two horses were attacked. On 1 September when two further animals were injured, the *Daily Express* suggested a £100 reward should be offered, but Captain Anson said this was not possible. On 5 September another letter purporting to be from Captain Darby said that a wager had been struck within the gang that within a given time ten horses would be maimed. He was paying four men £5,000 each. The attacks continued into the following year when in August more horses were injured. The Home Office took a detached view of the affairs. A memorandum of 13 June 1914 read 'the question of the identity of Darby scarcely concerns the Home Office except as a matter of curiosity'.

The attacks stopped with the outbreak of war but recommenced in the summer of 1915. Then a journalist, G. A. Atkinson, published a tuppenny pamphlet '*G. H. Darby*' *Captain of theWyrley Gang* and, on sending a copy to the Home Office, asked for an investigation. The Home Office dismissed the suggestion out of hand.

Edalji's father died in May 1918. He had been the vicar of Great Wyrley for more than forty years. He left an estate of slightly less than £150.

There were renewed claims for compensation when on 6 November 1934 Enoch Knowles pleaded guilty and received three years at Staffordshire Assizes to sending menacing and obscene letters. He had apparently been doing this for the past thirty years. Some of the letters were to judges and journalists, but others were to women after they had given evidence in criminal cases which he had read about in the *News of the World*. In one he described himself as 'Jack the Ripper of Whitechapel'.

Immediately Edalji wrote an account of his case for the *Daily Express*, but in June the next year the Home Office again turned him down. There were no grounds for thinking Knowles had written the Edalji letters. The Captain Darby letters had been written after Edalji was in custody and experts were sure that the Greatorex letters had been written by Edalji. The Home Office was sure that had Knowles written these letters he would have confessed.

Edalji continued to practise law in London in Borough High Street and then King's Cross as a solicitor, representing some notable underworld figures including members of the Sabini racecourse gang. He lived in modest circumstances in Paddock Close, Welwyn Garden City with his sister Maud until, now blind, he died in 1953 shortly after his brother Horace, who had changed his name to Magee and lived in Dublin. Maud continued to write to the Home Office claiming, after three men had been released after a wrong conviction in 1956, that there should be an inquiry into her brother's case. After all, Gladstone had been a cousin of the wife of the trial judge. She received short shrift. She died in March 1962 leaving all her papers in the case to the Law Society. They have been either destroyed or lost.

Rightly convicted or not, Edalji's case and the associated campaign were considerable factors in the creation of England's Court of Criminal Appeal in 1907.

Adolf Beck

One of the worldwide problems of the criminal justice system in the nineteenth century was that there was no accurate way of identifying criminals and matching them to their previous convictions. So, after his first conviction Smith would give his name as Thomas and then after the second Jones or Green and so on. It was only if the man appeared in the same court or was recognized by a police officer from a previous case that his previous convictions would become known, but it was very much a hit and miss affair.

In France things had not changed since the 1820s when the detective Eugene-Francois Vidocq had put together a card system with basic details of criminals. Then, in March 1879, Alphonse Bertillon, a clerk in the Sûreté in Paris, began comparing the photographs of prisoners, studying the ears and noses side by side. Now he decided that while people may have had similar measurements of their noses, ears and so on, they never had four or five characteristics that were the same. By August that year he had convinced himself, if no one else, that he had devised a simple system for the correct identification of a criminal.

It was not until February 1883 that he correctly challenged a man who gave his name as Dupont, then a common alias for French criminals, who had been arrested in December the previous year for stealing bottles. His real name, said Bertillon, was Martin.

In 1884 he identified another 300 recidivists and the

previously unsung Bertillon and his methods became fashionable. Britain's Home Office sent senior civil servant Edmund Spearman to Paris to meet him with a view to introducing his system into British prisons, and Louis Herbette, director of the French prison administration, now announced he was going to introduce Bertillon's system, which he called anthropometry, into French ones. On 1 November that year Bertillon, the new forensic genius, was unveiled to the public. 'Young French scientist revolutionises the identification of criminals', read one headline and his method was dubbed *bertillonage*. Journalist Pierre Brullard gushed, 'Thanks to a French genius, errors of identification will soon cease to exist not only in France, but also in the entire world. Hence judicial errors based on false identification will likewise disappear. Long live *bertillonage*. Long live Alphonse Bertillon!' Sadly they did not.

In 1895 a series of frauds occurred in London when about fifty women of the prostitute class were swindled. A man posing as a member of the aristocracy offered the women a position as his mistress and, telling them they would need better clothes and jewellery, either took their rings on a promise to return with better ones or borrowed money against which he deposited a worthless cheque. Then on 16 December 1895 in Victoria Street, one of the women, Ottilie Meissonier, who described herself as a language teacher, saw the man she believed had swindled her. A police officer was called and Norwegian businessman, fifty-four-year-old Adolf Beck, was arrested. The story Meissonier told was similar to that of all the other women.

She alleged that some months earlier she had been walking down Victoria Street when Beck approached her, tipping his hat and asking if she was Lady Everton. She said that she was not, but she was impressed by his gentlemanly manner and they struck up a conversation. According to her account, he introduced himself as Lord Willoughby and when she told him she was going to a flower show he said it was not worth visiting. He said that he knew horticulture because he had gardens on his Lincolnshire estate extensive enough to require six gardeners. When Meissonier mentioned that she grew chrysanthemums, he asked her whether he might see them and she invited him to tea the following day.

When he called he invited her to go to the French Riviera on his yacht. He insisted upon providing her with an elegant wardrobe for the voyage, wrote out a list of items for her and made out a cheque for £40 to cover her expenses. Then he examined her wristwatch and rings, and asked her to let him have them so that he could match their sizes and replace them with more valuable pieces. After he left she discovered that a second watch was missing. Suspicious, she hurried to the bank to cash the cheque, only to find that it was worthless.

Beck was placed on an identification parade with seven men brought in off the street and a Daisy Grant, who had also been swindled, and Meissonier's maid picked him out without hesitation.

He was charged and remanded in custody, protesting that it was a dreadful mistake. The story of his arrest appeared in the newspapers and now a number of women came forward complaining that they also had been the victims of similar frauds. In all, twenty-two women were invited to attend a rudimentary form of identity parades. Ten made a positive identification, one said he was definitely not the man and the others were uncertain. Kate Brakefield, who said she had been cheated the previous June, picked Beck out of a line-up of eight: 'I am satisfied he is the same man,' she said. Minnie Lewis, robbed in April, identified Beck from fourteen men: 'I have not a shadow of a doubt he is the man.' Juliette Kluth, swindled the previous March, went to a parade where eighteen men stood with Beck. 'Among them I recognised the prisoner at once.' Marion Taylor was 'quite sure' that Beck was the man. Fanny Nutt was just as confident: 'I should know him in a thousand.' Evelyn Emily Miller 'identified him at once without difficulty'. The police believed Beck was the same man as a German, William Weiss who, in 1877 as John Smith, had served five years for identical frauds.

At Beck's committal hearing PC Ellis Spurrell, one of the policemen who had arrested Smith eighteen years before, told the court:

On 7 May 1877 I was present at the Central Criminal Court where the prisoner in the name of John Smith was convicted of feloniously stealing ear-rings and a ring and eleven shillings of Louisa Leonard and was sentenced to five years' penal servitude. I produce the certificate of that conviction. The prisoner is the man . . . There is no doubt whatever – I know quite well what is at stake on my answer and I say without doubt he is the man.

Beck protested and insisted that he could bring witnesses from South America to prove that he was there when Smith was committing his frauds. He had come to England in 1865, working as a clerk to a shipping broker. In 1868 he moved to South America, where he made a living for a while as a singer accompanied by American composer and pianist Louis Moreau Gottschalk. He then became a shipbroker, also speculating in property. At first he was successful and on one deal netted £8,000 as commission from a sale of a Spanish concession in the Galapagos Islands. He returned to England in 1885 and engaged in various financial schemes, including an investment in a Norwegian copper mine. Unfortunately the mine was not a success, and he poured in more and more money until he had to put the mine up for sale. There were no takers and he was reduced to near poverty. By the time of his arrest he owed money for his room in a hotel in Covent Garden and had borrowed money from his secretary. Now the top hat and morning coat he sported were threadbare.

At his trial on 3 March 1896 he was prosecuted by Horace Avory, who later became one of the harsher judges in an era when judges were almost universally harsh.

The defence was that the frauds had been committed by the John Smith of 1877. Beck could show he was not John Smith and had been in South America. This was neatly circumvented by Avory and the judge, Sir Forrest Fulton. Avory dropped the charge against Beck of being a convicted felon, which he would have had to prove, and did not call Spurrell. Fulton refused to allow Charles Gill, appearing for Beck, to call evidence to show he had been in Peru when Smith was convicted in 1877.

The ten women identified Beck in court and Thomas Gurrin, a handwriting expert, gave evidence that the writing on the cheques and notes was that of Beck disguised. It was the same Gurrin who would give evidence in the flawed Edalji poison pen letter case. At the time Beck was not allowed to give evidence on his own behalf and those witnesses who were called to say they had known him in South America were not cross-examined about the dates. The verdict was inevitable. There was no right of appeal.

Beck was listed as a reconvicted man and given Smith's old number of Convict D523. He continually petitioned the Home Office complaining his conviction had been wrong, but, given that the Office received around 4,000 petitions a year from prisoners and 1,000 from their friends and relatives, unless new evidence was provided no attention was paid. Beck must have had some money left after paying for his counsel Charles Gill because T. Duerdin Dutton, his solicitor, continued to act for him over a number of writs brought against him for money owed and he did manage to provide the required new evidence, albeit in an oblique way.

After a struggle he managed to get the prison authorities to disclose that Smith was Jewish and had been circumcised. On 18 May 1898 a letter from the Home Office asked the governor of Portland Prison to inform them if Beck was similarly circumcised. The answer from Dr Treadwell was quite clear. 'No. He has not been circumcised.' This left the Home Office in something of a dilemma that was quickly smoothed over. The Home Office asked Sir Forrest Fulton for his opinion on this new evidence. Fulton wrote a minute dated 13 May in which he acknowledged that Smith and Beck could not be the same person, but he added that even if Beck was not Smith, he was still the swindler of 1895, and that he viewed the South American alibi 'with great suspicion'. Beck had, said Fulton, been convicted on overwhelming evidence.

His petition for release was therefore refused and the only immediate benefit to him was that he was now treated as a first offender. As a rider, in the absence of any agreed system of categorizing fingerprints, the Home Office thought the problem showed how necessary it was to adopt Bertillon's measuring system.

Beck was released in 1901 after serving nearly all his seven year sentence and began to try to find the women who had identified him to say they were mistaken. He would later tell an inquiry that some of those he saw failed totally to recognize him, as did PC Spurrell. He could not, however, get them to make written statements because, they said, they were afraid of the police.

Then three years later the frauds on prostitutes started up again with the perpetrator using exactly the same *modus operandi*. Pauline Scott, who had made a complaint about being swindled, was told to stand near Beck's lodgings in the Tottenham Court Road. When he left for work she identified him. Again he had more misfortune. Other women came forward and he was charged and once more committed for trial at the Old Bailey. In the week before the case he could not pay his solicitor, Freke Palmer, who withdrew. Another solicitor Matthew Williams did what he could in the remaining few days, but the barrister instructed did not know that Smith could not be Beck. He was tried at the Bailey in May 1904 and five women who had been defrauded picked him out. Gurrin again said the swindler's handwriting was that of Beck. 'Before God, my maker,' he told the jury, 'I am absolutely innocent of every charge brought against me. I have not spoken to or seen any of these women before they were set against me by the detectives.' He was duly convicted, but this time the judge Sir William Grantham had some doubts about the case and, despite assurances from both the Home Office and the police of Beck's guilt, deferred sentence until the July Sessions. He did not believe that Beck was of the criminal type and ordered a medical report. He also wanted the police to compare the 1896 prison photograph of him with the 1877 photograph of Smith.

At this point Beck's luck changed. Two more girls, sisters Violet and Beulah Turner, were swindled by a man using the name Turner who was arrested on 7 July while pawning their rings. An Inspector Kane, who had been involved in the Beck case, went to see him. He thought that while he resembled Beck he was older and stouter. He also had a scar on his neck, which Meissonier had mentioned in 1895. The man now gave his name as William Thomas, but it was clear he was Weiss alias John Smith. His landlord from 1877 identified him as his former tenant and Smith confessed. When Beck had been sent to prison the first time Smith had gone to America and returned in 1903 by which time he thought Beck would have served his sentence.

Now Gurrin unreservedly, if belatedly, changed his opinion. Of the five women, two had gone abroad and the remaining three admitted their mistake. Two of them picked out Smith from a large group of men. Hotel notepaper used by the swindler was found in Smith's possession as was a watch belonging to one of the girls. On 25 July 1904 the Home Secretary was asked in the House of Commons what action was being taken and had Beck been the victim of mistaken identity. Beck was released on £10 bail. Four days later he was given a free pardon and compensation of £2,000 raised, after a campaign led by journalist George Sims, to £5,000, roughly £300,000 today.

On 15 September 1904 Weiss, by now giving his age as sixty-five and describing himself as a journalist, pleaded guilty to the current crop of frauds and was sentenced to five years. The trial judge, Mr Justice Phillimore, said that while there was suspicion, there was no evidence that he had committed the frauds for which Beck had been sentenced.

In October 1904 a Committee of Inquiry, headed by the Master of the Rolls Sir Richard Collins, heard evidence from all those involved in the case including Horace Avory, who refused to accept any blame for the fiasco, and Sir Forrest Fulton. In its report it concluded that Adolf Beck should not have been convicted in the first trial due to the many errors made by the prosecution in presenting its case. The Committee also criticized Fulton saying he should have given consideration to the 1877 case, particularly because he was the one who had prosecuted Smith.

Fulton, who said he had no recollection of the earlier case, argued that his function was to limit the evidence to whether the defendant had committed the offences of which he was charged. In any event he believed the introduction of the 1877 crimes was more likely to harm Beck than help him. It was not an argument that sat well with his other remarks that he was deeply suspicious of Beck's South American story. The Committee found that he should have allowed that evidence to be called. It absolved Avory although, in retrospect, it is hard to see that he was acting in the best traditions of the Bar, knowingly cutting Beck's only defence from under his feet. It also criticized the Home Office, which had known as early as 1898 that Beck and Smith could not be the same man. The staff needed more legal training.

There had been nothing wrong, either, with the way the police had conducted the case. The real cause of the miscarriage – apart from the wrongful identification – was the omission in the prison records of 1877 and 1881 that Smith had been circumcised. Had this been known the Committee doubted the prosecution of Beck would ever have been commenced. Curiously, although it considered the question of establishing a Court of Criminal Appeal, it did not think it necessary. The opportunity to require cases to be heard by the Court of Crown Cases Reserved would be sufficient.

On 9 May 1905 E. G. Clayton, then secretary of the Prison Committee, wrote to all prison governors:

Governors are hereby directed to obliterate the particulars concerning Adolf Beck from the Weekly Convict lists which were forwarded to them for the week commencing 3rd July 1901 no 1782 he having been held to be innocent of the charge preferred against him and subsequently granted a free pardon.

A broken man, Adolf Beck died of pleurisy and bronchitis in Middlesex Hospital on 7 December 1909. It cannot have been much consolation that two years earlier a Court of Criminal Appeal had finally been established in England and Wales.

CHAPTER 4

Poison Pen

Mary Johnson; Rose Emma Gooding

Mary Johnson; Rose Emma Gooding

Adolf Beck was not the only person twice wrongly convicted of separate criminal offences. In 1912 Mary Johnson was convicted at the Surrey Quarter Sessions for sending obscene and threatening letters to a married couple named Woodman. She received six months and on her release the letters recommenced. The next year she was convicted of a similar offence against the Woodmans and this time she received nine months' hard labour. On Mrs Johnson's second release Mrs Woodman claimed the letters had started again and Mary Johnson and her husband Albert were once more sent to Surrey Quarter sessions, where this time they were acquitted. At this point the police and post office officials started to look at Mrs Woodman, who was caught posting three obscene letters. In her defence she denied she had written any of the previous 187 letters posted, of which 137 had been addressed to her. As for the three letters she was caught posting she claimed she had been forced to post them by a man named Charlwood, who had held a knife to her throat in her kitchen and threatened to cut it if she did not do so. In turn she was convicted and sentenced to eighteen months' imprisonment. Mrs Johnson now received £500 compensation, enough, if she had wished, to buy a row of terraced cottages.

Another crop of poison pen letters surfaced in Sussex in 1920 when a Miss Edith Swan, then aged around thirty, who worked as a laundress and was highly regarded in the neighbourhood, was living at 47 Western Road, Littlehampton in

Sussex, not far from the seafront. Her next-door neighbours were Rose Gooding and her husband William, a man respectfully referred to by the Home Office as Captain William. He was, in fact, the captain of a barge. Rose seems to have had at least one illegitimate child. With them lived her sister who also had an illegitimate child.

The trouble appears to have begun in May that year with a complaint by Miss Swan that the attractive Mrs Gooding was maltreating her sister's child. An inspector called and found there was nothing in the complaint, adding in his report that the house was 'good and clean'. Shortly after this Miss Swan received an obscene letter. And then more, signed somewhat surprisingly and variously: R; R.G.; 'Mrs Gooding's compliments'; and, to make sure there was no mistake, Mrs R. E. Gooding. Miss Swan went to see a local solicitor. Mrs Gooding was arrested and bailed on condition she provide sureties for her reappearance and good behaviour pending her trial. She could not find them and was remanded in custody.

The case was heard at Lewes Assizes in the December and, found guilty – there was no handwriting expert called – Mrs Gooding was sentenced to fourteen days' imprisonment and ordered to provide sureties in the sum of £40. This time she did not have to put the money down and she was released on 23 December.

The next letter to Miss Swan, delivered just after Christmas, read, 'I hope you get all the luck you deserve in the New Year for getting me sent to prison.' Sensibly, the Captain sent his wife to stay with her mother in Lewes, but the letters, always postmarked Littlehampton and posted at the Beach sub-post office, which was near Western Road, still continued. The Captain's ploy of sending his wife out of the immediate area failed. Miss Swan went to the police again claiming she had seen Mrs Gooding at a baker's shop in Littlehampton and also had seen her throw a letter on her doorstep.

Appearing in front of the thoroughly unpleasant and prosecution-minded Mr Justice Avory – who, in the fallout of the Adolf Beck case, had adopted 'The fault is not mine' attitude of Lord Cardigan after the disastrous Charge of the Light

Brigade – Rose Gooding was summarily convicted and on 2 March 1921 was sentenced to twelve months' imprisonment. Her appeal was dismissed on 11 April.

Still the letters kept coming and in May the Captain petitioned the Home Office asking the Home Secretary to reconsider the case. On 2 June 1921 a Home Office official noted, 'I have very little doubt that this woman has twice been wrongly convicted.' The police were not convinced, and there was a suggestion that the cunning Mrs Gooding might have left a stockpile of letters presumably for the Captain and her sister to post at intervals and so throw dust in the eyes of the Court of Appeal.

No chances were to be taken by the Home Office, however. The police were instructed to find out whether it was possible she could have written them in prison and smuggled them out to her husband during visiting hours. The answer was an emphatic 'no'. 'It is quite impossible she could have passed out libellous documents.' Or presumably any other. Morality, however, counted. Superintendent Seeley in his report thought that Miss Swan had a very good character while Gooding and her sister had illegitimate children. He could not believe Miss Swan wrote the letters herself.

Nevertheless, the attorney general referred the case back to the Court of Appeal with instructions to the barrister Eustace Fulton to assist the court rather than to try to have the conviction upheld. The hearing, with Rose Gooding represented by Travers Humphreys, who thought that 'miscarriages of justice were as rare as a black tulip', was something of a cover-up. No evidence was heard and no reason was given why the Home Office was satisfied that Rose Gooding was innocent. The publication of any details was said to be 'contrary to the interests of justice'. Mrs Gooding was released and in the August was awarded £250 compensation. The Captain had meanwhile lost his job when the shipyard at which he worked had closed down. But it was by no means the end of the affair.

Her release produced another sheaf of letters and the police now began to take a belated interest in Miss Swan. A policewoman hid in a shed that gave her a view of the alleyway between 45 and 47 Western Road and she saw Miss Swan drop a letter, which turned out to be obscene, in the garden of another neighbour, this time Lily May, the wife of a local police constable.

On 9 October, Caroline Johnson was fined £1. She had gone to Rose Gooding's home and pulled her hair and hit her in the face after telling her, 'I will teach you to talk about me and my friend Miss Swan.' Part of the mitigation was that she, Caroline Johnson, had received one of the indecent letters.

Edith Swan appeared at Lewes Assizes on 9 December and this time Travers Humphreys prosecuted. The trial judge Mr Justice Bailhache, who had had a commercial practice at the Bar, was known to dislike going out on circuit to try petty criminal cases which he thought would have been far better dealt with at Quarter Sessions. Miss Swan made a good witness with a modest answer for all Travers Humphreys' questions. When it came out that he had twice successfully prosecuted another woman for the same offence and nothing was mentioned about the subsequent Court of Appeal hearing, Bailhache declared that if he were on the jury he would acquit. Humphreys threw in his hand and Miss Swan walked free.

For the rest of the year nothing happened, but the letters started to flow again in early 1923. There was still a belief that the letters had not come from Miss Swan and so stamps were now marked on the back in invisible ink by post office officials above the name of the correspondent to be watched. On 23 June Miss Swan bought two penny-ha'penny stamps at the Beach sub-post office and the next day she posted two letters there. The sub-postmaster collected the letters as they dropped on a tray. One letter to her sister was in her ordinary handwriting. The second, in a disguised hand, was a libellous one addressed to the local sanitary surveyor. On the reverse of the stamp was WEB, the initials of W. E. Bowler of the post office who had sold the stamp, above S for Swan. At the committal proceedings she suffered the same fate as Rose Gooding in being unable to find sureties immediately and was remanded in custody.

Again Humphreys prosecuted and again the judge was

Avory. She claimed that the stamps she had bought had been the one used to her sister and one sent on another letter, posted earlier to another sister. Yet again Avory seemed to favour Miss Swan and did what he could to have her acquitted. The jury, however, retired for only a few minutes before convicting her. Given the misery she had caused, on 19 July 1923 Avory sentenced her to a most lenient eighteen months. On 12 August an application by her in person for leave to appeal against her conviction was dismissed.

CHAPTER 5

Mistaken Identity

Oscar Slater

Joe Hill

Walter Rowland

Mahmood Mattan

Patrick Meehan

Rubin Carter and John Artis; David McCallum

Oscar Slater

There was no doubt that Oscar Slater was a thoroughly un-desirable man with a number of aliases. He was a pimp, gambler, cheat and a dealer in stolen jewellery, but the question remains: was he a murderer?

Shortly after 7 p.m. on 21 December 1908 the body of Marion Gilchrist, a wealthy eighty-two-year-old spinster, was found in her flat at 15 Queen's Terrace, West Princes Street, Glasgow. She was a woman who kept her front door securely locked and bolted and, if her maid Helen Lambie was not with her, she took great care in identifying a caller before drawing the bolts. It was common for her to send Lambie out during an evening on errands or what the Scots called 'messages', and this evening she was sent out to buy a newspaper. On her return Miss Gilchrist's downstairs neighbour Arthur Adams intercepted her and told her there was an almighty row going on overhead and he feared his ceiling would break. As Lambie opened the Gilchrist front door a man walked calmly past her and Adams, and then rushed downstairs. In the dining room they found Marion Gilchrist's body. She had been battered to death, struck sixty or more times, possibly with a chair leg. Outside in the street a young girl, fourteen-year-old Mary Barrowman, said she saw a man rush past her. Initially none of the three said they could recognize the man.

Slater, also known as Leschziner, Sando, George, Anderson and Schmidt, fell under suspicion for a number of reasons. First, he was an outsider, a German Jew. Secondly, he was a pimp who claimed to be a gymnastics instructor as well as a dentist, something that, said the police, provided a cover for men to visit his home and his working mistress. Thirdly, he was unpopular with the police and had a conviction for violence in London, even though he had only been fined £1. Fourthly, and most significantly, the police were told he had pawned a diamond brooch shortly after the murder. Pawning a piece of jewellery was often a way of disposing of stolen goods to a receiver. There was never any intention to redeem the piece and it provided a rudimentary defence for the pawnbroker if he should be charged with receiving, or reset as it was known in Scotland.

When it came to it the brooch did not belong to Miss Gilchrist; it belonged to Slater's prostitute mistress Andrée Junio Antoine and had been pawned by him weeks before the murder when he was putting money together for a passage to America. Nevertheless, although the descriptions of the man given by Lambie and Barrowman did not resemble Slater, the police remained focused on him as the murderer. It was unfortunate for him that he had intended to go to America shortly after the murder, seen by the police as an escape from justice. In fact he had been there previously managing gambling saloons and now a friend had suggested there were opportunities for him in the Midwest. Using the name Otto Sando, and along with Andrée, he sailed on Boxing Day on the *Lusitania*.

Following him to America went the police, along with Lambie and Barrowman who had now changed their descriptions of the man they saw after being shown photographs of Slater. Although they shared a cabin in what must have been the greatest adventure of their lives, according to their evidence they did not discuss the case.

Slater was arrested when he arrived in New York to await the Glasgow police who wanted him extradited. Whether the police had a case of tunnel vision and were unwilling to look at any exculpatory evidence or whether this was a cynical exercise to solve a case and at the same time put away a man they disliked is open to question.

On 26 January 1909, along with Detective Inspector John Pyper, Lambie and Barrowman were outside the courtroom when a handcuffed Slater was brought from the cells for the extradition hearing. What happened next is a matter of dispute. According to Pyper the girls simultaneously touched his arm and said, 'Oh, there is the man away into the court.' The downstairs neighbour Adams who had gone with them refused to say he was positive the man he had seen at the murder scene was Slater, but both girls now said they were sure Slater was the man. Asked what had been going on outside the court, Lambie cheekily told Slater's advocate, 'It's none of your business' and was not reprimanded. Slater's American lawyers were convinced that an order for his extradition would be made and it would look far better before a Scots jury if he returned voluntarily. Accordingly he waived the proceedings.

Slater stood trial in Edinburgh in early May, prosecuted by a vitriolic Alexander Ure, the Lord Advocate. The only real evidence against him was that of identification and he called an alibi that he was at home with his mistress and their housemaid. The art of the advocate is to dominate the court and proceedings and Ure did just that. Addressing the jury he told them, 'I say without hesitation that the man in the dock is capable of having committed this dastardly outrage.' Unfortunately the trial judge Lord Guthrie was not a strong judge and made no attempt to curb Ure. To compound this, in his summing-up Guthrie also told the jury that because of Slater's character the general presumption of innocence applied with less effect than it would to a man of good character. The jury returned a split verdict. Nine thought he was guilty, five not guilty and one that the case was not proven. Slater was sentenced to death. Immediately voices were raised doubting his guilt and the fairness of the trial.

His lawyer, Ewing Speirs, gathered 20,000 signatures petitioning for commutation of the death sentence. Forty-eight hours before he was due to hang, Slater was reprieved and sent to the harsh Peterhead Prison, near Aberdeen. Over the years public support grew. Flushed with his success over the George Edalji case, Conan Doyle began to take an interest in

Slater. He found new witnesses and in 1912 published a pamphlet *The Case of Oscar Slater* in which he called for a pardon. There could be no retrial because at the time Scotland, unlike England and Wales, still did not have a Court of Criminal Appeal.

Now Mary Barrowman said she had been bullied and coached by the police. Helen Lambie was alleged by the experienced Glasgow detective John Thompson Trench to have told him that she had gone to Miss Margaret Birrell, Marion Gilchrist's niece, to say she knew who her employer's attacker really was.

Conan Doyle's intervention was sufficient for there to be a review of the case. Held in 1914, it took place behind closed doors and at it Trench gave evidence to say he had gone to Birrell's house and obtained a statement from her that Helen Lambie had given her the name of the man. Miss Birrell denied the conversation but Trench had made a note of it. According to him Lambie had said, 'Oh Miss Birrell I think it was A.B. I am sure it was A.B.' Miss Birrell had replied, 'My God, Nellie, don't say that . . . unless you are very sure of it.' For his display of disloyalty to the force, Trench was promptly dismissed and later, along with solicitor David Cook, was charged with reset after they had negotiated with a burglar to return stolen property to an insurance company in exchange for part of the reward. After his acquittal Trench rejoined the army. Slater remained where he was but the name of the suspect A. B. was divulged. It was Miss Gilchrist's nephew, Dr Francis Charteris.

In 1923 Slater passed the fifteen-year mark when a life prisoner in Scotland could reasonably expect to be released. He was not and it was not until two years later that Slater managed to get a smuggled note out of Peterhead to Conan Doyle, which revived his interest. In 1927 he wrote the introduction to *The Truth About Oscar Slater* by the crusading journalist William Park. In reviewing the book the *Solicitors Journal* thought, 'What is stated above, however, would seem to be sufficient to show the reasonableness of the demand that a new and thorough investigation into the whole matter should even now be made.' On 5 November that year Mary Barrowman wrote in *The Daily News* that she had been told what to say in evidence by James Hart, at the time the Procurator Fiscal of Lanarkshire. Slater was finally paroled in November that year.

Now began a fight for an appeal to the newly established Scottish Court of Criminal Appeal which could clear his name. Initially the legislation had only provided for appeals for those convicted after 31 October 1926, but the Act was amended so that the Secretary of State could refer suitable cases, that is Slater, to the Court of Appeal. Helen Lambie was by then living in America and refused to return to England, but John Pinckley, a New York detective, came to say he had watched as Slater was pointed out to her before she identified him. She did however write in the *Empire News* on 23 October 1927 that she had been persuaded by the police that Slater had been the murderer. Now she wrote, 'I am convinced that the man I saw was better dressed and of a better station in life than Slater.' Doyle continued to press for an appeal and it finally began on 8 June 1928 when Slater's counsel, Craigie Aitchison, painstakingly point by point destroyed the prosecution case in front of the five appeal judges.

The result of the appeal was not, however, the triumph in clearing Slater's name that his supporters had confidently expected. When the Lord Justice General read out the twenty-five-minute judgment, point by point he dismissed Aitchison's claims. The evidence of the New York detective about the identification was irrelevant, as was the fact that Slater had travelled quite openly to Liverpool after the killing. But what the judges could not get over was the trial judge's misdirection on the presumption of innocence. They thought that the verdict, effectively one of nine to six, might have been different without it. The conviction was quashed.

Next came the question of compensation and very reluctantly an *ex gratia* payment of £6,000 was made to Slater. That still left the costs of the appeal. The Jewish community raised £700 and Conan Doyle, who had paid for the appeal, was left £300 out of pocket. Relations between Slater and his champion were severed.

In 1936 Slater married Lina Schad and, apart from a period

during World War Two when he was interned, he lived the remainder of his life in Ayr, dying in 1948. He never re-offended. Francis Charteris, the man Helen Lambie suggested she had seen leaving the Gilchrist flat, retired in 1948 as Professor of Materia Medica and Dean of the Faculty of Medicine at St Andrews University. Most commentators elim-inate both him and Slater as viable suspects and suggest it was a casual robbery.

The noted Glaswegian lawyer Joseph Beltrami thought the case was one of the greatest miscarriages of justice in Scottish legal history, and there were many who agreed with him.

Joe Hill

On the night of 10 January 1914 John Morrison and his seven-teen-year-old son Arling were shot and killed in his Salt Lake City grocery store by one of two men wearing red bandanas as masks. No money was stolen nor even demanded, and so at the time it was presumed that the motive was not robbery. Morrison's younger son, thirteen-year-old Merlin, who survived the shooting, later said one of the men had called out 'We've got you now,' before he shot the grocer. Merlin said his brother had shot back hitting one of the men in the chest. The man ultimately charged with the murder was Joseph Hillström, the Industrial Workers of the World (IWW) songwriter better known as Joe Hill.

There had been power shifts in Salt Lake City, the home of the Mormons since the 1840s, in the first years of the twentieth century. The American Party in Utah had been formed to counter Mormon rule and from 1908 it had joined an alliance of other parties to oust them from political control in an attempt to separate business from religion. Graft and corruption were rife and now the Mormons joined opponents of the American Party to regain control. In 1911 the American Party did badly in the elections and disbanded. Two years later Mormon William Spry was elected Governor with a mandate to 'sweep out lawless elements', which included corrupt businessmen and IWW agitators 'or whatever name they call themselves'.

There is little doubt that Hill was Swedish-born, but much of the rest of his early life is clouded. His father was a train conductor who died when Hill was young, and his mother died in 1902. After suffering from glandular tuberculosis he seems to have come to the United States in 1901 and worked as an itinerant labourer, at the same time writing songs that were often parodies of gospel hymns, such as *In the Sweet Bye and Bye*. These were published as *The Little Red Song Book* by the IWW, known as the Wobblies, the militant union he joined in 1910. This was the time when the IWW was making great strides, if at some cost to their members, in organizing strikes to obtain better working conditions. Hill was in San Diego during the 'free speech fight' in early 1912, when the IWW, the American Federation of Labor (AFL) and church groups battled a city ordinance for the immediate cessation of public free speech rights. He was in San Pedro during the stevedores' strike the same year and was part of a failed attempt to found a workers' commune in Baja California. By 1913 he was blacklisted throughout California and travelled to Utah. He was there when the IWW organized a successful strike at the Bingham Construction Company.

When he arrived in Salt Lake City he lodged with the Swedish Eselius family, who also had another lodger, Otto Appelquist. A regular visitor and niece was Hilda Erickson who broke off her engagement to Appelquist after Hill's arrival. Hill was always well dressed and seemingly always had money in his pockets; his prison sheet in Salt Lake City listed four old gunshot wounds, three on his face and neck and one on his right forearm. As a result there were suggestions, never proved, that he made his living robbing small businesses.

It was not the first time the grocer Morrison had been attacked and one line of thought was that it related to his earlier career as a policeman. He had been threatened on a number of occasions. The last time had been as recently as 20 September 1913 after which he told the *Evening Telegram* that he knew one of the gunmen and was convinced he had not wanted 'my money, he wanted my life'.

After he was killed, given Morrison's brief career as a police officer, several men he had arrested were at first considered suspects. In all twelve people, including a career criminal Frank Z. Wilson, who also went by a variety of names including James Morton, were arrested and questioned before Hill was arrested and charged with the murder. Wilson had been seen not far from the Morrison store lying on the sidewalk and evidently in some pain. A bloody handkerchief had been found in his pocket. Nevertheless he had been released.

The information that led to Hill's arrest came on the following Monday morning after it was announced that there would be a $500 reward for information leading to the conviction of the murderer. Spurred by the possibility of reward money, Salt Lake City doctor, Frank McHugh, telephoned his friend Marshal Fred Peters and spilled the beans. Sometime after 11 p.m. on the evening of the Morrison killing, Hill had appeared on his doorstep with a bullet wound through the left lung. After McHugh had patched him up, Hill was taken back to his lodgings around 1 a.m. by Arthur Bird, another doctor who had called in on his colleague. Both men had noticed that Hill had a revolver with him. Hill generally shared a bed with Otto Appelquist and it turned out within the hour that Appelquist had left the house saying he was going to find a job. He was never seen in the state again.

By arrangement with Marshal Peters, McHugh called on Hill on the Tuesday night and gave him half a grain of morphine so that, he said in evidence, Hill 'might be arrested without hurting himself or anybody else'. His kindly action went unrewarded. When the police burst in on Hill, Peters shot him in the hand. By this time Hill had got rid of the revolver the doctors had seen. Overall, McHugh went unrewarded in every sense. Although he persistently claimed the reward money it does not ever appear to have been paid over.

While Hill was lodged in jail, Merlin Morrison was taken to identify him. There was no question of a line-up being arranged; it was simply a face-to-face confrontation. He made a partial identification, saying, 'I believe this is the man my brother shot.' Later the next day he was quoted in the *Tribune* as saying 'Hill is about the same size and height as one of the men who entered my father's store . . .' and ending 'the man whom I think resembles Hill crouched behind the end of the counter and shot my brother'. The local newspaper the *Evening Telegram* thought that Merlin 'fastens the crime upon Hillström without a doubt'. The *Tribune* thought the 'jubilant' police 'now believe that the circumstantial evidence all points with a deadly certainty to the guilt of Hill'.

There was also some more supporting identification evidence. Just before the shooting of Morrison, a Frank and Phoebe Seeley walking near the grocery had effectively been barged off the pavement by two men, one of whom had a scar on the side of his neck and wore a bandana. After another face-to-face confrontation Phoebe Seeley too thought the man looked like Hill.

On 24 January 1914 the *Deseret Evening News* printed an article, 'Hillström's Crime Record in California sent here.' It was a wholly misleading headline. The only criminal allegation was that he had taken part in one hold-up but had never been charged. As Hill's biographer William A. Adler put it, by the time he came to trial Hill 'was being treated as a murderous, larcenous, bomb-throwing alien anarchist who in his spare time wrote inflammatory, revolutionary songs for the I-Won't Workers'.

The prosecution based its case on one of those syllogistic fallacies that crop up in criminal trials throughout the world. A good example of a syllogism is 'Men are mortals, I am a man; therefore I am mortal.' And an example of a syllogistic fallacy runs, 'Some televisions are black and white and all penguins are black and white. Therefore, some televisions are penguins.' In this case it was 'Arling Morrison shot someone on the night of 10 January 1914; Joe Hill was shot that night; therefore Arling Morrison shot Joe Hill.' In fact, all told four men were known to have been shot that night in Salt Lake City and doubtless there had been others.

All Hill would say in his defence was that he had been shot in a quarrel over a woman. He did not name either the woman or the shooter but it was clear he meant Hilda Erickson and Otto Appelquist. As for his gun, it was not of the same calibre as the one used to kill Morrison. For their part, the prosecution decided Appelquist was the second gunman and, in his absence, charged him with murder.

At the preliminary hearing to establish whether there was a case for him to answer, Hill represented himself and asked only a few questions, but while he was awaiting trial a Wyoming lawyer, Ernest D. MacDougall, volunteered to act without fee. In turn MacDougall recruited Frank Scott, a local socialist-minded attorney. In the spring Hill wrote to the IWW Local 69 for help in establishing a defence committee. Now donations were solicited through an article in *Solidarity* and the appeal produced around $200.

Shortly before the trial MacDougall and Scott wrote in another issue of *Solidarity*:

> The main thing the state has against Hill is that he is an IWW and therefore sure to be guilty. Hill tried to keep the IWW out of it . . . but the papers fastened it on him. For this reason he is entitled to be helped and not allowed to hang for being an IWW. It should not be necessary for him to prove his innocence and it would not be if he was not an IWW.

But he was, and it was necessary.

The trial in June 1914 started badly and continued that way with Judge Morris Ritchie blaming the defence for the length of time it took – five-and-a-half days – to empanel a jury. So annoyed was he that he called three jurors from a previous case and summarily appointed them to the trial. One of them was a prominent Mormon, Joseph Kimball, and he and Ritchie were both members of the board of the Utah Society of the Sons of the American Revolution, a patriotic fraternal organization that had no truck with the Wobblies. Once the trial started Kimball became the foreman.

When the trial itself opened on 17 June the prosecution's objections were regularly sustained. Those made by Scott and MacDougall, when Elmer O. Leatherwood, the prosecutor, was putting leading questions to his witnesses, were just as regularly overruled.

Now Leatherwood literally led Merlin Morrison through his evidence, ending with:

Q: Does this man's general appearance correspond with that of the man who shot your father?
A: Yes sir.

Defence lawyers, particularly in high-profile cases, often walk a tightrope and now MacDougall felt that a kid glove approach should be used in the cross-examination of the boy. If he attacked Merlin head on he would no doubt make the boy cry, which might antagonize the jury. Hill vehemently protested, arguing that MacDougall wasn't mounting a full-blown attack and would not listen to the argument that such tactics might alienate the judge and jury even further. After a fairly pusillanimous cross-examination of Merlin by MacDougall, which led nowhere, Hill considered his position overnight and the next morning the pot boiled over – unfortunately publicly and bitterly.

This time the witness was state chemist Herman Harms. Even when scientists had made a significant discovery, either lawyers and police had not heard of it or they chose not to make use of it. Blood had been scraped from the sidewalk on Jefferson Street, south of Morrison's store. In 1900, a series of experiments by the German bacteriologist Paul Uhlenhuth, a professor at the University of Greifswald in north-eastern Germany, led to a serum that reacted to the presence of human blood but not to that of animals. In Hill's case however, no one seems to have thought of testing it. All state chemist Harms could say was that it was mammalian blood. The prosecution had said nothing, and whether co-counsel Frank Scott was going to make anything of the matter will never be known.

As Scott rose to cross-examine, Hill stood up and asked Ritchie, 'May I say a few words, your Honour?' 'You have the right to be heard in your own behalf ordinarily,' replied Ritchie, who should have sent the jury out of court at that point. Hill did not mince matters. 'I have three prosecuting attorneys here,' he told the judge. 'I intend to get rid of two of them, Mr

Scott and Mr MacDougall. See that door? Get out, you're fired.'

But Ritchie would not allow the pair to leave, and after further wrangling during which Hill snatched the papers from MacDougall saying they had been paid for and he would keep them, the judge decided the lawyers should remain as friends of the court, *amici curia*. Hill took over the cross-examination but when it came to it he only asked one ineffectual question of Harms and sat down.

Bolstering the identification made by Merlin, the next witness was Phoebe Seeley who had been near the Morrison store shortly before the shooting. At the preliminary inquiry she had told the court she could not be sure that Hill and the man she had encountered were one and the same. Now, led first by Leatherwood and then the judge she agreed that the 'thinness of his [Hill's] face is just the same as the man you saw'. Scott had already pointed out that the witness had been led into using the word scar but Hill seemed incapable of believing the lawyer could help him and commented out loud, 'My counsel seems to be very insistent upon holding the job.'

Finally Ritchie agreed there should be a half-hour adjournment and Hill was allowed to see two fellow Wobblies and also spend some time with Hilda Erickson. By the time the court reconvened an uneasy compromise had been reached. The lawyers would indeed stay on as *amici curia* and one would cross-examine each witness. Hill could also ask questions. But an incredible amount of damage had been done.

After the adjournment Scott made some inroads into Phoebe Seeley's evidence and finally forced her to admit that at the previous hearing her answer had been 'no' when asked, 'Are you able to state positively whether the defendant is the man or one of the men you saw there that night?'

That evening the *Deseret Evening News* hammered home the dangers of the IWW, pointing out that not only were they '... agitating for higher wages, shorter hours, more safety appliances in dangerous occupations but they also hope that the workers will acquire the necessary economic power to take "possession of the machinery of production".'

Worse, among their ranks were 'Women and children who are employed by factories, the black men of the South and the aliens who cannot become citizens until they have lived in the Country for a number of years.'

Help for Hill came from a slightly unexpected source. Virginia Snow Stephen, fifty-year-old, socially prominent daughter of a former president of the Mormon church and an art teacher at the University of Utah, travelled to Denver to ask Judge Orrin Hilton to appear for Hill. It appears that Stephen was a committed opponent of the death penalty but, with perhaps rather less foundation, was also convinced that anyone who could write poetry like Hill could not be a murderer.

Some years earlier Hilton had successfully defended another union leader, Vincent St John, in a murder trial in Telluride, Colorado, arguing that the charges were bogus, outdated and had been prompted by the Mine Owners' Association and the Citizens' Alliance for purposes of revenge against the union organizer. Now, Hilton told her he was committed to a Western Federation of Miners case in Michigan but, if necessary, would be available for any appeal. In the meantime he told her to get his Salt Lake City associate, Soren X. Christensen, to sit in on the case as additional counsel. His fees would be paid by the IWW.

Meanwhile the prosecution were calling more witnesses and an effort by MacDougall to pin the murder on Frank Wilson was thwarted by Leatherwood and Ritchie. First, Detective Cleveland said that Wilson did not resemble Hill and when MacDougall asked, 'In what respect does his appearance differ from that of the defendant?', Leatherwood objected saying the question was 'immaterial and irrelevant'. And when MacDougall wanted to know why the police had released Wilson without charge, after an objection by Leatherwood, Judge Ritchie soon closed this line of questioning: 'The court is not called upon to investigate the conduct of the officers, what they did, why they arrested this man or arrested another, unless it can be shown there is something beyond that.'

MacDougall soldiered on, arguing that the state was relying on indirect and circumstantial evidence and that the evidence befits 'other defendants against whom suspicion points with equal force and clearness'.'The objection is sustained,' said Ritchie. And that was the end of that.

One witness called by the defence partly escaped the prosecution's radar. Dr M. F. Beer, the Salt Lake City surgeon who examined Hill shortly before the trial, gave evidence that Hill's exit wound scar was inconsistent with a lead bullet, which typically mushroomed, leaving a wound two or three times the size of the entry wound. The wound, he said, was consistent with a steel bullet, which was not the ammunition used in John Morrison's .38 Colt. Curiously Leatherwood did not challenge him on what might have been thought to be a crucial point. He did, however, successfully object when Scott tried to have Dr Beer agree that Hill could not have been shot with his arms 'in any other position than directly over his head, and himself in a perpendicular position'. It was, said Leatherwood, beyond the scope of expert testimony and Ritchie agreed.

The question now arose whether Hill should give evidence. There is general agreement among lawyers that in criminal trials the peak of the defence case is at the close of that of the prosecution and that generally the defence goes downhill from there on. But murder cases are different. The jury wants to hear from the defendant. On the plus side was that Hill had no worthwhile convictions that Leatherwood could lovingly put to him. The downside was that he was going to have to explain how he came to be shot and no one would believe him if he failed to call some supporting evidence in the form of Hilda Erickson. It seems Hill's lawyers were divided. Scott and MacDougall wanted him to give evidence but Christensen advised against it. Indeed, one account is that he feared that Scott might somehow double-cross Hill and introduce damning evidence against his client. Since Hill did not want to give evidence and the IWW was paying for Christensen he took that man's advice.

In the biased forum of Salt Lake City, even without a hostile judge who allowed the prosecutor incredible latitude and stifled the defence whenever he could, whether Hill could ever have been acquitted is doubtful. What is certain is that he did himself no favours and in his closing speech MacDougall did him none either.

MacDougall rightly told the jury:

> The defendant may sit back in his dignity and demand that the state produce proof of his guilt. He is not bound to open his mouth or speak one word and the fact that he does not is of no concern of yours and you cannot consider it as evidence against him.

But then he rather weakened his position:

> It is true that if you or I were wounded and accused as this man is, we would take the stand and tell how it happened, but Hillström won't. He won't tell me how it happened ... What his reason is I don't know, but it is none of my business and none of yours.

Strictly speaking this was correct but Leatherwood would have none of it. Pointing at Hill he thundered:

> If you were an innocent man you would have told how you received that wound. Why in God's name did you not tell so that your name could have been cleared from the stain upon it. Because you did not dare, Joe Hillström! Because you were a guilty man and you could not tell a story that could not be corroborated. That is why.

In his closing speech over two days, not designed to make friends and influence people in his client's favour, MacDougall savaged Mrs Seeley, claiming that she was not merely mistaken but was a liar. Perhaps at the end of his tether in a trial in which every judicial decision had gone against him, he then foolishly attacked the Utah judicial system and, worse, those who took part in it, including the jury: 'I have seen where the court, judge, prosecutor and jury were but machines of the government to convict defendants – machines to make records for the prosecuting attorney and to do his bidding.'

Leatherwood was righteously incensed:

> When a man charges that courts are tools, that juries are corrupt and public officers are false to their trusts and intimates, that Utah is a state where a man cannot procure a fair trial, when he strikes at the very root of our American institutions of justice and freedom I resent it, I care not whether such criticism comes from pulpit or soapbox. I resent it.

Christiansen also addressed the jury, pointing out that the prosecution had failed to provide a motive and 'Men do not kill without a motive.' The prosecution had not alleged robbery and there was nothing to show that Hill had any reason to kill Morrison.

The whole case against Hill was circumstantial and Utah state law provided that the chain of proof 'must be complete and unbroken' and established beyond a reasonable doubt. If it was not, the judge was required to direct an acquittal. Ritchie's summing-up was a flagrant disregard of the requirement. He told the jury that the evidence was the equivalent of a cable of independent strands. If one broke it weakened the prosecution's case but did not fatally break it.

The jury retired at 7 p.m. on Friday, 26 June and two hours later had reached a verdict. At eleven at night, when the judge ordered them to be sequestered for the night, a first ballot confirmed it. No one changed his mind overnight and at 10 a.m. on the Saturday they returned a verdict of guilty with no recommendation of mercy. On Wednesday, 8 July 1914, as required by Utah law, Ritchie offered Hill the choice of death by hanging or by firing squad. He chose the latter saying, 'I'll take shooting. I'm used to that. I have been shot a few times in the past and I guess I can take it again.' Ritchie fixed the date for 4 September.

Now began the series of appeals orchestrated by Denver lawyer Orrin Hilton. The first was on 1 September when Ritchie denied a motion for a new trial. Christensen promptly filed notice of appeal to the Utah Supreme Court. Once the notice was filed the defence did not have to file the appellant brief for six months, something that annoyed Leatherwood intensely; he argued that it could easily be done in forty days. In a letter to the court, Hill continued to deny that the state had a right to inquire into the origins of his wound. Hilton himself represented Hill during the appeal, and he told the court: 'The main thing the state had on Hill was that he was an IWW and therefore sure to be guilty. Hill tried to keep the IWW out of [the trial] . . . but the press fastened it upon him.'

In an article for the socialist newspaper *Appeal to Reason*, Hill wrote, 'Owing to the prominence of Mr Morrison, there had to be a 'goat' [scapegoat] and the undersigned being, as they thought, a friendless tramp, a Swede, and worst of all, an IWW, had no right to live anyway, and was therefore duly selected to be "the goat".'

The case turned into a *cause célèbre* worldwide. In January 1915 the British chapter of the IWW called for his release, followed by a similar demand from the Australian branch who were at that time fighting a separate battle to defeat conscription. At a mass meeting 30,000 workers passed a resolution calling on Governor William Spry to free Hill. President Woodrow Wilson, Helen Keller (the blind and deaf author and fellow IWW member), the Swedish ambassador and the Swedish public all became involved in a bid for clemency. One woman who played a major part in the campaign was Elizabeth Gurley Flynn who, with her political and society connections, took up the case with Woodrow Wilson who, in turn, wrote to Spry and obtained a thirty-day stay of execution. The IWW was jubilant, not necessarily on Hill's behalf but believing it showed the power of the union. 'We have done it' was the key phrase.

On 28 May 1915 Hilton continued the argument that the evidential chain had been broken and that Hill should have been allowed to sack MacDougall and Scott. When he left the appeal court he was optimistic that the conviction would be quashed, but he was wrong. On 3 July, in a fudged verdict Chief Justice Daniel Straup wrote that, while acknowledging that Hill had a right to remain silent, his unexplained wound was 'a distinguishing mark', and that 'the defendant may not avoid the natural and reasonable inferences of remaining silent'.

This left an appeal to the Supreme Court of the United States or an application to the Utah Board of Pardons for a commutation. Hilton advised that the former was unlikely to succeed and Hill did not want to ruin the IWW with what would be prohibitive costs. He returned before Ritchie to be resentenced and again opted for a firing squad. Ritchie now fixed the date for 1 October.

Hill, who had spent his time churning out letters, articles and songs, did not like the word pardon, but his supporters urged him to go through with an application. On 18 September 1915 he appeared with Hilton before the Board of Pardons, which comprised Governor Spry, the state attorney general and three justices of the Utah Supreme Court including Straup.

The first four hours were taken up by arguments from Hilton, but at 6 p.m. Spry asked him, 'Say, Hilton, can't you make that fellow talk over there?'

Hilton: 'Well what do you want him to say?' Spry: 'Well, I want him to give an explanation of where he received the wound.'

Hilton: 'See? Still trying to make him prove himself innocent. He doesn't have to; that isn't the law. The people should prove him guilty, and I stand by that principle of law. I don't care, Joe can talk if he wants to but I am not going to ask him to, because he is right and you are wrong, and you know . . . there is not a textbook that was ever written but what contains that elemental doctrine.'

Now Hill shifted his ground slightly. If he was given a new trial he would tell all. Whether this was a bluff who can tell now? Probably he knew the Pardons Board could not in law grant him a new trial and as a result was safe in his demands for it. In a way he resembled the defendant who said he was going to ask the judge to allow him to have a lie detector test adding, 'Please God he won't let me.'

It seems the attorney general almost begged Hill to produce evidence, telling him, 'If there is any reason on Earth why you should not pay the penalty for the crime, this is the time to show it to us. I am in deadly earnest old man, and I want to do everything on Earth to save you if you are innocent. Won't you think it over and produce any proof you have here before us?' Hill was intransigent. 'I have thought it over. I know what I'm doing,' he replied.

Woodrow Wilson was persuaded to send another telegram and this time the Governor replied with some asperity, 'Forty-six days after the granting of the respite and at the eleventh hour, you, as the President, without stating any reasons therefore, again wire . . .'

On the evening of 18 November Hill sent a final telegram to Big Bill Hayward, the IWW leader in Chicago: 'Good-by [*sic*] Bill I will die like a true-blue rebel. Don't waste time in mourning – organize.' He also wrote: 'It is a hundred miles from here to Wyoming. Could you arrange to have my body hauled to the state line to be buried? Don't want to be found dead in Utah.'

At around 7.35 on the morning of 19 November 1915, Hill was taken before the firing squad. According to newspaper reports he did not go quietly, barricading himself in his cell and fighting off the guards with a broom, but he had calmed down by the time he was led to the execution point in the prison yard where, after, declining a shot of morphine and a tot of whisky, he made a short speech. 'Gentlemen I have a clear conscience. I have never done anything wrong in my life. I will die fighting and not like a coward.'

He had been granted permission not to wear a blindfold and is said to have called out to the squad, who had been given the command, 'Ready . . . aim . . .', 'Yes, aim. Let it go. Fire.' The day after the execution one of the members of the firing squad, the prose no doubt aided by a reporter, described it to the *New York Tribune*:

It seemed like shooting an animal. How my thoughts wandered! It seemed an age waiting for the command to fire. And then, when it came from Hillström himself, I almost fell to my knees. We fired. I wanted to close my eyes, but they stared at the white paper heart, scorched and torn by four lead balls. Four blackened circles began to turn crimson, then a spurt and the paper heart was red.

Hill left a handwritten will in the form of a poem:

> My Will is easy to decide,
> For there is nothing to divide.
> My kin don't need to fuss and moan –
> 'Moss does not cling to a rolling stone'.
> My body? Oh! If I could choose,
> I would to ashes it reduce,
> And let the merry breezes blow
> My dust to where some flowers grow.
> Perhaps some fading flowers then
> Would come to life and bloom again.
> This is my Last and Final Will
> Good Luck to All of You.
>
> Joe Hill

He gave his silk scarf to his friend Ed Rowan and a photograph of Gurley Flynn's son with his horse to Hilda Erickson. She had waited at the prison gate after being denied permission to witness the execution. To Gurley Flynn he dedicated a last song, 'The Rebel Girl'. She was later expelled from the union for favouring an individual over the cause.

His body was taken to a funeral parlour where it remained until it was carried in procession to the Oregon Short Line depot where it was put on the 5.25 train to Chicago.

On the following Thursday, a service was held at West Side Auditorium where around 5,000 heard Orrin Hilton deliver a two-hour speech in which he claimed his client had been brutally murdered. Hill's ashes were divided into 600 parts and the 150 IWW delegates were each given an envelope at a meeting on 19 November 1916 in Chicago; 450 other envelopes were sent worldwide to IWW locals. None was sent to Utah.

In the immediate aftermath Hilton was disbarred in Utah following the oration he gave at Hill's funeral. He went on to defend a number of other leaders of the Wobblies. In the back-lash Governor Spry was not renominated for the post the next year. Virginia Stephen, who had first approached Hilton, was dismissed by the university.

The death of Joe Hill marked both the high point of the IWW and the beginning of the end of the Wobblies. A series of arrests across America in a wave of anti-radicalism followed. Membership slumped and it never recovered from the so-called Palmer raids in which 10,000 supporters were arrested in January 1920 in various cities across the country. Given bail, Big Bill Hayward and other leaders fled to Russia.

By the late 1970s there were murmurs of appeals for a pardon and Merlin Morrison spoke out against any such suggestion. He was convinced he had correctly identified Hill. 'It was murder and nothing else,' he told the *Deseret News* in January 1977. However, in 1979 the Illinois Labor History Society began a campaign to exonerate Hill and it was joined by the American Federation of Labor and the Congress of Industrial Organization.

In a biography, published in 2011, William M. Adler concludes that Hill was probably innocent of the murders, but also suggests that he came to see himself as worth more to the labor movement as a dead martyr than he was alive. This real-ization may have influenced his decisions not to testify at the trial and subsequently to spurn all chances of a pardon. Adler claims that evidence pointed to the early police suspect Frank Z. Wilson being the killer, and cites a letter from Hilda Erickson which states that Hill had told her he had been shot by her former fiancé Otto Appelquist. Other earlier writers are divided, with James O. Morris suggesting in his monograph, *The Joe Hill Case,* that:

> The resigned defiant obstinacy of Hill protected no one but himself. There was nothing magnificent, no aspiration to martyrdom, no noble spirit whatsoever behind his desire for a new trial. He did not prove his innocence because he could not. Guilt dictated silence, not honour nor a fanatical belief in the principle of fair trial.

Was Hill actually innocent and if so why did he not tell the court of his relationship with Helen and the shooting by Appelquist? It seems to have been a mixture of stubbornness, the belief that the 'truth will out', a desire to protect the reputation of Hilda Erickson and, as the trial proceeded, a realization that whatever the evidence he was going to be convicted. As a result martyrdom loomed and here was a chance to give the IWW international coverage.

Warren Starr Van Valkenburgh, editor of the anarchist newspaper *Road to Freedom*, thought of him:

> He was a genius in the rough. A poet who wrote prose and verse that stunned his fellows like the gale an aspen leaf. Homeless, moneyless, friendless – in the larger sense – the undaunted champion of an unpopular cause, framed up, convicted on flimsy circumstantial evidence: foredoomed to destruction and true to himself to the very last.

Walter Rowland

On Sunday, 20 October 1946 the body of forty-year-old prostitute Olive Balchin was found battered to death on a bomb site in Deansgate, near the centre of Manchester. She had been badly beaten with a hammer, which was lying nearby. A piece of brown paper in which it had been wrapped was also on the site. In recent years she had been reduced to having sex on bomb sites for a few shillings a time and some tea and cakes.

The name of thirty-six-year-old Walter Rowland came into the frame both because he was known to have been seeing her and because he was known to have a violent temper. In the past three months since his demobilization he had been in the courts twice and was currently on probation imposed at Manchester Quarter Sessions for a breaking and entering offence. He was arrested after being interviewed about a coat he was said to have borrowed and kept.

When he was questioned he made a series of ambiguous but potentially damaging admissions. First that he knew the dead woman as 'Lil' and secondly that he had seen her on the eighteenth when he had bought her tea and cakes in Lillywhite's café in Piccadilly. They had had sex for which he had paid ten shillings. He had made a tentative arrangement to see her on the Saturday. Thirdly, on the day of the murder he discovered he had syphilis and believed he had contracted it from her. 'If I had been sure it was her, I would have strangled her. If she gave it to me, she deserved all she got.' In fact he had contracted the disease while serving in the army in Italy. He told the police he had been at a lodging house, 36 Hyde Park, on the Saturday night, but this was incorrect and he then clammed up, refusing to say where he had been.

Later he explained that the Hyde Park address was a mistake. In fact he had stayed there on the Sunday. With hindsight he should have had his solicitor correct it as soon as possible. Worse, when he did give details of where he had spent the night the register showed that he had signed out on the nineteenth rather than signing in. Nevertheless Frank Beaumont, the landlord at 81 Brunswick Street, Chorlton-on-Medlock, Manchester, said the register was wrong and was adamant that Rowland had spent the Saturday night there. There was no suggestion that he knew Rowland or that he had been bribed to give him the alibi.

The evidence against him was motive, the mistaken belief he had been infected by Balchin, and opportunity – his alibi was less than solid. There was a little forensic evidence – a spot of blood on his shoes and identification by a series of witnesses, then regarded as being far more certain than it is today. Rowland was put on an identification parade at Bootle police station on 27 October and was picked out by Edward MacDonald who ran a second-hand shop and who said he had sold Rowland the hammer on the Saturday afternoon. MacDonald had bought the leather-dresser's hammer on the morning of 19 October, put it in the shop window and sold it that afternoon. He had told the purchaser, who paid him 3/6d, that it was not a general purpose hammer but the man had said it did not matter, he was not going to do a job that night. MacDonald wrapped the hammer in brown crepe paper, which he identified as that found at the crime scene. At the preliminary hearing at the magistrates' court MacDonald at first failed to identify Rowland who was sitting with his solicitor as opposed to being in the dock. It was only when Rowland was asked to stand that he made the identification. MacDonald covered himself by saying he had failed to pick Rowland out because his head was down.

The prosecution's case was also that Balchin had been seen three times during the evening. The first was around 9.15

when she asked a Rita Leach for directions to Deansgate. Rita Leach walked part of the way with her and identified her through her hat and coat, which had distinctive buttons.

Elizabeth Copley, a waitress in the Queen's Café in Deansgate, said that around 10.30 p.m. a young woman, an elderly – sixty-to-seventy years old – woman and a man carrying a brown paper parcel had been in the café. She described the man as having black hair and wearing a black suit. The women had something to eat; the man just drank tea. At an identification parade on 27 October she said of Rowland, 'That looks like the man, but I'm not sure.' One problem with her evidence is that she continually referred to the woman she identified as Balchin as 'a young girl' or 'young woman'. Balchin was a worn forty-year-old with yellow hair turning grey, no teeth in her upper jaw and only a few septic ones in the lower.

Around midnight Norman Mercer, the licensee of a public house, said he was out walking his dog when he saw a couple arguing at the corner of Deansgate and Cumberland Street. At the mortuary he identified the woman through her coat buttons and, at an identification parade held in Strangeways Prison on 4 November, he picked out Rowland.

In effect there was no forensic evidence although the pathologist called by the prosecution said that there would have been a great deal of blood splattered over Balchin's attacker. It was agreed that Rowland had only one suit, given him on his demobilization from the army. There was a bloodstain on one of his shoes and dust and rubble in his trouser turn-ups as well as some grey hairs on his coat. Rowland's fingerprints were neither on the hammer nor the wrapping paper.

Rowland's final account of his movements was that around the Saturday lunchtime he had been out drinking in Liston's bar. He had later gone to collect his washing that his mother had sent to the post office. It was not there and so he decided to go to New Mills in Derbyshire to collect it. He arrived about 7.45 p.m. and picked up two shirts and a pair of overalls and then caught the bus back to Manchester. It terminated in Stockport and he went into the Wellington pub in Mersey

Square for a drink. The pub was divided into upper and lower levels and he went into the lower half, known as the Bottom Wellington. He then took another bus to Manchester, had some fish and chips and another drink and went back to his lodgings and bed.

The prosecution produced evidence to show that even if he had been in the Bottom Wellington he could still have caught the bus from Stockport and arrived in Manchester to be in the café with Balchin by 10.30 p.m. However, one piece of Rowland's story in his favour was that he said that while he had been in Bottom Wellington, two police officers walked through the pub at 10.30 closing time. And a Sergeant Jones confirmed that he had done so.

When the jury returned a verdict of guilty on 16 December, Rowland called out, 'May God forgive you, you have condemned an innocent man.' He was allowed to make a speech to the judge before the death sentence was passed. It was known as the *allocatur* and, since too many defendants were taking up too much time in haranguing the court and attacking the police evidence, its use was discontinued in the 1970s. In what has come to be regarded as one of the great extempore speeches by a defendant, Rowland told the judge:

> I have never been a religious man, but as I have sat in this Court during the last few hours the teachings of my boyhood have come back to me, and I say in all sincerity and before you and this court that when I stand in the Court of Courts before the Judge of Judges I shall be acquitted of this crime. Somewhere there is a person who knows that I stand here today an innocent man. The killing of this woman was a terrible crime, but there is a worse crime been [committed] now, my Lord, because someone with the knowledge of this crime is seeing me sentenced today for a crime which I did not commit. I have a firm belief that one day it will be proved in God's own time that I am totally innocent of this charge, and the day will come when this case will be quoted in the courts of this country to show what can happen to a man in a case of mistaken identity. I am going to face what lies

before me with the fortitude and calm that only a clear conscience can give. That is all I have got to say, my Lord.

After his conviction the jury had been told that in 1934 Rowland had been found guilty of the murder of his two-year-old daughter. He had been reprieved and sentenced to life imprisonment. Long-term prisoners were allowed out of jail if they agreed to join the army and so Rowland was paroled in 1945 to fight in Europe.

After Rowland was convicted and awaiting the hearing of his appeal, on 22 January 1947 David John Ware, a petty criminal who had a conviction for blackmail and was then serving a sentence in Liverpool Prison for stealing from the Salvation Army, asked to see the prison governor. He told him he was the killer of Olive Balchin and two days later made a detailed statement to an Inspector Stainton and in due course made a third confession statement to Rowland's solicitor in which he referred to the murder and his meeting with Olive Balchin, whom he called Balshaw.

At 6 p.m I met Olive Balshaw outside the Hippodrome. I spoke to her and suggested going to the pictures my idea was to kill time till it got dark.

'I went to a small Picture House near the Belle Vue stadium with her. We came out at 9 p.m. had a cup of coffee opposite the cinema and caught a bus to the centre of the City.

'I did not know whether to leave her or not but after finding a dark place not far from Piccadilly I decided to spend a while with her. The spot where we stopped was a place or building I took to be bombed in the war. We went inside the ruins & stood for a short while near the entrance. We were quite close to each other & being so near she took the opportunity of going through my pockets. I was aware of this but did not show her. I was ate up with hatred & felt I'd like to kill her. I realized I had the hammer [which he had bought earlier in the day] so suggested that I'd like to make water and went further in the building. In there I took the brown paper off the hammer and threw it in the corner.

I went back to her & suggested moving further inside where we could not be seen. She agreed to this & we moved further inside. She was on my left & with my right hand I got the Hammer out of my pocket. While she was still in front of me & had only a few paces to go before reaching the wall I struck her a violent blow on the head (I should say the right side). She screamed & before her scream lasted any length of time I struck her again this time she only mumbled. Her hands were on her head protecting it the second time she fell to the floor up against the wall & I repeated the blows. Blood shot up in a thin spray. I felt it on my face & then I panicked threw the hammer & left everything as it was. I made no attempt to get my money.

So the confession became a principal ground of appeal, but the Court of Criminal Appeal would have nothing to do with it. Dismissing the appeal on 10 February, 'It is not an unusual thing for all sorts of confessions to be made by people who have nothing to do with a crime,' said Lord Goddard, the Lord Chief Justice, in one of his early murder appeals since his appointment in the January. At the time the court had no power to order a retrial. Questions would have to be asked about Ware's mental state and if anyone was in a position to do so it would be the Home Secretary, said Goddard.

There was an outburst from Rowland when his appeal was dismissed:

I am an innocent man. This is the greatest injustice which has ever happened in an English court. Why did you have that man who confessed here and not hear him? I am not allowed to have justice because of my past.

Lord Chief Justice Goddard: 'Take him down.' But Rowland clung to the dock adding, 'It would have knocked the bottom out of English law to have acquitted me and proved my innocence. I say now I am an innocent man before God.'

The past to which Rowland referred had indeed been an unhappy one. In February 1927 he had been bound over for

theft and in the June was sentenced to three years' borstal training for causing grievous bodily harm to a Mary Ann Schofield.
He married in 1930 and his wife died in childbirth. The next
year he received two months' imprisonment for taking a motor
car. On his release he married Mary Ann Schofield and their
daughter was born in February 1932. In the October he received
twelve months for robbery and attempted suicide. He had drunk
Lysol. Then in May 1934 he was convicted of the murder of his
daughter Mavis, whom he had strangled. His defence had been
that his wife had killed the child. Nevertheless, 1,000 people
signed a petition for a reprieve and the sentence was commuted
to one of life imprisonment.

On 21 February 1947 the then incumbent Home Secretary
Maxwell Fyfe appointed John Catterall Jolly KC to conduct
an inquiry into Ware's confession and the evidence against
Rowland.

Writing specifically about the alleged miscarriages of justice
in the Derek Bentley and Timothy Evans cases, barrister John
Parris thought, 'The establishment is prone to appoint some
Queen's Counsel who is greedy for judicial appointment and
who will come up with a total whitewashing report.'

Many would say it was the same with Walter Rowland.
Certainly speed was the essence of the exercise. Jolly was assisted
by the Scotland Yard detectives Superintendent Alfred Barratt
and the dubious Herbert Hannam. Although Jolly did not have
much time with which to work there is no doubt he could have
asked the Home Secretary to respite the hanging. Years earlier it
had been done in the case of William Habron and more recently
in 1943, when the Canadian soldier Charles Guthier remained
in the death cell for eight weeks before being executed for
machine-gunning his girlfriend to death in Portslade, Sussex.
However Jolly preferred not to keep Rowland in the death cell
for any longer than need be.

Just as Rowland had done, Ware made a mistake in his dates.
He said he had travelled to Manchester on 19 October arriving
about 7.30 in the evening. He then went on to give details of
his movements the following day. They could not have been
accurate because 20 October was a Sunday and with Sunday

closing in force he could not have had his lunch in Woolworths as he said. He obviously meant he travelled on 18 October. Initially Ware stuck to his story but then, unfortunately for Rowland, he retracted his confession, in words that have all the hallmarks of a carefully taken police statement:

> I wish to say that the statements I have given confessing to a murder are absolutely untrue. I have never seen the woman Balchin in my life. I did not murder her and had nothing to do whatsoever with the murder. I made these statements out of swank more than anything.
>
> 'I had a feeling I wouldn't get very far with them. My health has not been too good since the outbreak of war and I really do feel I want some treatment. I also thought I was putting myself in the position of a hero. I wanted to see myself in the headlines. In the past I wanted to be hung. It was worthwhile being hung to be a hero seeing that life is not really worth living.

Ware told Hannam he had been to a cinema where he had seen a war film and had paid 2/9d (14p) for his seat. Other than that he could remember no details. He was equally vague about the rest of the day, saying he had been in the Oxford public house in Oxford Street and had later gone to Stockport to get a bed as he knew he would not get one in Manchester. How this was the case must be open to doubt. He had found one the evening before.

Worse, when Ware was put on an identification parade, MacDonald and other witnesses were adamant that he was not the man they had seen. Jolly even arranged a face-to-face confrontation but no one said they recognized Ware. Jolly delivered his report on 25 February.

There was no question of another reprieve. Rowland had already been reprieved once and that was quite sufficient By a coincidence he was placed in the same condemned cell as he had been after the murder of his daughter, until he was hanged on 27 February 1947.

In November 1951 Ware appeared at Bristol Assizes charged

with the attempted murder of Mrs Adelaine Fudge. In almost identical circumstances to the Rowland case he had bought a hammer in the afternoon and had later got into conversation with her. She agreed to go for a walk with him and when they sat on the grass together he produced the hammer and began to beat her with it. She managed to escape and he turned himself in at the police station saying, 'I have killed a woman. I don't know what is the matter with me. I keep having an urge to hit women on the head.' Found guilty at Bristol Assizes on 16 November 1951, he was sent to Broadmoor where he hanged himself three years later on 1 April.

Now questions were asked about the Rowland case in the House of Commons, and in December 1951 the Home Secretary Sir David Maxwell Fyfe defended the now dead Jolly against any criticism, saying what a careful and conscientious man he had been and that he had made 'an exhaustive inquiry'. There were 'no reasons to throw doubt on his conclusion'. There were also questions as to whether the police had withheld information favourable to the defence. Fyfe said he would make enquiries but, if he did, nothing seems to have come of them.

Mahmood Mattan

Sometime between 8.05 and 8.15 on the evening of 6 March 1952, forty-one-year-old Lily Volpert was killed in her shop in Bute Street in the notorious Tiger Bay area of Cardiff. Her throat had been cut, leaving a nine-inch wound. It was thought about £100 had been stolen. She had been burgled twice in recent months and was known to be letting only people she recognized into the shop. There was one unexplained find. In a drawer were a number of partially burned £1 notes wrapped in a newspaper dated 15 January that year.

Shortly after seven o'clock the next morning a road sweeper told a shop assistant he had found bloodstained clothes including a light blue shirt, a waistcoat of lighter material and a belt in the road. He asked the assistant what he should do and was told, 'Tell a policeman.' He misheard this as, 'I'll tell a policeman' and did nothing. By the time the police heard of the discovery, the shirt and waistcoat had disappeared.

On 7 March a witness, a Jamaican carpenter Harold Cover, said in his statement to the police:

... during the evening I was at the John Cory's Hall, Bute Street ... I am practically certain that it was 7.55 p.m. when I left the Hall. I walked slowly along Bute Street towards the Police Station. I was on the shops' side of Bute Street ... I saw two Somalis. One was standing against the glass window close to the doorway of Volpert's shop. The other was coming out of the shop doorway ... He passed right in front of me, causing me to move aside to let him pass. He turned to his right and went in the direction from which I had come. The other Somali remained by the window . . .

The Somali I saw leaving the shop I know well by sight. I have seen him in the Colonial Annex Dance.

I have seen him near a Somali Lodging House in Bute Street. I have also seen him walking in various parts of the Docks. The man I saw coming out of the shop I would describe him as 5' 10' in height, slight build, thin face. I am not sure if he has scars on his face. I think he has a gold tooth in his mouth. I'm not certain. He was not wearing a hat. He was not wearing any coat. Overcoat I mean . . . He was between 30 and 40 years.

The man standing by the glass window I would describe as between 25 and 30 years. Height, 6 feet, or a little more. Very young features, pleasant. He was wearing a gabardine mac, light colour [and] trilby hat . . . I've also seen this man around the dock's district once or twice.

I would certainly know the man coming out of the shop if I saw him again. I think I would know the man standing by the window.

On 10 March a Somali, Tahir Gass, who lived at 196 Bute Street, was interviewed by the police. He said he was in Miss Volpert's shop at 4.30 on the afternoon of the murder. He had passed the shop three times during the evening of 6 March. First, at a little after 7.30 p.m., when he was going to the Arab House in Sophia Street. Secondly, between 8.10 and 8.15 returning to 196, when he said everything was quiet outside the shop. Thirdly, later, when there was a crowd of people and police outside the shop.

The man who was allegedly seen leaving the shop around the time of the murder was the former seaman Mahmood Hussein Mattan, born in British Somaliland in 1923. When on one journey he landed in Wales, he left the ship and found work at a foundry in Butetown, Cardiff. He also met and married seventeen-year-old Laura Williams, a worker at a paper mill, and they had four children. As a mixed race couple

they suffered racist abuse from the community, so along with
their two sons they had moved to Hull for a year. By 1952
Mattan had been separated from his wife for the previous nine
months. Although she cited excessive sexual demands, the
split seems to have been reasonably amicable and he lived
across the road from her and her mother.

In early 1952 Mattan resigned his job at the steelworks.
From then on he seems to have lived through casual work
and betting in card games and on the local greyhound
tracks in Cardiff and Newport. In the January he had
received three years' probation at Cardiff Quarter Sessions
for stealing six shillings from a mosque. Prior to that he had
been acquitted of demanding money with menaces at the
Old Bailey in May 1951 and he was again found not guilty
of theft at Cardiff Magistrates' Court in the December. On
15 March he was arrested, charged with stealing a raincoat
and remanded in custody. Mahmood Mattan did not have a
gold tooth and generally wore not a trilby but a homburg
hat, known as an Anthony Eden after the politician. The
evidence against him on the murder charge was the identification by Cover, the evidence of a Mrs Gray who said she
had seen Mattan with £80–£100 in notes shortly after the
murder and what seemed to be minute spots of blood on
his shoes.

When the charge of murdering Lily Volpert was added on
17 March, he was asked by the magistrates if he wanted a
solicitor to defend him. He replied, 'Defend me for what?'
'Defend you on the two charges.' His response was, 'I don't
want anything and I don't care anything. You can't get me to
worrying.' Sensibly the magistrates gave him legal aid, and a
local solicitor Norman Morgan, handling only his second
murder case, was appointed. Later Morgan told an inquiry he
thought Mattan 'was a fool to himself' in claiming that all
prosecution witnesses were lying over unimportant matters.

Some officials had doubts about the case. On 27 March
before the committal proceedings were due to take place, a
member of the staff of the Director of Public Prosecutions
noted on the file after receiving the police reports, 'An

interesting case which cannot be called overwhelming. The Director should see these papers when he returns next week.'

Disclosure of material that might be helpful to the defence was different in those days. If the defending lawyer asked for it he might or might not get it. If he did not ask he certainly did not, and the prosecution did not disclose that Harold Cover, who was the principal witness against Mattan, had previous convictions. In 1947 he had attacked one of his daughters and was fined £25 for causing her grievous bodily harm. In 1951 he had slashed a man with broken glass from a milk bottle. He said it was in self-defence. Nor was an early interview with him disclosed to the defence.

Critics of the trial say that Mattan was denied an interpreter but, although he could not read or write English, he spoke it and understood it reasonably well. In fact he had acted as an interpreter in the local magistrates' court the previous year. Quite what the jury made of defence counsel T. E. Rhys-Roberts' closing speech in which he described Mattan as 'this half-child of nature, a semi-civilised savage' goes unrecorded.

Edmond Davies, prosecuting, made a speech of less than five minutes to the jury, telling them, 'If you believe Cover then you must find Mattan guilty.' The judge summed up in similar terms but warned the jury, 'however grave that suspicion that is not sufficient'. The jury retired for just over ninety minutes before returning a guilty verdict, which in those days had to be unanimous. Mattan was sentenced to death. The Court of Criminal Appeal gave him short shrift. 'A more model summing-up we have never read,' said Mr Justice Oliver.

The Home Secretary refused a reprieve and Mattan was hanged at Cardiff Prison on 3 September. Later his widow said she only discovered this when she went to visit him and saw the notice of his death on the prison gate.

The jury was never told that Cover would be able to share in the reward money or that four witnesses had failed to pick out Mattan in an identity parade. More shamefully, one of the investigating officers, Detective Inspector Ludon Roberts, who died in 1981, was aware that Cover's original description did not match that of Mattan, but that evidence was not put before the jury. In his statement the other Somali, Gass, later thought to be the most likely killer, had admitted visiting the shop earlier on the day of the murder but, again, the jury had not been told.

In 1969 David Wickham raised the case in the *People*: 'Was the wrong man hanged?' It followed the sentencing of Cover to life imprisonment for the attempted murder of another daughter with a razor.

On 1 June 1969 Laura Mattan's MP wrote to Home Secretary James Callaghan asking him to reopen the case. Later that month there was a very defensive letter from the Chief Constable. Cover's convictions were glossed over. Neither had involved a robbery and he had handed himself over to the police on both occasions. The Chief Constable very much wanted to know how much the newspaper had paid the new witnesses.

The Chief Constable summarized the evidence against Mattan: The reason a witness had made an identification from a photograph was that she was frightened to say it was a coloured man she had seen. Mrs Gray said Mattan had been in her shop in the Bute Street area and was wearing kid gloves and had a wallet with a roll of banknotes. There were the minute blood splashes on one of his shoes. He had been seen at local dog tracks carrying more money than usual. He said he had been at the pictures, but his mother-in-law and wife said he had visited them between 7.30 and 8 on the evening of the murder. Fellow lodgers said around 8.45 he was unusually morose. His dark overcoat had disappeared. He had a history of razor slashing and was out of work at the time. All the witnesses were said to have been impressive. Given this, Callaghan declined to reopen the case.

On 12 June 1954, Tahir Gass, who had made a statement in the Volpert murder case, now known locally as 'the crazy Somali', killed a local man George Jenkins whom he met by chance when Jenkins was leading home a horse he had bought. He had cut his throat. Gass was found guilty of murder but insane at Monmouthshire Assizes and was sent to Broadmoor from where he was released and deported on 5 October 1955.

In 1995 Mrs Mattan's campaign to clear her husband was taken up by Cardiff solicitors Bernard and Lynne de Maid. They now discovered that evidence was withheld from the defence at the original trial – a woman came forward to say that as a young girl she had not picked out Mattan in an identification parade. It was also disclosed that Cover only identified Mattan after a £200 reward – enough to buy a house in the city – was offered by the victim's family. In 1996 permission was granted to have the body exhumed and reburied, for which Mattan's family had to pay £1,400.

When the Criminal Cases Review Commission was set up in 1997 to correct miscarriages of justice, what was necessary was for a cast-iron case to be the first heard by the Court of Appeal. Two weeks before the Mattan hearing in February 1998 the prosecution furnished the defence with legible copies of entries by Detective Inspector Roberts. They were in a notebook, but not an official police officer's notebook. The prosecution believed that he made his notes at about the time of the committal proceedings. Their existence had been known to those representing Mattan some time earlier, but parts were illegible in the copies they had and the reference to Gass was not clear. Once a legible version was available, two entries became of great significance on this appeal. Roberts had written, 'The man seen by Cover was traced – Gass (Taher) and useless? Cover left Cory's Rest, 7.50 p.m., identifies the Somali in the porch as Gass.' In no written statement did Cover name either of the Somalis he says he saw.

The Gass murder of 1954 had not been linked to the Mattan case until the week before the new hearing. A wanted telex circulated at the time of the Jenkins killing had read:

A SEAMAN BORN IN BRITISH SOMALILAND 1920. 5FT. 7INS. SLIM BUILD. BLACK HAIR. BROWN EYES. DARK COMPLEXION. A MAN OF COLOUR.

GOLD TOOTH LEFT UPPER JAW ... HAS BEEN CONVICTED OF VIOLENCE.

The prosecution did not contest the appeal and giving judgement Lord Justice Rose said:

> In addition, the rules now applicable require far greater disclosure of material to the defence, by the police and prosecution, than was required in 1952. That said, this appeal must be allowed and the conviction quashed.
>
> 'We add this. It is, of course, a matter for very profound regret that in 1952 Mahmood Mattan was convicted and hanged and it has taken 46 years for that conviction to be shown to be unsafe. The Court can only hope that its decision today will provide some crumb of comfort for his surviving relatives. The case has a wider significance in that it clearly demonstrates five matters.
>
> 1. Capital punishment was not perhaps a prudent culmination for a criminal justice system which is human and therefore fallible.
>
> 2. In important areas, to some of which we have alluded, criminal law and practice have, since Mattan was tried, undergone major changes for the better.
>
> 3. The Criminal Cases Review Commission is a necessary and welcome body, without whose work the injustice in this case might never have been identified.
>
> 4. No one associated with the criminal justice system can afford to be complacent.
>
> 5. Injustices of this kind can only be avoided if all concerned in the investigation of crime, and the preparation and presentation of criminal prosecutions, observe the very highest standards of integrity, conscientiousness and professional skill.

Cover, who had been brought to court from prison, said afterwards that he had played no part in the killing and that he had always told the truth.

In May 2001 the Mattan family received £700,000 in

compensation. The money did not help all the family. In October 2003 an open verdict was returned on their son Omar who was found drowned on a remote beach in Caithness. He was said to have had financial difficulties and to have been drinking. Laura Mattan died in January 2008.

Patrick Meehan

Half a century after Oscar Slater, another thorn in the flesh of the Glasgow (and other) police was safe-breaker Patrick Meehan, a close friend of the city's gangleader Arthur Thompson. No one has ever suggested he was an attractive individual and comments on him from his former solicitors include, 'Meehan was a thoroughly unpleasant, ungrateful creature – there was no one single redeeming feature as far as I was concerned.' It therefore speaks well of the Glasgow lawyer Joe Beltrami that he spent many years fighting for Meehan's murder conviction to be quashed.

Although Meehan had no convictions for violence, he had a long and chequered criminal career and had received eight years at the Old Bailey for safe-breaking. He did not serve his sentence the easy way and after an initial unsuccessful escape attempt from Nottingham in August 1963, he wandered away when supposedly watching a prison cricket match and was off in a waiting car, first to Glasgow and then to Dublin and, according to his memoirs, to Germany where he was questioned about his ability to help free Russian spies. What is absolutely clear is that when he was recaptured he was sent to Parkhurst on the Isle of Wight, where he met a Lancastrian, James Griffiths. Meehan was released in August 1968 and returned to Glasgow. Griffiths turned up there the following summer selling stolen antiques. On 5 July 1969 the pair drove to Stranraer on Scotland's west coast to look at the possibility of burgling the motor taxation office there.

On their way back to Glasgow they had stopped to help a young girl who had been put out of a car by two youths who had driven off with her friend. Meehan and Griffiths drove after the youths and explained the facts of life to them before reuniting the girls.

On 8 July, seventy-two-year-old Rachel Ross died at the County Hospital, Ayr. Three days earlier, she and her husband Abraham had been the victims of a tie-up robbery at their home off Racecourse Road in the town, and one of the robbers had knelt on her chest. Abraham Ross had been hit with an iron bar and stabbed in the chest to make him disclose where his money was hidden.

Very much in the frame were Meehan and Griffiths because Abraham Ross said the men had called themselves Jim and Pat and, Ross thought, had Glaswegian accents. Meehan was arrested and put on an identification parade where he was asked to say, 'Shut up, shut up, we'll send for an ambulance.' He stood number one on the parade and once he had uttered the words Ross, who was in a wheelchair and under sedation, said that he was the man. After this no one else was asked to repeat the words.

Griffiths, who had a distinctive Lancashire accent, was never charged because when the police knocked down the door at 12 Holyrood Crescent where he was living he began shooting at them. In the subsequent chase and shoot-out that followed, one bystander was killed, and eleven civilians and five police officers were injured before Chief Superintendent Malcolm Findlayson shot Griffiths dead.

That left Meehan on his own adamantly denying any involvement, and the names being circulated in the underworld as the robbers were Ian Waddell and a man called Dick. Waddell had been spoken to by the police after the robbery and had been sufficiently disturbed to deposit the very substantial sum of £200 with a solicitor.

Beltrami later wrote, 'As one detective told me, "Waddell's name is mentioned a lot." A client said, "The dogs in the street are barking the names of Waddell and Dick. Even they know Meehan's innocent. The police must know it too."'

Under Scottish procedure if a defendant alleges that another has committed the crime he must impeach [name] him in pre-trial procedures, and Waddell and Dick were duly impeached by Beltrami.

There was one other problem for Meehan. The police said they had found pieces of paper in the possession of the dead Griffiths and these matched paper from the Ross household. Because Meehan had tied himself to Griffiths in his defence, this would link him to the paper. However since Beltrami could have no instructions about the paper – for example, had it been planted? – there was no way the police could be cross-examined about it.

Beltrami instructed the flamboyant Tory MP Nicholas Fairbairn and John Smith, later leader of the Labour party, for Meehan's defence and they were hopeful of at least the Scottish Not Proven verdict. Their troubles began with a hostile judge, Lord Grant. When Fairbairn tried to cross-examine Ross on the crucial question of the men's accents, Waddell was brought into court to say 'Shut up, shut up . . .' Ross said he was no longer sure, but Grant then rescued him, asking, 'Is your recollection as clear now, three months later, as it was when you went on the parade?' For the defence, Griffiths' girlfriend, with whom he had been living, gave evidence that he had a strong Lancashire accent.

Once they had impeached Waddell his name was put on the list of witnesses for both the prosecution and defence. If the prosecution had called him, then the defence could have cross-examined him, but they did not. Now the position was reversed and the defence was limited in the structure of the questions they could put.

As for an alibi, Waddell said he had been drinking at the home of a Donald Carmichael. When Carmichael gave evidence for the prosecution, Fairbairn asked him why, the moment the police contacted him simply to make a statement, he had telephoned Beltrami in the middle of the night. Again Lord Grant came to the rescue of Carmichael and the prosecution:

I imagine you realize whether you're guilty of an offence or not, a person who is summoned to the police station is always wise to consult his solicitor, and that solicitors always advise their clients to that effect – if they are reputable and able solicitors – and the court have said frequently that it is always desirable that a solicitor should be present if anybody is summoned to the police station in order to make a statement. Do you realize that?

Yes.

Grant was also there to give a helping hand when Meehan was asked, 'You're a self-confessed liar aren't you?'

Rightly, Meehan protested, 'I asked some months ago to be given a truth drug and to be interrogated under its influence.'

Grant: 'Can't you tell the truth without having a truth drug, Meehan?'

The judge allowed the prosecution to introduce evidence that Griffiths had been found guilty of robbery with violence, and it was suggested that picking up the girls had been a fiendishly clever way to fabricate a defence. Asked about the paper in Griffiths' pocket, Meehan could only reply, 'I can't answer for what was in Jim Griffiths' pocket.'

When Waddell was called to give evidence he was warned that he need not answer questions that might incriminate him, but curiously he agreed to answer questions about the £200 he had deposited with solicitor John Curtin. Foolishly he denied he had left any money with the lawyer. Fairbairn said that he would be calling Curtin, and Grant again intervened to say that dealings between a solicitor and client were privileged and the privilege could only be waived by the client. Amazingly Waddell agreed Curtin could be called, but when Fairbairn tried to introduce a conversation between Waddell and another witness, Grant stepped in: 'Mr Fairbairn, would you please not be more stupid than you really are.' Other prisoners were called by the defence to tell the jury that Waddell had admitted doing 'the Ayr job'.

When it came to his summing-up Grant withdrew the defence of impeachment from the jury's consideration:

Evidence has been led that Waddell made certain statements incriminating himself. He, however, in the box, denied having made those statements. Even if you accept the evidence that he did make those statements, that would not entitle you to hold, even on the balance of probabilities, that he was one of the perpetrators . . . So there is no evidence in law on which you could find a special defence of impeachment or incrimination established.

Meehan was found guilty by a majority. Sentenced to life imprisonment, 'You have made a terrible mistake,' he told the jury. An appeal was dismissed in quick time.

Beltrami never gave up. He had been half correct in impeaching Waddell and another man and the correct half was Waddell. His partner turned out to be another client of Beltrami, the safe-breaker William 'Tank' McGuinness, who began appearing uninvited in Beltrami's office and accosting him in the court precincts, to drop hints and ultimately make more or less frank admissions. By the time of his last appearance he had admitted that it was Waddell's responsibility to telephone for an ambulance for Mrs Ross but he never had done. As Waddell was covered in blood, McGuinness had gone to collect the getaway car.

Later in a report by Lord Hunter into the whole case he said that Beltrami should at this stage have gone to the police with McGuinness's statements but it is difficult to see how he could have done so. First, he would have thrown away the years of trust he had built up with his clients, some of a hard city's hardest men. And that was leaving aside any question of privilege. Anyway, once interviewed by the police, almost certainly McGuinness would have denied everything.

On 12 March 1976 McGuinness was beaten and left for dead close to Celtic football ground. He died thirteen days later in the Royal Infirmary without regaining consciousness. With permission from the McGuinness family, Beltrami now handed the statements over to the police. In May 1976 Meehan was pardoned. He was not the first person to be given a pardon in Scotland. The previous year, another of Beltrami's clients,

Maurice Swanson, was pardoned and given compensation after being wrongly convicted on identification evidence following a bank robbery.

Ian Waddell, who was serving three years for his perjury over the cash he deposited with Curtin, was charged with the Ross murder and, in turn, he impeached Meehan and Griffiths. He was acquitted by a majority verdict in just over an hour. That acquittal did him little good. In 1982 he was killed by his friend Andy Gentle in Blackthorn Street, Glasgow. The men had been involved in the killing of Josephine Chipperfield, who had been stabbed to death, and the prosecution's case was that Gentle thought Waddell would turn him over to the police. Gentle claimed a special defence that it was Waddell who had killed Mrs Chipperfield and that a George Forsyth had killed Waddell. He was convicted and sentenced to life imprisonment.

In his 1982 report on the Meehan case, something that had taken five years to compile, Lord Hunter suggested that, after all, the four men had all been involved and perhaps Meehan had been outside the house in case he was needed to blow a safe. Beltrami dismisses this idea, saying that Tank McGuinness, who was a far better and more experienced peterman [safe-breaker] than Meehan, would never have needed him.

Beltrami still continued to work on Meehan's behalf and obtained £50,000 compensation, declining to take any fees. Meehan was not grateful and in 1990 he wrote a book that blamed Beltrami for his conviction. Beltrami decided not to obtain an injunction, but the book was not stocked in the city's shops. Meehan was never again convicted and died in 1994. He had been suffering from throat cancer.

Rubin Carter and John Artis;
David McCallum

At around 2.30 a.m. on 17 June 1966 gunmen opened fire, killing barman James Oliver, and two others, sixty-year-old Fred Nauyoke and waitress Hazel Tanis in the Lafayette Bar and Grill, a bar patronized mainly by white European immigrants in the centre of a black district in Paterson, New Jersey. The evidence from William Marins, who was shot in the head but survived, was that two black men, one carrying a 12-gauge shotgun and the other a .32 handgun, went into the bar. Oliver, said to have been known for his bigotry, threw an empty beer bottle at them and they then opened fire. Hazel Tanis died almost a month later from injuries to her throat, stomach, intestine, spleen and left lung. Before she died she failed to recognize Carter and Artis. One theory was that it was a robbery, but a second theory, and the one which pervaded the subsequent trials, was that it was a revenge attack for the killing some six hours earlier of a black bar owner, Roy Holloway, by the white Frank Conforti. Conforti had sold him the Waltz Inn, but Holloway had failed to pay the full price.

There were witnesses who saw the getaway car. Among them a woman, Pat Valentine, who lived above the Lafayette, said she had seen two black males get into a white car, possibly a Cadillac or a Dodge, and drive away from the bar. She was sure it had out-of-state licence plates. A small-time criminal, Alfred Bello, who had been scouting a local warehouse to burgle, gave a description of the getaway car as white with 'a geometric design, sort of a butterfly type design on the back of the car', and with out-of-state licence plates with orange lettering on a blue background.

Boxer Rubin Carter, a one-time contender for the middle-weight championship of the world, was leasing a white Dodge Polara sedan at the time and within a matter of minutes he and his friend, nineteen-year-old John Artis, were stopped and arrested. They were questioned and taken to the hospital for a confrontation with Marins, who did not identify them.

When Detective Emil Di Robbio searched the Dodge he found a live .32 calibre pistol round under the front passenger seat and a 12-gauge shotgun shell in the boot. These were not however logged with a property clerk until five days after the shooting, although both were documented in a police report made seventy-five minutes after the murders.

Carter and Artis were given lie detector tests, which they seem to have passed satisfactorily. Both appeared before a Grand Jury but no indictments were handed down. Given that it is said a prosecutor can make a Grand Jury do almost anything he wants it does not seem as though there was any real evidence against the pair at the time.

There was a time when it seemed as though Carter, born on 6 May 1937, would become a world champion. At the age of eleven he had been sent to the Jamesburg State Home for Boys where he claimed the guards regularly beat and abused him. He escaped after six years and enlisted in the army where, turning to boxing, he won fifty of his bouts and lost only five. Thirty-five of his wins were by knockout and he became the army's European light-welterweight champion. On his discharge he returned to Paterson where he became a trailer driver but was arrested over his earlier absconding and sentenced to ten months in the Annadale Reformatory. He did not last long on the outside after his release. He was becoming a heavy drinker – vodka being his liquor of choice – and he attacked a woman, snatching her purse in a street robbery. This time he received four years. He took up boxing again in prison and the day after his release he began his professional career with a four-round win over Pike Reed for which he was paid $20.

With his shaven head, prominent moustache, unwavering stare and, above all, a damaging left hook, Carter was an intimidating man in the ring. As a boxer he was both fast and powerful, which earned him his nickname 'Hurricane'. Boxing has never been shy of hype and now Carter's prison record was used to promote his aggression. Instead of the ordinary dressing gown then favoured by fighters, he wore a hooded black-velvet robe trimmed with metallic gold thread, carrying the image of a crouching black panther on the back.

One problem he had in the ring was that at five foot eight he was short for a middleweight and as a result in his one title fight he was at a considerable disadvantage. Nevertheless his style made him a firm favourite at New York's Madison Square Garden and he appeared regularly in televised bouts. In 1963 the influential boxing magazine *Ring* named him as one of the top middleweight contenders after he knocked out eleven of his first fifteen professional opponents. One of his victims was Emile Griffiths, the welterweight champion, who was moving up a weight division. In 1964 Carter was given a shot at the world middleweight championship but his lack of height told against him and, although he claimed to have been on the wrong end of a racial verdict, he was comfortably out-jabbed and outpointed by the champion Joey Giardello.

Following that loss Carter tumbled down the rankings, losing seven of his final fifteen bouts and winning only one of his last five. In March 1965 in London he fought the Liverpudlian Harry Scott whom he was confidently expected to beat. Indeed *The Times* boxing correspondent was worried that Scott, who was not even the British champion, was over-matched and would take a bad beating. In fact, the bout was stopped when Scott received a cut eye, but it had been even at that stage. *The Times* still thought, 'Just because Carter appeared to have a bubble reputation it is no reason for gambles to be taken in this hazardous sport.' He lost a rematch the next month when Scott convincingly outpointed the once-fearsome Carter and in the May he was knocked down three times by the former world champion, Nigerian Dick Tiger. After the Grand Jury refused to indict him in the Lafayette case Carter went to Rosario, Argentina, where, in what would be his final contest in the ring, he lost over ten rounds to Juan Carlos Rivero.

While in London for the second Scott contest there was an incident when a gun went off in Carter's hotel room, but no prosecution followed. Despite claims made on his behalf that his criminal convictions deprived him of another chance to gain a world title, Carter had been clearly on the slide. Between bouts he was still drinking heavily. Outside the ring he wore bespoke suits and favoured a black Cadillac with Rubin Hurricane Carter engraved in silver by the headlights.

Several months after the Lafayette shooting the burglar Bello told police that he had had an accomplice during the attempted burglary, Arthur Dexter Bradley. Now they both identified Carter as one of the two men they had seen carrying weapons outside the bar on the night of the shooting. Bello also identified Artis as the other man. On Carter's return from Argentina, on 14 October 1966, first Artis and then Carter were arrested and charged with the murders.

Their lawyer Raymond Brown was able to point up discrepancies between the eyewitnesses and there were also a number of alibi witnesses who said Carter and Artis had been in a local bar, the Nite Spot, about the time of the shootings. Both men were convicted. The prosecution had asked for the death penalty but the jury recommended life sentences and Judge Samuel Larner imposed two consecutive and one concurrent life sentence on Carter, and three concurrent life sentences on Artis. Now began a campaign for their release.

In the summer of 1974 the New Jersey Public Defender's Office and *The New York Times* independently obtained recantations from both Bello and Bradley. Both men now said they had been mistaken in identifying the pair and claimed the police had pressured them into making the identifications. In a double-pronged attack the lawyers for Carter and Artis argued that Bello and Bradley had lied during the 1967 trial, when telling the jurors that they had made only certain narrow, limited deals with prosecutors in exchange for their evidence. In fact they had been promised considerably more. If so, the second 'ground' ran, prosecutors had either had an obligation to disclose this additional exculpatory evidence, or a duty to disclose the fact that their witnesses had lied.

On 10 December that year the appeal failed when Judge Samuel Larner said he did not believe Bello and Bradley when they said they had lied. Larner rejected the second argument as well but a further appeal to the New Jersey Supreme Court succeeded when the court unanimously held that the evidence of various deals made between the prosecution and Bello and Bradley should have been disclosed to the defence before or during the 1967 trial, as this could have 'affected the jury's evaluation of the credibility' of the eyewitnesses. 'The defendants' right to a fair trial was substantially prejudiced,' ruled Justice Mark Sullivan. In December 1976 the court set aside the original convictions and granted them a new trial.

Overnight, Carter was hailed as a civil rights champion, with a national defence committee working on his behalf and fund-raising concerts with the bills topped by Bob Dylan along with Joni Mitchell, Joan Baez and Roberta Flack at Madison Square Garden. The former boxer Muhammad Ali attended a pretrial hearing in Paterson in 1976 to show his support for Carter.

Carter was released on bail on 20 March 1976, but in just over a month he once more went from hero to nearly zero. This time he was alleged on 29 April to have assaulted Carolyn Kelley, a prominent community leader in the Essex County area who had been actively involved in raising funds for his defence. A Muslim for many years at the time of this assault, she had become the head of what was called the Carter Defense Fund – Freedom For All Forever. Quite what happened depends on who is speaking but it appears that Carter hit her during a quarrel over a hotel bill. He had, she said, been drinking. Very soon after the attack, the incident became known to counsel for the defence, the media people and others sympathetic to Carter. The Prosecutor's Office did not learn that any incident had occurred until the end of May 1976. Meanwhile

Carolyn Kelley later said that efforts had been made to persuade her not to disclose the matter. There was, said the prosecution, not sufficient evidence to bring charges. Mae Thelma Basket, whom Carter had married in 1963, divorced him after their second child was born, on the grounds of his infidelity. Now the celebrities who had flocked to campaign for him began to drift away.

On 31 August 1976, in an extraordinary development, the County Prosecutor wrote to their lawyer saying that if Carter and Artis took a polygraph test conducted by a person of unimpeachable nationwide integrity, to be paid for by the state, which clearly established their innocence, he would end the proceedings with a *nolle prosequi*. They did not agree.

From the defence point of view the second trial in December 1976 was something of a disaster. Both the prosecutor and the judge tried to help Artis to see that being tried together with Carter was against his best interests. He had no convictions and since there was no physical evidence linking him to the case, he had a good chance of being acquitted on the basis of reasonable doubt. Instead, Artis insisted on being tried with his friend and aligned himself with Carter's claim that the case was a police conspiracy. Then Artis's lawyer, Lewis M. Steel, spent much of the trial quarrelling with Judge Leopardi, which cannot have helped his client. Jurors as a body tend to side with the judge unless he is deeply unpleasant and not always even then, rather than with defence lawyers.

Now the prosecution resuscitated the alternative theory, alleging that rather than it having been a botched robbery the defendants had committed the Lafayette Grill murders in revenge for the earlier killing of the black tavern owner. Judge Leopardi allowed the prosecution to introduce evidence of a hostile black crowd outside the Waltz Inn, so offering the jury a racial motive. Arthur Bradley refused to cooperate with prosecutors and was not called as a witness. Bello resurfaced as a prosecution witness and recanted his recantation. Now he was the only witness who placed Carter and Artis at the murder scene. Again a number of witnesses provided Carter and Artis with an alibi.

Predictably, when Carter and Artis were found guilty a second time, their lawyers Myron Beldock and Lewis Steel accused the jury of being racist (against the defendants) and anti-Semitic (against them). Prosecutor Burrell Humphreys took a different view, saying, 'The best way to try a case is to stress reasonable doubt, and not antagonize the court, heap abuse on the prosecutor, and try to convince everybody the police are out to get you.'

Artis was released on parole in 1981 after serving fifteen years. He had been a model prisoner. The year before, Carter had heard from Lesra Martin, a teenager from a Brooklyn ghetto who had read his autobiography, and they began a correspondence. Martin was living with a group of Canadians who had formed an entrepreneurial commune and had taken on the responsibilities for his education. Before long Martin's benefactors, particularly Sam Chaiton, Terry Swinton and Lisa Peters, also developed a strong bond with Carter and began to work for his release.

Now their efforts intensified after the summer of 1983, when they began to work in New York with Carter's legal team, including the lawyers Beldock and Steel from the last trial and the constitutional scholar Leon Friedman. A defendant must exhaust all possible appeals in the state courts before he can apply to the Federal Courts for help and, over the next four years, numerous appeals in New Jersey courts failed. But now the indefatigable Canadians and Beldock, claiming that all proceedings had been exhausted at state level, petitioned the Federal Court for a writ of *habeus corpus*. When the issues were heard for the first time in a Federal Court on 7 November 1985, Judge H. Lee Sarokin of the United States District Court in Newark overturned the convictions on constitutional grounds.

> The extensive record clearly demonstrates that [the] petitioners' convictions were predicated upon an appeal to racism rather than reason, and concealment rather than disclosure.
>
> For the state to contend that an accused has the motive to

commit murder solely because of his membership in a racial group is an argument that should never be permitted to sway a jury or provide the basis of a conviction.

Sarokin ruled that prosecutors had 'fatally infected the trial' by resorting, without evidence, to the racial revenge theory, and that they had withheld evidence disproving Bello's identifications. The prosecution had effectively applied the syllogistic fallacy, 'Blacks generally attack whites; Carter and Artis are black; therefore Carter and Artis attacked the white victims.'

Sarokin said the trial had been so constitutionally flawed that Carter did not deserve to spend 'another day or another hour in prison'. The prosecution argued that he should remain in custody pending an appeal, but Sarokin refused their application. He also suggested that in view of the time lapse of twenty years the prosecution might not wish to retry the case.

It took another two years before the prosecution's attempts to reinstate the convictions were finally rejected by a Federal Appeals Court and by the United States Supreme Court. With a number of the state's witnesses dead by now they accepted Sarokin's recommendation and the charges against Carter and Artis were formally dismissed in 1988.

After his release Carter joined the commune in Canada that had financed, and worked so hard on, his appeals. The commune also worked on the appeals of Paul Morin, who had been convicted of the rape and murder of a young girl. After Morin's release the group changed the name of his defence committee to the Association in Defense of the Wrongly Convicted from 1993 to 2004 (AIDWYC), and Carter became the first executive director. He died in April 2014 after suffering from prostate cancer. By then he had left the commune and, still living in Toronto, was being cared for by Artis. The Committee issued a valedictory statement:

Rubin will be remembered by those at AIDWYC who were fortunate enough to have worked with him as a truly courageous man who fought tirelessly to free others who had suffered the same fate as he.

We will continue to fight against wrongful convictions, a battle that Rubin valiantly fought until the day he died. Rest in peace Rubin, your battle is over but you will never be forgotten.

In his book *Eye of the Hurricane*, Carter always accepted he was not perfect and admitted to a number of assaults and robberies – often seen by him through rose-tinted spectacles – but not the murders. Those earlier crimes, he claimed, were as a result of growing up under Jim Crow and happened when, in the words of the anti-slavery hymn 'Amazing Grace', he was blind. Of his time in prison and his work on improving the criminal justice system, Carter said, 'Those years in prison – maybe they were good for something, after all. But I wouldn't recommend it to anybody.'

Others remain unconvinced. Sarokin's decision has been roundly criticized, particularly by reporters Cal Deal and Paul Mulshine in the New Jersey *Star Ledger*, who have also amassed a series of answers to Sarokin's findings. Mulshine, who described Sarokin as 'an outrageously liberal judge who was a publicity hound', also points out that Carter's claim that he had been exonerated is strictly incorrect and that his conviction had been quashed rather than that he had been found not guilty. Boxer Joey Giardello sued the makers of the film *Hurricane* over his portrayal and received damages and changes in the film.

In the months leading up to his death, Carter had worked on behalf of David McCallum, a Brooklyn man convicted in 1985 on two counts of murder based on his confession. Two months before his death, the *New York Daily News* published 'Hurricane Carter's Dying Wish', an opinion piece in which he asked for an independent review of McCallum's conviction:

I request only that McCallum be granted a full hearing by the Brooklyn conviction integrity unit, now under the auspices of the new district attorney, Ken Thompson. Knowing what I do, I am certain that when the facts are brought to light, Thompson will recommend his immediate release . . . Just as my own verdict 'was predicated on racism rather than reason and on concealment rather than disclosure,' as Sarokin wrote, so too was McCallum's.

McCallum, then sixteen, together with Willie Stuckey had been convicted for the kidnap-murder of Nathan Blenner, whose body was found shot in the head in a Bushwick park in October 1985. McCallum claimed that he had been beaten and fed false facts by police officers before he confessed. Stuckey died in prison in 2001. McCallum's lawyers approached the District Attorney's Conviction Review Unit with evidence of another suspect who was questioned without the defence being told, and of DNA from a car used in the abduction, which matched other men. In October 2014 his and Stuckey's convictions were quashed. They were the ninth and tenth exonerations by the Brooklyn District Attorney during 2014.

CHAPTER 6

Race Hate

The Scottsboro Boys

The Scooba Three

The Scottsboro Boys

On 25 March 1931 a fight broke out between black and white youths who were riding a freight train near Stevenson, Alabama. It is not clear how the fight started. Possibly a white boy stood on the hand of a black one. Probably there was a good deal of racial shouting. Certainly it ended with eight of the black youths being sentenced to death for the rape of two young white women who were riding the freight in the same gondola-shaped open carriage.

During the fight, with one exception, the white youths were thrown off the train. The exception was Orville Gilley, who later described himself as a poet and musician. One of the youths thrown off telephoned the police at Paint Rock, Jackson County, and asked that the train be stopped and the boys arrested. By the time the train was halted only nine of the black youths remained along with Gilley and two women, Victoria Price and Ruby Bates, who were dressed in overalls and at first were thought to be white youths. The black youths were Roy Wright (aged thirteen) and his brother Andy (seventeen), Haywood Patterson (seventeen), Eugene Williams (twelve), Clarence Norris (nineteen), Olen Montgomery (seventeen), Willie Roberson (seventeen), Ozie Powell (sixteen) and Charles Weems (twenty-one). All were poor, most were illiterate; Montgomery was almost blind and Roberson was crippled by an advanced case of gonorrhea. He was also suffering from syphilis.

While she was being questioned by the stationmaster, Price

fainted, or at least pretended to, and when she recovered she made the allegation that she and Ruby Bates had been raped by the nine youths. At this time even the making of such an allegation in Alabama was sufficient to establish guilt. No corroboration was needed and it did not matter from what class the woman came. The thinking was that no white woman, even a prostitute, would demean herself by making such an allegation unless it was true. Making the allegation also had the benefit of deflecting probable vagrancy charges or a charge under the Mann Act of crossing a state line for immoral purposes. In a moment, she was turned from a female dissolute to a violated heroine; so much so that a local store provided her with a set of new clothes. The much less streetwise Bates simply went along with Price's claim. No matter that, despite their apparent ordeal, two doctors found neither mental nor physical evidence to back up their story.

Researcher Hollace Ransdall, sent by the American Civil Liberties Union (ACLU) to investigate the allegations, found:

> Victoria Price was born in Fayetteville, Tennessee. She has been married but says she is separated from her husband. She left him because he 'lay around on me drunk with canned heat', she said. She was known at the trial as Mrs. Price, though this is her mother's name, not her husband's. Her age was variously reported in Scottsboro as 19, 20, and 21. Her mother gave it as 24, and neighbors and social workers said she was 27.
>
> Victoria lives in a little, unpainted shack at 313 Arms Street, Huntsville, with her old, decrepit mother, Mrs. Ella Price, for whom she insistently professes such flamboyant devotion that one immediately distrusts her sincerity. This impression is strengthened by little side looks her mother gives her. Mrs. Price fell down the steps while washing clothes, and injured her arm, which is now stiff and of little use. Victoria says her mother is entirely dependent upon her for support.
>
> Miss Price is a lively, talkative young woman, cocky in manner and not bad to look at. She appears to be in very

good health. The attention which has come to her from the case has clearly delighted her. She talks of it with zest, slipping in many vivid and earthy phrases. Details spoken of in the local press as 'unprintable' or 'unspeakable' she gives off-hand in her usual chatty manner, quite unabashed by their significance. Like Ruby, Victoria spits snuff with wonderful aim.

Victoria and her mother, after some warm argument on the subject, agreed finally to the number of years that Victoria had worked in the mills as being ten. Eight of these years were spent doing night work, they said, on a twelve-hour shift. Victoria is a spinner, and used to run from 12 to 14 sides, she said with pride. 'Yeh, I used to make good money. I've made as high as $2.25 a day workin' the night shift before hard times come.' Now nobody is allowed to have more than 8 sides to run, and the average is 6, Victoria says. She gets 18 cents a side now, where she used to get 22 cents. 'I make on an average of $1.20 a day now, workin' two, sometimes three days a week. Every other week we are laid off altogether. You know nobody can't live on wages like that.'

Although Victoria, with a sly eye on me to see if I had heard of her record and would scoff, assured me that in spite of her low wage she never made a cent outside the wall of the mill. Her reputation as a prostitute is widely established in Huntsville, and according to the investigation of the International Labor Defense, also in Chattanooga. One of the social workers reported that Walter Sanders, chief deputy sheriff in Huntsville, said that he didn't bother Victoria, although he knew her trade, because she was a 'quiet prostitute, and didn't go rarin' around cuttin' up in public and walkin' the streets solicitin' but just took men quiet-like'.

Sheriff Giles, of Huntsville, said he had information that she was running a speak-easy on the side with a married man named Teller, who lived in the Lincoln mill village and had several small children, but was now running around with Mrs. Price and leaving his wife. The sheriff said he had been trying to catch them with liquor on them, but had not succeeded so far. He said that he had caught the Teller man in her house, however, and had given both of them a warning.

Mrs. Russell, a neighbor of the Prices, claims that Victoria is a 'bad one' and has been in no end of scrapes with married men. She was reported to be the cause of the separation of a Mr. and Mrs. Luther Bentrum, and was rumored to have received the attentions of a man named George Whitworth, until his wife threatened to kill her, and Victoria hurriedly moved out of the neighborhood. One morning after the Scottsboro trial, Mrs. Russell said she saw her lying drunk out in the back yard with a man asleep on her lap. Mrs. Russell is also authority for the statement that Victoria's mother was as notorious for her promiscuity in her day as Victoria is now.

These stories are typical of the sort that circulate continually among the mill workers of the group from which both Ruby and Victoria come. Whether true or exaggerated, they give some idea of the social background of both the plaintiffs in the Scottsboro case. Leaving out of consideration the matter of the conflicting and untested evidence upon which the Negro boys were convicted, and assuming what has by no means been proved, that the Negroes are guilty of the worst that has been charged against them, the question of whether a monstrous penalty has not been exacted for an offense which the girls themselves feel to be slight, can certainly be raised.

As for Ruby Bates:

Ruby lives in a bare but clean unpainted shack at 24 Depot Street, in a Negro section of town, with her mother, Mrs. Emma Bates. They are the only white family in the block. Of the five children in the family, two are married and three are living at home. Mr. Bates is separated from his wife and lives in Tennessee, according to the report of neighbors, who say that he comes occasionally to see his children.

The house in which the Bateses lived when I visited them on May 12, several weeks after the trial, had been vacated recently by a colored family. The social service worker who accompanied me on the visit sniffed when she came in and said to Mrs. Bates: 'Niggers lived here before you, I smell them. You can't get rid of that Nigger smell.' Mrs. Bates looked apologetic and murmured that she had scrubbed the place down with soap and water. The house looked clean and orderly to me. I smelled nothing, but then I have only a northern nose.

Out in front while we talked, the younger Bates children were playing with the neighboring Negro youngsters. Here was another one of those ironic touches which life, oblivious of man's ways, gives so often. If the nine youths on the freight car had been white, there would have been no Scottsboro case. The issue at stake was that of the inviolable separation of black men from white women. No chance to remind Negroes, in terrible fashion that white women are farther away from them than the stars, must be allowed to slip past. The challenge flung to the Negro race in the Scottsboro case was Ruby Bates, and another like her. Ruby, a girl whom life had forced down to equality with Negroes, in violation of all the upholders of white supremacy were shouting. As a symbol of the Untouchable White Woman, the Whites held high – Ruby. The Ruby who lived among the Negroes, whose family mixed with them; a daughter of what respectable Whites call 'the lowest of the low,' that is a White whom economic scarcity has forced across the great color barrier. All the things made the respectable people of Scottsboro insist that the Negro boys must die, had meant nothing in the life of Ruby Bates.

Yet here was Ruby saying earnestly, as she sat in a Negro house, surrounded by Negro families, while the younger members of her family played in the street with Negro children, that the Scottsboro authorities had promised her she could see the execution of the 'Niggers' – the nine black lads who were to be killed merely for being Negroes.

Ruby's mother, Mrs. Emma Bates, clean and neat in a

cheap cotton dress, talked with a mixture of embarrassment and off-handed disregard for her visitors' attitude toward her. She has worked in the mills for many years. She was employed by the Lincoln textile mill, the largest one in Huntsville, some time before the trial. When I saw her she was out of a job, but the neighbors reported that she had a 'boarder' living with her, a man named Maynard. They also gossiped that she frequently got drunk, and took men for money whenever she got the chance.

Neither mother nor daughter showed signs of regarding the experience Ruby is alleged to have been through as anything to be deplored especially. They both discussed the case quite matter-of-factly, with no notion apparently, that it had marred or blighted Ruby's life at all. The publicity which the case has brought to them, however, has impressed them greatly. They humbly accept the opinion of respectable white people; it never occurs to them, of course, to analyze the inconsistencies it makes with their own way of life. Accustomed to seeing Negroes all around them on equal status with themselves for all practical purposes, and looking upon sexual intercourse as part of the common and inescapable routine of life, they have no basis in their own lives for any intense feeling on the subject of intimate relations between whites and blacks. They have just fallen in with 'respectable' opinion because that seems to be what is expected of them, and they want to do the proper thing. There are so few times when they can.

The only strong feeling that Ruby showed about the case was not directed against the Negroes. It was against Victoria Price that Ruby expressed deep and bitter resentment. For Victoria captured the show for herself and pushed Ruby into the background, causing people at the trial to say that Victoria was a quick, clever girl, but Ruby was slow and stupid. It was easier for Victoria to talk than to breathe. Words came hard to Ruby. Victoria identified the six Negroes she claimed attacked her with a cock-sure, emphatic manner that much impressed the jurors and the trial spectators. She caught on at once to what was wanted of her

– identifications without any confusing hesitations to slow up the death sentences. Ruby, on the other hand, was annoying from the start because she could not say which ones attacked her. So Victoria with pert, condescending manner, passing looks with the prosecuting officials at such stupidity, told Ruby which ones she must say attacked her, in order not to get mixed up and identify some of those Victoria had previously said were 'her six Niggers,' as she put it.

Both Ruby and Victoria told me this, in their own words, when I interviewed them personally. Neither one had the slightest notion of the seriousness of what they were saying. The only opinion they had run across so far was that which said the 'Niggers' must get the death sentence at once or be lynched. Never having met any other attitude on the Negro question, they both assumed that this was my attitude, and therefore spoke to me as they thought all respectable white people speak.

Eighty years later it is possible to feel some sympathy for the girls and the dreadful lives they led, but Victoria Price, in particular, must have known that she was condemning nine young men if not to death then to decades of imprisonment.

Within a week of the youths' arrests the first trials before Judge Hawkins were all done and dusted. The defendants were represented by Stephen Roddy, a Chattanooga real estate lawyer with no experience of Alabama law, who said he was acting on instructions from friends of the boys. Roddy, who seems to have done the bulk of the work, was assisted by the elderly Milo Moody, variously described as being a low type and having a low practice, and as a mild village iconoclast. Roddy wanted Moody, who had not tried a criminal case in decades, to be the lawyer of record. A half-hearted petition for a change of venue by Roddy, on the grounds of local prejudice, was denied by Judge Hawkins who found the crowd, estimated to be between eight and ten thousand strong, had come to town in the spirit of going to a circus but without any malicious intent. He did not think it was significant that the defendants had been brought to court with an escort of 118 Alabama guardsmen armed with machine guns. Local reporter Mrs Ben Davis thought the crowd 'curious but not furious'. However one local, interviewed after the trials, gave Hollace Ransdall a different view of the townsfolk's feelings:

> A kind-faced, elderly woman selling tickets at the railroad station, for instance, said to me that if they re-tried the Negroes in Scottsboro, she hoped they would leave the soldiers home next time. When I asked why, she replied that the next time they would finish off the 'black fiends' and save the bother of a second trial. Then she told me a lurid story of the mistreatment suffered by the two white girls at the hands of those 'horrible black brutes', one of whom had had her breast chewed off by one of the Negroes.
>
> 'When I called to her attention that the doctor's testimony for the prosecution was to the effect that neither of the girls showed signs of any rough handling on their bodies, it made no impression upon her. Her faith in her atrocity story, which had been told to her 'by one who ought to know what he was talking about', remained unshaken.

Clarence Norris and Charlie Weems were tried first. During her evidence Victoria Price, who had clearly recovered well from her ordeal, claimed that she and Ruby Bates witnessed the fight, that one of the defendants had a gun, and that they had all raped her at knifepoint. During her cross-examination by Roddy, Price produced a string of repartee that brought roars of laughter.

Dr Bridges testified that his examination of Victoria Price found no vaginal tearing, and that she had had semen in her for several hours. Ruby Bates failed to mention that either of the girls were raped until she was cross-examined. The prosecution ended with evidence from three men who claimed the black youths fought the white youths, put them off the train, and 'took charge' of the white girls. The prosecution rested without calling any of the white youths as witnesses.

In retrospect it is easy to criticize Roddy, who was acting in a case well out of his depth and experience and one where there was a hostile judge and crowd. But, perhaps unusually, he called both his clients to give evidence and a fair disaster that turned out to be. Weems testified that he was not part of the fight, that Patterson had the pistol and that he had not seen the white girls until the train pulled into Paint Rock.

Clarence Norris stunned the courtroom by implicating the other defendants. He denied participating in the fight or even being in the gondola car where the fight took place, alleging that he saw the rapes by the other blacks from atop the next boxcar. Roddy called no more witnesses.

During closing, the prosecution thundered, 'If you don't give these men death sentences, the electric chair might as well be abolished.' Roddy made no closing argument at all – not even against the death penalty for his clients.

The court started the next case while the jury was still deliberating the first. The first jury deliberated less than two hours before returning a guilty verdict and imposing the death sentence on both Weems and Norris. With the return of guilty verdicts, a band outside struck up 'Hail, Hail the Gang's All Here' and 'There'll be a Hot Time in the Old Town Tonight'.

The next trial was that of Haywood Patterson. Victoria Price stuck with her story mostly, stating flatly that Patterson raped her. She also accused Patterson of shooting one of the white youths. Price also lied, 'I have not had intercourse with any other white man but my husband. I want you to know that.' Patterson was found guilty in short order.

The remaining defendants were tried consecutively and their cases were concluded in a day. Each successive jury could hear the cheers as the verdict of their precursors was announced. All but thirteen-year-old Roy Wright were convicted of rape and sentenced to death, then the usual sentence in Alabama for black men convicted of raping white women. Because of his age, in Roy Wright's trial the prosecution did not ask for the death penalty but eleven of the jurors wanted it imposed in any event. Only the foreman held out against them and the judge finally declared a mistrial on the sentencing phase.

The Communist-led International Labor Defense (ILD) had already been alerted by the editors of the Party's *SouthernWorker* and immediately after the death sentences were passed their board voted to take up the youths' case. Their interest was not wholly altruistic so far as the defendants were concerned. Here was a great opportunity for a symbolic crusade led by moral entrepreneurs in which the ostensible subject, in this case the release of the Scottsboro Boys, could be used to promote an entirely different aim; the advancement of the labour movement and the South's coloured population.

The cases were appealed and, unsurprisingly, the Alabama Supreme Court, whose justices included Thomas Knight Snr, the father of the prosecutor, affirmed seven of the eight convictions. It did however grant thirteen-year-old Eugene Williams a new trial on the grounds he was a juvenile. To his credit Chief Justice John C. Anderson dissented from the rejections, ruling that the defendants had been denied an impartial jury, fair trial, fair sentencing and effective counsel.

An appeal to the United States Supreme Court fared rather better. On 7 November 1932, by a majority of seven to two, the court overturned the convictions on the narrow ground that they had effectively been denied counsel and so the Due Process clause of the Fourteenth Amendment had been violated. Nothing was said about the improbabilities inherent in the girls' stories.

There had been suggestions that the great trial lawyer Clarence Darrow was going to take their cases at the retrials, but he withdrew when it became clear that, 'the case was controlled by the Communist party who cared less for the safety and well-being of those poor Negro Boys than the exploitation of their own cause. If I could not be free and completely independent, without political ties, I would have none of it.'

It was then William Patterson of the ILD wrote to the New York lawyer Samuel Leibowitz asking him to take the case without fee and paying his own expenses. Patterson had clearly learned his lesson because he wrote saying that, while their politics did not coincide, Leibowitz would be completely free to conduct the cases how he wished. The benefit to him would be that he had 'an opportunity to give best in a case which for its humanitarian appeal has never been equaled in the annals of American jurisprudence'. He could not help adding that while Leibowitz would be representing 'nine innocent boys' he would also be appearing for 'a nation of twelve million oppressed people struggling against dehumanizing inequality'.

Perhaps naïvely, Leibowitz had no conception of what conditions would be like in a biased Southern court.

It was after the first set of trials the Communist-led American Civil Liberties Union had sent young university graduate Hollace Ransdall to research the backgrounds of the two girls and she expanded this into an in-depth look at the conditions of the abject poor, both black and white, in and around Scottsboro. To a certain extent her report was slanted to what her employers wanted to read but, even allowing for this, it was a damning indictment of conditions for the local millworkers:

> All the mills were running on short time during the period of the Scottsboro case, and had been for some months before. Most of them had cut down to two, three, and four days a week. The Margaret had its workers on shifts employed only every other week, from two to four days a week.
>
> High standards of morality, of health, of sanitation, do not thrive under such conditions. It is a rare mill family that is not touched in some form by prostitution, disease, prison, insane asylum, and drunkenness. 'That's the kind of thing these mill workers are mixed up with all the time', complained one social service worker, 'I'm beginning to forget how decent people behave, I've been messing around with venereal disease and starvation and unemployment so long.'
>
> There was no father in evidence in the families of either Victoria Price or Ruby Bates.
>
> Husbands come and go in many cases, with marriage ceremonies or without. A woman who takes in a male boarder to help out expenses is unquestionably assumed to share her bed as well as her board with him. The neighbors

gossip about it, but with jealousy for her good luck in getting him, rather than from disapproval of her conduct. The distinction between wife and 'whore,' as the alternative is commonly known in Huntsville, is not strictly drawn. A mill woman is quite likely to be both if she gets the chance as living is too precarious and money too scarce to miss any kind of chance to get it. Promiscuity means little where economic oppression is great.

'These mill workers are as bad as the Niggers,' said one social service worker with a mixture of contempt and understanding. 'They haven't any sense of morality at all. Why, just lots of these women are nothing but prostitutes. They just about have to be, I reckon, for nobody could live on the wages they make, and that's the only other way of making money open to them.'

It should perhaps be mentioned that there are undoubtedly very many mill families in Huntsville to whom these things just described do not apply, but is also true that there is a large group of workers to whom the conditions do apply, and Ruby Bates and Victoria, with whom this part of the report is concerned, come from this group.

The second series of trials began on 28 March 1933 with Haywood Patterson in the dock, Thomas Knight Jnr again prosecuting and this time Judge James Horton presiding. Leibowitz now set out to show that the whole process was tainted because in the county there had never been a black man who had sat on a jury. The local view was summed up by the editor of *Scottsboro Progressive Age* when he wrote, 'Only a white man has the sound judgement which is essential for a fair and impartial jury.' Leibowitz knew that realistically there was no chance of his obtaining a black juror who, in any event, would almost certainly have been bullied into submission by the others. What he wanted was a solid ground of appeal. It was during the questioning of a potential black juror, fifty-five-year old John Sandford, a trustee of a Negro school, in an effort to show that he was fit to be called for jury service, that things boiled over. When Knight, asking him if he knew the meaning of 'esteemed', called him 'John', Leibowitz interrupted to say the correct form of address was 'Mr Sandford'. Knight replied he was not in the habit of doing that. Leibowitz then added for good measure that Knight should stop sticking his fingers in Sandford's eyes. That evening there were threats to lynch Leibowitz as well the Boys, and Knight tried to persuade Leibowitz's wife to go back to New York and safety. She refused. That night crosses were burned outside their lodgings.

Next day Judge Horton warned the courtroom spectators:

> It would be a blot on the men and women of this country, a blot on all of you if you were to let any act of yours mar the course of justice in this or any other case. I trust you will not show by discourtesy or violence anything but a proper regard for law and order. Your fellow-citizens would bow their heads in shame if any act of yours were to interrupt the course of justice.

There may have been no actual violence – all spectators were searched for weapons and one man found with a gun explained he had it 'just in case' – but the threats were still there. While Leibowitz was questioning one prospective juror, another, Fred Morgan, a member of the All Day Singers, a religious sect that believed its members could croon their way to heaven, complained to the court, 'Us jurors in Morgan County are not accustomed to taking the charge from the defendant's lawyer and we don't like it. I never heard the like of the way this man is questioning us white talesmen.'

Once the jury had been selected Leibowitz shredded the evidence of Victoria Price, showing that a boarding house in which she claimed to have stayed the night before her rape was wholly fictitious and the name of the owner had been taken from a character in a serial in the *Saturday Evening Post*. When, somewhat belatedly, Deputy Sheriff Arthur Woodhall gave evidence that he had taken a pocketknife from one of the Boys who told him he had taken it from Price, the prosecutor Thomas Knight began to applaud. Leibowitz moved for a mistrial:

Never in fifteen years of practice have I ever seen anything like this. The chief prosecuting officer for the State of Alabama told me that he intended to give these Negroes a fair trial, yet he jumps up, laughs, and claps his hands at something a witness says.'

Leibowitz's motion was denied. That night there was a Klan meeting at which there were renewed suggestions that Leibowitz should not be allowed to leave town alive. A leaflet 'Kill the Jew from New York' was sold at 50c. a copy. The next day Judge Horton told the court that the National Guard would be expected to shoot demonstrators.

Ruby Bates gave evidence for the defence at the second trial of Haywood Patterson. She had already written to a boyfriend, Earl Streetman, saying she had not been raped and she had gone via Montgomery to New York City. While she was there she visited the modernist preacher Harry Emerson Fosdick at his Riverside Church and he persuaded her to return to Alabama to 'tell the truth'. It probably did not matter, since the jury would have convicted a ham sandwich if the prosecution had asked them do so, but Knight tore her evidence to shreds. She told a string of lies trying to hide details of her past and, to an extent, what had happened before she boarded the train and she was ruthlessly exposed. She was accused of being in league with the communist party and having 'sold out for the gray coat and a gray hat', which she wore during the trial. At the end of her evidence she had to be smuggled away to avoid an irate mob.

A white youth Lester Carter, who had been on the freight, had been found and now he gave evidence that he had spent the night in the Chattanooga hobo jungle with Price and Bates, whom he had earlier met in jail. For his troubles he was derided by Knight as 'That's the prettiest Jew you ever saw – this Carterewsky.'

The final address to the jury by co-prosecutor Wade Wright, another of the All Day Singers, was a passionate attempt to inflame them. 'Show them that Alabama justice cannot be bought and sold with Jew money from New York.' Again,

Leibowitz's motion for a mistrial was denied. Surprisingly the jury was out for twenty-two hours before they laughingly returned the death penalty. Leibowitz lodged another motion, this time to set aside the jury's verdict, and now Horton agreed with him that it was impossible to continue the trials of the other youths in this atmosphere and granted a continuance. Leibowitz returned to New York where in June he heard Judge Horton had indeed granted the motion to set aside the verdict against Haywood Patterson.

In his written judgement Horton considered the medical evidence in particular, pointing out there was nothing to corroborate Victoria Price's claim. Unfortunately he did not, as he might have done, dismiss the case on constitutional grounds. Instead the case was set for a third trial and this time there would be no Judge Horton presiding. At the time it was possible for a judge in Alabama to be elected without any legal qualifications and Judge William Callahan was one. First on trial were to be Haywood Patterson and Clarence Norris.

Between the trials two Negroes in the custody of the sheriff had been lynched in Tuscaloosa cases; another named Royal was lynched in Decatur in August 1933 and a mob visited the Decatur jail to lynch a fourth. Only removal to Huntsville Jail before the mob arrived had saved him.

Leibowitz sent a telegram to President Roosevelt:

> We earnestly ask your good offices to persuade Governor Miller of Alabama to order out sufficient National Guardsmen to provide adequate protection for the nine Scottsboro boys and their attorneys who are to appear at Decatur tomorrow for arraignment of the defendants and for trial Nov. 27.
>
> At the previous trial this Spring, Circuit Judge Horton, presiding, took judicial notice of incipient mob action to lynch defendants and attorneys by ordering soldiers in open court to shoot if necessary to preserve the peace. Shortly after the trial, Judge Horton, who has since been supplanted, adjourned court on his own motion because of the temper of citizens.

Situation now infinitely more tense. Have affidavits naming many persons in Decatur and neighboring towns who have openly voiced intention of 'getting the niggers and their attorneys'.

Editorials today in Birmingham *Age*, *Herald* and *Post* show their appreciation of imminence of danger and urge officials to call out militia. Despite this situation, the Governor has rejected a plea for State troops to guard prisoners and attorneys. The probability of massacre of defendants and attorneys is extremely grave. We urge your intervention.

None came.

Judge Callahan's mission was twofold: to obtain the convictions of the defendants and to do so as cheaply as possible. The trial was costing $1,200 a day and that was several hundred dollars too much. Leibowitz and the defendants may have had a difficult time with Horton; now they faced a hostile Callahan. No, he would not allow evidence to show Victoria Price had been convicted of fornication, nor that she and Ruby Bates had been in a hobo jungle the night before the train ride. Objections were overruled and when Leibowitz complained that Price was looking at Thomas Knight for help with her answers he was rebuked for 'daring to insinuate such a thing'. The final blow came when the All Day crooner Wade Wright told the jury, 'If you let this here nigger go it won't be safe for your mother, wife or sweetheart to walk the streets of the South.' When Leibowitz objected Wright seemingly did not understand, telling the judge, 'I ain't said nothing wrong. Your Honor knows I always made the same speech in every nigger rape case.'

What Leibowitz had managed to establish was that the jury rolls had been tampered with to make it appear that Negroes could be called as jurors, and this is what saved Patterson and Norris on this occasion. They had been again convicted and sentenced to death and the Alabama Supreme Court had found there was no evidence their constitutional rights had been violated but, in July 1935, the Supreme Court of the United States reversed Norris's conviction and with it that of

Patterson. It was back to square one and in November 1935 a Jackson County Grand Jury re-indicted the defendants. The next month the Scottsboro Defense Committee (SDC) was formed and took over the defence of the boys from the ILD.

Leibowitz had other troubles. First, two detectives employed by the ILD had been charged with attempting to bribe Victoria Price. Secondly, the ILD was trying to oust him; he was not making enough effort on behalf of the underprivileged in general and the Boys were encouraged to dismiss him. There had been a third problem when in January 1936 another of the Boys, Ozie Powell, had stabbed Deputy Sheriff Blalock in what the authorities alleged was an escape attempt. Powell, who said he believed Blalock and other deputies were going to kill him, was shot in the head. Both he and Blalock survived. Now Leibowitz took something of a back seat, directing the action but leaving most of the advocacy to Southern lawyers.

At the end of the year Thomas Knight visited Leibowitz in an effort to find a compromise. Leibowitz suggested they should receive five years for assaults on the white youths on the train, something which would amount to time served but, back in Alabama, Judge Callahan would have none of it.

In January 1937 the Alabama Supreme Court affirmed Patterson's fourth conviction but by July that year it was time for a compromise. The trials were costing the state not only in monetary terms but also in adverse publicity. Norris had been sentenced to death after a third trial; Andy Wright received ninety-nine years; Charlie Weems received seventy-five years. Powell pleaded guilty to assaulting the deputy sheriff and drew twenty. Thomas Knight had become a judge and now the new prosecutor Thomas Lawson announced that the state had decided to drop the charges against Willie Roberson, Olen Montgomery, Eugene Williams and Roy Wright. But first there had to be some explanation of why a few years earlier they were enthusiastically sending the youths to the electric chair. There was, Lawson said, no doubt in his and the other lawyers' minds that those already convicted were guilty. Victoria Price's evidence had been '. . . corroborated by reputable witnesses so as in our opinion to convince any fair-minded man that these defendants did participate in throwing these white boys off the gondola car and raping her.'

In fact there had been considerable doubt in the minds of the prosecutors. In a closed-door session Price had been told that if she changed her evidence she would not be prosecuted for perjury, but she had refused.

Now for those Lawson was seeking to exculpate: Montgomery had told 'a plausible story' and was nearly blind. He had stuck to his story and it was possible that Price was mistaken in her identification. Roberson had also told 'a plausible story'. He was suffering from venereal disease and Dr Bridges thought not only would it have been very painful for him to have had sex but his condition would make it unlikely he would wish to. The other boys, Roy Wright and Eugene Williams, had certainly been on the boxcar but they had been twelve and thirteen respectively and the state had decided the six-and-a-half years they had served was sufficient. The four were smuggled out of town by Leibowitz and taken to Cincinnati to a storming welcome.

In July 1938, six months after Alabama's Supreme Court affirmed Norris's death sentence, Governor Bibb Graves did commute it to one of life imprisonment. Overall, as the years went by efforts to obtain early parole for the remaining youths failed, and it was not until November 1943 that Charlie Weems was paroled. He had done his sentence the hard way. Weems complained about being 'half fed' and said he spent a lot of time thinking about 'the ladies out in the world and I'm shut in here'. In 1934, he had been beaten and tear-gassed, causing permanent eye injuries, for reading Communist literature that had been sent to him. In 1937, he contracted tuberculosis. The next year he was stabbed by a prison guard who had mistaken him for his intended target, Andy Wright. Weems later took a job at a laundry in Atlanta.

Two months after Weems' release, Clarence Norris and Andy Wright were also paroled with a condition they remained in Montgomery. In September 1944 they broke their parole and left the state, but Norris was captured two months later.

In June 1946 Ozie Powell was paroled and went to live in

Georgia and assumed his brother's identity. In the September
Clarence Norris was paroled a second time. It was something
of a revolving door because in October that year Andy Wright
was recaptured and returned to prison. Again, Norris broke
his parole, leaving the state and going to work as a labourer
in Cleveland before moving to New York where in 1956
Leibowitz found him a job as a dishwasher. Over the years a
full-scale campaign for his pardon was mounted, and in 1976
Norris received it from Governor George Wallace. He died in
1989 aged seventy-six. He had been suffering from
Alzheimer's disease.

After Wright was first paroled in January 1944 he had
married a woman from Mobile later that year. He took a job
driving a grocery delivery truck, which he held for two years
before he left Alabama in violation of his parole. He was
arrested and for the next four years was in and out of the
Alabama prison system. The last Scottsboro Boy to be freed,
he finally left Kilby Prison on 6 June 1950. He moved to New
York, living in Albany and New York City, and the next year he
was accused of raping a thirteen-year-old girl. He had been
dating both the girl and her mother. He was acquitted by an
all-white jury.

Of the men against whom charges were finally dropped,
during his six years in jail, Olen Montgomery, who was severely
nearsighted in both eyes and nearly blind in one, wrote
frequent letters to his supporters asking for such things as six-
string guitars, hoping to become 'the Blues King' after his
release, and money to buy a night with a woman.

After his release in 1937, he said that he wanted to be a
lawyer or musician. Despite the assistance of the Scottsboro
Defense Committee, however, none of his career dreams was
realised. Montgomery bought a saxophone, then a guitar, and
practised as much as possible. He loathed most of the manual
job opportunities – dishwasher, porter, labourer – he was
offered, believing they were just getting in the way of his
musical career. He did agree to tour the country with Roy
Wright, who had been paroled in 1950, for the Defense
Committee and spoke at a number of Scottsboro Defense

Committee-arranged meetings. Over the years he bounced
back and forth between New York City and Georgia, drinking
heavily, and rarely keeping a job for more than a few months
until, in the 1960s, he settled for good in Georgia.

On his release, Roy Wright told Samuel Leibowitz that he
wanted to be a lawyer or a teacher. The dancer and actor Bill
'Bojangles' Robinson paid for him to attend vocational school
and, after going on a national tour for the SDC, he served in
the army, married, and took a job with the merchant marines.
In 1959, after returning from an extended stay at sea, Wright
became convinced that his wife had been unfaithful. He shot
and killed her and then himself.

In July 1948 Haywood Patterson escaped from Kilby. He
and other inmates were working on a prison farm when he
took off, running through tall rows of corn, then out into the
woods. Cornered in a creek by three dogs, he drowned two of
them. The third got away. He made it to Atlanta and then back
home to Chattanooga. Eventually he made his way to the
home of his sister in Detroit, Michigan. There, in 1950, with
Earl Conrad he wrote a book, *Scottsboro Boy*. When in June
that year Patterson was found in Detroit by the FBI, the
Governor of Michigan refused to extradite him. Five months
later he was charged with the murder of a man in a bar-room
fight. He did not help himself. His first defence was that he was
not in the bar, his second that he was in the bar selling copies
of his book and took no part in the fight. The third version was
self-defence. Convicted of manslaughter, he was sentenced to
six to fifteen years. Suffering from cancer, he died in August
1952 at the age of thirty-nine. Clarence Norris was pardoned
in 1976. He died in 1989.

It was hoped that Eugene Williams would enter the Baptist
Church but there is no record that he did so. Instead, after a
brief entertainment career he moved to St Louis where a relative helped him adjust to a relatively stable life.

In 1977 Victoria Price lost an action for defamation against
the National Broadcasting Company over her depiction in the
film, *Judge Horton and the Scottsboro Boys*. She died in 1982.
Overall the shy and intimidated Ruby Bates behaved very

much better. She joined the ILD making speeches on behalf of the Boys and apologizing for the damage she had done. She also spouted a good deal of the party line, saying she had been 'intimidated by the ruling class of Scottsboro'. She married Elmer Schutt in Washington State and changed her name to Lucille. She returned to Alabama in the 1960s and died in October 1976 aged sixty-three, two days after Norris was granted parole.

Labelled a 'nigger lover', Judge Horton was defeated in a re-election campaign two years after the case. He died a broken man five years later. Leibowitz went on to have a glamorous legal career in New York before being appointed to the bench.

On 19 April 2013 Alabama Governor Robert Bentley signed a pardon exonerating all nine Scottsboro Boys. On 21 November 2013, Alabama's parole board voted to grant post-humous pardons to them all.

The Scooba Three

Three years after the Scottsboro Boys were first convicted came another civil rights landmark case, this time in Scooba, Mississippi. On 30 March 1934, unmarried, white, sixty-year-old cotton farmer Raymond Stuart was found dying in the living room of his farmhouse. A lamp had been smashed and part of his face and shoulder had been burned. His head seemed to have been struck with an axe-like instrument. 'Beaten to Pulp' headlined the local paper. The motive was thought to have been robbery; the suspects were any black persons who had been in the neighbourhood.

One witness Henry Wallace recalled:

> The white men all got together in a kind of vigilante group and went right through the community going to black men's houses and taking them out and trying to make them talk. At the time they were drag[ging] them out they didn't even know Mr Raymond Stuart was dead.

In the 1930s DeKalb, around 150 miles from Scottsboro, in Kemper County, known as Bloody Kemper, was a centre for lynching black suspects at a rate of twice the remainder of the state. In September 1930 a double lynching had taken place in an effort to obtain confessions from two black men, 'Pig' Lockett and Holly White, suspected of robbing a white couple. When they were taken from DeKalb Jail to Scooba, three miles away, for a preliminary hearing, a lynch mob comprising leading local citizens captured them and tied them to the branches of two trees, which were allowed to spring up. One died before he confessed and the other was hanged shortly after he did. Coffins were kindly provided by a churchgoing member of the mob who thought it would be sacrilegious not to have given the men a decent burial.

It was therefore with some pride among members of the Scooba community that when the principal suspects in the Stuart murder case, Ed Brown, one of his tenant farmers, Henry Shields and Arthur 'Yank' Ellington were arrested, they were not lynched on the way to the county jail in Meridian some thirty miles away. Nor were they pulled out of the jail and hanged. Deputies had guarded them with tear gas bombs, machine guns and sawn-off shotguns. The sheriff had been prepared to call in the National Guard, but no attack came.

A week later, on 5 April, represented by John A. Clark and three other local lawyers, all appointed by Judge J. I. Sturdivant, the men went on trial for Stuart's murder. Crowds who had come to Stuart's house had hopelessly contaminated the crime scene and the only evidence against the men was confessions they had made to the chief of police B. B. Hyde and other officers in the gaol.

When he was shown a bloodstained jumper and a pair of overalls said to have been found at his home with strands of hair similar in colour to those of Stuart, Shields was said to 'have broken down and implicated Brown', who in turn admitted his part in the robbery and murder. Now they admitted that the dying Stuart had been thrown into the cotton-seed room of his house and they had attempted to burn the body. The local newspaper thought that if convicted the earliest they could be hanged was 11 May. The trial lasted just over a day and, after a retirement of less than half an hour, an all-white jury found the trio guilty.

The *Meridian Star* was thoroughly pleased, both with the result and the way the trial had been conducted by Judge Sturdivant. The defence lawyers came in for praise and there was a particular nod towards District Attorney John Stennis who had conducted the prosecution with a 'character that added to the brilliant distinction that he has already won during his administration of the office'.

Overall the local white population was quite pleased with itself. At a time when Mississippi led the country in the lynching of blacks, largely following allegations of assaults on white women – six in 1934 alone – another had been avoided and justice had been seen to be done. Gallows were built and the prisoners, who reportedly spent their time praying and singing gospel songs, became something of a tourist attraction.

But what the local paper had not reported was how the men had come to make their confessions. In fact, the only evidence against them had been beaten out of them. Ed Brown told the court that he had confessed after Deputy Sheriff Cliff Dial '. . . told me that he had heard I had killed Mr Raymond. I said: "I declare I didn't kill Mr Raymond." He said, "Come on in here and pull your clothes off, I going to get you." They bent me over a chair and I had to say yes, I couldn't help it.'

Asked by defence lawyer Clark if that was the reason why they told Sheriff Adcock of Meridian that they killed Raymond Stuart, Brown replied, 'Yes, sir, that is the reason. If you could see the places [on his body as a result of the beating] you would say a train didn't move any lighter.'

Ellington told the jury, 'They got me out of bed and carried me to Mr Raymond's house. They tied me up there with my hands to a tree and whipped me. They tied me and whipped me good. Then they hung me, they pulled me up twice.'

Deputy Sheriff Dial was quite open about the whipping. He thought it was, 'Not much for a Negro, not as much as I would have done if it was left to me.'

At first Clark had been convinced the trio were guilty of Stuart's murder, and it was only after the details of the beatings were admitted by the witnesses that he began to have some sympathy for his clients. He had not been well and would admit later that he was 'simply going through the form of a trial'. Now he took up their cause with vigour. First, he declined any payment from the court. In fact he had received nothing because although the defending lawyers were entitled to $25 a client, Judge Sturdivant had feared reprisals from the locals and had refused to authorize it. Clark did, however, receive a small sum from the National Association for the Advancement of Coloured People (NAACP).

Clark and his wife, both of whom had political ambitions, were warned that these would be in jeopardy if he continued with the case but, nevertheless, he took it to the Mississippi Supreme Court where he obtained a partial success. Although the appeal was dismissed, Justice Anderson dissented, holding, 'Without the confession the court would have been forced to direct a verdict of not guilty. Yet the appellants were driven to confess their guilt by the most brutal and unmerciful whippings. The Third Degree or its equivalent is still in use.'

Clark may have avoided the crosses burned before Sam Leibowitz's lodgings in the Scottsboro case but it broke his health and he was now in a state of both mental and physical collapse. He wrote again to the NAACP and when the secretary Walter White and the board discussed the case, the chairman Louis Wright noted that 'anytime a white lawyer in Mississippi says things are bad and he needs help, then we have to help'.

On 12 December 1937, John Clark's wife wrote to the noted civil rights lawyer Arthur Garfield Hays: 'He has been very unjustly criticized and has worried quite a bit because of the lack of help he has had in the hard fight he has waged. He has fought a good fight and kept the faith. I have encouraged him in every way possible.'

Clark handed the case over to his friend Earl Brewer, the one-time Governor. Early in his career Brewer had represented the widow of Jonathan 'Casey' Jones, the legendary railroad engineer killed trying to stop the Cannonball Express crashing into a stationary train, and obtained for her an out-of-court settlement with the Illinois Central Railroad. It was Brewer who, financed by the NAACP, took the men's case to the United States Supreme Court which, in the celebrated decision *Brown v Mississippi*, quashed the convictions and sent the case back for a retrial.

If the trio thought that was the end of their troubles they were mistaken. It had been hoped and even anticipated that a *nolle prosequi*, staying the proceedings, would be entered. This would have meant their release but would also have allowed the state to bring further proceedings if more evidence came to light. However, there was to be no *nolle prosequi*. For two years Brown, Shields and Ellington were held in the prison expecting a court date that was never decided upon. Finally, on 28 November 1936, the men agreed to a plea bargain, pleading *nolo contendere* to manslaughter, and their nightmare was finally over. They agreed to seven-and-a-half years for Brown, two-and-a-half years for Shields and six months for Ellington.

The Jackson *Daily Clarion-Ledger*, by no means convinced of their innocence, pointed out that Brown, Shields and Ellington 'have stood within the grim shadow of the hangman's scaffold several times since the dark and dreary night in March 1934 that Raymond (Stuart) was bludgeoned to his death.' The editorial continued:

> The results may seem illogical to many citizens who are not lawyers. The three Negroes either were guilty of murder deserving the death sentence, or they were innocent of all crime ... A 'compromise' ends the notorious and costly 'Kemper county' case which gave Mississippi so much undesirable national notoriety ... It is closed, but its lesson should be long remembered by all Mississippi law officers and prosecutors. The lesson is that the use of torture or coercion to obtain confessions not only violates the rights of the accused persons but also jeopardizes Justice.

The case did John Stennis, the prosecutor, no harm at all. He later served forty-two years as a United States senator, running for office in Mississippi thirteen times and never losing.

CHAPTER 7

Incompetent Lawyers

James Fisher; Richard Glossip; Russell Tucker; Reginald Love Powell; Ann Marie Boodram

James Fisher; Richard Glossip; Russell Tucker; Reginald Love Powell; Ann Marie Boodram

Those who deal with the initial trial in death penalty cases know that if their client is convicted, then ten or twenty years down the line when all other appeals are exhausted, they will be accused of incompetence and this is the ground of appeal of last resort. Usually this is a routine tactic, but over the years there have been some spectacular and irreversible miscarriages of justice caused by the defence lawyers' incompetence or sheer disregard for their clients.

High on the list would be former Oklahoma's State Senator Melvin Porter, whose defence of James Fisher for the 1982 murder of Terry Neal was described by the Tenth District Court as 'grossly inept'.

Neal, who was found dead in his apartment in downtown Oklahoma City on 12 December 1982, had been stabbed in the neck with a broken bottle. The police learned that Neal was a bisexual who occasionally solicited sex from men in a certain area of the city. Their investigation then led to the arrest of Fadjo Johnson, a baby-faced teenager who was seen getting into a car with Neal on the night of the killing, and it was he who was initially charged with the murder.

Before long, however, the prosecution dropped the charges and Johnson became their key witness, claiming that a man named 'James' had actually committed the murder. On this information, the police began investigating Fisher, who had been drifting around the South at the time of the murder. Fisher was arrested on 10 January 1983, in Buffalo, New York, and was extradited to Oklahoma for trial on the charge of first-degree murder.

The prosecution relied almost exclusively on Johnson's evidence in convicting Fisher. His evidence was that he met Fisher on the night of 11 December 1982, in an area of downtown Oklahoma City that was known to be frequented by homosexual prostitutes. There, Neal picked up both of them and took them back to his apartment. Johnson claimed that he went into another room while Fisher and Neal had sex, but he came back in time to see Fisher hit Neal on the head with a wine bottle and stabbed him several times in the neck with the broken end of it. Johnson's evidence was that Fisher then told him to take Neal's television, which they sold before Fisher dropped Johnson off near his house. The only other incriminating evidence against Fisher came from a Buffalo Police detective, who said that when Fisher was arrested he admitted that he had hit 'someone named Terry' over the head with a wine bottle, but had not killed him. The state had no physical or forensic evidence that linked Fisher to the crime.

Although the case basically rested on Fisher's word against that of Johnson, Fisher's lawyer, Porter, indicated several times that he believed what Johnson was saying, and even sympathized with him for having had to witness such a horrible crime. Although Johnson admitted in his direct evidence that he had earlier been charged with the murder, Porter failed to drive home this admission on cross-examination. Later, when a police officer denied that Johnson had ever been charged with the murder, Porter did not bother to challenge him. He did not even ask Johnson whether he had agreed to give evidence in exchange for the state dropping the charges. A guilty verdict duly followed, and Porter did even less during the sentencing phase when he only spoke nine words. 'Waive. Rest. Judge, I object to that. We waive.' Worse, Porter was hopelessly prejudiced against his client, later saying he had allowed his 'personal feelings' towards Fisher to affect his representation. 'At the time,' said Porter, 'I thought homosexuals were among the worst people in the world.'

The Oklahoma Court of Criminal Appeals was 'deeply disturbed by defense counsel's lack of participation and advocacy during the sentencing stage,' but not disturbed enough to reverse the conviction or sentence. It rejected a claim of ineffective assistance of counsel, holding that despite the incompetent representation, there was not a reasonable probability that without the errors by the lawyer the result of the proceedings would have been different. It did, however, allow the appeal on other grounds.

Things were no better for Fisher at his retrial. The evidence was not strong, but this time he received possibly even less help from his new lawyer, Johnny Albert, who was drinking heavily and abusing cocaine and who, said his colleagues, was 'neglectful of his cases', and spent 'less time working on cases and more time drinking beer and playing pool during work hours'. Albert missed court appearances and avoided clients. He also physically threatened Fisher at a pretrial hearing and, as a result, Fisher refused to attend his own trial. He was again convicted and once more sentenced to death. Four years later, the Oklahoma Court of Criminal Appeals held that Fisher had again been denied his right to counsel. This time it vacated the conviction because the prosecution's case against Fisher had not been strong. Prosecutors agreed to his release in July 2010, provided that he leave Oklahoma forever. He had served a mere twenty-six years.

Nor was Richard Glossip helped by his counsel when he went on trial for the January 1997 murder of motel owner Barry Van Treese. Glossip was the manager of Van Treese's Best Budget motel in Oklahoma City where he lived with his girlfriend D-Anna Wood. The motel was in a poor state of repair and he employed a handyman, the emotionally dependent Justin Sneed, to do maintenance work in return for his board and lodging. There were also serious shortfalls in the accounts, and the state's case was that when Van Treese came to the motel to undertake an audit Glossip, afraid he would lose his job, persuaded Sneed to kill him. Sneed pleaded guilty

and was given life without parole. He then gave evidence
against Glossip, who was convicted.

Four years later Glossip's conviction and death sentence
were overturned because his trial counsel's conduct was 'so
ineffective that we have no confidence that a reliable adver-
sarial proceeding took place'.

Unfortunately Glossip was reconvicted and resentenced to
death at a second trial and among his grounds of appeal he
cited the incompetence of his new counsel. This time, in 2007,
the court dismissed his allegations and his appeal in general,
saying that while some of the trial decisions might be questioned it would not say there had been incompetence. In July
2013 the 10th U.S. Circuit Court of Appeals ruled unanimously against Glossip's claim that he did not receive a fair
trial. Since then he has fought a battle to stay his execution, at
one point scheduled for November 2014 but subsequently
deferred to await another round of appeals.

On his website Glossip claimed:

> I never had a chance at a fair trial. If you don't have money
> and can't afford a good attorney you don't stand a chance.
> But even after all that I have never given up hope. My first
> attorney said he had a deal with the judge that would save
> me from the death penalty, but I would have to confess to
> the crime. I could not do that, because I didn't commit the
> crime, and I would be lying. The [Second] Appeals Court
> turned me down, after a split decision, because they said
> that while the problems with the trial were real, they were
> not bad enough.

Then there is the case of the North Carolina lawyer who
disliked his client Russell W. Tucker, convicted of shooting a
security guard and a taxi driver in a botched robbery, so much
he could not bring himself to file an appeal against the conviction and imposition of the death penalty on the man. 'I decided
that Mr Tucker deserved to die, and I would not do anything
to prevent his execution,' said Greensboro lawyer David B.
Smith. Appointed to post-trial representation of Tucker in

February 1998, Smith and another Greensboro lawyer went to
see Tucker on death row in Raleigh. 'At the end of the visit,'
Smith said in an affidavit in support of an application for an
appeal against sentence out of time, 'I decided that I did not
like Mr Tucker.'

He continued:

> My own beliefs against capital punishment were severely
> challenged as I read the trial transcripts in preparation
> for post-conviction relief . . . I shared with my therapist
> my feelings and the consequences of my inaction, but I
> could not bring myself to act in a professional and
> responsible manner.

Fortunately in Tucker's case the Supreme Court later vacated
the execution.

In fairness to Smith he was only following a century-old
precedent. When Maryland lawyer Senator Reverdy Johnson
joined in the defence of Mary Surratt, charged in 1865 with
conspiracy following the assassination of Abraham Lincoln, he
first announced:

> I am here to do whatever the evidence will justify me in
> protecting this lady from the charge upon which she is
> being tried for her life. I am here detesting from the bottom
> of my heart everyone concerned in this nefarious plot . . .
> And I am not here to protect any one, whom, when the
> evidence is offered, I shall deem to be guilty, even her.

It was not a ringing endorsement of his client and he carried
out his threat a few days later when he left the courtroom,
abandoning his client to what was ultimately her hanging.

Kansas City public defender Mary Ann Marxkors, assigned
to the case of Reginald Love Powell, became so emotionally
involved with him that she completely failed to organize the
defence of the nineteen-year-old man who had an IQ of sixty-
five. Testing also indicated that Powell suffered from an
Auditory Selective Attention Disorder. In March 1988 he was

convicted of stabbing two men with a butterfly knife while mugging them for a take of $3 and a packet of cigarettes. She had persuaded him to plead not guilty even though the offered plea bargain would have saved him from the death penalty. Nor did she put him on the witness stand when it might have become clear that he had a serious mental impairment.

Ms Marxkors, who had been in therapy for fifteen years, accepted she had written Powell a series of letters described as 'varying in tone from a junior High School romance to the smutty and obscene things you read about in *Penthouse*'. She had also had sex with him on three occasions in his cell. Later she told a reporter, 'It was my first death penalty case and I spent a lot of time with him to gain his trust. I came to know a lot about where he came from, what his life had been. Yet, he was always caring to me.'

The Mississippi Appeal Court, which could never be described as lily-livered, ruled this was no reason why he should be reprieved and Ms Marxkors remained in touch with the unfortunate Powell during his time on death row in Potoski where he was eventually executed. 'Am I in love with him? Part of me wants to think I'm not,' she told a reporter from the *Reading Eagle* shortly before Powell's execution in February 1998.

She was warned by her Bar association that her conduct was 'inappropriate', but was neither suspended nor disbarred. She later gave up the law and studied for a master's degree in social work. 'Love and emotions can be so powerful,' she said defending her conduct. 'Anyone can be blinded. The initial physical part was very emotional and driven by vulnerability and this shared thing. It certainly wasn't anything I ever planned.'

Of course negligence and incompetence are not confined to any one jurisdiction. In England, however, it is very difficult to mount a successful appeal against poor defence. Indeed, the courts will twist and turn in an effort to avoid criticism of counsel. In Trinidad, Ann Marie Boodram was extremely unfortunate on a 1998 retrial for the murder of her husband Alston by feeding him curried chicken laced with paraquat in January 1989. It was only near its end that her counsel realized this was the second time around; even then he did not attempt to obtain a transcript of the first hearing. She had made a confession only, she alleged, after a police inspector had raped her. At the first trial the judge had excluded the confession but unfortunately had not given his reasons. Convicted again and sentenced to death for a second time, in her case however the Privy Council ruled her counsel's conduct was so extreme that the conviction was quashed.

> In the present case Mr Sawh's multiple failures, and in particular his extraordinary failure when he became aware on 17th February 1998 that he was engaged on a retrial, to enquire into what happened at the first trial, revealed either gross incompetence or a cynical dereliction of the most elementary professional duties . . . it is the worst case of the failure of counsel to carry out his duties in a criminal case that their Lordships have come across. The breaches are of such a fundamental nature that the conclusion must be that the defendant was deprived of due process . . . The conclusion must be in this exceptional case the defendant did not have a fair trial.

The Privy Council ruled that since she had been on death row for seven years a retrial would be inappropriate.

CHAPTER 8

The Power of the Press

Joseph Majczek

Dr Sam Sheppard

Joseph Majczek

It was 11° below zero on 9 December 1932 in Chicago's southwest side near the stockyards, when twenty-nine-year veteran Traffic Police Officer William D. Lundy went off duty in mid-afternoon and into Vera Walush's speakeasy, where he was a regular visitor. He went through into the dark kitchen in the rear, where he stood beside the coal range. A trucker John Zagata came in and, as Walush herself poured them each a shot of moonshine whisky, two gunmen appeared in the kitchen entrance. Lundy tackled one of them and the other shot him six times in the back, killing him. The men took money from the till and escaped in a car bearing Ohio plates.

As well as a desire to revenge a colleague there is always press and public pressure to solve a police officer's murder, but there were additional reasons why it was particularly strong in Lundy's case. First, during the month he was killed there were another five unsolved murders in Chicago. Second, the Century of Progress exposition, intended as a sign that the city was now out of the Depression, was scheduled to open the next spring. As a result, action was demanded from Mayor Anton Cermak, who had been elected in the previous year on a promise to clean up the city's crime. After meeting with a delegation of businessmen, he called a press conference and with the police superintendent at his side, announced, 'A war on crime.'* And there was no

---

* Ironically on 15 February 1933, Mayor Anton Cermak was shot in the lung and seriously wounded while shaking hands with President-elect

better place to start than clearing up the murder of a policeman, albeit an off-duty one who was in a blind pig.

At first Walush told police she had no idea who the killers were, but after several hours of questioning she said one of them could have been a man she knew only as Ted. When police discovered that Theodore Marcinkiewicz lived in the neighbourhood he became a prime suspect, but by then he had disappeared. Two weeks after the shooting a local bootlegger was arrested with a case of whisky in his car. In exchange for not being charged, he told police that Marcinkiewicz had been staying with the Majczek family. When police went to the Majczek home on 22 December 1932, there was no Marcinkiewicz and in default they arrested Joseph Majczek, married to Helen and with one young son, Joey. Marcinkiewicz gave himself up the next day and both the men went on trial in November 1933.

Majczek was represented by the mob lawyer, W.W. O'Brien, who had been shot and badly injured in 1926 when mobster Hymie Weiss had been killed in an ambush. To ease the pain from his wounds he had been drinking heavily ever since.

Their convictions rested primarily upon the evidence of Vera Walush, whose occupation for the purposes of the trial was sanitized and throughout she was referred to as the manageress of a 'delicatessen'. At the trial she said she had

---

Franklin D. Roosevelt at Bayfront Park in Miami, Florida. At the time it was thought the gunman Giuseppe Zangara was aiming for Roosevelt but Lillian Cross, a doctor's wife, had hit the gunman's arm with her handbag and spoiled his aim. In addition to Cermak, Zangara hit four other people, one of whom, a woman, also died of her injuries. Zangara told the police that he hated rich and powerful people, but not Roosevelt personally. Cermak died three weeks later.

Another version of the shooting was that Zangara was not a loner but was a contract killer hired by the mob to shoot Cermak, as his promise to clean up Chicago's rampant lawlessness posed a threat to Al Capone and Chicago's organized crime syndicate. Yet a third was that the shooting was to avenge an earlier attempt on the life of mobster Frank Nitti. Zangara was executed in Florida's electric chair on 20 March 1933.

identified Majczek at the first identification parade she had attended on 23 January. Majczek said he had been arrested on the twenty-second and she had failed to pick him out from two earlier line-ups, but the police records showed his arrest to have been on the twenty-third. Walush later positively identified Marcinkiewicz when he surrendered on 23 January.

Two other somewhat doubtful witnesses provided damaging testimony against Marcinkiewicz. Bessie Barro claimed he had told her he was going to rob Walush's speakeasy, while Bruno Uginchus told the jury that after the murder Marcinkiewicz said 'he had a little trouble'. Although neither of these statements related to Majczek, O'Brien failed to object to their admission. He also failed to cross-examine Vera Walush on her initial inability to identify his client.

Both men called alibis. Majczek's brother, another relative and a deliveryman placed him at home at the time of the crime. Four witnesses placed Marcinkiewicz at his home at that precise time, and two others placed him a little later at a neighbourhood saloon where, timewise, he could not have been had he taken part in the robbery.

They were both found guilty but, very surprisingly, were not sentenced to death and received ninety-nine years. O'Brien handled the appeal, in which he did not raise the admissibility of the evidence against his client.

Majczek made the most of his sentence, learning to read and write English. Over the years he wrote a thirty-page account of his arrest, his trial and the failings of his lawyer. He also wrote the remarkable story of how the trial judge Charles P. Molthrop had invited him to his chambers and said he would work to obtain a retrial for him.

In 1940 Helen Majczek divorced her husband and married Ed Bartosiewicz. Several years later they had a daughter.

Then, on 10 October 1944, Majczek's mother, Tilly, who had put the money together working as a charwoman, placed a classified advertisement in the *Chicago Times*:

$5,000 REWARD FOR KILLERS OF OFFICER LUNDY ON DEC. 9, 1932. CALL GRO 1758, 12–7 P.M.

In fact, she had been running the advertisement every year, steadily increasing the reward as her savings grew. This time it was brought to the attention of the city editor Karin Walsh by John J. McPhaul, one of the paper's rewrite men. Walsh then assigned police reporter James McGuire to call the number. By the next day, in what started out as a human interest story, McGuire had seen Majczek's mother.

McGuire later wrote, 'I wrote a story making the 60-year-old scrubwoman the heroine, tossed in a couple of lines from Kipling's "Mother o' Mine", and figured that was that.'

It was not. Instead, next he went in search of John Zagata, the man in the speakeasy at the time of the robbery. Zagata repeated his story that he thought the killers were both much taller than Majczek, adding, 'There was not enough light in that back room to recognize anybody.'

He also said that Judge Molthrop had called him in some days after the verdict and questioned him about the identification. Zagata confirmed the judge saying he was going to get a retrial for the two men.

On 12 October the *Chicago Times* had the story:

Is Mrs. Majczek's battle for Joe's vindication based on anything more than a mother's blind faith in a son? Is there anything in the history of Policeman William D. Lundy's murder or Majczek's trial that might indicate she has sound reasons for believing in her son's innocence?

'The *Times* has undertaken an investigation to determine whether there are any facts – hidden or overlooked – that may be regarded as supporting the mother's contention.

'As a beginning, the *Times* is able to reveal today that Timesmen have obtained corroboration of an astounding statement by Majczek that the trial judge who sentenced him to serve 99 years doubted his guilt.

'The statement was given to the *Times* by James Zagata, coal truckdriver. It is his first public statement on the case since the trial in November 1933, and his first public disclosure that he believes Majczek is innocent.

From then on the *Times* ran a campaign for Majczek's release under the banner 'Is he guilty? Would you convict Joe Majczek?' The paper also reported that Walush had been running a speakeasy rather than a delicatessen and that she had been threatened with arrest if she refused to give evidence against Majczek and Marcinkiewicz. The reason, the paper claimed, that Judge Molthrop had failed to come to his promise to grant the defendants new trials was that he had been warned by prosecutors that granting a new trial would end his career in Democratic politics.

McGuire tracked down Walush in the Polish neighbourhood but she refused to alter her statement of eleven years earlier. However, he found the original arrest slip in a police warehouse. It showed Majczek had indeed been arrested the day before Walush had identified him and gave considerable backing to the allegation that the police had used the time to coax a statement out of her.

In November McGuire arranged for Majczek to take a lie detector test with the expert Leonard Keeler, who reported, 'After careful analysis of this subject's polygrams, it is the opinion of the examiner that he is not guilty of the Vera Walush robbery or the William Lundy murder.'

The next morning the paper's banner headline read 'Lie Detector Clears Joe'. Now the paper hired the well-known lawyer Walker Butler to seek a pardon for him. In addition to the claims that Majczek appeared to have been framed, Butler also developed a substantial body of evidence to show that his trial lawyer, W.W. O'Brien, had been incompetent. The former court bailiff at the trial said he was not surprised, adding that O'Brien had been drunk throughout the proceedings. Butler later said, 'Joe's defence had been so badly botched as to constitute a criminal offence in itself. His counsel failed to take elementary steps that would have been obvious to a first year law student.'

On 15 August 1945, based on Butler's petition, Governor Green granted Majczek a full pardon based on his innocence. Marcinkiewicz, though, did not benefit. A seemingly forgotten man, he remained in prison until, just before Green left office in 1949, he offered to commute Marcinkiewicz's life sentence to seventy-five years, which would have made him eligible for parole in 1958. Marcinkiewicz turned down the offer. He was wise to do so, for he was legally exonerated through a state *habeas corpus* proceeding in 1950.

The Illinois legislature approved special funds to compensate both men for the time they spent in prison – $24,000 for Majczek and $35,000 for Marcinkiewicz. A state legislator who sponsored the $24,000 award now demanded a kickback of 20 per cent. In June 1948, although they remained friends, Helen divorced Ed Bartosiewicz and remarried Majczek. They moved to Oak Lawn, Illinois and had two more sons.

In 1948 20th Century Fox made Majczek's story into the film *Call Northside 777* with James Stewart as McGuire and Lee J. Cobb as the city editor. In 1950 Vera Walush, now Kasulis, sued Fox. Four years later the suit was settled by paying her $25,000 and agreeing never to show the film locally in Chicago or on local television.

In July 1978, coming home from a Walgreen's drugstore, Majczek drove past the intersection of 103rd and Kilbourn Street, killing a young man on a motorcycle. 'It was a very graphic accident that really affected Joe,' wrote his son Jim, saying that afterwards his father was scared he might have to face another trial. Majczek suffered from insomnia and began to have nightmares similar to the ones he had had in jail. He also suffered a mild heart attack. He died in a mental hospital aged seventy-three in 1983. His mother Tilly had died in July 1964. Ted Marcinkiewicz committed suicide in April 1982. He was losing his sight and did not wish to be confined once again in an institution. The real killers of Officer Lundy were never found.

Dr Sam Sheppard

Every lawyer needs a case to bring him to prominence and for F. Lee Bailey it was that of osteopath Dr Sam Sheppard who was convicted of the murder of his wife Marilyn. On 4 July 1954 she was found battered to death in their bedroom at their house in Lake Road, Bay Village, a wealthy suburb of Cleveland.

Sheppard's father had been a general surgeon specializing in osteopathy before founding a clinic in downtown Cleveland. Sheppard went to Cleveland Heights High School before qualifying as a doctor and studying neurosurgery. By 1949 he had joined his father who had set up Bay View Hospital in Bay Village. Sheppard and his family were regarded somewhat as outsiders. For a start he did not join the local medical association. The family had also made an enemy of Dr Sam Gerber, the coroner of Cuyahoga County, who, referring to the clinic, had gone on record as saying, 'I'm going to get them someday.'

In November 1945 he married Marilyn Reese in Los Angeles and they had one son, also named Sam but known as Chip, born two years later. Their marriage deteriorated after that. Apparently she lost interest in sex and was fearful of a second pregnancy. Sheppard began a string of affairs, which, since adultery was a crime in Ohio at the time, if discovered left him vulnerable to prosecution and also to a serious decline in his practice.

On the evening before Independence Day 1954 the

Sheppards dined at home with their friends and neighbours Don and Nancy Ahern. Sam Sheppard had been operating at the Bay View Hospital earlier in the day and after dinner fell asleep on the sofa, apparently something which was not unusual. Marilyn, now four months pregnant again despite her fears, and Nancy watched a film on television. Don Ahern listened to a baseball game on the radio. The Aherns left around midnight, after which, according to Sheppard, Marilyn locked the door to the lakeside entrance. By this time the Sheppards' dog Koko was back in the house.

At 5.45 a.m. Sheppard telephoned his friend John Spencer Houk, Mayor of Bay Village, who lived a hundred yards down the road, saying, 'For God's sake Spen, come quick! I think they've killed Marilyn.' When Houk and his wife Esther arrived they found the front door open. A medical bag and equipment were strewn over the floor and a desk drawer was pulled open. Sheppard was in a chair in his study in pain from a neck injury. His trousers were wet and there was a smudge of blood on them. Upstairs Marilyn was in her single bed, half covered with a sheet and with severe head injuries. There appeared to have been no forcible entry and a later examination of the room found no fingerprints except those of the family. There was no bloodstained weapon and no one had heard Koko bark.

At 6.30 a.m. Sheppard was taken to the family hospital. By 9 a.m., under sedation and being treated for neck injuries, he was questioned by the Coroner, saying:

> I think that she cried or screamed my name once or twice, during which time I ran upstairs, thinking that she might be having a reaction similar to convulsions that she had had in the early days of her pregnancy. I charged into our room and saw a form with a light garment, I believe, at that time grappling with something or someone. During this short period I could hear loud moans or groaning sounds and noises. I was struck down. It seems like I was hit from behind somehow but had grappled this individual from in front or generally in front of me. I was apparently knocked out. The

next thing I knew, I was gathering my senses while coming
to a sitting position next to the bed, my feet toward the hallway . . . I looked at my wife, I believe I took her pulse and
felt that she was gone. I believe that I thereafter instinctively
or subconsciously ran into my youngster's room next door
and somehow determined that he was all right, I am not
sure how I determined this. After that, I thought that I heard
a noise downstairs, seemingly in the front eastern portion of
the house.

On 7 July, in a wheelchair and wearing a neck brace and dark
glasses, he went to his wife's funeral. His lawyer, William
Corrigan, advised him against taking a lie detector test because
he feared the police might manipulate it.

Somehow Sheppard had also incurred the enmity of the
crusading Louis Benson Seltzer, editor of the *Cleveland
Press*. Seltzer, always keen to expose political and police
laxity and corruption, now ran a malign campaign against
him. In what writer Colin Evans described as 'the dreadful
power of a runaway media', on 21 July 1954 a front-page
editorial entitled 'Do It Now, Dr. Gerber' called for a public
inquest. Hours later, Gerber announced that he would hold
one the next day.

It took place in the gymnasium of the local high school.
Gerber refused to allow witnesses to have legal representation
and, when lawyer William Corrigan protested, he was evicted
from the proceedings to great acclaim from the public.
Sheppard gave evidence over an eight-hour period during
which he denied he had committed adultery in California with
a 'Miss X'.

A week later on 28 July the paper ran another front-page
editorial, 'Why Isn't Sam Sheppard in Jail?' which in later
editions was headlined, 'Quit Stalling and Bring Him In!'. The
article continued, 'You can bet your last dollar that the
Sheppard case would have been cleaned up long ago if it had
involved "average people".' Sheppard was described as a liar.
'Still free to go about his business, shielded by his family,
protected by a smart lawyer.' So much for innocent until

proven guilty. Two days later a crowd tried to storm his brother Richard's house where he was staying. That night, Sheppard was arrested.

The trial opened before Judge Edward Blythin at the Common Pleas Court in Cleveland on 18 October 1984. And, with Corrigan keen to keep divorced or separated wives off the jury, selection took ten days. A motion to have the trial moved out of Cleveland to avoid local prejudice was rejected.

During the trial, a popular radio show broadcast a report about a New York City woman who claimed to be Sheppard's mistress and mother of his illegitimate child. Since the jury was not sequestered, two of the jurors admitted to the judge that they had heard the broadcast but Blythin did not dismiss them. From interviews years later, it seems highly likely some jurors were contaminated by the press before the trial, and perhaps during it.

The prosecution's theory was that Sheppard killed his wife because he wanted to be free to remarry and that he had staged the killing as a burglary. Now, Sheppard claimed he had confronted a bushy-haired man whom he chased to the lake shore and with whom he had struggled before being knocked out. Almost all the evidence or lack of it could cut both ways. The prosecution claimed they had found the 'imprint' of a medical instrument on Marilyn's bloodstained pillow but no one could identify what the instrument was. The medical bag might have been emptied by Sheppard or by a burglar looking for drugs. One of Sheppard's T-shirts had been found near the lake, but it bore no bloodstains.

Three witnesses, however, told against him. First, Nancy Ahern said she thought that 'Mrs Sheppard always seemed very much in love with her husband but I was never quite sure about Dr Sam.' Secondly, Mayor John Houk said that Richard Sheppard had asked his brother, 'Sam did you do this?' Richard Sheppard denied it, saying 'I am positive I never said such a thing.' But the damage was there.

It was the third witness who did the most serious harm to the defence. Miss X turned out to be twenty-four-year-old

Susan Hayes, who had been a laboratory technician at Bay View Hospital. The affair had begun in Los Angeles three years after they met. She told the jury, 'He said that he loved his wife very much but not as a wife and was thinking of getting a divorce.'

Sheppard did not come across well in front of the jury. He wore staid suits, white shirts and sober ties throughout the trial and did not give an impression of any warmth. He said he had lied to protect Susan Hayes and not himself. There was, however, some supporting evidence in his favour. First, two witnesses gave evidence that they had seen a suspicious bushy-haired man near Lake Road that evening. Richard Sheppard told the jury that Marilyn had told him Mayor Houk had been pestering her for two years. Backing this was evidence from the Sheppard's maid that the mayor would visit Marilyn in her bedroom when she was alone in the house. There was also evidence that a fragment of tooth found in the bedroom did not come from either of the Sheppards. Footprints of a woman had been found on the beach near the house and under Marilyn's fingernails were a small piece of red leather, wool threads and a chip of nail polish not used by her.

The jury retired at 10 a.m. on 17 December and did not return a verdict until 4 p.m. on 21 December when they found Sheppard not guilty of first-degree murder but guilty of murder in the second degree. He was sentenced to life imprisonment and so began a series of appeals. In January 1955 Corrigan hired eminent criminalist Paul Leland Kirk of the University of California to examine the Sheppard property, and in April that year he produced a 10,000-word report. His conclusion was that that there had been a fourth person in the house that night. The pattern of bloodstains on the walls showed the killer had struck Marilyn with the left hand. Sheppard was right-handed. There was blood on the wardrobe door that did not match that of the Sheppards, and the fragments of teeth on the carpet could not have been as a result of the blows to Marilyn's head. He concluded she had bitten her attacker and there were no bite marks on Sheppard. Kirk was convinced that if Sheppard had been the killer his trousers would have been soaked in blood.

On 10 May Judge Blythin refused to grant a retrial on the basis of Kirk's analysis of the evidence and on 20 July the Ohio Court of Appeal upheld the conviction. It later refused a retrial, praising Kirk's originality and imagination, but saying his report was speculation. On 19 December the United States Supreme Court also upheld the conviction.

Sheppard's family then went to the so-called Court of Last Resort run by the thriller writer Erle Stanley Gardner, creator of Perry Mason. Members of the family took and passed the lie detector test and Sheppard was given permission to take it. But before he did, a Donald Wedler, serving a ten-year sentence for attempted armed robbery, confessed to Marilyn Sheppard's murder. Coroner Gerber and two detectives interviewed him in prison in Florida and denounced the confession as a complete hoax. A lie detector expert from the Court of Last Resort saw Wedler and reported he was telling the truth 'or what he believes to be the truth'. Permission for Sheppard to take the test was promptly revoked and Gardner withdrew from the case.

In 1959 Richard Eberling, who had cleaned windows at the Sheppard home, was arrested when some of his cleaning service customers began complaining that he was stealing from them. Eberling confessed to robbing a number of families. Among the stolen property he had with him at the time was a ring that had once belonged to Marilyn Sheppard. Eberling had, he said, stolen it from her sister-in-law's home.

During his questioning Eberling told officers he had cut his hand in the Sheppards' home days before Mrs. Sheppard's death. The wound, Eberling allegedly said, had dripped blood throughout the house. The officers brought Eberling to the attention of Cuyahoga prosecutors, but this did not fit into their theory and Eberling simply received a suspended sentence for the thefts.

Sheppard's lawyer Corrigan died in August 1961 and a Chicago journalist who had written *The Sheppard Murder Case* approached the young, flamboyant lawyer F. Lee Bailey to take the case. A great champion of the lie detector, Bailey began a campaign to allow Sheppard, who had been refused parole, to take one and unsuccessfully tried to enlist the support of Sheppard's nemesis, editor Louis Seltzer, to support him.

It was not until April 1963 that Bailey petitioned the US District Court – a federal rather than a state body – to reopen the case and fifteen months passed before, on 15 July 1964, Judge Carl Weinman, describing the original trial as a 'mockery of justice' and denouncing the trial judge and the *Cleveland Press,* ordered the release of Sheppard and a retrial. Sheppard was bailed.

Celebrity criminals attract attention and Sheppard had been no exception. He had been in correspondence with the wealthy, German-born Ariane Tebbenjohanns, whose half-sister had married Josef Goebbels, Hitler's minister for propaganda. She had been visiting him in prison and three days after his release he married her. Meanwhile the prosecution appealed Weinman's decision and the US Sixth Court of Appeals overturned the verdict. They did, however, allow Sheppard his freedom pending a further appeal and, on 6 June 1966, the US Supreme Court upheld Weinman's decision.

The prosecution chose to retry Sheppard on the second-degree murder charge and the retrial began on 24 October that year. Bailey did not call Sheppard, who by now was heavily into drugs and alcohol, and his principal witness was forensic scientist Paul Kirk. Before he called Kirk, Bailey had destroyed the evidence of the coroner Sam Gerber who had admitted he had never found, in twelve years' research, a surgical instrument of the type that had made the impression on Marilyn's pillow.

BAILEY: 'Well, now, Dr Gerber, just what kind of surgical instrument do you see here?'
GERBER: 'I'm not sure.'
BAILEY: 'Would it be an instrument you yourself have handled?'
GERBER: 'I don't know if I've handled one or not.'

BAILEY: 'Of course, you have been a surgeon, have you, Doctor?'

GERBER: 'No.'

BAILEY: 'Do you have such an instrument back at your office?'

GERBER: [Shakes head to indicate no.]

BAILEY: 'Have you seen such an instrument in any hospital, or medical supply catalogue, or anywhere else, Dr Gerber?'

GERBER: 'No, not that I can remember.'

BAILEY: 'Tell the jury, Doctor, where you have searched for the instrument during the last twelve years.'

GERBER: 'Oh, I have looked all over the United States.'

BAILEY: 'And you didn't describe this phantom impression as a surgical instrument just to hurt Sam Sheppard's case, did you Doctor? You wouldn't do that, would you?'

GERBER: 'Oh no. Oh no.'

But Gerber had been destroyed and now Bailey also called Eberling to explain how his blood could have been found on all three floors of the Sheppard home.

Bailey made a typically barnstorming speech, saying the prosecution's case was 'ten pounds of hogwash in a five-pound bag'. The jury retired for twelve-and-a-half hours on 16 November before, after five ballots, returning a verdict of not guilty. On the first ballot four members had voted for a guilty verdict. In all he had served twelve years. A week later Sheppard's autobiography *Endure and Conquer* was published.

After his release Sheppard was left owing thousands of dollars to his lawyers and was drinking quantities of vodka. He obtained the return of his medical licence, but in December 1968 a professional negligence suit was settled against the Youngstown Osteopathic Hospital where he had worked, on an undertaking that he resigned. The next year he was divorced by Ariane Tebbenjohanns who claimed mental cruelty, gross neglect and who 'feared for her safety'. After the decree was granted she described him as 'that maniac', saying she had never been happy during their four-year marriage.

Now he turned to small-circuit professional wrestling in places such as the high school Waverley, Ohio, to pay his debts. Sheppard married for a third time in 1969; his bride was Colleen Strickland, his manager's twenty-year-old daughter. He said he had never been happier, but privately he told his friends he wished he was dead. He died following a heart attack in March 1970.

The Sheppard estate has maintained that the murderer was, in fact, the window cleaner Richard Eberling, who was later convicted of killing an elderly widow, Ethel May Durkin, who died after a fall in her home in 1984. Her death was first thought to be an accident until in 1987 a Florida woman told police that she had helped Eberling fake Ethel Durkin's will. Eberling and his long-time companion, Oscar 'Obie' Henderson III, who had inherited the bulk of Durkin's $1.5 million estate, were convicted of second-degree murder and sentenced to life in prison.

In 1988 Eberling was ordered to provide DNA tests and Sheppard's body was exhumed so tests could be made on that. New genetic tests provided 'conclusive evidence' that blood found on Dr Sam Sheppard's trousers and in his home was not his own, pointing toward an intruder. Nor was it Sheppard's blood which had been found in several other spots around the home – including a bloodstain on a wardrobe door less than two feet away from where Marilyn Sheppard's body was discovered. DNA comparison of Eberling's blood with blood found at the murder scene proved to be inconclusive.

In 2000, Sheppard's son, Sam Reese 'Chip' Sheppard, who was seven at the time of his mother's murder, brought an action against the state of Ohio for his father's alleged wrongful imprisonment. The verdict he sought was that his father was innocent and, to obtain it, a higher standard of proof than a mere 'not guilty' was required. After a ten-week trial, a civil jury returned a unanimous verdict that he had failed to prove his father had been wrongfully imprisoned. On 22 February 2002, the Eighth District Court of Appeals ruled unanimously that the civil case should not have gone to the jury, as a wrongful imprisonment claim could be made only by the person actually imprisoned, and not by a family member. On Sheppard's death the claim died with him.

The highly popular 1963 television series *The Fugitive* is said – although denied by its creators – to have been loosely based on the Sheppard case.

CHAPTER 9

Three Who Got Away

John Bodle

Harold Loughans

Tony Mancini

John Bodle

In 1833 James Marsh, a chemist working at the Royal Woolwich Arsenal as an assistant to Michael Faraday, who later discovered electromagnetism, gave evidence in the trial of young John Bodle, accused of poisoning his eighty-one-year-old grandfather George, a retired farmer living at Plumstead, nowadays a south-west London suburb but then in the country. He had, said the prosecution, gone over to his grandfather's home and poured arsenic into the kettle used to make the family's breakfast coffee. At one time John Bodle had run a coffee shop, but when that venture failed he worked on his grandfather's farm from which, for a time, he was banned for an unspecified offence.

On Saturday, 2 November 1833 the whole Bodle family – George, his wife, her deaf and dumb daughter by a previous marriage, a married daughter, Elizabeth Evans and a young servant, Sophia Taylor – experienced vomiting and diarrhoea. They did nothing about it until the evening when they called in a doctor and told him they thought they were suffering from cholera, possibly caused by a toad in the water. The doctor, however, thought they were suffering from arsenic poison served up in their coffee and he prescribed white of eggs as an antidote. They all took it except for George Bodle, who only took a small sip and instead, on the Sunday, drank a pint of beer. Unfortunately he also ordered the kettle should be scrubbed. Before he died on the following Tuesday, holding his stomach in pain, he now said he believed he had been poisoned and knew who had done it.

The next day, his son John, who lived nearby, told magistrates appointed to inquire into the death that he believed his servant Mary Higgins could give information that would be helpful. In turn she told the magistrates that on the Saturday morning she had seen Bodle's grandson, confusingly also named John, sitting by the fire around 6 a.m. when she came down to start her day's work, something she had never seen before. He had then gone over to his grandfather's house and returned an hour and a half later. She also said that on the Saturday evening she had heard young John Bodle tell his mother that he wished his grandfather and father would die on consecutive days so he could have an income of £1,000 a year, and that he would not mind poisoning people he did not like. George Bodle had substantial freehold and leasehold properties, as well as stocks and shares which would pass to his son. George's maid, Sophia Taylor, told how young Bodle had arrived on the Saturday morning at his grandparents' house and had, unusually, taken the kettle out into the yard to fill it for her.

When John Bodle Jnr was questioned he showed Police Constable Morris where he could find two packets of poison. Preservation of evidence was not a priority for Morris, who would later tell the inquest that he had taken the packets of arsenic around various public houses showing them to drinkers, one of whom had rubbed some on his chin. Morris also admitted he had become 'quite intoxicated' and that the packets might have been opened and examined in other taverns. He was later dismissed from the force.

The chemist who supplied Bodle Jnr with the arsenic packets said there was a quantity missing from one of them. Asked why he had bought arsenic, at first Bodle said it was to kill rats but later he admitted using it as a rudimentary treatment for venereal itch, brought into the house, he said, by his father.

The coroner was not pleased with the jury when it returned a verdict of wilful murder. Committing John Bodle Jnr to Maidstone Gaol to await trial, he added, '... and I trust that better success will attend you there than it has here.' *The Times* was particularly supportive of young Bodle and commented that at the funeral wake his father, who effectively had turned his son in, seemed the least concerned of the party.

The defence lawyers did not dispute there had been a poisoning. So far as they were concerned the only question was who had administered it. At the Assizes young Bodle's mother denied he had talked about killing his father and grand-father, and a long statement written by his lawyers was read by Bodle, who was not allowed to give evidence. His lawyers firmly put the blame on his father, who had convictions for malicious damage. The defence also implied he was in a conspiracy with the servant Mary Higgins. It was a view shared by the judge, who asked the jury whether they wanted to hear any more evidence. Three minutes later, to great applause, they acquitted the youth. The following Sunday he attended a service at Plumstead Church where a public thanksgiving for his acquittal was conducted by the vicar.

The judge and jury had it wrong. In February 1844 John Bodle Jnr, now known as James Smyth, was convicted of demanding £30 with menaces by threatening to accuse Thomas Robinson, Lord Abingdon's butler, of an unnatural crime, then a capital offence. He claimed he had been taken by Robinson to a bedroom and had dropped his wallet containing three £5 notes. When the butler refused to pay, Bodle remembered that it was three £10 notes and said if they were not repaid at once he would have to contact Lord Abingdon. Sentenced to twenty years' transportation, while in the hulks he confessed that he alone had poisoned his grandfather. Earlier, Bodle had disappeared after stealing £80 from one of his sisters.

Early writers on the case seem, rather unfairly, to have blamed James Marsh for the failure of the prosecution. He had performed what was then the standard test for detecting ar-senic by passing hydrogen sulphide through the suspect fluid. It has been suggested that by the time the case was heard the sample had deteriorated and that Marsh did not explain his findings simply enough to be understood. The case, however, was not fought on the grounds that George Bodle had not been poisoned, simply whether it was by his son or grandson. Marsh, however, took the criticism personally.

Three years later in 1836 he published the results of his analytical toxicology analysis in *The Edinburgh Philosophical Journal*. Relying on Carl Wilhelm Scheele's 1775 demonstration that zinc and arsenic mixed in an acid solution formed a gas (arsine), and on Johann Daniel Metzger's experiments two years later converting arsenic vapours into a metallic arsenic deposit, Marsh devised a simple apparatus to capture arsenic. So sensitive was the test that it could detect as little arsenic as 1/120 of a grain (0.5 mg). He could now separate 'very minute quantities of arsenic from gruel, soup, porter and other alimentary liquors'. The scrubbing of the Bodle kettle would not have been sufficient to hide the arsenic. One problem with the test, however, was that it was so sensitive, great care had to be taken over possible contamination. For instance the body might have been placed on wood that could have been painted with a green arsenical colouring, and then there was the problem of arsenic in the soil and the copper pots in which potentially poisoned body parts were boiled. Another problem was that the procedure took seven hours to complete. A third was that not everyone applying the test knew how to do so or how to interpret the results.

Harold Loughans

What comes around, goes around. In the early years of finger-prints being accepted as evidence in American courts, juries there were still sceptical, so in May 1911 New York police officer Joseph Faurot gave a demonstration of the art during the trial of the well-known burglar Caesar Cella, then facing a charge of breaking into a hat shop. Cella's defence was an alibi: he had been to the Hippodrome theatre with his wife and then to bed.

Faurot had found and photographed the prints of several dirty fingers on the shop window and identified them as those of Cella from prints he had given in 1907. He enlarged them so the jury could see the points of identification clearly. During Faurot's evidence Judge Rosalsky stopped the case, ordered him from the room and arranged for lawyers and jurors to press their fingers on panes of glass in the courtroom window. One man placed a fingerprint on a glass desktop. When Faurot returned he made the correct identifications and Cella changed his plea to guilty.

Before sentencing him, Rosalsky promised there would be no indictments against his alibi witnesses if Cella would tell the court if he had really committed the crime and how. 'It is most important in the cause of justice and science that you tell the whole truth. It is invaluable to us to know whether the expert testimony given during this trial is correct.'

Cella said the alibi had been partly correct. He and his wife had indeed been to the Hippodrome but later, when she was asleep, he had left their bed to commit the burglary. He received six months. Before his plea seven jurors would have convicted on the basis of his bad record; five would have acquitted because of the strength of his alibi witnesses. 'That is beautifully characteristic of the jury box – conservatism,' commented *The New York Times* on 20 May.

In 1943 a case arose in England in which there was scientific evidence ranged against a defendant who had a perfect alibi. Towards the end of his career the celebrated pathologist Bernard Spilsbury appeared more and more for the defence and, just as when he had been for the prosecution, his charisma and reputation often triumphed over science and indeed even logic. On 28 November 1943 Rose Robinson, who had run the John Barleycorn Public House at 518 Commercial Road, Portsmouth for forty years, was strangled in her bedroom. She was a creature of habit and was known to keep the takings in cash under the eiderdown on her bed, ready to pay the brewery for the beer. That weekend the takings amounted to some £450. Around 10.30 p.m. her barman had heard her put the bolts in place before he walked away from the pub. Her killer had ransacked her room leaving behind a small black button.

A fire-watcher heard breaking glass around 3.30 in the morning and a neighbour, Louise Smitherman, at 514 Commercial Road, reported that she had seen four men in the street and that her own back window and door had been smashed.

A month later police stopped Harold Loughans, who had a deformed right hand missing most of three fingers, when he was trying to sell a pair of new shoes in a café in the Waterloo Road, south London for twenty-five shillings (£1.25). The deformity was the result of an accident some years previously when his hand had been caught in a machine and the tops of his fingers had been ripped away as he tried to get it out. When questioned about where he had obtained the shoes he first of all said that they were a present from his brother and then he told the police, 'I'm wanted for more serious things than this. It's the trapdoor for me now.' First, he admitted a string of burglaries and then that he had killed Rose Robinson. 'It's a relief to get it off my mind,' he told the police. 'I didn't mean to kill the old girl, but you know what it is when a woman screams.'

Later he made a statement, which ended:

> When I got back to London I gave £50 to a young lady and the rest of the money I kept in a suitcase. I told the young lady who I was with that if ever I was arrested she was to take the suitcase and money and go away. She saw me arrested on the 21st December and I gave her the tip to go.
> I do not wish to give any more information about the young lady or the man who drove the car.

Now, he led the police a merry dance changing his story so that it appeared another man had killed the landlady. First, he persuaded the police that if they would take him back to the café he would try to identify his driver and the girl to whom he had given the suitcase and money. Neither appeared at the café nor at the Hero of Waterloo next door. They then took him to a house in Clapham but no one there knew the girl. They arranged that he should attend an identification parade at Brixton Prison to see if he could pick out the man he now said had killed Mrs Robinson, but he failed to make any identification.

Forensic evidence matched the thread on the button found in Mrs Robinson's room to that of Loughans' jacket sleeve. Fibres on one of his boots matched those in a mat beside Mrs Robinson's bed, and a feather similar to feathers in her eiderdown was found on his coat, which had no buttons. Now he said that when he discovered he had lost one he pulled them all off. Pathologist Keith Simpson gave evidence that she had been strangled by a right-handed man who had left a single deep bruise on her throat with a thumb and three lighter bruises from fingers.

In a report of 7 January 1944 Simpson thought, 'Though it [Loughans'] is a deformed hand its dimensions are adequate, the stumps of the index, middle and little fingers are sufficiently long and capable of the stretch necessary to effect the grip described above.'

At committal proceedings, however, Loughans said the police had made up his confession. He now maintained that with his deformed right hand he could not grip with sufficient strength to have strangled Mrs Robinson.

On remand at Winchester Prison, Loughans underwent the usual examination to see whether he was fit to plead and on 21 February Dr Thomas Christie wrote:

> Examination showed he is somewhat below average gener-
> ally in intelligence but he would appear to have developed
> his intelligence in such a way that he is able very quickly to
> exploit any situation to his own advantage. In a peculiarly
> cunning way he will anticipate questions and where they
> are leading.

Cunning he certainly was. On remand he tried to put the blame on a fellow inmate, a deserter George Gaskin, curiously the brother of Louise Smitherman, whose door had been forced the night of the murder. Loughans asked to see the police, telling them about the man. If he was allowed to stand outside Gaskin's cell door and ask a question the response would be such that they would know he was the killer. The police checked Gaskin's alibi and were satisfied he was not involved. Their thought was that local gossip had mentioned his name as a suspect and Loughans had latched on to it.

Loughans also told the police that he could prove he was in Huddersfield in Yorkshire four hours before the murder. He had come out of Parkhurst Prison on the Isle of Wight on 15 October 1943 where he had completed a three-year sentence for housebreaking. He had gone back north but the police could not trace him until early November when he took a job in Halifax. He had, he said, left on the evening train on 28 November for London. Next day he had reported as a convict on licence to New Scotland Yard, telling them where he was staying that night. Whether he was trying it on or merely had the day wrong he certainly did catch the night train and report, but it was on the Saturday, the night before the murder. To pay for his fare he had conned a local Methodist minister out of the money, saying he had tuberculosis and wanted to go to a sanitarium in the south. After visiting Scotland Yard on the Sunday morning he had gone to the Methodist Central Hall at Westminster where he saw Sister Lily Sweet and arranged to come back the next day. He did not. He clearly had come into some money because the police could trace him staying at the Strand Palace Hotel and also at the Winston in Jermyn Street off Piccadilly.

At his trial at Winchester Assizes in March 1944 he produced an alibi that three people had seen him in Warren Street underground station in central London, which was used as an air-raid shelter, on the night of the murder. All were of good character and none apparently knew each other. Edith Hatcher said she remembered seeing Loughans sitting on a bunk talking to her friend Mrs Edith Costas and that was when she saw his deformed hand. He had nursed her baby and she had shown him to a bunk bed near to hers. He had turned in about twenty minutes past midnight. She had to get up during the night and said she saw him asleep just before 3 a.m. He was still asleep at 5.15 a.m.

Rachel Pickering said she remembered asking Loughans, who had a strong Yorkshire accent, if he wanted some cocoa. She had lent him a pillow and pulled it from under his head at 5.45 a.m. when she left the shelter. He was still asleep. There is always the possibility that while an alibi witness may be telling the truth, he or she may have the day wrong, but these witnesses could not be shaken.

Next came James Rycroft, a rail-track mender who confirmed he had seen Loughans that night talking to the three women. He had particularly noticed the man's deformed hand. Confirming the date as a Sunday night, he said that he remembered it because Sunday was the day for relaying track. He was bolstered by William Bull who brought a Record of Work book that showed the only night Rycroft had worked at Warren Street in November was that Sunday.

Faced with the confession on the one hand and this seemingly cast-iron alibi it is not surprising the jury disagreed.

Loughans' retrial took place a fortnight later, this time at the Old Bailey, and with it came a surprise witness for the defence. Sir Bernard Spilsbury was called and said he had examined Loughans. He gave evidence that his right hand was incapable of exerting any pressure. He had had Loughans put his hand round his throat and the stumps had barely touched the skin. They did not even have the power to leave a scratch. Unfortunately for the Crown, on this occasion Keith Simpson was not a good witness, admitting that, given the exigencies of the war, he had not seen Loughans personally and had made his findings from examining a plaster cast of the hand.

It may seem difficult to believe that Loughans could have left the shelter, driven to Portsmouth in the blackout with only slivers of light from the headlights, robbed and killed Rose Robinson and driven back to be in his bunk at daybreak. But what was curious was that the prosecution had already arranged for two officers to make a test drive to see if Loughans could somehow have managed the run. On the night of 20 March, in what were described as worse conditions than those of 28 November, the officers set off from Warren Street in a 12 hp Riley. They went via Purley and arrived in Portsmouth just before 2 a.m., left at half past and were back at Warren Street at 4.35 a.m. This evidence would have severely damaged Loughans' alibi, but for some reason which he did not explain in his memoirs, *A Lance for Liberty*, J. D. Casswell KC for the Crown had decided not to use it in the first trial.

The seemingly bona fide alibi was called again and this time Loughans was fortunate with his judge. Mr Justice Cassells would not allow Casswell to call evidence of the detectives' journey to Portsmouth. Cassells was also one of the first, and few, judges to comment adversely on the general habit of detectives making their notebooks agree word for word, saying, 'It has always appeared remarkable that two police officers not in collaboration were able to produce an identical note of a particular conversation.'

Defended by John Maude, taking time off from prosecuting Helen Duncan in the next court, on 4 April 1944 Loughans was acquitted after the jury had retired for just over an hour.

He was arrested immediately after and tried for an attempted murder and robbery at St Albans where he had tied Helen Lewis, a semi-paralyzed woman, to a chair with wire and kissed her several times. This time he received five years to be followed by a further five years of preventive detention.

It was not the end of the matter. On 18 December 1960 the *People* newspaper published a version of J. D. Casswell's memoirs. In his book he had been careful to say that 'Not for a moment do I wish to impugn the utter and complete vindication of Loughans at the trials', but the article in the *People* was headlined 'This is the Perfect Murder'. According to Loughans he had been in prison when a warder told him he should sue over the article and he wrote to the Labour MP, solicitor Sydney Silverman, who came to see him and took the case on. Now he sued Odhams Press, publishers of the *People*, its editor Renton Campbell and Casswell for libel.

In November 1962, in an application for an adjournment of the libel trial, Neville Faulks appearing for Loughans had told the court, 'The defendants boldly said that it [the article] did not mean that [he was guilty of the murder] but, if it did then, by Jove, he did murder her.' He went on to say that Spilsbury – whom he described as, 'I am Sir Oracle. When I speak, let no dog bark' – had died and Loughans' alibi witnesses could no longer be traced. Faulks wanted to call Dr Francis Camps, who had now seen Loughans' hand, but he was then in South America. For the defence, opposing the application for an adjournment, Gerald Gardiner's position was what was called a 'rolled-up plea'. The paper had accurately set out the facts of the two trials; there was no innuendo implying guilt and they denied anyone reading the accounts would come to the conclusion that the plaintiff should have been convicted. But, if they did, then the paper said yes, he did it. Simpson was available for cross-examination. The case was stood over until January 1963.

So that year Loughans effectively stood trial for the murder of which he had been acquitted; the first time a newspaper had accused a man, acquitted of murder, of being nonetheless guilty. It is probably best not to know where Loughans found the money to pay for his solicitor and his barrister Patrick O'Connor QC. Legal aid was not available for libel actions and in those days solicitors could not take cases on a no-win no-fee basis. By the time the case was heard Loughans was back in custody, and from Brixton Prison, against the advice of the Governor or his assistant and without the knowledge of Silverman, he wrote to the solicitors for the *People* saying he would accept £150 and an apology. They replied saying he could have the £150 but no apology. The defendants then paid £250 into court, which he did not accept.

For eleven days the jury heard evidence of the old murder – with Loughans still protesting his innocence. 'You are asked to try again a murder in the guise of a libel action,' his lawyer complained to the jury. 'A foul lie,' Loughans called the *People* article. Like so many criminals Loughans, now being treated for cancer, was not a good witness, prevaricating, contradicting himself and at times becoming abusive. Simpson was there to give evidence for the defence and this time he bolstered his failure to examine Loughans in person saying one of the reasons he had not done so was that he might have been trapped, 'in the way he trapped Sir Bernard'.

Francis Camps, who had maintained a long-standing personal antipathy towards Keith Simpson – he expressly requested that on his death Simpson should not carry out the post-mortem – gave evidence for Loughans, but even at his best he never carried the aura of Spilsbury and he was obliged to admit Loughans' hand was strong enough to strangle an elderly woman. Harold Harris, a surgeon who had also examined Loughans, accepted that he had a grip of 14 lbs, which twenty years earlier would have been much stronger. He also agreed that Loughans would have had the strength in his right hand to strangle Rose Robinson, but he added, 'I don't think you could strangle with that hand in the way the strangulation was carried out.' The jury found that there had been an implication that Loughans had killed Mrs Robinson and that indeed he had done. Verdict for the defendants.

The case had one further twist. In May 1963 Loughans,

now again out of prison, walked into the newspaper's office to sell his confession to the murder. Spilsbury had been completely fooled by him. Loughans admitted, rather as Cella had done in New York in 1911, that after being seen at the Warren Street air-raid shelter he left, went to Portsmouth and was back before dawn to be seen again in his bed. He wrote a statement with his deformed hand:

> I remember seeing a lot of money around at the John Barleycorn so I stole a jeep that I might rob the place. I was on my own. I got into the pub by the back entrance. I thought I would find the money downstairs. There was none there so I crept up the stairs but I think they must have been rather creaky for when I went into Mrs Robinson's bedroom she was sitting up in bed clutching the bags.

He had driven back to Warren Street and when he realized no one had seen him go or return he thought he had a cast-iron alibi.

The *People* added rather sanctimoniously, 'We gave him a few pounds to help him on his way because it is no part of a newspaper's duty to be vindictive against a dying man.'

But Loughans was still not finished. On 21 October 1963 he received three years at Hertfordshire Quarter Sessions for theft and obtaining goods by false pretences. He had found a vicar's chequebook and with it, in the days before backup debit cards were required, had treated himself to stays in the Hilton Park Lane and the Hyde Park Hotel. He had bought two cars, rented a flat in Chelsea, ordered £1,000 of goods from Harrods and tried to buy a Bentley. He appealed to the Court of Appeal asking to be allowed out for Christmas since this would be his last and he had spent the previous thirty-four Christmases in prison. The appeal was refused on 20 December 1963. He died the next year.

Quite what was the truth will remain a mystery. Loughans must have learned of Rose Robinson's money after his release from Parkhurst and before he went north. Whether he was on his own must be questioned. If Louise Smitherman is correct, she heard four men in the street around the time of the murder. Was there ever a girl to whom he gave the money or was he laying yet another false trail? One thing is certain: aided by Spilsbury, Loughans got away with murder.

Tony Mancini

Sometimes the sheer brilliance of a defending counsel can temporarily blind a jury. Clarence Darrow was able to do this in the Leopold and Loeb case, saving his clients from the electric chair, and one of the great examples in England is that of Norman Birkett KC in his defence of Tony Mancini in what was known as the Brighton Trunk Murder of 1934. Of course, it could be argued that the miscarriage that followed was the failure by the prosecution to put together an indestructible case.

In fact there were three Brighton Trunk Murders. The first was in 1831 when John Holloway, also known as Goldsmith, a smuggler and painter on the Royal Chain Suspension Pier built as a landing stage for packet boats, strangled his wife, nineteen-year-old Celia, with the help of his bigamous wife Ann Kennett. He then wheeled Celia's body in a trunk to Lover's Walk in Preston Park on the outskirts of the town, where he buried the remains and where a thunderstorm uncovered the body within a week.

Holloway had been obliged to marry Celia when she became pregnant and she had been something of an encumbrance. A contemporary report described her as being only four foot three inches, 'in reality almost a dwarf'. Her head was of an extraordinary size in proportion to the rest of her body and her hands turned outwards like the paws of a mole. She was, according to Holloway, sexually very active and had certainly charmed the landlord who, Holloway claimed, he had seen having sex with her in their nightshirts and, worse, that she was apparently enjoying it.

Celia had been to the magistrates and had obtained a maintenance order of two shillings a week. She was again pregnant, as was Ann Kennett. In fairness to Holloway he did everything he could – after his mother suggested it – to exculpate Kennett who had also been arrested. He said the woman in the dock was not the Ann Kennett who had helped him trundle Celia's body to Preston Park. Possibly because the Ann Kennett in the dock was seven months pregnant, the jury acquitted her.

He was convicted at Lewes Assizes and hanged on 16 December 1831 at Horsham Gaol. His body was returned to Brighton where more than 23,000 were said to have gone to the Town Hall to see it on display.

The second trunk murder, which was never solved, was that of an unidentified girl whose body was found in a trunk left at Brighton Station on 6 June 1934. She had possibly died following a botched abortion. It came to light when porter William Joseph Vinnicombe investigated a smell coming from an unclaimed plywood trunk deposited at the left luggage office eleven days earlier. He called the police, and when they opened the trunk they found the dismembered torso of a woman. When other stations were alerted, a suitcase at King's Cross railway station was found to contain the legs. The head and arms were never found. The press named the victim 'The Girl with the Pretty Feet' or simply 'Pretty Feet' because she had recently been to a chiropodist. Sensibly the local chief constable called in Scotland Yard in the form of Chief Inspector Ronald Donaldson.

The post-mortem report prepared by Sir Bernard Spilsbury read:

Internal examination of the torso had not revealed the cause of death; the legs and feet found at King's Cross belonged to the torso; the victim had been well nourished; she had been not younger than twenty-one and not older than twenty-eight, had stood about five feet two inches, and had

weighed roughly eight and a half stones; she was five months
pregnant at the time of death.

Curiously Spilsbury seems to have found nothing to suggest
the girl died following an abortion, but based on what the
police knew about him Donaldson suspected a local doctor
and abortionist Edward Massiah, and asked officers to keep
observation on him. One, drafted from Hove, confronted
Massiah, expecting him 'to come quietly' as the expression
goes. Instead, the doctor wrote a list of names and pushed it
towards the officer. Many of them he recognized: they belonged
to important people in Sussex, national celebrities, members
of the nobility and wealthy and well-placed businessmen. The
doctor explained that these were people who, if he were ever
threatened with court proceedings, would do all in their power
to protect him and ruin his accuser or accusers. According to
crime historian Jonathan Goodman, displaying a touch of
purple prose, '. . . it seemed to the policeman that the sun had
gone in: all of a sudden the consulting room was a place of
sombre shadows . . .'.

The officer did not tell Donaldson of the meeting and the
Chief Inspector only heard of it when he was warned by a
senior officer to back off the investigation. Massiah moved to
London where the following year a young woman died after
visiting his surgery. Spilsbury again performed the autopsy
but it did not lead to charges being brought. 'Only a small
proportion of cases of alleged abortion go any further than the
coroner's court,' said Spilsbury, which in itself must have been
a miscarriage of justice. Nor did the General Medical Council
take action because Massiah remained on the General Medical
Register. His name was only removed when he failed to
re-register in 1952 after his retirement, some years earlier, to
Port of Spain, Trinidad.

The third of the Brighton Trunk Murders was that of the
dancer Violette Kaye, whose body was found in a trunk in a
house in Kemp Street on 15 July 1934. Possibly one of between
nine and sixteen children, Violette was once married to George
Saunders, whom she had met while both were working in the

theatre in Pontypridd. On the music hall stage she had danced first in Miss Watson's Rosebuds then in the Parisian Pinkies and finally as half of Kay & Kaye, Pep, Punch & Personality and had lived with the other half, Tony 'Kay' Fredericks, for three years. After the act and relationship broke up, possibly because of her predilection for drink and morphine, he joined the British Union of Fascists and she drifted into low-level prostitution.

Now aged forty-two, and working the Leicester Square area of London, she met petty criminal, RAF deserter and pimp Cecil Lois England, better known as Jack Notyre and ultimately even better known as Tony Mancini, in Sadie's Café. Mancini, sixteen years her junior, and who had assumed that name to give himself some status in London's criminal milieu then dominated by Italian interests, was not a handsome man. He had a sallow complexion, a cast in one eye and a slight stutter. Nevertheless, he clearly had some fascination for women because over the years he ran a string of prostitutes. As time went on the papers dubbed him 'The Sea-Front Romeo' and 'The Dancing Waiter'.

Violette and Mancini first lived in Bayswater before moving to Brighton where she worked the promenade and at the racecourse. Mancini would absent himself when she brought men back to their lodgings, which they changed twelve times during their first six months in the town.

In May 1934 he decided to apply for a job. Whether this was to give himself some sort of independence rather than rely wholly on the earnings of Violette or that he wanted to get out of the house because of her constant drinking is not clear, but he started work as a waiter-cum-kitchen hand at the Skylark Café at the bottom of West Street, not far from the seafront. Like other cafés in the town the Skylark had been suffering from troublemakers and Mancini was also there as a bouncer. It was in the café that he met young waitress Lizzie Atterill and it was not long before, on 10 May, Violette turned up drunk in the middle of the day to make a scene.

When a fellow worker mentioned it a week later Mancini said Violette had left and gone to work in Paris. Her sister had

intended to come to stay on 14 May but she received a telegram dated 11 May, 'Going abroad. Good job. Sail Sunday.
Will write – Vi.' Her sister's address was misspelled.
Meanwhile, Mancini took Lizzie out dancing and back to the
Park Crescent flat. He also gave her some of Violette's clothes,
saying she had left them behind. Lizzie noticed there were no
sheets or blankets on the bed and Mancini said that was
because he was about to move and had sold them. He was
correct about moving. He had seen an advertisement on a
card in the window of the Skylark for a room to let and had
taken it.

Now, he bought a second-hand trunk in Brighton market
for 7/6d (37p) and, with the help of a friend from the Skylark,
took his belongings to 52 Kemp Street. Although the trunk
stank of cleaning fluid, the elderly couple from whom he
rented do not appear to have noticed but others asked if he
was keeping rabbits. Eventually the landlady complained that
the trunk was oozing fluid and he explained this away saying it
was French polish.

By 14 July the Brighton police noticed that Violette was not
working her usual beat and Mancini told them she had gone
off with another man who could afford to keep her. It was a
perfectly reasonable explanation; allegiances shifted quickly in
the demi-monde and it was accepted.

Then almost immediately came the announcement that the
police were conducting a house-to-house search for the missing parts of the girl in the earlier Trunk Murder. Mancini
panicked and went to stay in a Salvation Army hostel in Poplar
using the name Swintey. On 15 July the police opened the
trunk at Kemp Street and discovered the decomposing remains
of Violette Kaye. Two days later Mancini was arrested near
Blackheath and taken back to Brighton.

Questioned about the body he said he had returned to the
Park Crescent flat and found Violette dead on the bed with a
handkerchief tied around her neck and the sheets covered in
blood. He believed one of her clients had killed her and added,
'I knew they would blame me and I couldn't prove I hadn't
done it.'

The holiday crowd outside Brighton police station bayed for his blood and now there was speculation in the press that he was responsible for both of the Trunk Murders. His trial at Lewes Assizes opened on 10 December 1934 with the crowd again jeering as the prison van drew up. The prosecution was led by J. D. Cassels, who would later become a High Court judge, and Mancini was defended by Norman Birkett who privately thought he was 'a despicable and worthless creature' but who did not translate his feelings into inaction as David Smith did years later in North Carolina.

The evidence against Mancini was formidable. Spilsbury, then at the height of his fame, said that Violette had died from shock brought on by a depressed fracture of the skull. She had been hit with a heavy, blunt weapon and a partially burned hammer was found in the cellar of the Park Crescent flat. One end fitted the fracture perfectly. Thomas Gurrin, the handwriting expert, claimed that the handwriting on the telegram form sent to Olive Watts matched the handwriting on a menu Mancini had prepared at the café. In turn Olive said it was not the writing of her sister.

There was worse to come. Mancini must have had some power over women. For the day or so while he was on the run in Poplar he had tried to persuade seventeen-year-old Doris Saville that he was wrongly suspected of murder and asked her to provide a false alibi. They were supposed to have met on Brighton seafront and gone to tea with a woman, clearly Violette, at Park Crescent. They left her when she had told them she was expecting three men and when they returned they found her dead. He also tried to persuade her to work for him but, although she did have sex with him, she refused. In the end she gave evidence for the prosecution.

Added to this there were small bloodstains on his clothes, although since he agreed he had moved the body it would have been surprising had there not been.

There was also some supporting evidence from men who had been with Mancini at an amusement arcade, Aladdin's Cave, near the pier. He had claimed to have given Violette a beating, adding, 'Why knock women about with your hands? You only hurt yourself. Hit them with a hammer and slosh her out, the same as I did.'

There was some luck for Mancini with Thomas Kerslake, the driver for a local bookmaker Charlie Moores, who was the last person to see Violette alive. Birkett coaxed him into agreeing that she had appeared to be drunk or drugged and was also extremely frightened. Mancini was also fortunate in that all the prosecution witnesses who knew the pair said they had never seen them quarrel and they had had what appeared to be a loving relationship.

Spilsbury was the immediate problem and Birkett tried to persuade him that Violette, who had been taking morphine in 'more than a medicinal dose', had fallen down the narrow steps leading to the basement flat. Grudgingly Spilsbury agreed this might be possible but he preferred the hammer explanation. A blow from either end could have caused the depression.

Then in what was a masterstroke Birkett asked Chief Inspector Donaldson about Mancini's convictions, and pretty insignificant they were – bound over for stealing silver; three months for loitering with intent to commit a felony and six months for stealing clothes from a dwelling house.

Q: There is nowhere any record of a conviction for the crime of violence?
A: No sir.

Nor, Donaldson agreed, was there any possible connection with the other Trunk Murder.

As for the defence, there was no doubt that Violette had been a prostitute, which allowed Birkett to speculate that it might have been a client who had killed her. One client, the bookmaker Charlie Moores, she knew as 'Uncle', but unfortunately shortly before her death he had been admitted to a mental hospital. Another had a limp and was known as Hoppy.

As was usual Mancini was the first witness for the defence and as he took the oath he was seen to remove something

from his pocket. It was a rosary and when the judge asked
him if he was a Roman Catholic he said shamefacedly that he
had been. It was one of the early examples of the now well-
known trick of buying the sympathy of a jury through a
display of religion.

He made a good witness. His biggest problem was why he
had not gone to the police when he found Violette dead on
the bed.

A: I considered that a man who has been convicted never
gets a fair and square deal from the police.
Q: In what respect did you fear you would not get a square
deal? Because of your convictions?
A: Because I thought they would say 'Very well, you must be
the man. You have been living with her. She has been keeping you. You are a convicted man and you found her.'

Nor could Cassels shift him in cross-examination.

Q: When you knew she was dead, why did you not call
assistance of any kind?
A: Because I was afraid, as it is now proved, I should be
blamed for it.
Q: Perhaps with reason?
A: There was no reason.
Q: You say people convicted never get a square deal from
the police?
A: Yes, it happens every day.
Q: You suggest they would not have given you a square
deal?
A: I am sure of it.
Q: Are you saying they have not done so in this case?
A: That is not for me to say.

In his final address to the jury Birkett began by saying how
unfair the rules were that because he had called witnesses as
to the fact the Crown had the right to address the jury after
him. He then made much of Mancini's lack of motive in

killing Violette, the person who was providing him with money. He was perhaps fortunate that no one pointed out that he was seeing another younger woman, Lizzie Atterill, whom he would no doubt have attempted to put on the game had the opportunity arisen.

What Birkett cleverly did was to put Mancini and the witnesses in an almost subhuman strata where the behaviour of decent people such as the jury did not apply.

> This man lived upon her earnings and I have no word whatsoever to say in extenuation or justification. None. You are men of the world. Consider the associates of these people. We have been dealing with a class of men who pay eight pence for a shirt and women who pay one shilling and sixpence or less for a place to sleep. It is an underworld that makes the mind reel. It is imperative that you should have it well in mind that this is the background out of which these events have sprung.

Closing his speech to the jury he told them:

> I think I am entitled to claim for this man a verdict of Not Guilty. And members of the jury in returning that verdict you will vindicate a principle of law, that people are not tried by newspapers, not tried by rumour, but tried by juries called on to do justice and to decide upon the evidence. I ask you for, I appeal to you for, and I claim from you a verdict of Not Guilty.

He paused, looked at the jury and added after a moment, 'Stand firm.'

It has been generally regarded as one of the greatest closing speeches to a jury in an English criminal trial. Mancini was also fortunate in his judge. Not from Mr Justice Branson the rantings that Mr Justice Stephen heaped on Florence Maybrick nor those of Mr Justice Shearman on Edith Thompson's immorality in 1922. Instead he warned the jury:

This is not a court of morals but a court of law and you must not allow the natural feeling of revulsion which one must feel against a man who so supports life to affect your judgement against this man. Do not feel any kind of resentment against him which would lead you to draw an inference against him which you would not draw against a man who had not spent his days in that kind of life.

The jury returned a verdict of not guilty after a retirement of two and a half hours. Then Birkett, showing just how out of touch the Bar was with real life, told Mancini, 'Now go home and look after your mother. She has stood by you and been a brick.'

Before the trial one newspaper had claimed that Mancini had been involved in the stabbing of a man in Soho, as clear a libel as possible. His solicitor, F. H. Carpenter, wrote a letter to the newspaper threatening proceedings that would have resulted in substantial damages. Instead of letting his lawyers handle the case, Mancini reverted to type and could not resist taking the 200 ten-shilling notes that the paper's representative enticingly counted out before him in exchange for an acknowledgement that this was in full and final settlement of any claim.

He was married a week after his acquittal to a woman whom he had met at Aladdin's Cave, and the next summer he was touring fairgrounds billed as 'Toni Mancini, the Infamous Brighton Trunk Murder Man'. As part of his act he pretended to use a guillotine to cut off the head of his pretty wife. In the September he received three months with hard labour for stealing a watch from a Tonbridge jeweller. On his release he joined the navy. He married twice more and lived in Liverpool before returning in the 1970s to London.

And so for the next forty years there was speculation about whether Birkett had indeed obtained the acquittal of a guilty man. It was thought to have been resolved at the end of November 1976, when Mancini confessed to *News of the World* reporter Alan Hart that during a blazing row with Violette she had attacked him with the hammer he had used

to break coal for their fire. He had wrested the hammer
from her, but when she had demanded it back, he had
thrown it at her, hitting her on the left temple. The story
appeared as 'I'VE GOT AWAY WITH MURDER'. In it he
also claimed to have been a member of the Italian Sabini
racecourse gang and to have chopped off a man's hand and
put another's in a mincing machine on behalf of the notorious Harryboy Sabini.

Two years later he gave another, more detailed version of
the story to journalist Stephen Knight in which he said that
Violette had picked up the hammer and tried to hit him
with it. 'So I hit her. I'd never hit her before . . . I don't hit
women . . . I just got hold of her shoulders and was banging
her head on the floor like that. I said "Don't you spit at
me!" And I don't know how long I was like that. And when
I came out of my rage, she was lying like that . . . quite still
you see.'

The account did not fit Spilsbury's analysis of how Violette
had died but now the Director of Public Prosecutions considered a charge of perjury. It was rejected because of the length
of time that had elapsed since the case and also because there
was no corroborative evidence. It would have been an easy
defence for Mancini to say the story was false and he had
made it up for Knight to swallow.

In July 1986 Carolyn Robertson, a reporter on the Brighton
Evening Argus, traced him to south London where he told her
that he had, in fact, been innocent all along and vowed to fight
the lies told about him. He died the next year.

Before his death Mancini wrote to the crime historian
Jonathan Goodman asking whether he would read his autobiography. It was handwritten and Goodman was astonished
to find there was no reference either to the Trunk Murder or to
Mancini's later life. Almost as soon as Goodman received the
book, Mancini telephoned him demanding its return, saying
that if Goodman did not comply, although he was no longer in
the life, he knew plenty of hard men who were.

Back in 1935 when he filed his report on the case, a very
disgruntled Chief Inspector Donaldson, who believed that

Mancini had been schooled in his evidence during the time between committal and trial, wrote that the acquittal was due '. . . to the vagaries of a jury who can be swayed and have their visions distorted by the eloquence of Counsel'.

CHAPTER 10

Fit-ups and False Confessions

Alfred Dreyfus

Ameer Ben Ali 'Frenchy'

Reggie Dudley and Bobby Maynard

The Darvell Brothers; the Cardiff Three;
Idris Ali

The Mickelberg Brothers

Arthur Allan Thomas

The Maxwell Confait Case

Warren Billings and Tom Mooney

Colin Ross and the Gun Alley Tragedy

James Finch and John Stuart

Alfred Dreyfus

When judges deride defence allegations that there has been a conspiracy between a number of police witnesses who have fabricated the evidence, saying the greater the number of police the less likely it is there has been a conspiracy, they would do well to look at the massive cover-up in the case of the young French officer Alfred Dreyfus.

In early autumn 1894, at a time when Germany and Italy were allied with Austria in a military union (the Triple Alliance) hostile to France, the French Intelligence Services, headed by the director of intelligence Colonel Jean Sandherr, were monitoring supposedly secret correspondence between the German and Italian Military Attachés Maximilian von Schwartzkoppen and Alessandro Panizzardi.

On 26 September the long-serving French espionage agent Marie Bastian, known as *l'agent Auguste*, found a piece of paper, or *bordereau* as it was called, in the wastepaper basket of von Schwartzkoppen at the embassy on the rue de Lille in Paris, which led to the Dreyfus scandal.

On the face of it Bastian worked for the *Service Renseignements* as a cleaning lady supplying all foreign embassies with maids, as a result of which their wastepaper baskets were searched on a daily basis. She had previously been involved in stealing a document from the safe of another German military attaché, which led to the arrest of Guillaume Schnabelé as a spy in the spring of 1887, and a subsequent diplomatic incident between Germany and France.

The paper she found this time contained information about the hydro-pneumatic brake of a gun, a note on covering troops, proposed modification in the formations of artillery, an outline of a proposed firing manual for field artillery and details of a proposed invasion of Madagascar. The writer of the *bordereau* had signed off saying he was about to go on manoeuvres.

Colonel Sandherr took it for granted that the culprit was a general staff officer trained in artillery and General Auguste Mercier, the Minister of War in the Charles Dupuy Cabinet, agreed. Their initial problem, however, was that no one who was shown the *bordereau* recognized the handwriting. Principally because of his supposed expertise in graphology, Major Armand du Paty de Clam, attached to the General Staff, was appointed to head the investigation to find the spy and a three-week investigation threw up six possible suspects. Then a suggestion was made that it was not necessarily from a general staff officer but from a man who had some knowledge of the four different bureaux of the ministry. Could it be from a *stagière*, a trainee staff officer seconded as part of his training to all four bureaux?

And a suitable culprit who fitted that particular bill was Alfred Dreyfus, the son of a wealthy Jewish textile manufacturer, a young artillery officer originally from Alsace. What was against him was that he was austere, personally wealthy and, worst of all, Jewish at a time when whole swathes of the French were, and would remain for decades, anti-Semitic. Philippe Bunau-Varilla, who had been at college with him, wrote, 'I recall his very characteristic Jewish look which was rather unprepossessing,' before adding that despite this he was a decent fellow.

There was already a black mark against his name. At the War College examination in 1892 one of the members of the panel, General Bonnefond, felt that 'Jews were not desired' on the staff, and gave Dreyfus poor marks for *cote d'amour* or likeability. Bonnefond's assessment lowered Dreyfus's overall grade, and he did the same to another Jewish candidate, Lieutenant Picard. The two officers had lodged a protest with the director of the school, General Lebelin de Dionne, who expressed his regret for what had occurred but said he was powerless to take any steps in the matter.

Du Paty de Clam and his superior officers now fixed upon Captain Alfred Dreyfus as the writer and by the middle of October General Mercier, along with the head of the General Staff, General de Boisdeffre and General Gonse, his deputy in charge of Intelligence, now convinced themselves that Dreyfus had had access to the information that had been passed to the Germans. In order to obtain a definitive handwriting sample, du Paty de Clam, now in charge of the investigation, called Dreyfus and dictated him a letter based on the wording of the *bordereau*.

It did not matter that Dreyfus was not eligible to go on the manoeuvres mentioned in the *bordereau* nor that Alfred Gobert, the Bank of France's graphologist, said that someone other than Dreyfus could have written it.

Experts create self-perpetuating myths in which they cloak themselves. Now the authorities called on the notably anti-Semitic Alphonse Bertillon, who had developed the then current system for measuring and identifying criminals, which was later superseded by fingerprinting, to confirm the hand-writing was that of Dreyfus. He knew little or nothing of handwriting but he did know what was wanted of him. Yes, said the darling of the French press, it was Dreyfus who had written the *bordereau*.

On 13 October 1894 Dreyfus was arrested and charged with communicating French military secrets, including details of the new Howitzer gun, to the German Embassy. He was remanded to the Cherche-Midi military prison for further investigation. Now, following a leak from military headquarters, the newpapers *Le Soir* and *La Libre Parole* began a virulent anti-Dreyfus and anti-Semitic campaign. On 3 December Major d'Ormescheville recommended Dreyfus should be court-martialled.

The trial, which began on 19 December, was a foregone conclusion. But even without Bertillon, it is doubtful in the atmosphere surrounding the case that Dreyfus would have been acquitted. Du Paty de Clam, who also gave evidence at the court martial, was promoted to lieutenant-colonel as a reward for obtaining the conviction of Dreyfus.

Others were not so convinced by Bertillon. Roland Strong, the *New York Times*' correspondent, described his evidence:

> 'In the meanwhile M. Bertillon, with gestures and in the shrill pitched voice of a quack at a country fair, continued his monologue producing every minute fresh paper covered with wonderful hieroglyphics, copies of which he presented to the Judges who, with an expression of owllike wisdom carefully examined them.
>
> 'He then said he would give a practical demonstration and, putting his high hat on the floor, took ten minutes copying the *bordereau*.'

Writing of the affair later, French forensic scientist Edmund Locard thought that Bertillon had become so obsessed in his belief that Dreyfus was guilty he had forgotten his role as a scientist, but he had given his evidence as an 'expert'. Locard claimed that Bertillon's convoluted and flawed evidence was a significant contributing factor to what was the miscarriage of justice.

Inevitably found guilty on 22 December, Dreyfus was sentenced to life imprisonment on Devil's Island off the coast of French Guiana. His appeal was dismissed on 31 December and on 5 January 1895, he was publicly stripped of his army rank in the courtyard of the École Militaire before silent ranks of soldiers while a large crowd of onlookers shouted abuse against him from behind railings. He did not go down without protest, saying, 'I swear that I am innocent. I remain worthy of serving in the army. Long live France! Long live the army!' He arrived on Devil's Island on 13 April. Back in France, his family continued to protest that he was innocent.

In March 1896 Lt Colonel Georges Picquart, the new chief of French military intelligence following the retirement of Sandherr, was sent a second note, '*le petit bleu*', which had been retrieved by Marie Bastian. Picquart compared the handwriting with that of the *bordereau* and was convinced that

Dreyfus was not guilty and that the traitor was an army major, Ferdinand Walsin Esterhazy, who was improperly using the title of Count and was a gambler with an expensive mistress. Esterhazy had first offered his services to the Germans a month before delivering the first *bordereau*.

This was not a scenario that pleased the High Command. 'What does it matter to you if that Jew stays on Devil's Island?' the deputy chief of the General Staff allegedly asked Picquart, after evidence of Esterhazy's guilt had come to light. 'If you keep quiet, no one will know.' Picquart replied, 'What you're saying is vile. I don't know what I will do, but of one thing I am certain – I will not take this secret to the grave.' On 27 October 1896 Picquart was rewarded with a transfer out of Paris and later to the dangerous southern desert of Tunisia where there was an uprising against French colonial rule. Four days later in a cover-up, the French counter-intelligence under Colonel Hubert-Joseph Henry arranged for the master penman Lemercier-Picard to fake documents – a letter allegedly from the Italian Embassy to the German attaché specifically naming Dreyfus as their contact – so that the evidence once more pointed to him. This would be later known as '*le faux Henry*'. That month *Le Matin* published a copy of the original 1894 *bordereau*.

It was not a situation that was allowed to go unchallenged and the writer Émile Zola, whose novels such as *Germinal* and *Nana* had scandalized French society, and the future President Georges Clemenceau began a campaign to overturn the conviction. In August that year Esterhazy was retired by the army and the next month du Paty de Clam warned him that he was now seriously under suspicion. On 23 October 1897 Esterhazy had his last meeting with Schwartzkoppen and later in the day met du Paty de Clam in the Parc Montsouris; he promised him his support. The next month, with Henry or du Paty de Clam's approval, Esterhazy sent anonymous letters to Picquart's friend and Dreyfus supporter, politician Auguste Scheurer-Kestner, requesting clandestine meetings. He then had his mistress, Marguerite Pays, send notes signed 'Speranza' and 'Blanche' to Picquart. Forged messages were also planted in Picquart's file to make him appear as the fabricator of the '*petit bleu*', which he himself had discovered in March 1896.

Some days later, on 11 November, a stockbroker from South America saw a facsimile of the original *bordereau* on sale at a newspaper stand and realized that the handwriting matched that of one of his clients, Major Esterhazy. He immediately contacted Dreyfus's brother, Mathieu.

The newspapers were not all anti-Dreyfus and on 25 November 1897 Zola wrote to the sympathetic *Le Figaro* calling for his release. Three days later the paper published letters between Esterhazy and a discarded mistress, Madame de Boulancy, in which he expressed his contempt for the French, even dreaming of becoming an uhlan so he could kill as many French soldiers as possible.

An inquiry into the allegations against Esterhazy came to nothing when General de Pellieux, who had conducted it, exonerated him. That was followed by a second inquiry, this time conducted by Major Ravary, which on 1 January 1898 also cleared Esterhazy. Three handwriting experts said that the writing in the second *bordereau* was not his, but it was decided the best way to clear him in the public's eyes was after an official trial. On the second day of a trial behind closed doors beginning on 11 January, Esterhazy was duly acquitted. Now Picquart was indicted for revealing military secrets to civilians and sent to the Mont-Valérien military prison.

On 13 January 1898, Zola's *J'accuse* was published on the front page of the Paris daily *L'Aurore* run by Ernest Vaughan and Georges Clemenceau, who decided that the controversial piece would best be in the form of an open letter to the President, Félix Faure. It accused the highest levels of the French army of obstruction of justice and anti-Semitism, writing, 'At the root of it all is one evil man, Lt. Colonel du Paty de Clam, who was at the time a mere Major. He is the entire Dreyfus case.' By the end of the day 200,000 copies of the paper had been sold.

Now began the 'Dreyfus Affair', which divided French society. There were those who supported Dreyfus, such as writers Marcel Proust and Anatole France, scientist Henri Poincaré and Georges Clemenceau, and those who believed him to be guilty.

Zola's intention was that he should be prosecuted for libel so that the new evidence in support of Dreyfus would be made public, and he got his wish. Zola went on trial for criminal libel at the Cour d'Assises de la Seine in the Palais de Justice in Paris with Clemenceau's brother and the great lawyer Fernand Labori as his defence. Now an anti-Semitic mob stormed the court. Zola was convicted on 23 February, sentenced to one year's imprisonment and removed from the ranks of the *Légion d'honneur*. The conviction was quashed in April, but when he was convicted a second time in July, rather than go to jail, he fled to England with only the clothes he was wearing. After an unhappy stay in London, in June 1899, he was allowed to return in time to see the government fall. During the trial, however, General de Pellieux inadvertently acknowledged the existence of the secret file that had been distributed to the judges at Dreyfus's military trial of 1894 and had mentioned the document the *'faux Henry'*, produced by Henry on 31 October 1896, paving the way for a retrial for Dreyfus.

Meanwhile on 5 March 1898 Picquart, on bail, and Henry had fought a duel with swords at the riding school of the École Militaire in which Henry was slightly wounded in the wrist. The public at every level of society took sides and there was rioting in Paris.

In August 1898, the Minister of War Godefroy Cavaignac, curiously an anti-Drefusard, ordered Captain Louis Cuignet to examine the documents in the case. Cuignet soon discovered that the most damning evidence, the 'faux Henry' brought to the court in 1896, was in fact a forgery using two separate documents, to ensure the required result. When Henry was questioned on 30 August by Cavaignac he confessed within the hour. The next day Colonel Henry cut his throat after drinking most of a bottle of rum in his cell at Fort Mont-Valérien. On 3 September Esterhazy shaved his moustache, crossed into Belgium and then sailed for England where he continued to write anti-Semitic articles for French papers until his death in Harpenden, Hertfordshire, in 1923. Generals de Boisdeffre and de Pellieux, admitting they had been deceived by the forgery, requested they be relieved of their duties.

Following the campaign for his release, Dreyfus's first conviction was quashed on 3 June 1899 and he was returned to France for a retrial at Rennes on 7 August. On his way to court his lawyer Fernand Labori was shot in the back and took a week to recover. His attacker was never found. At the trial itself Bertillon again gave evidence. This time, diplomat and historian Maurice Paléologue, who watched the second court martial, thought Bertillon was 'certainly not in full possession of his faculties'. Paléologue went on to describe Bertillon's argument as 'a long tissue of absurdities', and wrote of 'his moonstruck eyes, his sepulchral voice, the saturnine magnetism' that which made him feel that he was 'in the presence of a necromancer'. For his pains now Picquart was charged with forging the second *bordereau*.

At the second trial Dreyfus, lulled into believing the court was on his side, told the tribunal:

> I am absolutely sure, I affirm before my country and before the army, that I am innocent. It is with the sole aim of saving the honour of my name, and of the name that my children bear, that for five years I have undergone the most frightful tortures. I am convinced that I shall attain this aim to-day, thanks to your honesty and to your sense of justice.

Dreyfus was mistaken. By a majority of five to two he was again found guilty, this time 'with extenuating circumstances', and sentenced to ten years. However, after the German Embassy agreed to release documents showing Dreyfus was not the writer of the notes, in a deal which anticipated that of the 'Lockerbie bomber' Abdelbaset al-Megrahi by a century, on 19 September 1899 he was pardoned by President Emile Loubet when he withdrew his appeal. Exiled from Paris, Dreyfus went to live with one of his sisters at Carpentras, and later at Cologny, but he was by no means grateful for the clemency, saying, 'The government of the Republic has given me back my freedom. It is nothing for me without my honour.' It was not officially cleared until 1906 when the Cours de Cassation quashed the conviction.

By then the charges against Picquart had also been dropped, and he had been promoted to brigadier-general, a position an officer of his seniority and experience could normally have expected to reach had his career not been interrupted by the Dreyfus affair. He became War Minister in Clemenceau's cabinet from 1906–09 and died in 1914 after a fall from his horse.

Zola died from carbon monoxide poisoning in October 1902, apparently caused by faulty chimney ventilation at his home at Melun. There had been previous attempts on his life and his enemies were blamed but nothing could be proved. Zola's widow begged Dreyfus not to attend her late husband's funeral and reluctantly he agreed. He was right to do so. Feelings were still running high against him. Henri Rochefort wrote in *L'Intransigeant*:

> Although M. Dreyfus and his general staff of sub-traitors will have every facility to enter the cemetery under the protection of the police he must come out [of it] again and the carriage of the German Emperor's spy will be exposed to suffer the same fate as that of M. Zola which often narrowly escaped being rolled over the banks of the Seine on leaving the Assize Court.

In 1908 military journalist Louis-Antoine Gregori shot Dreyfus twice in the arm when he attended the ceremony moving Zola's ashes to the Pantheon. Gregori told the press:

> I did not wish to kill Dreyfus. It is true I aimed at him, but I only wanted to graze him. My object was to protest against the participation of the army in the glorification of Zola and the rehabilitation of Dreyfus. My blow was aimed less at Dreyfus than at Dreyfusism.

After a trial during which he repeatedly and unsuccessfully tried to reopen the Dreyfus case, Gregori was acquitted and died on 26 October 1910. Du Paty de Clam died in the battle of the Marne in 1916.

Reinstated in the army, Dreyfus fought with great distinction in the First World War, both at Verdun and the Chemin des Dames. He died on 12 July 1935. One result of the Dreyfus fiasco was that for a time serious counter-espionage in France effectively ground to a halt. Another was the inexorable decline of Bertillon, whose system of classifying criminals had been overtaken when the method of classifying fingerprints had finally been agreed.

In September 1995 in a gesture of reconciliation the French army at least publicly admitted that Dreyfus had been framed. General Mourrut told the Jewish Consistory (French Jewish Central Council) that 'the affair was a military conspiracy which ended in the deportation of an innocent man and was partly founded on a false document'.

Ameer Ben Ali 'Frenchy'

In 1891 New York had its own Jack the Ripper case with the murder of the ageing and increasingly drunken actress Carrie Brown. Known as Old Shakespeare and now reduced to low-level prostitution, she would act out the bard in waterfront bars for the price of a few drinks. On 23 April she took a client, who signed the register as C. Knick, to Room 31 at the East River Hotel on the south-east corner of Catherine Slip and Water Street. Another prostitute, Mary Miniter, generously described as an assistant housekeeper, later said he had a foreign appearance, was about thirty-two years old, five foot eight tall, of slim build, with a long sharp nose, heavy moustache of light colour, and wearing a dark-brown cutaway, black trousers and a dented black derby. Even so, Miniter claimed she did not get a good look at him; he seemed 'anxious to avoid observation'. Others described the man with Brown as medium sized with blond hair, stocky and of a seafaring appearance.

The next morning C. Knick was gone, leaving behind Carrie Brown's remains on the bed where the night manager Eddie Harrington discovered them around 9 a.m. when he unlocked the room. The coroner found she had first been strangled and the murderer had then mutilated her body in a frenzy of stabbing and cutting. Dr Jenkins, who performed the autopsy, thought the killer had attempted to carve the abdomen out of her body.

By 25 April, among the numerous men under arrest was

Ameer Ben Ali, variously known as George Frank and 'Frenchy', an Algerian Arab who professed to neither speak nor understand English. On the night of the murder, Frenchy, an habitué of the East River Hotel, had occupied Room 33, across the hall from Room 31. The rules of the hotel were curious. Single men could not stay in it and, possibly to reduce allegations of theft, women were not allowed to leave during the night. But rules are made to be broken and on the night of the murder Frenchy had simply bribed Harrington to let him in.

Five days later Chief Inspector Thomas Byrnes, described by journalist Lincoln Steffens as 'simple, no complications at all – a man who would buy you or beat you, as you might choose, but get you he would', triumphantly announced that Frenchy was the killer. Byrnes alleged that after C. Knick had left, Frenchy had crept across the hall, robbed and killed Carrie Brown and crept back into his own room. There were blood drops on the floor of Room 31 and in the hall between Rooms 31 and 33; blood marks on both sides of the door to Room 33 as if the door had been opened and closed by bloody fingers; bloodstains on the floor of Room 33; on a chair in that room and on the bed blankets and the mattress (apparently the East River Hotel did not provide sheets). Blood had also been found on Frenchy's underwear and socks. Scrapings from his fingernails indicated the presence of blood. He had given false explanations as to how the blood came to be on him.

He was arraigned on 30 April and held in The Tombs prison until his trial opened on 24 June. As he could not afford an attorney, the court appointed Abraham Levy who was appearing in his first murder trial. The court had found Emil Sulta, a cigar dealer, apparently from the same Algerian village as Frenchy, to interpret and *The New York Times* thought 'he earned his money'. District Attorney DeLancey Nicoll and a chief assistant, Francis Wellman, prosecuted. Byrnes and four officers testified for the prosecution. According to journalist Edwin Borchard, so did numerous witnesses 'from the lowest stratum of New York life', to prove that Frenchy had been living a 'sordid life', and, particularly, that he was accustomed to staying at the East River Hotel, wandering from room to room at night. Two men gave evidence that while in The Tombs they had seen Frenchy with a knife.

Three medical experts testified that a chemical analysis of his fingernail scrapings, bloodstains on the bed in Room 31 and on his socks showed 'intestinal contents of food elements, all in the same degree of digestion – all exactly identical'. They inferred from this that the bloodstains resulted from blood flowing from the abdominal injuries of Carrie Brown.

Apart from calling a police officer to say that Frenchy had not carried a knife in prison, Levy lacked the resources to conduct a thorough investigation. He had to rely on his client, who was a dreadful witness. He sometimes seemed to understand English; at other times, he claimed not to understand questions even after they had been translated into his native dialect. He consistently denied killing Brown, but Francis Wellman later wrote in *The Art of Cross-Examination*, that the prosecution 'badly tangled' Frenchy 'time and time again upon cross-examination'. In a compromise verdict he was convicted of second-degree murder and, on 10 July, was sentenced to life imprisonment in Sing Sing. The first jury ballot had been eight to four on a count of first-degree murder. A second had been eleven to one.

The New York Times was unhappy with the verdict, writing on 3 July that very few people were:

> Satisfied of his guilt either by the evidence, the arguments or the verdict. The Algerian's character and behaviour were against him and the conduct of his counsel was not calculated to produce a favourable impression but a conviction for crime should be established upon facts, clearly established by evidence and that upon which this verdict was rendered was of the flimsiest circumstantial kind.
>
> The head of our detective force is undoubtedly a keen and energetic officer but he has shown more than once that

success in catching and convicting somebody is more to
him than the demands of exact justice.

The belief on the street was that he had been framed. There
were two rumours. One was that the murderer, a blond sailor,
had sailed for the Far East. The other was that Old Shakespeare
really had been murdered by Jack the Ripper. Although most of
the Ripper murders were committed during the late summer
and autumn of 1888, Frances Coles, also known as 'Carrotty
Nell', was butchered in Whitechapel in February 1891, only
two months before Carrie Brown took C. Knick upstairs.
Steamers had reduced the travel time from London to New
York to roughly a week. The writer Herbert Asbury
suggests many investigators believed that Jack the Ripper had
accepted Byrnes' challenge to come to New York where he
would arrest him, and that the police had charged Frenchy to
save the inspector's professional honour. In turn Byrnes hinted
that he had some documents in his possession to show that
Frenchy had been in London at the time the Ripper was operating but he never produced them.

On 15 July one witness, Mary Healey, who said she had had
drinks and dinner with Frenchy when he ate a meal of cabbage
and corned beef but had refused to go with him to the East
River Hotel on the night Brown was killed, was rewarded for
her evidence. A charge against her that she had hit a woman
Anna Johnson with a bottle was dismissed.

Over the years there were regular petitions for Frenchy, now
in the Matteawan State Hospital for the Criminally Insane, to
be pardoned. During his time there he learned English and
behaved well except for beating another inmate with a potato
masher, causing an injury that required ten stitches.

Nearly eleven years after his trial, in 1902 Governor
Benjamin B. Odell received another pardon application
for Frenchy based on new evidence and supported by a
number of high-profile petitioners. Apparently, a man who
matched the description of C. Knick had worked for several
weeks in the spring of 1891 at Cranford, New Jersey, about
fifteen miles from the city. He had been away from Cranford

on the night of 23 April 1891, and disappeared entirely several days later. Among the objects left in his room were a brass key bearing a tag with the number 31 and a bloody shirt. The key matched the keys of the East River Hotel. No evidence ever connected Frenchy to the key.

Journalist Jacob Riis then filed an affidavit stating that when he had visited the hotel on the morning after the murder and before the coroner's arrival, he had not found blood on the door of either room or in the hallway. Why he had not given this evidence at the time of the trial is not clear. The governor of New York, Benjamin Odell, inferred from the affidavits of Riis and other observers that the bloodstains, which had been found by the police only on the day after the murder, had been made at the time of the visit of the coroner and the crowd of reporters when the body was examined and removed. Even the police had testified that there was no blood on or near the lock or knob of the door to Room 31, which presumably the murderer had had to unlock, open, close and relock.

On 22 April 1901, Frenchy was released. Asked to comment, Byrnes was unabashed. 'The records show that I landed him and the records show, too, what his personal record was. I haven't got time to go into the details of his career. The governor can pardon whom he likes. It's nothing to me.' No compensation was paid to the unfortunate man, who was due to be deported to Italy – other reports say to Algeria.

One suggestion has been that Brown's killer was in fact the Ripper suspect Dr Francis Tumblety, who had jumped bail in England and had arrived in New York shortly before the killing. There is no evidence to support the theory, nor indeed that Tumblety, who was also arrested in connection with the assassination of Abraham Lincoln, was indeed the Ripper.

In December 1903 another prostitute, Sarah Martin, who worked the Cherry Hill district, was murdered in James Kelly's Raines Law Hotel, at 11 James Slip, Manhattan, known locally as Slaughter House Point. Like Carrie Brown she had been badly mutilated and had been disembowelled almost certainly while she was asleep or drunk. In 1904 Emil Nielsen, also known as Totterman, a Swedish sailor, was convicted of her murder and sentenced to death. He was reprieved the next year.

Reggie Dudley and Bobby Maynard

North London has never had the social status in criminal circles granted to the East End but, nevertheless, from the pre-First World War days, when a team known as the Titanics ruled the area, it has always had a good number of high-class villains including the bank robber and first modern supergrass Bertie Smalls.

In his lifetime the gaunt and gangling north Londoner Billy Moseley was a relatively successful bank robber. Standing well over six foot, when he and his equally tall half-brother George Arnold were arrested for a raid, soldiers from the nearest Guards' barracks had to be sent as foils so that a realistic identification parade could be held.

Moseley was probably not quite top class and he went to prison in the early 1970s following a failed armed robbery. Before then he had been having an affair with Frankie, the wife of robber Ronnie Fright, who was himself serving a seven-year sentence at the time. This, at the very least, was regarded as bad form and certainly worth a bad beating, even a non-fatal shooting. On his release Moseley took up once more with Frankie. He also discovered that his close friend Bobby Maynard had begun to associate with Reggie Dudley, a man he certainly disliked, and although he had badly beaten him in a fight some time earlier he now probably feared him.

The lean and saturnine Reginald Dudley was a thoroughly undesirable character. He was a receiver and police informer, traits that often go together. Despite rumours of his being a grass he was well respected in the criminal fraternity. One police officer recalled, 'I always thought he could go as far as the Krays and the Richardsons. He had a team and he had ability and the sense of purpose to do to north London what the Krays did to east London.'

Another story about him was that after his wife had in some way offended him he had chained her to the pilings on Brighton Pier and left her there for the tide to come in. True or not, he had certainly served a six-year sentence for slashing her face.

By the middle of the 1970s he would only deal with high-quality stolen goods and it was suggested that he was also working with the corrupt police officer Alec Eist, shaking down robbers and relieving them of their proceeds.

Robert 'Fat Bob' Maynard was much more rotund and far jollier. He had been hit over the head with a plank in a fight in a club in London's Tottenham Court Road, resulting in brain damage that affected his speech. He would stammer over the telephone, 'H-hello it's Bob-by M-mmay—. . .' and when interrupted would ask, 'H-how d-do y-you kn-now it's m-me?'

Together Dudley and Maynard were known as the Legal and General Firm after an advertisement of the time for the insurance company that showed two men in overcoats, something they both habitually wore. The name was said to have been coined by Dudley's friend Eist.

On 26 September 1974 Moseley set off for a meeting at 6.30 p.m. with Ronnie Fright 'to clear the air' at the Victoria Sporting Club in Stoke Newington, a rather less grand venue than its name suggested. He was never seen alive again. A week later parts of a body began to surface in the Thames near Rainham in Essex. The head and hands were missing, which in the pre-DNA days made identification extremely difficult, and for a time it was thought to be that of the IRA robber Kenneth Littlejohn who had escaped from Mountjoy Prison in the March. However, Moseley had suffered from a rare skin disease as well as from gallstones. An X-ray taken while he was in Bedford Prison showed the gallstones, and blood samples from the body matched those of his children. As a result the not always reliable pathologist Professor James 'Taffy' Cameron identified the body as that of Moseley.

Another friend of Moseley was Micky Cornwall, an armed robber known as 'The Laughing Bank Robber' who was released from his eight-year sentence for robbery on 18 October that year. Back in 1962 another robber, Ray Barron, had been convicted with Colin Saggs and Cornwall of a bank robbery in Barnet. He had met Reggie Dudley in prison and had taken up with Dudley's daughter, Kathy.

Cornwall was also involved with Kathy Dudley, once married to a John Dann, known as 'Doughnuts', possibly because he was once a baker and possibly because he cut holes in people who offended him. Her marriage to Dann had broken down and it was then she had taken up with Barron. When he went back to prison she began her association with Cornwall. Neither her father nor Ray Barron seem to have taken umbrage.

As so many criminals do, in the short time he was in circulation Cornwall was looking for 'one last big one'. He also had a new girlfriend, Gloria Hogg, with whom he wanted to buy a home in the country. Meanwhile he contented himself with a string of hotel robberies and rented a room from Colin Saggs, now a police informer. Cornwall confided his plans for a 'final job' to another north London criminal John Moriarty, who also turned supergrass after he had been shot in the leg for a second time. It seems Cornwall left his digs for 'the big one' on 3 August in a mustard-coloured Range Rover. Some days later two men, identified by Saggs' fourteen-year-old daughter, Sharon, as Dudley and Maynard, came asking for him. Moriarty claimed to have seen Cornwall at a bus stop in Highgate, north London, on 23 August and that seems to have been the last sighting of him before his body was discovered by picnickers in a newly dug grave in Hatfield, Hertfordshire. He had been shot in the head.

During the next year the *Islington Gazette* published an ambiguous letter signed 'Fat Bob'. 'It's been said that Mick was asking too much about Bill's death. The police seem to have forgotten Billy. They may forget about Mick.' Maynard went to their offices to complain, saying he had never been interviewed by the police about the death or the letter. He certainly had not written it. The paper published an apology, but said they had been told by the police it was genuine. Maynard also received a .22 bullet wrapped in cotton wool. So had an acquaintance, car dealer Phil Luxford.

Meanwhile an inquest into Moseley's death was held and Professor Cameron told the coroner that Moseley had been tortured before his death. He had been burned with a naked flame and his toenails had been pulled out. Cameron also told the coroner that he thought Moseley had been killed with a gunshot to the still-missing head.

Initially the Hertfordshire police had absolute control of the inquiry into Cornwall's death, but when no progress was made and such leads as there were led straight back to London and the name Moseley, a joint Hertfordshire and London squad was assembled. The officer in charge of the inquiry was Scotland Yard's Commander Albert Wickstead, known as Bert and a man who, as with many other policemen around the world, liked to be called 'The Grey [or Silver] Fox'. Wickstead had come to prominence when, after the trial of the Kray twins, he had tidied up London's East End with successful prosecutions of a minor protection gang run by George and Brian Dixon and a feud between the Tibbs and Nicholls families which had threatened to get out of hand. He was known for his success rate in clearing up cases but was not regarded as being overly fussy about the quality of the evidence, provided it stood up in court. 'A horrible man,' recalls one detective sergeant who worked with him. 'He hated everyone and everyone loathed him. You look at all his cases and it's the same the whole way through. Everything was verbals and he blew cases up for more than they deserved.'

It was not until nearly eighteen months later, on 22 January 1976, that Wickstead swooped. Eighteen people were taken to Loughton police station and seven were finally charged. Dudley and Maynard were charged with the two murders, as were Ronnie Fright, Ernie Maynard (Robert's brother) and George Spencer. Charlie Clarke, a market stall holder, and

Kathy Dudley were charged with conspiracy to murder. Others who were rounded up but not charged included Ernie Maynard's wife Sylvia and the grass John Moriarty.

The trial opened in November 1976. 'The story I have to tell is a terrible one. The evidence will disclose no shortage of cruelty and no shortage of sheer evil,' Michael Corkery dramatically told Mr Justice Swanwick and the jury in his opening speech for the prosecution. He was keen to point out that he was not obliged to provide a motive and this indeed was a problem for the prosecution. Eventually a selection of motives to suit all tastes was offered: 1. Moseley had an affair with Frankie Fright and had to be punished; 2. He had fallen out with Dudley ten years earlier; 3. He had been suggesting Dudley was a grass; 4. He, Moseley, was sitting on the proceeds of a large jewel robbery; 5. Sheer sadism; 6. Cornwall had set out to avenge Moseley's death; 7. He had discovered Maynard and Dudley were the killers and so had to be silenced; 8. He had had more than a brief liaison with Kathy Dudley and had to be punished as well. Corkery was 98 per cent sure that Moseley had been killed with a single shot to the head, which was still missing.

The case against Ronnie Fright was that he was deliberately late for his meeting with Moseley outside the Victoria Sporting Club and so had lured him to his death.

Much of the evidence against the defendants was delivered by a ragbag of serving prisoners who, having seen The Light (and the prospects of an early release), were able to give evidence against their former cell-mates. Principal among them was thirty-year-old Tony Wild, who asked the judge if he could sit down to give his evidence because he had an anal fissure. He had, he said, been raped as a young man and apart from contracting syphilis, he had this permanent reminder of the experience. His criminal career had begun as a shoplifter, car thief and office breaker before he graduated to armed robbery and a series of attacks on Securicor vehicles. The proceeds had disappeared into the Golden Nugget casino in Piccadilly, major London hotels and on a fur coat that cost him £1,200.

Bertie Smalls had paved the way for supergrasses to obtain a semi-official five years for their crimes instead of up to twenty and Wild took advantage of this when he was caught on another Securicor vehicle raid which stood to net him over £7,000. He shot at the guards and escaped, crashed his Volvo and was arrested hiding in a field. His co-accused picked up eighteen years. As thanks for his evidence in the case Wild, who was fortunate not to have been charged with attempted murder, received a mere five. In his cell he kept a record of alleged conversations with other inmates including Brighton publican Oliver Kenny, then landlord of the Horse and Groom in the Hanover area of the town and an old friend of Dudley. When he offered these to the police there was initially no reaction and he wrote:

> Although I have passed on information that I believe would be useful to your inquiries, I have received from your office not even an acknowledgement of the receipt of my letters let alone a routine questioning as to the validity of their content. Perhaps you feel that I am trying to work a ticket or something.

Next he offered them Reggie Dudley, writing to Wickstead, 'I hope you will appreciate that I have been very forthright in this letter and that, in itself, will indicate to you that I have other more serious matters to impart to you.' And when he did make a statement, 'It's almost a relief to be in the police cell and get it off my plate. I am caught and am going to spend a long time in prison. When I come out I only want to spend the rest of my life quietly with those I love.' Now where have we heard that before?

Wild told the police that Dudley had boasted about killing Cornwall, saying, 'He went up in the fucking air, didn't he boys?' And as for Maynard he had apparently said, 'I didn't know guys would squeal like a pig.' But the most damaging revelation came from his conversation with Oliver Kenny who, Wild said, had told him he nearly died of fright when Dudley brought Moseley's head into the pub one night.

Wild held his own during cross-examination. Attitudes in the 1970s were different and Michael West, for Dudley, suggested that real men such as Dudley would have had nothing to do with a disgusting pervert such as Wild. Dudley would not have given him the time of day, let alone a confession.

Wild, who had a good line in psychological gibberish, would have none of it:

> I have been to bed with literally hundreds of women and I could call five hundred into this court to testify to that fact. My crimes, I know, have got progressively more serious, ending up with armed robbery. I would interpret that as an attempt – or at least a subconscious attempt – to regain my manhood.

As for Fright, Frank Read, a fellow prisoner in Pentonville, said he had confessed saying, 'We done one, we sawed one up.' This evidence was effectively destroyed when two other prisoners said that they were sure Read was perjuring himself. An assistant governor at the prison told the jury that the police had tried to trap Fright by putting him in a cell with a known grass. Yet another prisoner said the police had tried to recruit him to get a confession out of the defendant George Spencer.

Wild apart, the only evidence against the defendants was a certain amount of circumstance and their apparent and hotly disputed half-admissions to Wickstead. They had been kept in custody and interviewed over a period of four days. According to the police, Dudley had, during a journey in a police car, said, 'The cunt [Moseley] had it coming. He tried to fuck me so I fucked him good and proper.' Later Dudley was said to have told the police questioning him about Cornwall, 'You can take it from me it is not on my conscience . . . He deserved what he got and that's it.' Maynard had supposedly told the police after his arrest, 'It's about time you came for me.' He was also alleged to have said of Cornwall, 'I told him if he had sex with her [Kathy] I would kill him.' Maynard, asked why he had gone to Saggs' house looking for Cornwall, had replied, 'It was business.' Had he told Fright to be late for the meeting at the Victoria Club? 'I'm not answering that, otherwise I'm finished.' Kathy Dudley was alleged to have said of her father, 'Now he's got us into murder.' Charlie Clarke had admitted his involvement but said he had thought the pair were only going to be beaten up.

What was so surprising was that there had been the opportunity to tape record most of these interviews thereby eliminating any doubt. There had been a recorder fitted into Wickstead's desk at the police station, but it had never been switched on. Why not? 'I am a police officer who believes in police methods and tape recorders are not used in police interviews.'

Another officer went on to explain that tape recording was not an option because it would not have been admissible. In which case why have one? And that the street noise would have made the answers inaudible, as would the noise of officers scraping their chairs and coughing. The room was, in fact, carpeted.

The case, initially estimated for eight weeks, had dragged on until 17 June 1977 at which point, summing up, Swanwick told the jury:

> In no case here, none of the cases against any of the accused, is there any physical evidence directly connecting any of them with any of the crimes charged. There is no evidence of where or exactly when either Moseley or Cornwall died. There are no eyewitnesses of any crime; there was no forensic evidence, no finger prints, no blood stained clothing, no murder weapon to connect any of the accused with either killing, and no written and signed confessions. The evidence against the accused consists largely, and in some cases almost wholly, of alleged oral confessions to police and others. So you must consider – such questions by themselves would not be sufficient – motive and opportunity, relationships, previous and subsequent conduct and see whether in each case they support and confirm the alleged

confession or make it less likely to have been made or to have been intended as a confession.

The judge directed the jury to find Ernie Maynard not guilty. Dudley was found guilty with a unanimous verdict. Bobby Maynard was found guilty by an 11–1 majority of killing Moseley and by a 10–2 majority of the murder of Cornwall. Ronnie Fright had already been acquitted, as had George Spencer. Dudley and Maynard each received life with a minimum of fifteen years; Kathy Dudley, convicted of conspiracy, received two years suspended. Charlie Clarke received two years but not suspended.

On 28 July, six weeks after the trial ended, Moseley's head was found in a public lavatory in Islington, thawing in a plastic bag along with a copy of the London *Evening News* dated 16 June 1977, the day the jury began to reach their verdicts. On 18 October that year Professor Cameron told an inquest that Moseley's head had been kept in a deep freezer possibly for up to three years. It had also previously been buried and, because of paint traces, had possibly been kept in a garage. There was no evidence it had ever been in the sea. He now thought Moseley had not been shot in the head but had choked on his own blood.

It seems the police were not interested in who had been keeping the head over the years because when investigative journalist Duncan Campbell asked Scotland Yard what inquiries were being made, he was told there were none in progress.

Immediately after the appeals were dismissed in April 1979, Moseley's widow, Ann, and his eldest son became keen members of the campaign led by Maynard's wife Tina to have the guilty verdicts reversed. Leaflets and badges 'MDC – Not Guilty, Right √' were distributed and in September that year a march took place from Camden Town to Hyde Park Corner.

In 1980 Wild was released from prison and told Duncan Campbell that he had made up his evidence about the head in the pub following a scenario police officers had outlined for him. On 23 April 1982 he received a further ten years for another five armed robberies. His luck was still in. Although he had fired shots in the raid the trial judge accepted he had done so only to frighten. He was paroled in a little over three years.

The years went by and Maynard, Dudley, Clarke and Spencer took truth drug tests and Kathy Dudley a lie detector test. All passed but the results were not admissible in court. Wild was released again and in 1995 made further statements. Initially he would not go to court but, offered an indemnity against prosecution for perjury, he said, 'I would like to make it clear that the whole of my evidence against Reg Dudley, Bob Maynard and other co-defendants was entirely false in so far as it relates to comments made by them that were incriminatory.'

In 1991 Liberty, formerly the National Council for Civil Liberties, adopted the Maynard–Dudley case as one for special consideration in a campaign against wrongful convictions.

It took another eleven years before the case finally came to court. In that time scientific techniques had developed to include the technique of ESDA (Electrostatic Detection Apparatus) and it was now possible that there was a chance to prove that the compromising remarks to police were never made. If writing is fashioned on a sheet of paper resting upon other pages, the indentations or impressions produced are transferred to those below. These transferred impressions, although often invisible to the human eye, can be detected using an electrostatic detection device. Dudley and Maynard applied for access to the interview notes, but the Metropolitan Police replied that the papers had unfortunately been destroyed by a sergeant who had been told to make space.

After his retirement from the bench, Swanwick generously gave his time to listen to and discuss the case with some of the campaigners, and in later years was certainly not convinced of the rectitude of the convictions. He died in June 2003.

In the appeal in 2002 there was new evidence to the effect that a statement said to have been taken by the police could not have been written within the times stated. Although it was timed as from 4.05 p.m. it was said to have commenced at 4.28 p.m. and concluded at 5.18 p.m. The statement was handwritten. However, an independent document examiner stated that studies had shown that the number of characters written in the statement could not have all been handwritten in fifty minutes. The average person can write 140–150 characters a minute. One or two people can do 180, but 250 is impossible. By this time, though, Wickstead and the note-taker Trevor Lloyd Hughes were both dead.

Resisting the new appeal Victor Temple QC, for the Crown, submitted that it was obvious that either the commencement time of the interview or the finishing time must have been noted down incorrectly and that the jury would have appreciated that point. The court said that while it accepted that such an explanation could well have been a possibility, it also appreciated that there could have been other, less innocent, explanations.

Temple argued that Dudley had came across as 'prone to angry outbursts, challenging and arrogant' at the trial, and these same traits could be found in his answers to questions put in the interviews. But Lord Justice Mantell replied, 'Just because the person in the dock is a known villain and thoroughly unpleasant, it does not mean his convictions are therefore safe.'

The court said that it was not for it to determine which scenario was correct. Once it had determined that there had been a defect in the evidence not disclosed at trial, and that defect might have affected the decision of the jury, then the court was obliged to overturn the verdict. Indeed, the court ruled that the defect in one statement could have led the jury to look at other pieces of evidence against the other co-accused differently. As a result, they overturned all four convictions, even though the statements given by the others appeared to be without such defects. The court said the suggestion that the jury concluded that the police had made a mistake would require the appeal court to look into the minds of the jury and to speculate as to their reasoning in a way that is clearly forbidden.

Dudley and Maynard had not been thought suitable for early release because they had refused to accept their guilt.

Dudley had been finally paroled in 1997 having served twenty-one years, and Maynard, who had been given bail in November 2000, had served twenty-five. Kathy Dudley and Edward Clarke also successfully overturned the verdicts against them.

'If you look at Wickstead's cases, they're all the same. They're these verbal half confessions, never signed,' said one detective who knew him.

Certainly there was one embarrassing case in his career when Arthur John Saunders was jailed for fifteen years for his part in a raid on Barclays Bank in Ilford. His conviction was based on partial admissions in questions put to him by Wickstead. Two years later bank robber and supergrass Bertie Smalls turned Queen's Evidence and provided details of the many robberies in which he had been involved, including the Ilford one. He was adamant that Saunders had not been on it. If this was not accepted the whole house of cards built around Smalls' evidence must tumble.

In an appeal heard in October 1973 Lord Widgery commented:

> In the course of this interview as recounted by Police Superintendent Wickstead, one does not find Saunders positively admitting that he had anything to do with the Ilford bank robbery; on the other hand there is a noticeable absence of any positive denial of such association and indeed many of the answers which I have read, equivocal in themselves were certainly, one would have thought, answers which did not lie readily in the mouth of an innocent man, who would have asserted his innocence in a positive way.

Rather than find Wickstead had fabricated the confession, His Lordship decided Saunders had been drinking before the interview and was boasting. His conviction was quashed and he was awarded compensation. He later led what was called 'the Grandfather Gang' of bank robbers and received fifteen years.

Dudley and Maynard were finally awarded six-figure sums in compensation and Dudley died in 2008. Neither was ever reconvicted. For some years Billy Moseley's ashes remained on the mantelpiece in Tina Maynard's house in Camden. Ronnie and Frankie Fright were reconciled. Wickstead died in 2001, aged seventy-seven.

The Darvell Brothers; the Cardiff Three; Idris Ali

On 19 June 1986 Sandra Phillips, a thirty-eight-year-old mother of four and manageress of the Private Shop, a Swansea sex shop, was sexually assaulted and beaten to death before her attackers made an attempt to set fire to her shop, spraying petrol to cover their traces.

A report on one suspect, Wayne Darvell, read, '[He] is on the borders of normality. [He is] susceptible and with limited intelligence and a compulsive confessor.' At the special school Darvell attended as a boy, his former teacher, Byron Doel, described him as someone who loved to be the centre of attention, a fantasist. 'He was forever confessing things he hadn't done,' Doel told the BBC radio programme *Rough Justice*. 'If he confessed, the teacher's problem was solved and he was happy.' Darvell also hung around police stations, saluting officers and volunteering useless information. A psychologist who later examined him said he was 'suggestible and gullible' and would name others if it earned him points from those in authority. Before the Phillips murder he had already confessed to the murder of a dentist in which he could not possibly have been involved. Detectives also ignored warnings from two local uniformed officers that statements made by Wayne Darvell could never be relied on. Now he implicated his brother Paul and both were charged with the murder.

Based on the confession, the brothers were convicted at Swansea Crown Court in 1986 when both received life sentences; Paul to serve a minimum of twenty years and Wayne fifteen.

Their case was taken up by JUSTICE and the subsequent appeals were based largely on evidence gathered by Devon and Cornwall police. When the case came before the Court in July 1992 the Crown did not contest the appeals.

Using ESDA (Electrostatic Detection Apparatus) testing, the Devon and Cornwall police had discovered a stack of irregularities. Detectives' notes of their questioning of Wayne Darvell, which they said in evidence had been contemporaneous, had not been compiled until long afterwards and the originals had been destroyed. The statement of susceptible Wayne had been written to look as if he had been supplying information rather than simply agreeing with what the police had told him.

The confession had been based on a 150-page statement by a detective, which, he had said on oath, was made after the interviews. Counsel for the Darvells said the 'doctored' statement was a blueprint for the interview notes.

Another detective who took part in the Wayne Darvell interview and claimed the notes were written up immediately afterwards was found to have made them in a pocketbook that had not been issued until two months later.

Officers had also secretly taped conversations between the brothers in their cell in between questioning but had not told their lawyers. The tapes contained statements that the men would have been unlikely to have made if guilty and would have supported the defence case.

Statements by two detectives that they saw the Darvells near the scene of the murder on the day were also wrong because examination of their diaries proved the policemen to have been elsewhere at the time.

One crucial piece of evidence, that of a bloody palm print found on a payphone attached to the wall near Sandra Phillips' body, was neither hers nor that of the brothers. This information had not been passed to the defence, who had been told that tests had been insufficient for a positive identification.

Although it was never proved, it was alleged that an earring – similar to one possibly worn by the victim – which was found in a police car after it had been used to take Wayne Darvell to the police station, had been planted.

Following their release in 1992 the brothers were awarded £80,000 each in compensation for the seven years they spent in prison. In 2005 Paul Darvell was found dead of natural causes at his home; he was forty-two.

On 14 February 1988, twenty-one-year-old prostitute Lynette White was killed in a derelict flat above a bookmakers at 7 James Street in Butetown, Cardiff, where she and her friend Leanne Vilday took their clients. In the days before her death she had fallen out with her pimp-cum-boyfriend Stephen Miller, known as 'Pineapple' because of his distinctive hair-style, and had disappeared.

She was also due to give evidence in two criminal cases, the first of which was against Francine Cordle, a member of a powerful Cardiff family, who was alleged to have stabbed another prostitute Tina Garton. The second involved an allegation against Robert Gent and Eric Marasco of attempting to procure a thirteen-year-old girl for prostitution. At first it was thought that White's death might have been in connection with either of these cases but both Francine and her mother Peggy Farrugia were eliminated from the inquiry, as were Gent and Marasco.

When White disappeared, the police began actively searching for her and a judge issued a warrant for her arrest to ensure that she attended the first trial, which was due to commence at Cardiff Crown Court on 15 February 1988. Her body was found the day before the trial.

She had died in a frenzied attack in which she had been stabbed fifty times. Her throat had been cut and her head and one breast had been almost completely severed and there were defence wounds to her hands. There had been no attempt at rape or genital mutilation.

The pathologist, Professor Bernard Knight, described it as 'a mutilating attack with sexual overtones' and identified a

total of sixty-nine wounds. Although she had been stabbed
seven times in the heart he concluded that it was the throat
injury that had killed her, saying, 'It would require considerable force because the skin, muscles, larynx and voice box had
been cut right down to the neckbone.' Asked how the wound
could have been inflicted, he said it was a normal reflex for a
person to keep their head down in such a situation, and her
head may have been forcibly held back for the knife wound to
be inflicted. One of the two T-shirts Lynette was wearing was
'absolutely lacerated. It looked like a colander'. Knight believed
the murder weapon to have been five inches long and that she
had died between midnight and 4 a.m. Her wristwatch had
stopped at 1.45 a.m., leading the police to conclude that this
was the most likely time of her death.

White's body was discovered between the foot of the bed –
the room's only furniture – and the window, still clothed but
with one shoe off. Unsurprisingly there was heavy bloodstain-
ing to the base of the bed, the carpet and the walls of the room.
There was very little blood on the mattress, where an opened
but unused condom was found. Forensic examination found
150 different sets of finger and palm prints in the flat.
Azoospermic (exceptionally low level) semen was present
both in White's vagina and on her underwear, which pathologists determined had been deposited there within six hours of
her death. Some of the blood found on White's clothing,
including her exposed sock, was found to be from a male with
the blood type AB.

The only immediate help for the police was that a schoolgirl
had seen a white man covered in blood about 100 metres from
the James Street flat shortly before the body was found. On 17
March 1988 DCS Williams appeared on the BBC television
programme *Crimewatch UK* to say that the police believed this
man was responsible for White's murder. 'This man almost
certainly had the blood of the deceased on him.' South Wales
Police issued a photofit but it produced no positive result.
Over the months the police questioned a number of potential
suspects including, naturally, Stephen Miller.

Then in December Leanne Vilday, Lynette's friend and

owner of the flat where her body was found, and another working girl, Angela Psaila, told the police that they had been present when the killing took place and they had been forced to slash the body. As a result five men of mixed race – Lynette's pimp Stephen Miller, Tony Paris, Yusef Abdullahi and two cousins, Ronald and John Actie, the latter of whom was regarded with serious disfavour by the local police – were arrested and charged with the murder.

What, if any, corroborative evidence was there of the girls' statements? After many hours of repeated and bullying questioning with one pair of police officers playing bad cops and another pair playing good cops, Steve Miller, who had a borderline IQ of seventy-five, confessed. To back that up he also apparently confessed to a man Ian Massey, on remand with him, who helpfully went to the police. As for Yusef Abdullahi, his girlfriend Jackie Harris put him in the frame saying he had told her he was in the room when Lynette was stabbed. There was no corroborative evidence against the Acties. Nor, from a room that must have been littered with forensic clues, was there any forensic evidence against any of the men. The motive was thought to be a revenge on Lynette for her treatment of Stephen Miller.

Boiled down, the prosecution's case was not without its flaws. The police were afraid that Psaila and Vilday would not come up to proof on their statements. Vilday had already named a Martin Tucker as one of the killers and had then withdrawn the allegation. She had been taken to a hypnotist, something by now discredited in England. Psaila, who also made an allegation against another man and had withdrawn it, displayed racist tendencies, calling the defendants 'black monkeys' at the committal proceedings.

Because of potential prejudice the first trial was heard at Swansea and ended when Mr Justice McNeill died following a heart attack when he was about to begin summing up. The second trial before Mr Justice Leonard lasted 197 days, then the longest murder trial in Britain. The crucial question was how Miller had come to make his confession, which had been recorded on a series of tapes. Before he had made it on tapes seven and eight, he had denied being involved on more than three hundred occasions before he was gradually coaxed into a confession. During this time he had a solicitor present who had not tried to halt the questioning as Miller became more and more hysterical. In the second trial Miller's original counsel was not available and he had been replaced by Roger Frisby, a man of great charm and experience, but who was now definitely not what he had been. Unfortunately in a pretrial hearing to exclude the confession, Frisby did not have the crucial tapes containing the most bullying questioning played to the judge.

Leonard warned the jury about convicting on the evidence of the girls alone and they must have listened to him at least because they acquitted the Actie cousins. Abdullahi, Miller and Paris received life imprisonment. Now began the campaign for the release of the Cardiff Three, as they became known. For any campaign to succeed there must be help from the press and indeed the Three were indebted to journalists Satish Sekar, John Willams and Duncan Campbell who kept their case alive in the newspapers. Sekar, in particular, spent days investigating the case.

When the case came before the Court of Appeal almost everything focused on the confession of Stephen Miller. By then Jackie Harris had withdrawn her statement against Abdullahi, saying he often said weird things and she had made her statement to the police to hurt him. It had also turned out that the helpful Ian Massey was something of a supergrass. He had given evidence against Ged Corley, a Manchester policeman, whose conviction for robbery had been quashed on appeal. Massey had clearly benefited from his cooperation with the police. A man with a record for violence and serving a fourteen-year sentence, he had been granted parole on his first hearing after serving only a third.

In 1992 in allowing the appeals, the Lord Chief Justice, Lord Taylor, commented that,

> Short of physical violence, it is hard to conceive of a more hostile and intimidating approach by officers to a suspect.

If you go on asking somebody questions, and tell him he is going to sit there until he says what you want, there will come a time when most people will crack. Oppression may be of the obvious, crude variety or it may be just by relentlessness.

The Cardiff Three were released.

In October 1995 South Wales Police reopened the case and agreed to carry out DNA testing on the surviving forensic evidence, but did not use the most sensitive method of testing that was then becoming available in the field. When the preliminary tests failed to produce usable profiles, journalist Satish Sekar, recognizing that the technology to extract profiles from such poor samples would eventually become available, urged the police to cease testing before they used up the remaining samples.

Testing was halted in 1998 and, in January 2002, after the development of the Second Generation Multiplex Plus (SGM+) test, forensic scientists were finally able to obtain a reliable crime scene DNA profile. Now, using the process of familial searching, a partial match was eventually made with the profile of a fourteen-year-old youth who was known to the police but who had not been born at the time of the murder. This led to the arrest on 28 February 2003 of his uncle Jeffrey Gafoor. On 4 July that year Gafoor pleaded guilty at Cardiff Crown Court to White's murder. He was sentenced to life imprisonment, with a minimum of twelve years and eight months to be served. He maintained he had acted alone and later said he still could not remember how or where he met Lynette White, or what he did with the murder weapon, or where he went for a drink, or how he got home. He could not even be sure whether he had ever had sex with her.

Asked how he felt about five innocent men being arrested, Gafoor said, 'I am not responsible for anyone else being implicated. The law may say otherwise but I don't think I am.'

In 2004 the Independent Police Complaints Commission (IPCC) began a review of the conduct of the police during the original inquiry. Over the next twelve months around thirty people were arrested in connection with the investigation, nineteen of whom were serving or retired police officers.

In February 2007, four witnesses who gave evidence at the original murder trials were charged with perjury. In December 2008, three of them, Angela Psaila, Leanne Vilday and White's neighbour Mark Grommek, were found guilty of committing perjury and each were sentenced to eighteen months' imprisonment. A fourth was found to be 'unfit to stand trial'. Sentencing them Mr Justice Maddison said, 'It has been submitted on your behalf, accepted by the prosecution, and I accept it myself ... you were seriously hounded, bullied, threatened, abused and manipulated by the police during a period of several months leading up to late 1988, as a result of which you felt compelled to agree to false accounts they suggested to you.' However, he continued, perjury was 'an offence which strikes at the heart of the system of the administration of justice'.

In 2009 two further witnesses from the original trial were also charged with perjury and, along with eight former police officers, charged with conspiring to pervert the course of justice; they stood trial in July 2011. It was the largest police corruption trial in British criminal history. A further four police officers were due to be tried on the same charges in 2012 when, in November 2011, the case collapsed after the defence submitted that copies of files that they said they should have seen had instead been destroyed. As a result, the judge ruled that the defendants could not receive a fair trial and all fourteen including the supergrass Ian Massey were acquitted.

In January 2012 the apparently destroyed documents turned up, still in the original box in which they had been sent to South Wales police by the IPCC.

There was one more Welsh case of concern. It was one in which forensic scientists had combined together to produce a stunning identification of a victim. However, work may have been partially undone by the subsequent police investigation. In 1989 the body of Karen Price, dubbed 'Little Miss

Nobody', was found by workmen wrapped in a carpet in a shallow grave in a back garden during a building renovation in Cardiff. Dr Zak Erzinçlioglu, whose speciality was entomology, was able to say from soil and the carpet around the skeleton, which had attracted a colony of woodlice and bluebottle fly eggs, that the death had occurred at least five years earlier, and quite possibly several years before that. The body had not been buried immediately after her death. This eliminated any young women who had disappeared since 1984. Then, Professor Bernard Knight concluded that the skeleton was that of a teenage girl around five foot four in height while David Whittaker, a forensic dentist, thought the girl had been aged around fifteen-and-a-half, which narrowed things further. Anthropologists Christopher Stringer and Theya Molleson suggested the skull belonged to a white girl, although possibly not purely British. In fact the body had an Eastern Mediterranean ancestry.

The next link in the chain was provided by Richard Neave of Manchester University, a medical artist specializing in reconstructions of faces of those long dead from the study of their skulls. His reconstruction was shown on television and photographs were published in the newspapers. A social worker said it was Karen Price, who had run away from a children's home near Pontypridd eight years earlier. Another social worker found a photograph of Karen that closely matched the reconstruction.

Karen Price's dental records were obtained and Dr Whittaker found they matched the teeth in the skull. Then Dr Peter Vanezis used video techniques to superimpose images on the photographs and the skull, producing an exact match.

Neave had hoped to carry out DNA fingerprinting on the remains and compare the results with DNA from Karen's parents, who were Cypriot and Spanish, but this was thought to be impossible in view of the age of the remains. Erzinçlioglu knew of work undertaken on mammoths and Egyptian mummies that showed it was not the age of the remains that mattered so far as the preservation of DNA was concerned but the physical properties of the surroundings in which they had been lying. Dr Erika Hagelberg, of Leicester University, was next up to the plate. One of the leading authorities on ancient DNA, she extracted a sample from the skeleton, which was 'amplified' using the technique of polymerase chain reaction, which generates sufficient DNA material for analysis. The results showed that the likelihood of the skeleton being the child of Karen Price's parents was in excess of 99.99 per cent.

It was now known who had died but there was no clue as to the killer. That emerged through old-fashioned policing. The BBC programme *Crimewatch UK* showed the model of the case and it appears this was seen by Idris Ali, a small-time burglar who was watching television with his friends; he had remarked that he had been at a special school with Karen. Apparently at Ali's request, a friend telephoned the police to say, 'There's a bloke in the house that knew Karen Price.' The prosecution's case was that Ali had been using the girl as a prostitute and that, when she refused to pose for pornographic photographs at a sex party at 29 Fitzhamon Embankment, Riverside, Cardiff, Ali and another pimp and bouncer Alan Charlton had beaten and strangled her. The body had been buried after being kept in a cupboard for four days.

Ali, who was regarded as having a borderline learning disability, was interviewed extensively; first as a potential witness and then, when the police did not believe him, as a suspect. Ali eventually admitted having been present during the murder and having a limited involvement in the girl's death. By this time he had been at the police station for fourteen hours without any opportunity to rest. He was again extensively questioned, and during yet another interview that was not contemporaneously recorded he said that he had been forced to strangle the girl at Charlton's instigation. There were a total of fourteen taped interviews, during which there were repeated breaches of the police Codes of Practice and improper procedure, including delays in cautioning him, absence of contemporaneous records and insufficient time for rest. The defence argued unsuccessfully that the trial judge should exclude the interviews following the improper procedures, but they were admitted into evidence. Ali's confession was virtually the only evidence against him. A friend of Price who had been at the party gave evidence that she had seen the killing and basically supported his version of events. Both Ali and Charlton were convicted of murder. Charlton was sentenced to life imprisonment and an appeal was dismissed. After Ali's conviction was quashed and a retrial ordered, he pleaded guilty to manslaughter and was released on the basis of time served. He was later jailed for nine years for robbery and while in prison he led a cell-block riot that left two guards severely injured. This time he was jailed for twelve years. He absconded from a bail hostel in 2010.

In February 2014 it was announced that the Criminal Cases Review Commission had asked the Court of Appeal to review Charlton's conviction, citing concerns with the South Wales Police's investigation and possible 'oppressive handling of witnesses'.

The Mickelberg Brothers

In Perth, Australia, the deaths of two retired officers on 1 September 2001 led to yet another re-examination of a case that had long caused problems for the Western Australian Police. The deaths were those of Don Hancock, one-time head of the Perth Criminal Investigation Branch, and his friend and former colleague Louis 'Lou' Lewis. They followed the shooting of Gypsy Joker biker Billy Grierson. The case that was re-examined was the Perth Mint robbery of 1982 and the convictions of the Mickelberg brothers, Peter, Ray and Brian.

On 22 June 1982 three different couriers, each with false cheques, arrived at the Mint on Hay Street in the middle of the city and collected gold bullion weighing 68 kilos, then worth A$653,000. In today's terms it would be valued at more than A$1.5 million. The couriers and the gold promptly vanished. In many ways it was an attractive crime and one that appealed to the Australian psyche – daring, well thought through and, best of all, there was no violence involved. In charge of the investigation was Hancock, then a sergeant and one of many officers worldwide who revelled in the soubriquet 'Grey Fox'.

Although they had only one previous conviction between them – Peter had been fined A$50 for possessing an unlicensed firearm – high on the list of suspects were the Mickelberg brothers who worked as abalone divers and pilots. Ray Mickelberg was a former SAS commando in Vietnam and, given the military precision with which the raid had been carried out, was regarded as the potential mastermind.

On 26 July Peter Mickelberg was driving home to the north Perth suburbs when a police car pulled in front of him, forcing him to stop. He was taken to Belmont police station where he was interviewed by Hancock and another officer, Tony Lewandowski. This was regarded as an odd choice of police station as there was a headquarters in the city specially set up to deal with the robbery. Other odd features of the arrest were that all other officers attached to Belmont except one had left the station by the time Mickelberg arrived. The one remaining officer Bob Kucera, later the West Australian Health Minister, left shortly after.

According to Peter Mickelberg – denied until after Hancock's death – Lewandowski first of all told him that no one knew where he was and that as far as others were concerned he could be dead. Then Hancock told Lewandowski to make the prisoner strip and he punched Mickelberg in the solar plexus and throat. Years later Lewandowski claimed he told Hancock that they really had no evidence but Hancock replied, 'Don't worry, it will get better.' According to the two policemen, Peter Mickelberg's confessed to his involvement and implicated his brothers. The confession was, as is often the case, unsigned. The prosecution also claimed that a fingerprint of Ray Mickelberg was found on one of the fraudulent cheques. The defence claimed that, since one of his hobbies was casting hands – there were about twenty casts found when his home at Marmion Beach was raided – it would have been easy for the police to obtain a mould of Mickelberg's finger and to have planted the print. In 1983 the brothers were found guilty; Peter received six years six months and Ray Mickelberg a massive twenty years. Brian served nine months before his conviction was quashed.

The Mickelbergs also had another problem following their discovery in 1980, two years before the mint robbery, of a fabulous gold nugget 'The Yellow Rose of Texas', named by an American seaman who won A\$200 in a competition run by engineer Bryan Pozzi.

The discovery of the Rose, the second largest gold nugget ever found in Western Australia, had been made by the

Mickelbergs' mother Peggy while prospecting near Kalgoorlie. Now, wearing a wig and glasses and without her false teeth, said to have been taken out because she felt sick on the flight, she left the light aircraft carrying the nugget to be photographed by the alerted press.

The nugget was duly and wrongly authenticated by experts and was sold to Australian entrepreneur Alan Bond for A$350,000. During the course of the Mint investigation the police discovered photographs of the nugget, which, far from being found in the goldfields, had been created by Ray Mickelberg and Brian Ponzi. The Mickelbergs and Ponzi refused to sign what were alleged to be confessions about the Rose, but these were admitted in evidence against them. The Mickelbergs claimed the whole thing was a joke and publicity stunt for an adventure business they were running, but the authorities were not amused. On 19 May 1984 Peggy Mickelberg received an eighteen-month sentence, of which she served nine; Ponzi and Ray were ordered to serve five years with a minimum of thirty months; Peter and Brian were sentenced to thirty months with a minimum of eighteen. Their father Malcolm was found not guilty. With his sentence tacked on to the end of the Mint swindle Ray now had the longest sentence of any serving Western Australian prisoner.

Over the years Peter and Ray Mickelberg made a total of seven appeals – six to the Western Australian Court of Criminal Appeal – and all were rejected. In 1989 some 55 kg of the gold was left in a Perth suburb, something which certainly cannot have been done by the brothers; Brian Mickelberg had died in a mysterious helicopter crash in 1986 and the others were still in prison. A gold bar and two containers, later tested and identified by the Perth Mint, were also sent to a local television station together with a note that the Mickelbergs were innocent and had been framed. The note claimed a prominent Perth businessman was behind the swindle.

A campaign in 1995 by journalist Avon Lovell, saying the brothers had been the victims of a miscarriage of justice, came to a temporary halt when Lewandowski sued Lovell and put a stop to sales of his book, *The Mickelberg Stitch*, which had sold

17,000 copies in a week. The Police Union imposed a A$1 a week levy on its members to fund Lewandowski's action. There were also allegations that the Union prevented Lovell getting a job with the *West Australian*, telling the paper that if he did, no officer would work with it.

After a further rejected appeal in November 1989 police commissioner Brian Bull told the press that the decision 'totally vindicates the actions of the police in their investigation into the Perth Mint swindle'. Peter Mickelberg was released that year and Ray two years later.

Regarded as a man who knew how to get results, and described by one officer as a 'take no prisoners sort of bloke', Don Hancock became the head of the Perth CIB on the back of the successful prosecution of the brothers. Shortly before the 1983 trial a recording, which was never played at the trial, was made by Ray Mickelberg of a conversation with Hancock at Mickelberg's home:

Hancock: 'I'm not a mean person, but I'll tell you what: I've done things in my life that you never did, and harder things, worse things, and if I've got to do them again, well I'll do them again.'

RM: 'In the line of duty?'

Hancock: 'That is, yes. What I believe is my line of duty – to get the job done.'

Of course, this sort of conversation can be interpreted in a number of ways. Hancock may simply have meant he was prepared to associate with informers and general scum to obtain information, but there are less generous explanations.

When he retired in the late 1990s Hancock went back to the Kalgoorlie goldfields where he had grown up and ran a public house in the remote town of Ora Banda as well as working a claim. There, on 1 October 2000, he met with trouble from the local biker gang the Gypsy Jokers, one of whom, William Grierson, was banned by the hot-tempered Hancock from his hotel after he and other bikers insulted Hancock's daughter, Alison – asking her to 'cream her pants' for them. Hancock promptly shut the hotel down for the evening.

Later that night Grierson was shot dead at a nearby

campfire, hit in the shoulder and his spine severed. By the time the police interviewed Hancock, known as a fine shot, he had showered and changed his clothes. He refused to hand over his clothing and ate an orange, something that would mask gunshot residue. He then returned to Perth and took legal advice, declining to assist with police enquiries. Over the next few weeks his home was firebombed, as was a store he owned, and the hotel was blown up.

In the spring of 2001 the police heard that some Jokers were mounting surveillance on Hancock's home and that there was a plot to kill him at a Kalgoorlie race meeting where he had a horse running. They managed to persuade Hancock not to go and instead, along with Lou Lewis, on 1 September he went to Belmont racetrack in Perth. Probably while they were at the races, a bomb was placed in Lewis' Holden station wagon. They stayed late at the track because Hancock wanted to listen to the last race at Kalgoorlie in which his horse ran third. As Lewis drove them back to Hancock's home the bomb was remotely detonated, killing the men and blowing a large crater in the road. On 28 March 2002, thirty-eight-year-old Sidney John Reid, a full member of the Gypsy Jokers, pleaded guilty to the murders.

It was only after Hancock's death that Tony Lewandowski, now estranged from his wife and son, broke ranks and swore an affidavit admitting he had lied and had taken part in the beating of Peter Mickelberg:

'I have had enough. Now that Don Hancock is dead I can't harm him and I am now telling the truth . . . a couple of times I wanted to come clean but there was no way I could go against Don.'

Lewandowski, who said that while he admitted fabricating evidence he still believed the brothers to be responsible for the robbery, asked the Director of Public Prosecutions for immunity but, while it was being considered, he left the country for Asia.

He returned to give evidence by video-link on 27 September 2002 at a preliminary hearing of yet a further appeal by the Mickelberg brothers. On 2 July 2004 by a majority of two to one this time the court allowed the appeals, quashed the convictions and indicated there would be no retrial. It is difficult to see how there could have been. Hancock was dead and so now was Lewandowski, who had committed suicide at his Perth home in May that year. It was not, however, a unanimous verdict. The Chief Justice David Malcolm and Justice Christopher Steytler were in favour of allowing the appeal. Justice Michael Murray was not, holding that no miscarriage of justice had occurred. The Western Australian Police were unwilling to accept the verdict and Assistant Police Commissioner Neil Hay said there was an abundance of evidence linking the brothers to the crime. In their turn the brothers asked for A$11 million compensation, a claim that was eventually settled for rather less than that.

Arthur Allan Thomas

Sometime before 22 June 1970 but probably on the wet and cold evening of Wednesday the seventeenth, Harvey Crewe and his wife Jeannette disappeared from their 365-acre farm at Pukekawa, Bitter Hill, forty miles south of Auckland. Their neighbour Julie Priest had heard three shots some-time between 8 and 8.30 that evening. She did not hear any the following evening and was able to pinpoint that particular night as she had gone to bed early after going out on the Tuesday.

Although Harvey Crewe was said to have a bad temper, the couple were generally well regarded in the community, a township of around 600 people. They were, however, reclusive – dinner invitations were not returned – and so there was no real comment when he failed to appear for the Saturday football match or when neither turned up for a dance that night. Nor does the milkman seem to have been worried that the milk and bread he delivered on the Thursday had not been collected on the Friday. Nor did he report that it had still not been collected on the Monday.

They had not been heard of for five days when Jeannette's father, Len Demler, who had a neighbouring farm, drove over after getting no replies to his telephone calls. What he found was their two-year-old baby daughter Rochelle in her cot, hungry and in soiled nappies but by no means starving or suffering from hypothermia. Other used nappies were found on the fridge, in her cot and in other parts of the house. These were quite obviously not left there by Jeannette Crowe, who kept a bucket with nappy wash next to her washing machine.

There were bloodstains on the carpet and a meal laid out on a table, but of the Crewes there was no sign. In the yard the Crewes' dogs had been fed and watered. Curiously, Demler returned home leaving things as they were and telephoned his stock agent to cancel a collection of sheep. The man was out and Demler waited for him to return the call before calling on his neighbour, Owen Priest, for help, telling him, 'The bugger's killed her and done himself in.' It was about 2.20 that afternoon that Priest telephoned the Tuakau police. Demler later went to a party instead of joining in the search for his daughter and her husband.

A crucial element in the case was whether Rochelle had been fed and, if so, when. Dr Thomas Fox, who first examined her, thought there was no need for her to be sent to hospital and she was left in the care of an experienced local mother. The doctor thought she had been unattended for a maximum of seventy-two hours and a minimum of forty-eight. If left for four to five days she would have been seriously ill. However, another doctor, Ronald Caughey, thought she had not been fed at all. Initially Detective Inspector Bruce Hutton, in charge of the case, thought she had been fed after her parents disappeared, but then in 1977 he changed his mind, saying she had not.

Supporting the theory that Rochelle had indeed been fed was a local man, Bruce Roddick; he said he had seen a woman about five foot ten or five foot eleven tall with brownish hair cut short and wearing dark slacks outside the Crewes' house on the Friday morning. He had seen her driving the Crewes' car sometime before and she had waved at him.

On 16 August, almost two months to the day of their disappearance, the body of Jeannette Crewe was discovered at a spot known as Devil's Elbow in the flooded Waikato river. It had been wrapped in bedclothes and bound with wire. She had been shot through the head with a .22 bullet. The body also appeared to have been beaten but there was no sign of any sexual attack. Fifteen fragments of the bullet were recovered from her head, including one large fragment on the base of which the number eight was embossed. These were immediately sent to Dr D. F. Nelson of the Department of Scientific and Industrial Research (DSIR) for comparison with bullets test-fired from rifles collected from relatives and associates of the Crewes, from residents within five miles of their farm and from other persons who had in some way become involved in the inquiry. A search for a .22 cartridge case was also carried out in the house and enclosure, but nothing was found.

The next day a .22 rifle belonging to a local farmer Arthur Allan Thomas was collected by the police. No .22 rifle was collected from Demler because he was not registered as an owner. Nor, despite a thorough investigation, could the police establish that he had had any access to a .22 at the time the Crewes were killed.

On 17 September, almost a month to the day after his wife's body was found, Harvey Crewe's body was fished from the same river. He also had been shot in the head. His body had been weighted down with an axle, which was traced as registered to a 1929 Nash motor car in 1958 and then in 1965 to a trailer. The axle had been owned by Arthur Thomas' father and in 1965 its axle assembly had been removed from the trailer. It might, or might not, have been replaced.

There had been a series of earlier incidents on the Crewes' farm. First, in 1967 there had been a burglary but only some of Jeannette's jewellery had been taken. The next year Crewe had returned home to find a bedroom on fire and in 1969 a hay barn was torched.

The initial suspect for the killings was Jeannette's father Len Demler. There had been ill feeling in the family over the will of his wife Maisie, who had cut another daughter from inheriting because of what she saw as an unsuitable marriage. In turn Demler cut Jeannette from his will. Quite why that would make him wish to kill her and her husband is unclear. However, Crewe was negotiating to buy Demler's half share in his farm, which might have resulted in his being evicted. Some of Jeannette's blood was found in Demler's car, which was, perhaps, more reason to suspect him.

There was some talk of a murder/suicide but that would

have required someone to dispose of the bodies. And there was also the question of who, if anyone, had fed Rochelle and the Crewes' dogs.

Suspicion then turned towards Arthur Allan Thomas, who was known to have been fond of Jeannette both at school and before her marriage. The police had test-fired barely 3 per cent of similar rifles belonging to residents in the Pukekawa district, but of those tested, all but two rifles were eliminated as possible murder weapons. One of these two rifles belonged to Arthur Thomas.

Despite his rifle not being excluded as the murder weapon the rifle was returned to him on 8 September 1970, the day after the interview when it had actually been put to him by officers that the rifle was the weapon used to kill the Crewes.

On 27 October, the garden at the Crewe house was searched for a third time and this time a cartridge case was found. The case carried marks which, said the police, showed it had been fired from Thomas's rifle. In November, he was arrested and charged with the two murders.

Although Thomas seems to have met Jeannette Crewe in the street only a few times since her marriage, the prosecution's case was that he was obsessed with her and resentful of Harvey Crewe. It was alleged that Thomas, without any real supporting evidence, had had in the late 1950s a 'passion' for Jeannette; that he had pestered her at dances and followed her to Maramarua at a slightly later stage when she working there as a teacher.

In support of this obsession the prosecution claimed that a brush and comb set had been taken in the burglary. Some years before her marriage Thomas had given her such a set, but his present was discovered unopened in a spare bedroom after the murders.

Now the theory ran that with an ever-growing resentment he had staged the burglary, set fire to the bedroom and finally killed them. There was also a suggestion that the Crewes were relatively wealthy while many local farmers including Thomas were having a hard time during the winter of 1970 and this was another cause of deep-seated resentment.

At his first trial in 1971 it was generally agreed that the time

of the shootings had been between 7 and 9.30 on the evening
of 17 June and Thomas was able to provide an alibi for that
period. Mr Justice Henry suggested to the jury that the killer
might be a stranger to the district, 'a passing burglar', but the
jury went with the police and the finding of the cartridge in the
garden. Thomas was found guilty and sentenced to life imprisonment. In June that year his appeal against his conviction was
dismissed. Almost immediately a campaign was launched on
his behalf and, in February 1972, a petition was lodged which
resulted in the Court of Appeal quashing the conviction and
ordering a retrial.

In April 1973 Thomas was reconvicted at the second trial.
This time evidence was given of a visit made by him to a
fortune-teller years earlier to find out how, if at all, his relationship with Jeannette Demler was likely to develop. It was again
inferred at the trial that this passion may have endured up
until 1970, despite Thomas's marriage in 1964, Jeannette's
marriage in 1966, and the fact that there was no evidence of
any but the most casual association or rare contact between
the two in the intervening years. For the defence, the respected
forensic scientist Dr Jim Sprott gave evidence that the cartridge
case found in the Crewes' garden did not match the bullets
that had killed the couple. The jury retired for just under two
and a half hours before convicting Thomas a second time. It
seems at first three jurors had voted for a not guilty verdict.

After the second trial, in 1973, on Detective Inspector
Hutton's instructions, Detective Sergeant Stan Keith dumped
a number of key exhibits at the Whitford tip. They included
the cartridge case found in the garden.

At this juncture Thomas's supporters, including Pat Booth
of the *Auckland Star*, began another attempt to overturn his
conviction. Sprott's key contribution came after retired detective Jack Ritchie, who ran a gun shop in Dannevirke, came up
with a theory that the bullets used to kill the Crewes were never
in the type of cartridge that police alleged they found in the
Crewes' garden.

Ritchie sent examples to the Thomas retrial committee
chairman Pat Vesey, who passed them to Sprott. In turn Sprott

advertised in the press and on radio at his own expense, asking the public for as many cartridge cases as possible of the type involved. He received about 26,000 and examined most of them himself.

There were no matches between the type of cartridge case and the bullets used in the killings. And now it appeared that the cartridge case had been planted at the scene. Next the author David Yallop wrote *Beyond Reasonable Doubt?*, exposing substantial flaws in the prosecution case.

On 17 December 1979 Thomas was released from prison following the grant of a free pardon by the Governor-General of New Zealand. On 24 April 1980 a warrant for a Royal Commission into the case was issued. The proceedings were to be in public and anyone wishing to make a submission was advised how to do so.

On 21 May 1980 the Commission's proceedings were formally opened in Auckland. On 9 June it began hearing evidence, generally sitting in public but occasionally in private. The hearing took sixty-four days and ended on 30 October. For security reasons the room was swept for bugging devices each morning before the hearing.

The Commission dismissed the prosecution's theory of obsessive jealousy, concluding:

We raised the question as to the relevance of the burglary and the fires, there being no evidence that Mr Thomas committed any of them. We received the following reply from counsel for the Police:

'These are relevant in that taken together with the murder itself they suggest a connected and regular course of conduct in each year of the Crewe marriage by a local person with a continuing grudge against either or both Crewes, the grudge being of a personal nature in that as with the murder, there was evidently no monetary motive (nothing of value stolen except items of personal significance to Jeannette, suggesting possible sexual or romantic significance), a person with particular interest in the brush and comb set, someone not acting on an impulse, but on the

338 *Fit-ups and False Confessions*

basis of personal animosity of depth and long standing, and a person other than Demler, in that he had an alibi for at least one of the nights in question.'

That this submission should come from experienced counsel demonstrates the lack of any reasonable answer to Thomas's contention that he never was on the Crewe farm that night. Even taking all the Prosecution evidence at its face value however, we are unable to see that it suggests any more than that Mr Thomas had at one stage a romantic interest in Jeannette Demler; that in common with many dairy farmers in a year of drought he had a degree of financial difficulty in 1970; and that a burglary and two fires occurred in the Crewe house in the early years of their marriage.

The Commission went on to say that to link the three factors together into a motive for Thomas killing the Crewes was quite unjustified:

We are of the view that the Prosecution evidence utterly fails to establish any motive on the part of Mr Thomas to kill Mr and Mrs Crewe. It follows that it in no way supports the proposition that he might have been on their property on 17 June 1970 to deposit exhibit 350 [the cartridge] there.

Instead, the Commissioners found that the cartridge case relied on to convict Thomas had been created by firing bullets taken from the Thomas farm using his seized gun and the cartridge had been planted by Detective Inspector Bruce Hutton and Detective Sergeant Lenrick Johnston outside the Crewe house. The inquiry found there was misconduct by Hutton and Johnston in the prosecution of Thomas and that his arrest and prosecution had been unjustified. He was awarded NZ$950,000 compensation for his time in jail and loss of the use of the farm.

Despite the Royal Commission describing the conduct of Hutton and Johnston as an 'unspeakable outrage', on the advice of the Director of Public Prosecutions that no conviction would be likely, the New Zealand police never laid charges against any police officer involved in the investigation and prosecution of Thomas. Lenrick Johnston died in 1978; Bruce Hutton in 2013.

With the rapid developments in forensic science over the past forty years, in 2010 Rochelle Crewe now asked the Prime Minister, John Key, to have the case reopened. As a result a number of members of the Thomas family were re-interviewed and asked to provide alibis.

In 2012 Ian Wishart wrote *The Inside Story*, in which he debunked the theory that if it was not Arthur Thomas it must have been Demler. Instead he leaned towards the theory that it was either the son of a prominent New Zealand family or the psychotic police officer Johnston who, he claimed, had been blackmailing Jeannette over a false burglary claim. Another far-fetched theory, which has circulated without any evidence to support it, is that Jeannette shot her husband, and her father helped her dump the body. She then committed suicide and again Demler disposed of the corpse.

Then in September 2013 it was announced that ten uniden-tified fingerprints taken from the Crewe house had gone missing. Prints from their car had also apparently been lost. Researcher and author Chris Birt commented:

> From my perspective, having researched the Crewe murders and the Police investigation for thirty-nine years, there can be no innocent explanation for this disappearance. A cynic may be excused for believing that this is another act by a member, or members, of the New Zealand Police aimed at preventing the resolution of this most famous of cold cases.

In 2014 a 328-page review of an investigation conducted by Detective Superintendent Andy Lovelock reported that 'there is a distinct possibility that (the rifle cartridge found at the scene) may be fabricated evidence, and that if this is the case, that a member of police would have been responsible'. It concluded that Rochelle had not been fed after her parents' murder and that a possible sighting of a woman on the farm had been incorrect. The report offered no suggestions as to whom the killer might be, but it did eliminate Demler. It also regarded as extremely significant that the axle used to weight down Harvey Crewe's body had at one time been on the Thomas farm. There was, however, nothing further to be done. Memories would have faded and many witnesses were dead.

The Maxwell Confait Case

Over the years most famous murder cases have been known by the name of the accused – Harvey Hawley Crippen, Joe Hill, O. J. Simpson, the West Memphis Three and so on – but the 1972 killing of a homosexual transvestite prostitute in south London has always been known by the name of the victim, Maxwell Confait. It was a case that would have enormous repercussions for the English legal system.

Around 1.20 in the morning of Friday, 22 April 1972, firemen called to a blaze at Doggett Road, Catford found the body of a man in an upstairs bedroom. He was identified as twenty-six-year-old Maxwell Confait, who preferred to be called Michelle, and who was well known in the gay community of south London. He had been strangled.

Confait's landlord was Winston Goode, a married West Indian who lived in the same house and shared Confait's penchant for wearing women's clothes. He was awakened by the sound of the fire and, after getting his wife and children out of the house, went to Catford Bridge railway station to telephone the police. Goode was later questioned by the police and denied having a homosexual relationship with Confait or being jealous of him. Some days later he was admitted to Bexley Psychiatric Hospital, unable to remember the traumatic events of the fire. He later committed suicide, swallowing cyanide.

The first medical man at the scene was Dr Bain, the police surgeon, who, because of Confait's way of life, did not take a rectal temperature to establish the time of death. Nor did Dr

James Cameron, the Home Office pathologist who arrived later. Both thought that Confait had been strangled between 6.30 and 10.30 p.m on the evening before the fire.

Two days later a police officer saw two boys running away from a fire that had been started in a shed in a local park. He passed on this information and on 25 April three local boys, Colin Lattimore, Ronnie Leighton and Ahmet Salih, were arrested.

Lattimore was eighteen and said to have a mental age of eight. He had been diagnosed educationally subnormal and later psychiatrists would say he was highly suggestible, to the extent that 'the slightest indication of the expected answer will produce it'. Leighton was fifteen and, though considerably brighter than his friend, was described as 'borderline subnormal' and 'really an immature, inadequate simple dullard'. Salih was reasonably intelligent. He was just fourteen. All were questioned without a solicitor, parent, guardian or a responsible adult being with them.

Lattimore and Salih complained the police had hit them. Lattimore suffered a nosebleed and Salih had cried. Leighton also claimed to have been a victim of police violence. By the end of their questioning Lattimore and Salih both admitted starting the Confait fire. Lattimore and Leighton also admitted killing Maxwell Confait, while Salih only admitted watching the murder.

At the committal proceedings to find whether the boys had a case to answer, the prosecution's medical evidence was that Confait had died between the times Cameron and Bain had suggested. Under the Criminal Justice Act 1967 a defendant had to give an alibi notice if he wished to call witnesses to support it at the trial. All three had alibis but Lattimore's was watertight. Independent witnesses could trace his movements from 6 p.m to 11.40 p.m. Another saw him at home at 11.45 p.m. and his father could place him at the house at and after 12.35 p.m. This destroyed the case against all three boys. If Lattimore had not killed Confait then the others could not have helped or watched him.

This presented the prosecution with a serious problem. The time of death had been based on the medical evidence on the onset of rigor mortis. It had never been the intention of the Act to improve the position of the prosecution by giving them a chance to rearrange things in their favour, but what was now necessary was that the time of death had to be shifted so that Lattimore's alibi was worthless. And shifted it was.

So at the trial in November that year, medical evidence was called in the shape of Cameron, whose evidence in the Australian Chamberlain case was later discredited, to say that based on the temperature of the fire, which would have speeded up the process of rigor mortis, Confait could have been killed as late as 1 a.m. And that was the end of the alibis. Worse, the trial judge Mr Justice Findlay admitted the youths' confessions in evidence.

The judge also took the opportunity to tell the jury that they were to put out of their minds any feelings they had about youth crime in general and youths causing trouble at football matches in particular, both of which were on the rise. It was akin to the notice in saloons during Prohibition, 'Do not add water to this otherwise you will make beer.'

After three-and-a-half hours' retirement the jury came back with verdicts against the boys. Lattimore was found guilty of manslaughter on the grounds of diminished responsibility and convicted of two counts of arson. He was detained under the Mental Health Act and sent to Rampton. Ronnie Leighton was found guilty of arson at Doggett Road and Ladywell Fields, and also of burglary at a nearby house. He was ordered to be detained at Her Majesty's Pleasure. Salih was found guilty of arson and burglary and sentenced to four years' detention.

On 26 July 1973, Lord Justice James refused leave to appeal saying that 'there was no misdirection in the summing-up to the jury and no representation of facts which can be relied upon as justifying the grant of leave to appeal'.

The families did not accept the verdicts. In particular, Lattimore's father wrote a series of letters to the Queen and the Prime Minister, while his local Member of Parliament, Carol Johnson, also wrote to the Home Office.

To an extent the boys were fortunate. After the Labour victory in the General Election in February 1974 Roy Jenkins was appointed Home Secretary and the radical barrister Alex

Lyon came into the Home Office. Both were committed to reviewing miscarriages of justice. Lattimore's new Member of Parliament for Lewisham was Christopher Price, who had been working for Thames Television and was another man who campaigned against miscarriages. The National Council for Civil Liberties had also become interested in the case and, with Price, contacted one of the leading pathologists in the country, Professor Donald Teare. A thirty-minute documentary of the case was made for Thames Television during which Teare gave his unequivocal opinion that Maxwell Confait had died between 6.30 p.m. and 10.30 p.m. Another noted pathologist of the day, Professor Keith Simpson, broadly agreed with Teare.

On 18 June 1975, Roy Jenkins announced in Parliament that he was referring the case to the Appeal Court. Again the boys were fortunate in that the humane and liberal-minded Lord Justice Scarman was sitting. The effect of the new medical evidence was:

> ... to destroy the lynch-pin of the Crown's case and to demonstrate that the version of the admission relied upon by the Crown cannot be true. Even if correct the confessions could not be regarded as sufficiently reliable evidence, standing as they do to justify the convictions for arson, which were based solely upon them.

Scarman also criticized the police for their handling of the case, saying that they should have put more emphasis on the fact that there had been no struggle. This suggested that Maxwell Confait had known his killer. He said he had known of cases where auto-eroticism was used as a stimulus for the homosexual act. Scarman queried, was Maxwell Confait killed by a lover in a tragic accident?

In any event the convictions were overturned and the boys freed. Jenkins then ordered a further police inquiry into the case, undertaken by the Derbyshire police, but no arrests were made and the case remained unsolved.

Recriminations followed. How could the boys have confessed to a killing they could not have committed and, moreover, how could Sir Norman Skelhorn, then the Director of Public Prosecutions, have authorized the prosecution? Now Sir Henry Fisher, a former High Court Justice who had unusually left the bench to forge a career in the City, was appointed to hold an inquiry.

In his report at the end of 1977 he found that Detective Superintendent Graham Stockwell, one of the interviewing officers:

> ... gave his evidence [to the inquiry] convincingly and made a favourable impression on me. He has a frank and open manner; he seemed calm, steady, careful and intelligent (as his posting to the Fraud Squad indicates). I judged him to be wholly trustworthy.

That was not the case with Ronnie Leighton who had had a quick spat with Donald Farquharson, who represented the police at the inquiry. Early in his cross-examination when Farquharson asked why he started fires, Leighton replied, 'I tell you I don't know. If you keep on, mate, I will knock you on.' He then left the room saying, 'I have fucking had enough of this.'

Fisher was critical of the way the prosecution was conducted:

> So far from trying to make the time of death more precise ... Detective Chief Superintendent Jones, Mr Williams (of the Director of Public Prosecution's office) and Mr [Richard] DuCann (Treasury Counsel who conducted the prosecution at the trial) made every effort to keep it as vague as possible. The reason for this was that they were concerned to establish a case which rested wholly or mainly on the confessions which could not be entirely true unless the time of death was outside the brackets given by Dr Bain and Dr Cameron, the pathologist.

Fisher's curious findings went as follows:

(a) Lattimore's alibi was genuine and he could have taken no part in the killing.

(b) Leighton and Salih could have taken part in the killing.

(c) All three could have set light to 27 Doggett Road.

Fisher would not accept that the confessions could have been made without at least one of the boys having been involved in the killing and the arson. The most likely scenario, he thought, was that Lattimore's confession to his part in the arson was true; that he had been persuaded to confess to the murder by Leighton and or Salih; that Leighton and Salih's confessions to the arson were true and that they had structured their answers to questions about the killing to implicate Lattimore.

The experienced former judge Sir Henry could not have been more wrong. In January 1980 the new Director of Public Prosecutions, Sir Thomas Hetherington, received further information about the case and eight months later, Sir Michael Havers, the attorney general, told the House of Commons that he was satisfied that Confait had died even earlier. He was also satisfied that if Sir Henry had had this information before him he would not have come to the conclusions he did. There was, however, insufficient evidence to prosecute anyone else.

The new evidence had come from Inspector Eddie Ellison, who had been investigating a complaint by a man that he was being blackmailed over a murder he was alleged to have committed. Two men, each blaming the other, said they had seen Confait being killed. There was no independent evidence and therefore no prospect of a successful prosecution. The next year the three youths were offered a total of £65,000 compensation.

What Fisher did get right was the need for changes in the way suspects were interviewed as well as the need for an 'analysis and evaluation of a case by a legally qualified person at as early a stage as possible'. In the Confait case there had been clear breaches of the so-called Judges Rules, which governed the police interrogation of suspects. The questioning of Lattimore had been unfair, said Fisher. The investigating officer should have waited until someone, a parent or friend, could have been present at the interview. He thought that the DPP's man Williams had done as much as prevailing practice expected of him and if that was so then prevailing practice was wrong.

The case was the beginning of the road to the introduction of the Police and Criminal Evidence Act 1984, which provided very considerable safeguards for suspects through the recording of interviews and the provision of legal representation. It was followed by the establishment of the Crown Prosecution Service in 1985, which removed the right of the police to prosecute their own cases, so lessening their ability to persuade defendants to plead guilty at an early opportunity and also eliminating, at least in theory, the opportunity for police corruption over matters such as arranging bail and interfering with evidence.

It is said that DuCann never prosecuted again. In Tom Tullett's adulatory biography of James Cameron, *Clues to Murder*, there is no mention of the Confait case at all. In Norman Skelhorn's *Public Prosecutor*, published in 1981, he wrote:

'In . . . view of the developments that have now taken place, resulting from fresh evidence having come to light – which was apparently not available at the time of the prosecution or at the time of Sir Henry's inquiry – I do not think that any useful purpose would be served by now dealing with these matters. Sir Henry's report was of course published appreciably later than my retirement, but in so far as he suggested possible revision of procedures both by the Department and by the police, I feel sure they will have received careful consideration.'

Warren Billings and Tom Mooney

In anticipation of the United States' imminent entry into World War One, on 22 July 1916 San Francisco held a parade honouring Preparedness Day. The procession, which started at 1.30 p.m. and which was expected to last three and a half hours, had over 51,000 marchers from 2,134 organizations as well as fifty-two bands. Military, civic, judicial, state and municipal divisions were followed by newspaper, telephone, telegraph and streetcar trade unions. Many of the following marchers came from other cities in the San Francisco Bay area. The starting signals were 'the crash of a bomb and the shriek of a siren'. It was not a wholly popular parade with the radicals and an unsigned anti-war pamphlet, circulated throughout the city in mid-July, read in part, 'We are going to use a little direct action on the 22nd to show that militarism can't be forced on us and our children without a violent protest.'

About half an hour into the parade, just as marchers from the Grand Army of the Republic and Sons of the American Revolution were passing a crowded street corner, a time bomb, in the form of a cast steel pipe filled with explosives, was detonated on the west side of Steuart Street, just south of Market Street near the Ferry Building. Ten people were killed and more than forty injured.

Although there were suggestions that two Mexican-looking men planted the bomb, for the police aided by an old Pinkerton Detective Agency man Martin Swanson, it was simply a question of rounding up the usual suspects. And the suspects this time included Warren Billings, Tom Mooney, his wife Rena, taxi driver IsraelWeinberg and Edward Nolan, president-elect of the Machinists' Lodge 68. Four days after Swanson joined the investigation the five were arrested.

Born in Chicago, the son of Irish immigrants, Thomas Mooney was an active member of the Socialist Party and an enthusiastic campaigner for the Industrial Workers of the World (IWW) leader Eugene Debs's campaign for the presidency of the United States. Mooney also edited the radical newspaper *Revolt* and was friends with a number of anarchists, many of whom argued that violent acts could be useful instances of 'propaganda by the deed'. Warren K. Billings, born at Middletown in 1893, one of nine children, and who worked in a shoe factory, also had a reputation for promoting direct action.

Martin Swanson had been on the trail of Mooney and Billings for some years after they had incurred the wrath of the Pacific Gas and Electric Company during a 1913 strike. They had been arrested for, but were never convicted of, conspiring to dynamite power lines. This had been followed by an unsuccessful attempt to convict Mooney in Contra Costa County on a charge of unlawful possession of explosives.

On 11 June 1916, a high-voltage tower of the Sierra and San Francisco Power Company, which served the Union Railroads of San Francisco (URR), had been dynamited in the San Bruno hills. Soon afterwards the URR offered a reward of $5,000 for information leading to the arrest and conviction of the dynamiters. Two days later Swanson interviewed Israel Weinberg, who had often taken Mooney to trade union meetings, offering him a share of the $5,000 reward if he could provide evidence that would convict Mooney of the San Bruno bombing. Weinberg refused.

After that Swanson had approached Warren Billings. If he would provide information connecting Mooney with the bombing then, as well as a share of the $5,000 reward, he could have a job with the Pacific Gas and Electric Company. Billings also refused and reported the approach to Mooney and George Speed, secretary of the IWW.

Billings had been earlier convicted for carrying dynamite on
a Sacramento streetcar and received two years, which he
served in Folsom. Both men always maintained their arrests
had been as a result of a frame-up by the gas company's detectives, including Swanson.

During the four separate trials over the Preparedness Day
bombing the prosecution's case rested on a ragbag of five
disparate witnesses. Frank C. Oxman, apparently an Oregon
cattleman, claimed to have seen the defendants at the scene of
the crime, as did an itinerant waiter John McDonald who
placed Billings at Steuart and Market at the crucial time. John
Crowley, who gave evidence only at the Billings trial, placed
him at Steuart and Mission during the march. Estelle Smith, a
prostitute, said she had seen the defendants at 721 Market
Street and her mother Mrs Kidwell gave evidence to the same
effect. Mellie Edeau and her daughter Sadie, who had
contacted the police after the bombing, also said the defendants were at 721 Market. The prosecution's case was now that
the defendants had intended to place the bomb at Market but
had then changed their minds and had driven to Steuart.

The show trials that followed were conducted in a lynch
mob atmosphere, encouraged by the prosecutors, District
Attorney Charles Fickert and his deputy Eddie Cunha.
Mooney and Billings were convicted in the first two trials.
Mooney was sentenced to be hanged. Billings received life
imprisonment. In April 1917 Rena Mooney was acquitted, as
was Weinberg in the November. Nolan was released after nine
months in prison without being brought to trial.

After Mooney was sentenced to death, the Socialist Party
tried to expel him, but his local branch successfully warded off
the threat. Then US President Woodrow Wilson became
involved. Without informing Mooney's defence committee,
Wilson telegraphed California Governor William Stephens
asking him to commute Mooney's sentence to life imprisonment, or at least stay the impending execution. To his credit,
and possibly thinking of the Joe Hill furore in Utah, Stephens
commuted the sentence.

After the trial, letters came to light regarding the principal

witness, the rancher Oxman. The trial judge Franklin A. Griffin
had thought him to be by far the most important witness:

> His testimony was unshaken on cross-examination and his
> very appearance bore out his statement that he was a rep-
> utable and prosperous cattle dealer and landowner from the
> State of Oregon. There is no question but that he made a
> profound impression upon the jury . . .

But appearances can be deceptive. While Mooney's appeal for
a new trial was pending it was discovered that Oxman had
written to Ed Rignall, a friend from his home town of Grayling,
Illinois, which he had not visited in the previous twenty years.
It urged him to 'Cum to San Frisco as an expurt witness in a
very important case.' It continued, 'You will only hafto answer
3 & 4 questions and will Post you on them. You will get mileage
and all that a witnss can draw Probly 100 in cleare so if you
will come ans me quick, in case of this Hotel and I will mange
the Balance.'

This letter and others came to light because Rignall did
come to San Francisco, but when he discovered he was
required to commit perjury he returned to Grayling where he
told lawyers what had happened. In turn they wrote to
Mooney's lawyers.

At first the exposure of Oxman, involving as it did the
district attorney's office, seemed almost to guarantee that
Mooney and Billings would be granted a new trial and initially
Fickert agreed he would not oppose one. Cunha accepted he
knew of Oxman's deception and promised to see that justice
should be done. Judge Griffin lost no time in officially suggesting there should be a new trial and the attorney general of the
state, Hon. Ulysses S. Webb, in a request filed with the Supreme
Court of California, urged similar action.

It now seemed the men would obtain a new trial; however, a
series of events wrecked their hopes. In May 1917 Oxman was
put on trial for perjury. Fickert found counsel for him and, it
is alleged, arranged his acquittal. There was then a sudden
change of mind on the part of Fickert who backtracked,

possibly influenced by the power companies. When challenged
on the Oxman trial Fickert said that there was another page of
the letter which told Rignall only to come if he had seen the
incident, but unfortunately it had been lost. Now he denied
that he had ever agreed to a new trial, and his subsequent
efforts were now a clumsy attempt to whitewash Oxman and
justify his own motives and conduct throughout. The final
blow was a decision of the Supreme Court to the effect that it
could not go outside the record in the case – in other words,
that a judgement could not be set aside merely for the reason
that it was based on perjured evidence.

In November 1920, either in a fit of remorse or with an eye to
his future, Draper Hand, of the San Francisco Police Department,
went to Mayor James Rolph and admitted that he had helped
Swanson and Fickert to frame Mooney. He told Rolph:

> Swanson sent for me and asked me to take Oxman to the
> North End station and show him Weinberg's auto. They had
> taken the car out there. I took Oxman to see the car. It was
> his first and only sight of the car. Oxman was very much
> concerned, when he saw the car, to find out if it were pos-
> sible for a man to sit in it and hold a suitcase as he was going
> to describe in court. He had me get in the car and let my
> hand hang down over the side, as if I were holding a suit-
> case. He wasn't satisfied till I got in and did as he wanted;
> after that he thought his version was all right – that the
> defence wouldn't prove it impossible.
>
> There wasn't any license plate on the car when I took
> Oxman to see it. If the plate had been there it would be bad
> for the prosecution if Oxman were asked if he hadn't got the
> number when he saw the car at the police station. Cunha
> had had the plate taken off that car. It was in a drawer in an
> inner office at the station. Cunha told me to copy the
> number. I did that and gave it to him. As far as I know
> Oxman never saw the license plate itself.

Later Edgar Rignall and Earl K. Hatcher provided evidence
that Frank Oxman was 200 miles away during the bombing

and could not have seen what he told the court at the Mooney trial. In February 1921 John McDonald confessed that the police had forced him to lie about the planting of the bomb. Despite this new evidence the Californian authorities still refused to grant a retrial.

Then William Wilson, Secretary of Labor under Woodrow Wilson, ordered J. B. Densmore, the former Federal Director of Employment, to make a report. It was a damning indictment of the state's prosecuting attorney and his methods.

Densmore found that the witness Mrs Kidwell had a husband in prison for forgery and had given evidence in exchange for a promise he would be released. The working girl Estelle Smith had first told the story of events at 721 Market to newspaper reporters but then changed her story at the trials and it now contradicted McDonald. She later said that she had been told by Fickert and Martin Swanson to coach the others how to give their perjured evidence and was threatened with prison if she refused.

Mrs Edeau had gone to the police to say that she had seen the men at the scene of the bombing but had failed to pick out Billings and Mooney. She later said that she saw them at 721 Market and not at the scene of the bombing. When this discrepancy was pointed out she said it was their astral bodies that had been at Steuart. McDonald later admitted he had never seen the defendants before he saw them in prison. John Crowley had a long police record and in turn his evidence contradicted that of McDonald.

Shortly before Governor Stephen commuted Mooney's death sentence, Densmore had planted a dictagraph in Fickert's office. As a result of the recording Densmore thought that Fickert was an associate of men with interests of such a nature that it was unbelievable he could be either impartial or honest in a case of this nature. He had also been cooperating with notorious jury fixers; he and his associates had conspired to frame cases, and in particular conspired to frame Mrs Mooney and attempted to intimidate and blackmail a woman witness.

As for Assistant DA Cunha, he was recorded as saying:

If I knew that every single witness that testified against Mooney had perjured himself in his testimony, I wouldn't lift a finger to get him a new trial. If the thing were done that ought to be done the whole low-down bunch would be taken out and strung up without ceremony.

Densmore concluded his report:

The basic motive underlying all the acts of the prosecution springs from a determination on the part of certain employer interests in the city of San Francisco to conduct their various business enterprises upon the principle of open shop. There has been no other motive worth talking about. As to their plan of operations it was simplicity itself. A terrible crime had been committed and popular indignation and horror glowed at fever heat. From the standpoint of the unscrupulous element among the employer interests the opportunity seemed made to order. To blame the outrage on certain agitators in the labor world seemed not only possible but, owing to various concomitant plausibilities, doubtless appealed to the foes of organized labor as possessing all the elements of a stroke of genius.

A 1919 Grand Jury refused to find a True Bill against Fickert from the charges made by Densmore over the framing of Mooney and Billings, and separately for his having conspired with bondsman Pete McDonough in arranging for wealthy defendants to be given bail. Times had changed and now President Theodore Roosevelt declared, 'anyone assailing Fickert for prosecuting anarchists should be deprived of citizenship'.

Fickert continued literally to fight his corner, first against an old critic, the Democrat Francis Heney at the Olympic Club, and later against newspaper editor Fremont Older at the Palace Hotel. Older, who had spent twenty years fighting for the release of Mooney and Billings, had originally believed Mooney was guilty but had changed his views. He disliked

Mooney, thinking him worthy of jail for real crimes, but not for the bombing at Steuart and Market.

And so Billings and Mooney remained in jail until, on 28 August 1928, a petition was presented to Governor C. C. Young asking him to pardon Tom Mooney. However Young, while promising to study the case carefully in his spare time, replied, 'While, like many other people, I have been dissatisfied with some of the aspects of the trial, I have never been able to bring myself to a belief in the innocence of the accused.'

By now there were few people, including the trial judge Franklin A. Griffin, who had become part of the campaign along with nine out of ten of the living jurors who said they had been misled by the perjured evidence, who still believed Mooney and Billings were guilty.

Nevertheless successive Republican governors over a period of twenty years – William Stephens (1917–23), Friend Richardson (1923–27), Clement Young (1927–31), James Rolph (1931–34) and Frank Merriam (1934-39) – all refused to order the release of the two men.

In 1935 Mooney finally filed a writ of habeas corpus which was heard by the United States Supreme Court. Even though he presented evidence that his conviction was obtained through the use of perjured testimony and that the prosecution had suppressed favourable evidence, his writ was denied because he had not first filed one in state court.

The pair had to wait until the election of a Democrat as governor for their release, and Mooney was finally pardoned in 1939 by Culbert Olson. The Sunday after his release he walked in a parade up Market Street from the Embarcadero to the San Francisco Civic Center, accompanied by an honour guard of one hundred longshoremen with their hooks and led by Mooney's own union, Local 164 of the International Molders' Union.

Although over the years the two men had become estranged, Mooney then campaigned for the release of Billings, who never quite achieved the martyr status accorded Mooney. For a time Mooney travelled around the country making speeches and drawing a full house at Madison Square Garden in New York City, but his years in prison had taken their toll physically. He was also separated from his wife and in love with another woman, a member of the Communist party. Rather callously he wrote, 'the lives of Mrs Mooney and myself are now and have been for the past sixteen years totally and completely incompatible'. Many of his former colleagues in the labour movement thought him to be selfish and conceited.

Billings was also released in 1939, a few months after Mooney left San Quentin, when his life sentence was commuted to time served – twenty-three years. The commutation of sentence meant he could not vote, own or inherit property or obtain a driver's or marriage licence. He was by law, if not in fact, a dead man.

Finally, in 1961, another Democrat, Governor Pat Brown, granted Billings a full pardon. It was, however, on the grounds that he had been 'rehabilitated', rather than because he was innocent of a crime that no one really believed he or Mooney had committed.

After leaving prison, Billings began working as a watch repairman, a trade he had learned in prison, and later set up his own repair business at home. He resumed his labour activism as a member of the Watchmakers Union executive board and delegate to the San Mateo Labor Council. He was active as well in the anti-Vietnam War movement and various other political, economic and social causes.

After attempting a lecture tour, Mooney collapsed. The California Federation of Labor turned down a resolution to pay his hospital bills as his politics were deemed too radical. Dying impoverished in a San Francisco hospital, Mooney at fifty-nine had only a few visitors and letters sending money from friends. From his bed he acted as Chairman of the 'Citizens' Committee to Free Earl Browder', a Communist who had been jailed for passport frauds.

He died at Saint Luke's Hospital in San Francisco on 6 March 1942 after a fourth operation to remove part of his stomach. His funeral concluded with the singing of 'The Ballad of Joe Hill'. After his death Rena Mooney took in boarders and eked out a living giving violin and piano lessons. She died following a heart attack when doing the ironing on 11 August 1952. Warren Billings died on 4 September 1972. Their persecutor Fickert had died from pneumonia in October 1937.

There have been many alternative theories put forward about who planted the bomb – Mexicans, the IWW, a madman Dane Chris Lassen who was sent to a mental hospital after he said the Kaiser had told him to plant it – even Swanson and Fickert in an effort to discredit the unions. Curt Gentry, in his exhaustive analysis of the case *Frame-up:The Incredible Case of Tom Mooney and Warren Billings*, leans towards the theory that it was the work of the German Louis Witzke, described as 'the most dangerous spy in the world', on the orders of his spymaster General Franz Von Bopp. Witzke was sentenced to death for another unrelated piece of spying in America but his sentence was commuted and he was released in 1923. If Gentry is correct, Lassen's account may not have been too far from the truth.

Colin Ross and the Gun Alley Tragedy

One of the problems of the forensic scientist in the early days came when he (they were very rarely women) stepped outside his discipline, often with disastrous consequences. One man who did so was Australian chemist Charles Alfred Price who, given a microscope, provided much of the crucial evidence in what became known as the Gun Alley Tragedy in Melbourne.

On Friday 30 December 1921 the naked body of pretty, auburn-haired twelve-year-old Alma Tirtschke was found in the dead-end Gun Alley in central Melbourne. Known as the Eastern Market, it was a collection of cheap shops, fortune-tellers, bars and curtained doorways that led to brothels. The girl had been raped and her body washed. The police inquiry was led by the experienced if dubious officers John Brophy and Thomas Piggott, who believed that the washing had been done to remove clues as to the killer's identity.

Described by lawyer T. C. Brennan as a 'modest, obedient, intelligent, quiet child', Alma, wearing a box-pleated overall, a white blouse with blue spots and a panama hat with her high school badge on it, had left her aunt's home at Jolimont between 12.30 and 12.45 p.m. to go to Bennet and Woolcock's butcher's shop in Swanston Street, half an hour's walk away. She was to collect a parcel of meat from her uncle who worked there. He seems to have been out and she left the shop about fifteen minutes later carrying the meat, which weighed around 8–9 lbs.

For some reason she did not return to her aunt straight away. She was seen in nearby Little Collins Street and well after 2.15 p.m. she was seen by two women – a Mrs and Miss Edmonds – about fifty yards from the entrance to the Eastern Arcade. They saw her go into the Alley and did not see her again. According to the women, Colin Ross, who owned a wine bar in the arcade, was standing in front of the door to his premises. Mrs Edmonds put the time at 2.45 p.m.

Alma had also been seen by Stanley Young and his wife coming out of the Arcade, walking across the street and standing near a lodging house. They put the time as between 2.30 and 3 p.m. One question that has never been satisfactorily answered is what she was doing in the area at all, carrying around that amount of meat on a hot summer's day, an hour and a half after she should have finished her errand. All the streets where she was seen are within around ten minutes' walk of each other.

What was a child of her sort doing in and around the Eastern Arcade? This was delicately explained by the *Argus* on 7 January 1922:

> Great importance is attached by the detectives to the infor-
> mation given by the girl's relatives that she suffered from an
> organic weakness which might have caused her to visit the
> arcade. Previously the detectives had been at a loss to under-
> stand why a girl of her temperament and character, could
> have been induced to enter such an unattractive quarter.

Without doubt, the detectives in the case, John O'Connell Brophy* and Thomas Frederick Piggott, described many years

---

* Brophy's career came to an end in May 1936 when he was admitted to St Vincent's Hospital with gunshot wounds. Initially it was put about that he had accidentally shot himself while cleaning his revolver but it emerged he had been with two women on a deserted road near Melbourne Zoo when he was attacked by gunmen. There was considerable speculation that one of the gunmen was the husband of one of the women. After a public inquiry the Chief Commissioner Thomas Blamey, who had earlier lied on Brophy's behalf, was required to resign and Brophy followed him some months later.

later as Batman and Robin, were the scourge of the Melbourne underworld. Of them Squizzy Taylor, the leading light in the 1920s milieu, wrote, 'Ashes to Ashes, Dust to dust, if Brophy don't get you, Piggott must'. They were regarded as none too scrupulous as to how they came by their evidence and indeed some years later, like Lucifer, Brophy fell headlong from grace.

From the start they came under pressure from the press. The *Argus* summed up local feeling:

> As each day passes the grievous disappointment of the public at the failure of the police to track down the murderer of the child Alma Tirtschke grows more profound . . . The detectives and police force of Melbourne are on their trail and no matter how exacting they may find the ordeal they must realise that the public will not tolerate failure on their part.

Initially there were stories that a Chinese man had been arrested and then a German. Both were incorrect. Significantly the *Argus* also carried a story that around 3 p.m. on the afternoon Alma disappeared a man had heard a girl screaming in fear.

Rewards were posted, with the government putting up £1,000 and the Melbourne *Herald* another £250. In all, that sum would have bought five inner suburb houses at the time.

As the owner of a wine bar just over a hundred yards from where the body was found, Colin Campbell Ross, a man with a row of gold teeth and suffering from gonorrhea but with no criminal convictions, was one of the men the police interviewed the next day. When the police went to see him they found the floor of the bar had been recently scrubbed but, although he was one of the first to be questioned about the killing, Ross seems to have been unconcerned. Asked bluntly by Piggott, 'Ross, how much do you know?', he replied, 'I do not know anything.'

On 5 January three more men were arrested and released. The police saw Ross again that day, this time at his home in Footscray – the wine bar had been shut down at the end of the year. They saw him again on 8 January when he was at the

Detective Office in Russell Street for eight hours, at the end of which he made a statement. He said he had seen a child answering Alma's description and gave the detectives details of an alibi, saying he had been with a friend, Gladys Linderman, who also went by the name Wain; she had arrived at his bar about 4 p.m. and stayed an hour. They had been in its private room. Apparently, although the saloon was a haunt of prostitutes who were regularly moved on by the police, 'respectable' women took their children there and sat in the private room.

Ross had made an appointment to see Gladys that evening around 9 p.m. in nearby Little Collins Street, and after he had shut his bar and gone home for tea he returned to meet her. They had gone back to the wine bar and stayed there until 9.45, after which he had taken her back to her home in nearby King Street. He then went to catch a train at Spencer Street station to go back to Footscray. He had one Yale key to his wine bar and his brother Stanley had the other.

This was one of those cases in which the police relied heavily on the evidence of known criminals and people with a grudge against Ross. His troubles had actually begun earlier in the year. His wine bar, which he ran in partnership with his brother Stanley, was inhabited by the local low life and the police suspected that he was rolling drunken clients, taking their wallets when they went to use the urinal in the alley.

On 13 October 1921 a commercial traveller, John Bayliss, had been shot in the shoulder in the lavatory in the market. A Frank Walsh, said to be American or British (reports varied), was charged with the shooting and he gave up Ross to the police. He told the detectives Ross had helped the drunken Bayliss to the dunny in the passage and found he had a roll of money on him. They would go fifty-fifty if Walsh took it off him. He gave Walsh a gun and told him to use it if he had to. One of the witnesses against them who put them both right in it was a girl, Ivy Matthews. She had been a waitress working for Ross and she claimed she had been with Phyllis Grey, Walsh's *de facto*, when he told her about the robbery.

Ross was found not guilty but Frank Walsh received nine months. Immediately after the trial Ross made another serious mistake and sacked Ivy Matthews, probably in a squabble over her share of the money. Bayliss went downhill and in the winter of the next year he was found asleep in the Eastern Market. By then he was more or less a derelict covered in lice and still wearing the coat he had worn when he was shot.

The robbery, coupled with the saloon's generally unsavoury reputation, was sufficient to have Ross's liquor licence withdrawn and it was to be closed on 31 December that year; the day after Alma's murder.

Overall Ross was not an attractive character and does not appear to have done the best for himself. He clearly never thought he should have a solicitor, and after he made his statement following his eight-hour detention he returned to see Piggott and challenged him to tell him who had been telling lies about him.

On 10 January the police questioned the man who said he had heard a girl's scream around 3 p.m. He had not come forward earlier because he had been in poor health but since no one else had done so he decided he must. The man could not say from which building the screaming came and Piggott decided it had been shrill laughter by girls or that of an ill-tempered child rather than a young woman. That particular line of inquiry lapsed.

But by then Olive May Maddox, a twenty-one-year-old married but separated woman who worked as a prostitute, had come forward to tell the police the story they wanted to hear. She had, she said, known Ross and the saloon well, visiting it on a daily basis until the time of the robbery and the dismissal of Ivy Matthews, after which her visits dropped off to perhaps 'five times a week at the most'. She had been at the wine bar on the day of the murder just before five with another girl, Jean Dyson. She looked in the parlour and saw a third girl, Lil Harrison. As she passed the beaded curtains of the small compartment on the right she saw a young girl who, if her story was correct, must have been Alma. The girl had a glass in front of her but Maddox could not say if it was empty. There were two men drinking nearby, and after speaking with Lil Harrison she went back to the bar and Jean Dyson and said to

Ross, 'Hello Col, she is a young kid to be drinking.' He replied, 'Oh if she wants it she can have it.' About a quarter past five she wandered off and when she returned just before six the girl was gone and she did not see Ross.

She saw him again on 5 January when, according to her, Ross made a number of telling remarks, saying first of all that she should tell the police nothing and then adding, 'The papers all say that she was a goody-goody but that is for the sake of the public. She was a cheeky little devil.'

Five days later she spoke with her friend Ivy Matthews who told her she should go to the police, something she was reluctant to do because she had absconded her bail.

Many people were in and out of Ross's wine bar that afternoon but Ivy Matthews was the only other person to have seen the girl there, and when she was in the Melbourne Hotel the next day for a 3 p.m. appointment, she read in *Truth* magazine of the murder. She had gone straight to Ross's saloon and confronted him saying, 'Why did you do it?' For a time he had denied Alma was in the room, but when pressed he said she had asked him for a drink and he had given her some lemonade. Matthews had said, 'Why did you take her in the little room? I know how you are with little children.' Finally he said, 'On my life Ivy, I did not take her in there with any evil intention, but when I got her there I found she knew absolutely what I was going to do with her if I wanted her.' He went on to say he had outraged her between six and eight in the evening when his brother Stanley and Gladys Wain had left. He also went on to say she was not a virgin. He left the body in a blanket, which Matthews described and, after Gladys Wain had come and gone, he went home but then returned by car between one and two to dispose of the body. At first he had thought of putting it where Italians might be blamed and then in the room of a man, McKenzie, whom he disliked, but had finally just left it in the street. He had said, 'I did not mean to kill her but it was my passion that did it,' adding a 'disgusting comment', which she eventually wrote down for the court, 'He said, "You know what a kid means to me, Ivy. I had fucked her before I knew what I had done. She played about with me through the afternoon and she'd been well fucked before I got to her.'''

Ross was arrested on 12 January and appeared, again unrepresented, in the magistrates' court the next day. He objected to a remand saying he had already given his alibi. Remanded in custody he said in a surly fashion, 'This is the country's justice. It is a great country; there is no doubt about it.' He then contacted Napthali Sonnenberg, the solicitor who acted for major Melbourne villains, who in turn instructed barrister George A. Maxwell with T. C. Brennan as his junior. In his day Maxwell had been one of the great advocates of the Victorian Bar but now he was nearly blind and he was not regarded as a strong cross-examiner.

It was while he was on remand that Ross apparently made his third confession, this time to Sidney Harding who was facing what prisoners called The Key, an indeterminate life sentence, and so had every reason to curry favour with the authorities. According to Harding this came over a number of meetings in the exercise yard and directly contradicted the confession he had made to Ivy Matthews. He had given the child a few glasses of sweet wine. He had not strangled her during the sexual act but a little later when she began calling out. When he had gone back to the wine bar during the night it had been by bicycle and not by car. At least one part of this confession could be disproved. There was no trace of alcohol in Alma's stomach.

There were two scientific pieces of evidence and the crucial one was the red-golden hairs, found a fortnight after the killing, on a rug at Ross's home. Now the chemist Price, rehearsed by his assistant Charles Taylor, identified them as matching Alma's. There were no bloodstains on the blanket, nor on the floor of the bar. There was the evidence too that Ross suffered from venereal disease, but there was no trace of a transfer of the infection to the girl. Curiously both a sister of Ross and Gladys Wain had reddish hair but Price was adamant they were not similar. On 30 January Sonnenberg asked to be allowed to have an analyst conduct an independent examination of the hair samples and was refused.

Ross's trial, which began on 20 February, lasted five days and, fuelled mainly by the Murdoch-owned *Herald*, was carried out in an atmosphere of almost total public hostility towards him.

Olive Maddox, who had been kept out of the way by the police in case criminals such as Squizzy Taylor tried to get her to change her evidence, appeared in court wearing a navy frock of jersey silk and a navy silk hat with matching ostrich feathers, grey gloves and a gold bangle on each wrist. One newspaper reported her as having a high colour. Was it rouge or TB or alcohol?, it wondered. How had she come to go to the police? She had been advised to go by her friend Ivy Matthews who had spoken to the fortune-teller Madam Ghurka, who had a stall in the alley.

Her friend Ivy Matthews was a very odd witness indeed. She really would not give a straight answer about herself. For a start she would not say where she lived and when the address 25 Rathdown Street was forced out of her she was reluctant to say who lived there. In fact the person who owned the property was a Julia Gibson but no, she said, she did not feel obliged to say if Gibson was Madam Ghurka. She did not know she was a fortune-teller. She admitted she herself might have gone by a variety of names. She was married but would say nothing of her husband, whom she would not name, except to say he was a sick man who lived in Queensland and who sent her money. She claimed to have been a partner in Ross's wine saloon. But no, there was no bad feeling between them after her sacking although they were engaged in litigation.

Ross's defence rested heavily on the shadowy figure of Gladys Wain but their stories didn't entirely match. He maintained she was his girlfriend. She said she was nothing of the sort. She was a married woman separated from her husband but still living in the same house. Her connection with Ross had only been to buy linoleum and other fittings from his wine bar she knew was closing. She had neither removed her hat nor lain down on the couch – which rather ruled out it being her hair on the rug. She was not fond of Ross and could not understand why he had described her as his girl. It was an absolute lie she had 'a certain disease', but under cross-examination she admitted she had been treated for VD. What that had to do with her honesty is not immediately apparent unless it could be said that the disease carried with it a propensity to lie.

The jury took over twenty-four hours to find Ross guilty. 'My life has been sworn away by desperate people. If I am hanged, I will be hanged as an innocent man,' he told the court.

The tenor of the summing-up had been how could people be so wicked as to condemn a man to death by their false evidence ? But it has been done year in year out over the centuries. For a start Sidney Harding, who was totally discredited in the witness box, was one such person. Harding was so deep in trouble there had been every reason for him to try to shift the odds in his favour. As for the girls, here on offer was the equivalent of nine inner city houses in reward money to be shared. There is also little doubt that Ivy Matthews held a grudge against Ross and she and the manipulative fortune-teller Madam Ghurka could mould the malleable Olive Maddox.

As is often the case, after the trial some witnesses came forward to support Ross's story. One man said that he had been in the bar and the girl could not have been on the premises without being seen by him. A taxi driver said he had heard a child scream. He had looked for the source but although he could not find it he was sure that the cry had not come from Ross's wine bar. In March the Court of Appeal refused to hear the witnesses and perhaps unsurprisingly dismissed T. C. Brennan's argument that an alternative verdict of manslaughter should have been left to the jury. It had not been argued by counsel at the trial and the court saw no reason why the judge should have taken it upon himself to do so. The introduction of a manslaughter verdict when Ross had denied all along that Alma had been in the wine shop seemed like a desperate throw of the dice.

One of the witnesses whom it had been intended to call if there was a new trial was Hannah Livy Mackenzie. She told the Court of Appeal that she had seen a man with black rolling eyes, a swarthy complexion and black and grey hair taking the girl along Russell Street on the afternoon of 30 December. She was told he was Mr Murdoch, the girl's uncle. Unfortunately there were no photographs of Murdoch for the court and, inconveniently, he was in another state. However Senior Detective Brophy was on hand to reassure the court that Murdoch was not swarthy, he was not tall and thin as Hannah Mackenzie said but was of medium build and rather stout. His hair was brown rather than black.

Although Ross intended to petition the Privy Council in England he was hanged before he could do so. To his death he continued to protest his innocence, saying he had been framed by the Melbourne police. Shortly before he was hanged he received a letter:

You have been condemned for a crime which you have never committed, and are to suffer for another's fault . . . My dear Ross, if it is any satisfaction for you to know it, believe me that you die but once, but he will continue to die for the rest of his life. Honoured and fawned upon by those who know him, the smile on his lips hides the canker eating into his soul. Day and night his life is a hell without the hope of reprieve. Gladly would he take your place on Monday next if he had himself alone to consider. His reason, then, briefly stated is this: A devoted and loving mother is ill – a shock would be fatal. Three loving married sisters whose whole life would be wrecked to say nothing of brothers who have been accustomed to take him as a pattern . . . It is too painful for him to go into the details of the crime. It is simply a Jekyll and Hyde existence. By a freak of nature he was not made as other men . . . This girl was not the first . . . With a procuress all things are possible . . . In this case there was no intention of murder – the victim unexpectedly collapsed. The hands of the woman, in her frenzy, did the rest.

The letter bore the postmark of a small country town. The writer was never traced.

On the night before his execution Ross wrote to his family:

Good-bye, my darling mother and brothers. On this, the last night of my life, I want to tell you that I love you more than ever. Do not fear for tomorrow for I know God will be with me. Try to forgive my enemies – let God deal with them. I want you, dear mother, and Ronald to thank all the friends who have been so kind to you and me during our trouble. I have received nothing but kindness since I have been in gaol. Say goodbye to Gladdie for me and I wish for her a happy life. Dear ones, do not fret too much for me. The day is coming when my innocence will be proved. Good-bye all my dear ones. Some day you will meet again your loving son and brother. COLIN xxxxxxxxxx

The hanging did not go well. For some reason the authorities had decided to experiment with a four-stranded rope rather than the tried and tested three-stranded European hemp. Ross did not die immediately because his spinal cord was fractured, not severed. Although his windpipe was torn and obstructed by his destroyed larynx, he continued to struggle with rasping breaths and convulsed on the rope. It is thought his death by asphyxiation took between eight and twenty minutes.

After his death Ross was championed by his barrister, T. C. Brennan, who, until his own death in January 1944, believed evidence would be forthcoming which would clear Ross.

On 10 August 1924 the body of eleven-year-old Irene Tuckerman was found hidden in chaff bags at Khartoum Street, Caulfield, Melbourne, in circumstances resembling the Gun Alley murder. Piggott investigated but no charges were ever brought.

The witnesses were duly rewarded with Ivy Matthews receiving £350; Sidney Harding was given £200, Olive Maddox £170 and, presumably for her part in persuading Maddox to come forward and housing Matthews, Madam Ghurka received £25.

Spared The Key in reward for his efforts, Harding and his wife went to Sydney where on 16 June she was given twelve months for theft. The next year he was reported to be in London claiming he had been robbed while feeding pigeons and begging for money for his return fare to Australia.

In 1926, then going under the name of Sutton, Ivy Matthews was charged with obtaining goods worth £110 from Myers Emporium with a worthless cheque. She claimed she did not know her account had been closed and was found not guilty.

In fact Ivy Matthews was an abortionist with a record of convictions beginning in 1933. Over the years as Irene Cholet, Irene F. Sholet, Nurse Mack, Florence Mackie, Irene Mackie, Irene Smith, Patricia Cholet and Irene Patricia Florence Sutton, she appeared in court on charges of abortion, unlawful possession and using insulting words.

In March 1938 she lost a slander action. She claimed sixty-four-year-old Walter Studd, to whom she owed money that he had lent her to set up a hotel, had defamed her, calling her a thief and a murderess. Her husband at the time of the Ross case had died and she had remarried. During her evidence she admitted she had been known as Nurse Mack and had run what she called a 'rest home', which was described as a one-room hospital. She received a much rougher time than she had in the Gun Alley case:

Gamble (for Studd): 'What is your maiden name?'
Witness: 'I would rather not answer.'
Judge Stretton: 'Do you admit that it was not Ivy Matthews?'
Witness: 'My maiden name was not Ivy Matthews.'
Gamble: 'In the Colin Ross case you said that that was your maiden name.'
Little (for Matthews): 'I object.'

Gamble said that he wanted to establish that the witness had given false evidence not only at the trial but in certain documents. It was essential that he should get her correct name now to establish this. Little said that he did not object to the name being given in writing. She had apparently given the name Ivy Matthews in the Colin Ross case as the result of an arrangement with the police.

Judge Stretton had not been impressed with her evidence:

I have come to the conclusion that the plaintiff is mentally agile and an extremely dishonest person who would do anything to suit her own interests and would stop at nothing where her vindictiveness was concerned.

'She is the most extremely vindictive woman I have ever seen in a law court. As to the other witness called to corroborate her, I do not believe him. If I had to go so far as to say that the defendant had established his innocence I would do so unhesitatingly. I accept his evidence.

In 1963 she was arrested as Irene Cholet in Kew in the act of carrying out an abortion. She had a heart attack and died in September 1964 before standing trial.

Olive Maddox left Melbourne in the November following the case. She had been shot at and, she said when she appeared on a charge of soliciting, attacked by other girls. She acquired a conviction in Perth and was soon back in her old haunts where she was sometimes known as Lily Stevens.

Madam Ghurka continued her successful career as a fortune-teller and professional litigant. In May 1951, quite amazingly, she was awarded £1,000 against the *Herald*, which had said she was a notorious fortune-teller, then a criminal act. One of her seven sons became a journalist with *Smith's Weekly*.

Overall the Gun Alley trial was seen as a great success. The foul murderer of a young girl had been convicted and hanged. The streets were safe again. The status of Brophy and Piggott rose immeasurably.

In May 1922 newspaper magnate Keith Murdoch, well pleased with himself, wrote to Lord Northcliffe:

You remarked to me that when a sensation comes, you would get all the readers you want. Perfectly true. I had only put on 8,000 when we got a murder mystery, an unprecedented one, leading to such scenes as mounted police having to be called out to check the crowds about the residence of the supposed murder. That left us with a steady 125,000. Then came the trial when we were averaging 230,000 or thereabouts. We are left with a steady 140,000 now and I hope for a bit more.

It was not until the middle 1990s that, two years after he began researching the case, journalist Kevin Morgan found a file of the Office of Public Prosecutions containing the original hair samples, which had been thought lost. He began a long administrative struggle for the right to submit the hair samples for DNA testing, finally achieving his aim in 1998. Two independent scientific authorities – the Victorian Institute of Forensic Medicine and Dr James Robertson of the forensics division of the Australian Federal Police – found that the two samples of hair did not come from the same person, thereby disproving with certainty the most damning piece of evidence against Ross. By now it had been accepted that the evidence of the witnesses, in particular that of Ivy Matthews, was not safe.

On 4 October 2005, the families of both Colin Ross and Alma Tirtschke jointly submitted a thirty-one-page petition of mercy and a year later the Victorian Attorney General Rob Hulls forwarded it to the Chief Justice, Marilyn Warren, requesting her to consider the plea for Ross. The subsequent posthumous pardon on 27 May 2008 was the first in Victoria's legal history and at present is the only instance of a pardon for a judicially executed person in Australia.

In 1996, Kevin Morgan had interviewed Viola, Alma's sister, and in his book, based on his conversation with her, he provides a very viable alternative suspect for the murder.

James Finch and John Stuart

The time and day: 2 a.m. 7 March 1973. The place: the crowded club, the Whiskey Au Go Go, a discotheque on the first floor of a building in Amelia Street, Fortitude Valley, an inner suburb of Brisbane's run-down strip of brothels and nightclubs.

The clubbers had gone to the Whiskey to hear the Delltones, well known for their surfing songs such as 'Hangin' Five' and 'Mr Baseman'. The support band was Trinity, playing for the first time. It was while they were on a break that two men dropped two nine-litre drums of petrol just inside the doorway to the club. The petrol spilled out from half-loosened caps and one of the men threw a match. When the people in the club began to smell smoke and the air-conditioning system took in the fumes and recirculated them, there was a general panic. Two of the exit doors seemed to be locked and the fire took hold of carpets and timber. Ten men and five women, including two waitresses and two members of Trinity, died in a matter of minutes.

From early in January that year stories had been circulating that Sydney criminals were looking to take over the nightclubs in Fortitude Valley. One version was that the principal targets were to be the Whiskey Au Go Go and Chequers, said to be the plushest in Queensland when it had opened the previous year in Elizabeth Street. The source of the rumours was a local criminal, John Andrew Stuart, who was feeding the story to a Brisbane journalist, Brian Bolton.

Both clubs were owned by the brothers Brian and Ken

Little, and Ken Little had told the *Sunday Sun* newspaper that a loaded gun had been put to their heads and they had been threatened. They had another problem. Chequers was in financial trouble at the time. There were also stories that up to A$50,000 had gone missing and a creditors' meeting was in the offing. On 11 January the car of Bill McAlary, then acting manager of the Whiskey Au Go Go, was torched and as a result armed guards were sent to protect the home of John Farr, the manager of Chequers.

There was a bomb blast at another Fortitude Valley club, Torino's, on 25 February, said by the *Sunday Sun* to be the first shot in an enormous extortion racket by the Sydney underworld. Later another club, Alice's, was targeted. The paper thought that up to forty clubs would be targeted and made to pay a then massive A$15,000 a week for protection. Sydney's Mr Big – who could then have been either Lennie McPherson or possibly nightclub owner and brothel keeper Abe 'Mr Sin' Saffron – was said to be casing Queensland and at least three Sydney gunmen were wandering around the Valley trying to avoid each other. Coupled with the news that a prominent Sydney criminal had been arrested after the blast at Torino's, it was sensational stuff.

But as it turned out, unfortunately the police failed to heed the warnings. Later John Bell, manager of the Whiskey, told the paper he had warned the police two and a half hours before the explosion. The paper recounted proudly that it had told the authorities on at least eight occasions of the likelihood of serious trouble and that the Whiskey would be the first target. At first the authorities denied there had been any such warnings but later admitted that while there had been, they had been unspecific.

Initially the police believed the Whiskey fire was the work of a maniac and there was no suggestion of it being the work of southern criminals. But within hours their attitude changed and on 10 March they said they wanted to interview Sydney-based Linus 'The Pom' O'Driscoll, a member of the Toecutters gang, who at the time had disappeared and was in hiding. They published mugshots of him. They believed the killer might have been acting as an intermediary agent for extortion-ists but there was no question of the involvement of a Mr Big from Sydney. Indeed, ignoring the maxim that little fish are sweet, they thought that southern criminals would have no interest in Brisbane, which, in the early 1970s, was regarded in criminal terms as little more than a country town.

In fact throughout the 1960s and 1970s there had been an interchange by corrupt police in Queensland and the south of their favourite criminals. After a serious quarrel with Jack 'Ratty' Clarke – shot and killed in August 1974 by John Stuart Regan – for a time the standover man Donnie 'The Glove' Smith was not welcome in Sydney. As a result, in exchange for a Queensland man, he was sent to Brisbane by detective Fred Krahe to run the Interlude club in the Valley.

Linus The Pom was soon discarded as a suspect and atten-tion turned to Stuart, a man said to have an IQ of 160 and a tendency towards arson. Later a former girlfriend said he liked setting fire to wheatfields.

In the aftermath of the Whiskey bombing John Stuart gave another long and self-exculpatory interview to the *Sunday Sun*, this time saying that while he had spent over half of his thirty-two years in prison he had not been involved in the blast and the people who had been were animals.

Wheatfields apart, Stuart had had a long and distinguished criminal career. He had served two years in Westbrook, a long-closed borstal boys' home near Toowoomba where the physical and sexual brutality of the regime was legendary. In 1962, while serving a sentence in Queensland, he had sawn through a hardwood beam in the security section of the Royal Brisbane Hospital and escaped. For the next three days he drove round the city in a car stolen from a policeman before he was captured in a shoot-out in the foyer of the Regent Theatre.

On his release he went to Sydney where he became the offsider of the dangerous Ducky O'Connor who, in May 1967, apparently shot himself in a Sydney nightclub while standing at the table of Lennie McPherson.

In 1965 he and O'Connor, dressed as police officers, moved in on two prostitutes, an approach that resulted in a charge of rape, reduced to one of having carnal knowledge by false pretences. He was sentenced to five years for his pains. He had also been one of the men who had gunned down Jackie 'Iron Man' Steele in November 1965 on behalf of McPherson, after Steele had been bad-mouthing Mr Big saying he was a police informer.

In April 1966 Stuart attacked a detective interviewing him in Long Bay Gaol, Sydney, fracturing his cheekbone, for which he received three years. The same year he stabbed another prisoner but there were no official repercussions. In 1967 he was found wandering in Long Bay looking for Steele who, at the time, was inside for possessing an unlicensed pistol. On his release Stuart moved back to Queensland. While in prison in Sydney he had met an Englishman, James Richard Finch.

Born in Bow on 20 December 1944, one of six children, Finch had been placed in a Dr Barnardo's home in November 1952 at the request of a children's care officer. He was selected for migration in 1954 and arrived in Sydney on 13 October. A good cricketer and boxer, he was placed in the Barnardo establishment at Picton, New South Wales. In May 1961 he was sent to Mount Penang Training Institution after charges of breaking and entering. From there it was downhill all the way.

In December 1966 in Sydney, Finch shot the celebrated and seriously dangerous standover man and killer of Ratty Clarke, John Stuart Regan, known as 'Nano the Magician' because of his ability to make those who crossed him vanish. Ever game, the next day Regan went to a police station with a lawyer to deny he had been shot. Sensibly he would not allow the police to examine his chest. It did Finch little good. In October 1967, described as a young criminal who was mixing with some of Sydney's heaviest, he received fourteen years and was deported back to England at the end of his sentence.

In the weeks before the Whiskey fire, Stuart invited Finch back to Australia and he arrived using a false passport. Finch was arrested three days after the blaze when Stuart's brother Dan gave him up, telling the police where they could find him. On Sunday, 11 March 1973 Stuart and Finch were both charged with fifteen counts of murder and Stuart was additionally charged with attempting to wound Detective Patrick Glancey. Nothing was left to chance when the pair appeared in court on the Monday morning. It was not a dignified debut. They were both handcuffed to the dock rail and there was Detective Glancey standing on Stuart's seat, holding him in a headlock. Another officer held his left arm, two his right and two more were at the dock gate. Stuart claimed that he had been beaten up, but the magistrate said he did not think it an 'appropriate time' to consider the allegation. Bail was not granted.

The case was long and drawn out. On 28 May the first committal proceedings were adjourned after Finch swallowed wire and claimed to have bitten off his own finger in a demonstration of his innocence. In fact a prisoner had cut it off for him. The trial was set for 28 August and then Stuart swallowed twisted paper clips bound with rubber bands. When they rotted the clips uncurled and stuck in his intestines.

The trial finally began on 10 September, but a week later Stuart dismissed his barrister and swallowed some more clips. What he really wanted was a separate trial from Finch, thinking he stood a better chance of an acquittal on his own. The trial judge, however, was having none of it and so, for the first time in Queensland's legal history, a major trial went ahead without one of the defendants in the dock. After an operation to remove the clips Stuart swallowed more, and from then on had no real part in the proceedings except for a visit by the court to his bedside at the Royal Brisbane Hospital to ask whether he wanted to give evidence. He said nothing and it was left to barrister Jeffrey Spender for Finch to salvage what he could from the wreckage. Throughout the trial Finch himself was handcuffed to the bar of the dock or, when he gave evidence, to the witness box. It cannot have helped him in the eyes of the jury. Nor can they have been pleased to be segregated throughout the whole trial, being taken for drives or on fishing trips at the weekend. For some reason the defence rather than the prosecution always get the blame for these inconveniences. 'I hope they find them guilty soon,' said one woman in the public gallery. Her husband was on the jury and she was missing him. It did not augur well for Stuart and Finch's chances.

What was the evidence against the pair? In fact there was no scientific or identification evidence at all. It was a question of winks and nods, verbals and jailhouse snitches. Stuart had told Bob Bottom about 'hophead' criminals and the journalist thought he might be trying to set up an alibi. Stuart had also told John Bell of the Chequers nightclub that Lennie McPherson had gone old and soft and wasn't interested in Brisbane, but that a Sydney gang wanted to move into the clubs. He, Stuart, was to be a frontman, something he did not want. He was, he said, the meat in the sandwich and did not know how to avoid getting bitten.

Overall the prosecution produced a motley crew of witnesses, including the finest collection of Sydney villains assembled since the police found the notorious Double Bay Mob having a meeting the previous year. Among the luminaries was Lennie McPherson, then rated as a top criminal in Sydney, there to tell the court he had no interest in Brisbane clubs. At the time he had a home at nearby Surfers Paradise looked after by his henchman, the one-eyed Lennie Guy naturally known as 'Cyclops'. Nor had James 'Paddles' Anderson, acquitted of a murder back in Melbourne in 1940 and regarded as one of, if not the, leading Sydney identities of the time, any interest in clubs in Queensland.

Anderson was keen to distance himself from McPherson. As a child they had gone to the same barber but he rarely saw him nowadays. Indeed, as opposed to the 'bad old days', he told the jury, he was now accepted in the best circles, whatever that might mean. The murderous 'Nano the Magician' Regan was also there. He was, he said, a company manager who had no interest in baccarat clubs in either Sydney or Brisbane. He had, however, an interest in land development. There was no mention of his earlier career as a pimp or his current one as an enforcer and killer. His previous run-in with Finch was not mentioned. Nor was there any mention of the fact that two years earlier he had come to Queensland to kill the pimp Leslie

Grigler, who had taken a prized Sydney prostitute, Cheryl Ann Mitchell, away from him.

In fact, Regan did indeed have an interest in land development in Queensland, but it was fraudulent and he was associated in the scheme with the one-time court clerk turned major drug dealer and police informer John Milligan. Regan was also thought to have been running call girls with Milligan. But, of course, with the criminal records of Finch and Stuart hovering and waiting to be put in evidence if there was an attack on the character of the prosecution's witnesses, the jury never heard any of this.

Perhaps the most interesting of all the southern witnesses for the prosecution was, however, the informer Graham James Miller, who denied he had any criminal connection with the underworld and told the court he was a self-employed salesman of toys and blankets, a business that was doing very well. Now the shoots of the defence began to sprout, albeit weakly.

Yes, Miller had known both Stuart and Finch nine years ago and, yes, out of a sense of generosity he had bailed Stuart out of Parramatta Prison the previous year. Strange for a man who hadn't seen him for years? No, just the decent thing to do. No, he didn't work for Lennie McPherson. Indeed the last time he had seen him was about fifteen years earlier in the Singapore By Night club. He knew Regan but didn't go around with him. No, he didn't know Paddles Anderson. Yes, he had a conviction when he was placed on a bond for three years for possessing a hand grenade but he had had no intention of throwing it. He hadn't been to jail for years.

These were clearly the Sydney heavies whom Stuart would have liked the jury to believe were behind the bombings. Had they been aware that McPherson was known as Mr Big in Sydney and had once, annoyed that his mother had not invited him to her birthday party, torn the head off a live white rabbit and thrown it at the terrified one-legged woman; that Regan had convictions for rape and had run a string of girls from the age of eighteen and had become one of Sydney's most feared killers; that Paddles Anderson was a member of the Double Bay Mob, Sydney's criminal elite; and had they had a crystal ball to see that the next year Miller would be in court yet again, things might just have worked out differently for Stuart and Finch.

But trouble also came from within the Stuart family. There was Rosalie Mary Stuart who told the jury that her brother-in-law had spoken of getting A$100 a week from three clubs in Brisbane and that he would never have to work again. She didn't think much of that. Why should people pay him for nothing? She hadn't liked it either when after the fire he'd told the press about the bomb explosion three years earlier that had cost informer and tattooist Billy Phillips' wife Tracy her hands. And there was also Stuart's brother, Dan, Rosalie's husband who had been arrested on a drugs charge just before the case, and had turned his brother in. Stuart, making one of his rare appearances in the dock, screamed, 'Dan ... you are lying ... you're lying for the reward.' Dan's son would later describe his father as 'the really sick puppy'.

As far as Finch was concerned, one serious problem was what he was doing in Brisbane in the first place, when he should have been safely tucked up in his Essex home in England. His story that he had come under a false name to see Stuart's ill mother one last time wasn't a good one. Then there was his unsigned confession, taken in the presence of New South Wales detective Roger Rogerson in his prelapsarian days, and seemingly on secondment to Queensland. According to Superintendent Buchanan, when interviewed Finch had been remorseful, thumping and kicking a wall in the police station saying, 'Kill me, kill me. I deserve it.' Indeed the fatherly Buchanan had had to tell him to quieten down and moderate his language in case women and children in the street outside heard him. Although a tape recording of a confession had been made earlier by Constable Glenn Hallahan in the case of the multiple murderer Carstens, one had not been made for Finch's confession. Verbals? What verbals? This was the first time in thirty-seven years on the force that Buchanan had ever been accused of verballing a man.

The most amazing of the prosecution's witnesses was

undoubtedly the jailhouse informer Aboriginal Arthur James Murdoch from Palm Island, a bisexual rapist who was serving seventeen years. One prison officer later described the man, dubbed 'The Black Stallion', as:

> The perpetrator who was straight out of the movie 'planet of the apes'.[sic] The raped victim was bleeding from the anus, and had massive bleeding bite marks all over his neck, shoulders, back and buttocks with visible teeth marks. This rabid tree ape with its knuckles dragged on the ground was caged in double spaced mesh, so that he could not grab and rape other prisoners. He has now been released back into his aboriginal community after serving decades incarcerated in solitude.

Murdoch told the unlikely story of how Finch had found him to be a sympathetic shoulder and had confided in him about the fire in the prison yard. No, he had not even thought of getting parole or any other favours, on the back of his appearance in court. Later it was suggested he received $50,000, part of the reward money. Whether or not it was his evidence that earned him his discharge, Murdoch had only been let loose nine days before he raped again. This time he was jailed for life.

The defence suggested that the club owner and man-about-Brisbane John Hannay had a motive for firing the disco. Hannay was a curious man. Later named by Australian Labor Party member Kevin Hooper as one of four Queensland mafia godfathers – the others were Geraldo and Antonio Bellino and Luciano Scognamiglio – Hannay had had an up and down relationship with Ken and Brian Little who owned the Whiskey and had left them after allegations of a shortfall of between A$20,000 and A$50,000 while he was the manager. He had been attacked and beaten in an alleyway a few days before the fire. Hannay had also been the manager of Alice's where he unfortunately kept the books of the Whiskey, and had changed the insurance of Alice's on 4 January, thirteen days before that club was fired. He had given the insurance business to a friend of one of the employees. When he was called to give evidence

Hannay told the jury he had recently fallen off a horse and since that accident could remember nothing.

At the close of the prosecution's case the trial judge Justice Lucas went to see Stuart in the prison hospital to try to discover whether he would give evidence, but he simply turned his face to the wall.

When it came to his summing-up, Lucas did not look kindly on the allegations of verballing by the police:

> In fact on Finch's story it is a conspiracy on the largest scale involving members of the police forces of Queensland, New South Wales and Victoria . . . It has always seemed to me that the larger a conspiracy becomes and the more policemen involved in it the less likely the story of a conspiracy is true.

On this point Justice Lucas was wrong. In fact verballing and the scrumdown (known in England as swifting) was practised worldwide. It involved one officer writing a sort of screenplay for the officers involved, each of whom would then write his own particular part in his notebook. Each notebook would interlock with those of the other officers.

It was not until *McKinney v R* in 1991 that the Australian High Court made up its mind about the necessity of warning a jury that unsigned confessions might actually have been fabricated. Before that there had been conflicting judgements about what was required, but now by a majority decision, the court, which actually took note of the developments in technology that could be used to record interviews, took a firm line.

On 22 October the jury, which had been sequestered for some six weeks, took a bare two hours to find both Stuart and Finch guilty. Stuart was brought to court to hear the verdict and spat at the prosecutor. Afterwards his brother Dan tearfully denied he was a Judas. He had had to do what he had had to do. Shortly afterwards he bought himself a $25,000 powerboat. It may, of course, have come from the sale of his house at Jindalee.

There was no thought in the mind of press or public that the convictions were unsafe and that the wrong men had been convicted. One theory was that when no one believed the stories Stuart had fed the journalist Bolton, he had had to take action himself:

> Stuart very deviously used an old Brisbane journo Brian Bolton. Stuart used to feed him these bullshit stories about the heavies from down south and, of course, crap like that in the newspapers made people sit up and take notice. It added to the atmosphere of fear. The trouble was that no one really believed him, so he had to do something about it.

Were there any other credible suspects? One thing was clear and that was that Finch and Stuart could not have set fire to Torino's. Stuart was in prison and Finch had not arrived in the country. Suspicion for that was levelled at a curious crew dubbed the Clockwork Orange Gang whose leader, Ian Hamilton, was said to have been the getaway driver. Hamilton, a former boxer, later disappeared and Billy Stokes, editor of the *Port News*, was convicted of his murder. Gradually, however, the blame for Torino's came to be put on the shoulders of a Brisbane drug dealer, Vince O'Dempsey, and his one-time associate Billy McCulkin, who was said to have been contracted to undertake the job for A$1,000 and then farmed it out to the Clockwork Orange Gang for A$500, a sum with which its members were well pleased.

In an interview with the *Brisbane Telegraph* on 6 July 1979, O'Dempsey denied any involvement in the Whiskey fire or any other deaths, saying, 'I have never murdered anyone. Nor do I intend to murder anyone.'

Meanwhile the Whiskey case rumbled on with both Finch and Stuart consistently refusing to accept their convictions. One prison officer Tom King thought it was because of the quality of the snitches who had been used against them:

> Police fell for information fabricated from within Boggo Road using a criminal who was a notorious dog and pimp [police informer] to augment the case, with alleged

admissions first made by Finch to an inmate known to
others as a jail dog, Arthur, then by Stuart.

Without this he thought they would 'probably have copped it
sweet'.

Over the years both Finch and Stuart regularly tried to
have their convictions quashed. In August 1974 their appeal
to the Court of Criminal Appeal was dismissed and in the
November they were refused special leave to appeal to the
High Court of Australia.

Then in June 1977 the bisexual rapist Murdoch, who had
given evidence against Finch, changed his evidence, making a
very long and detailed statement admitting that he had told a
pack of lies, saying he had only given it on a promise to be
allowed back into the general prison population. He had, he
said, never really spoken to either man.

An immediate appeal by Stuart and Finch to the Governor
of Queensland for the exercise of his pardoning power was
rejected and in September 1978 a further application for leave
to appeal to the Court of Appeal was also turned down. In
May 1981 yet another application by Finch for Special Leave
to the High Court was rejected.

The next year Stuart staged a rooftop protest at the prison
using bricks to spell out, 'Innocent – victim of police verbal'.
His mother then told the papers she had received telephone
calls saying he would be poisoned by warders.

On 17 January 1979 he was found dead in his cell. 'I was at
the jail seeing some clients,' recalls a Brisbane solicitor, 'and
they told me Stuart had been playing merry hell and the screws
had belted the shit out of him.' Aged thirty-nine, he had
suffered a heart attack. Some drugs were found in his body
but they had not contributed to his death. The year after
Stuart's death a report was made alleging misconduct by a
group of senior prison officers, but no action was taken.

Finch soldiered on. In May 1984 the Commonwealth
Attorney General had successfully restrained him from
proceeding in an application to the Privy Council and in
March 1985 another petition for pardon, this time based on

the evidence that the confession must have been fabricated, was also rejected. It had been based on a 1984 study by a phonetics expert, Scotsman the Reverend Arthur Morton, who said there was only a one in 236,000 chance that the confession was in Finch's original words.

Throughout the decade opinion varied over Finch's guilt with the *Sun* journalist Dennis Watt leading a campaign for a reinvestigation of the confession. Unsurprisingly Detective Sid Atkinson, who had been involved in the interrogation, was against him. As far as he was concerned Finch was the criminal dictator of Boggo Road. All this about being the Birdman of Boggo Road, looking after his budgerigar, was rubbish. The Boggo Road governor, Ron Stephenson, backed Atkinson. So far as he was concerned the crafty Finch was far more devious than the straightforward Stuart. 'You knew what he was doing when he swallowed rubber bands and paper clips but Finch was another story. The Pom spoke educated English as well as criminal slang,' something which Stephenson, rather curiously, thought proved his guilt.

Finch, as is often the case with good-looking high-profile prisoners who protest their innocence, and even those who do not, became the target of romantically inclined females. In 1986, while still in prison, he married his leading campaigner, Cheryl Cole, who suffered from a wasting disease and whom he called 'Chirpy'. It was her third marriage.

This led to a belief in at least his reformation and at best his innocence and a campaign, Friends of Finch, was started for his release. The National Freedom Council took an interest and some A$30,000 was raised, sufficient money to instruct Gold Coast lawyer Christopher Nyst to gather evidence for an appeal to the Attorney General. Clamour grew for his release.

In February 1988 Finch was paroled and again deported to the United Kingdom. He and Cheryl, said now to be terminally ill, went to live in Basildon where he was greeted by a newspaper front-page headline, 'Welcome Home Killer'. It was only a few months before Cheryl, unhappy with England in general, and her husband in particular, returned to Australia.

And then the wheels came off. It was never quite clear what made the journalist Dennis Watt of the *Sunday Sun* decide to go to England to spend five days cosying up to Finch, probably good old-fashioned journalistic instinct. It was then that Finch told him that he had, in fact, started the Whiskey fire. Worse, he told Watt how he had only married Cheryl out of sympathy and that he was fed up with catering for her every need and whim. Not only had he had to carry her to the bath but he had had to brush her hair with 100 strokes a night and, if he missed, with 200 strokes the next night. He had expected her to be long dead but she was showing no signs of it. Finch's wrongful conviction campaign collapsed.

Back in Australia the loyal Cheryl would not believe her husband had actually set the fire and suggested he needed rehabilitation. And there are still some who think that Finch, who had not adjusted to life on the outside, had simply lashed out, complaining that no one cared about him personally, only about the campaign.

Two days after the article appeared Finch went on television to retract his confession, saying he was confused and that he had only confessed for the money. After all, in theory, there were still another fourteen murders on which he could be extradited and tried. In November that year Finch told Bruce Stannard of the *Bulletin* yet another version of events. The firebombing had been ordered by a senior policeman, whom he named. Drug dealer Vincent O'Dempsey was the planner, Ian 'Clockwork Orange' Hamilton was the accomplice who actually lit the fire and Billy McCulkin was the getaway driver. It was an allegation McCulkin and O'Dempsey vehemently denied. Hamilton was already dead.

Then three officers, all disguised, came forward to admit that Finch had been verballed. The Queensland Attorney General asked them to make an official statement but none did, although one gave a long interview to Stannard saying that when the men had been arrested Stuart would not make a statement and so they had decided to lumber Finch. According to the unnamed officer, Finch was given a continued beating in an effort to make him confess. One officer gave Finch a 'terrible hiding'. It was a worldwide, tried and tested way to obtain a confession. 'Some blokes you kick them in the balls and straight away they start squealing and they'll tell you everything.' By the end the police officer had some grudging respect for him. 'Finch was handcuffed to a chair and we knocked the shit out of him . . . He didn't even whimper.' Later Finch would say that while he had been verballed by the police, in their position he would have done the same.

Finch might as well have saved himself the pain. With no confession forthcoming, he was simply comprehensively verballed. Another man did the typing. 'He was an excellent typist, very clean, very fast. We all contributed bits and pieces to the statement. It was the sort of thing we'd all done many, many times in the past,' said the unnamed officer. Later there were fears that the man, a devout Catholic, might crack under the strain, but he remained staunch. The officer who gave the interview was unrepentant, believing Stuart and Finch were 'dangerous animals to be taken off the streets for public safety'.

Over the years many people have put in their penny's worth over who actually started the blaze. They included prison governor Roy Stephenson who published his autobiography *Nor Iron Bars a Cage*. He had never been a Finch supporter and wrote that Finch did it all by himself, dropped a lighted holder of matches and ran. Finch then went into the bush for four days and only came out after he heard Stuart had initially been released. Then he went and stayed under the assumed name of Doug Jones with Danny Stuart, John's brother. He maintained Finch was the brains and had actually planned the whole thing from England.

Danny Stuart Jnr thought about writing a book on his uncle's troubled life and in doing so shed a little more light on his father Danny Snr who had given evidence in the trial. In December 2010 Frank Robson interviewed Danny Stuart Jnr who still maintained his uncle was innocent. Shortly before she died, Stuart's mother said she had forgiven Danny for turning his brother in. Cheryl Finch died in 2002. Tony Murphy, the police officer alleged to have been involved in the fire, was named in a dossier compiled by officers known as the

Group of Eight who complained about corruption in the force and Murphy in particular. It was forwarded to the Chief Commissioner but was not acted upon.

Over the years the Whiskey's one-time manager John Hannay had something of an eventful career, surviving an organized hit on his life in 1996. He also served a prison term for misappropriating a superannuation payout. At one time he owned Daydream Island in the Whitsundays and, by 2000, was the proprietor of the Beat Club in Brisbane and was helping his nephew run another. In 2005 he was banned from managing corporations for five years by the Australian Securities and Investments Commission after he was found to have been a director of eight failed companies, including the one behind the Beat Club.

In both 2013 and 2014 there were suggestions that the investigation into the fire would be reopened. In October 2014 O'Dempsey and his friend Garry Dubois were charged with the murders of the wife and daughters of Billy McCulkin. They have denied any involvement in the deaths.

CHAPTER 11

The Road to Abolition

Derek Bentley

Ruth Ellis

Derek Bentley

On 2 November 1952 PC Sidney Miles, a married man with two children, was one of a number of officers called to an attempted break-in at a confectionary warehouse at 27 Tamworth Road, Croydon, south London. Around 9.15 p.m. a young girl had seen two men climbing over a gate and up a drainpipe to the roof of the warehouse. She told her mother who called the police. The two youths found on the roof were sixteen-year-old Christopher Craig and nineteen-year-old Derek Bentley.

The police, in the form of Frederick Fairfax and Norman Harrison, were soon at the premises where they had to climb a drainpipe just as Craig and Bentley had done. They were joined there by Miles and the overweight PC James Christie McDonald, who had trouble climbing the pipe. Miles went to find the keyholder.

There may well have been a third youth. On the next evening the London tabloid the *Star* wrote, 'Police are looking for a third youth believed to be on the roof of Messrs Barlow & Parker's premises when PC Miles was shot.'

Barrister and author John Parris, who defended Craig in the subsequent trial, wrote there were five youths who went out together to burgle a butcher's shop from which Bentley had stolen the keys. Two had gone home rather than try to break in to the confectionery warehouse. Parris believed that the young girl's mother, Mrs Edith Ware, saw not Craig and Bentley but Bentley and another youth because Craig was already in the premises.

In 1960 Parris, convinced there was another boy on the roof, wrote:

> It would be unfair at present to disclose the name of the third youth who was on the roof-top that night when Fairfax and the other officer got there, or to give other details from which he could be identified; but he should take warning that, if he continues to boast about it, as he is at present doing, he may yet find himself in the dock on a capital charge.

Later the two boys who had left before the break-in went to a master they trusted and he told them to go away and forget about things because he saw no useful purpose in their going to the police.

About twenty minutes after the first call by Mrs Ware, Miles, who had arrived back with the keys to the premises, unlocked the door to the roof. It was then Fairfax called out that he was a police officer and Craig replied, 'If you want us fucking well come and get us.' Fairfax ran over and grabbed Bentley. Craig backed away and by now Harrison had climbed onto an adjacent roof. It was alleged that Bentley then broke away from Fairfax shouting, 'Let him have it, Chris.'

Fairfax grabbed hold of Bentley and, using him as a shield, advanced on Craig who began firing wildly, hitting Fairfax in the shoulder, probably because the bullet ricocheted off the concrete roof. He then shot Miles between the eyes.

McDonald was then helped onto the roof by Fairfax while Bentley stood quietly by. After shooting Miles, Craig yelled, 'I am Craig. You've just given my brother twelve years. Come on you coppers, I'm only sixteen.' He fired the remainder of his ammunition and called out, 'Give my love to Pam,' before he swallow-dived off the roof, crashing into a greenhouse, which partly broke his fall, and breaking his wrist, breastbone and spine. Before he passed out he is said to have boasted, 'I wish I was fucking dead. I hope I've killed the fucking lot.'

Later, while in hospital after his operations, and with a police guard at his bedside, he was alleged to have made a series of damning remarks including, 'You coppers. The other one's dead with a hole in his head. I'm all right. All you bastards should be dead.' Three days later he sealed his fate with:

'If I hadn't cut a bit off the barrel of my gun I would probably have killed a lot more policemen. That night I was out to kill because I had so much hate inside me for what they did to my brother.'

As for Bentley, he was alleged to have said on the way to Croydon police station, 'I knew he had a gun, but I didn't think he'd use it. He's done one of your blokes in.' At the station, when cautioned he replied, 'I didn't have a gun. Chris shot him.' He had already made a long statement, which was written down for him and which he attempted, unsuccessfully at first, to sign.

The press and public hostility towards the pair was overwhelming. Craig was carried into Croydon Magistrates' Court on a stretcher while the crowd shouted insults at him. The Home Secretary showed his solidarity with the police by attending Miles' funeral.

Derek Bentley was born on 3 June 1933; his twin brother died shortly after birth. Another brother suffered from Downs' Syndrome and died in infancy. At the age of four Bentley fell off a lorry and from then on suffered from intermittent epileptic fits. During the war he was buried in debris when a flying bomb hit the family home. By the time he was eleven he was still totally illiterate. Sent in 1948 to Kingswood, an approved school in Bristol, for stealing builders' tools, an IQ test gave him a mark of sixty-six, which put him in the then category of 'feeble-minded'. It was his third visit there.

Bentley was released early and worked as a road sweeper for the council and then for a second-hand dealer. At the medical examination for his suitability for National Service he was given a Grade IV rating as being subnormal and rejected. He was thoroughly indulged by his parents who allowed him to keep twenty-four cats, three dogs, sundry rabbits and a chicken. He would not eat meat.

After Bentley started going out with a girl whose sister was the girlfriend of Craig, his father believed he was under Craig's malign influence. In an effort to stop his son associating with him, Bentley's father had been to the police station at Norbury where he spoke to the desk sergeant about the problem only to be told that nothing could be done as no crime had been committed. On the fatal night Bentley had been allowed to go out with two other youths who had called at his home, but Craig was waiting round the corner.

Christopher Craig came from a respectable family of eight. His father, a cashier at a bank in Victoria Street, had served in the London Scottish regiment in the First World War and had been a company commander in the Home Guard in the second. All the family were well-behaved as children. Then his elder brother, Niven Scott Craig, whom he adored, went off the rails, serving five years for robbery while in the army in Austria. He was ultimately sentenced to twelve years on 31 October, two days before his brother's attempted warehouse-breaking.

Niven Craig broke out of prison in 1961 and remained out for six weeks. He was finally released on parole in 1966 after his case was debated in Parliament, when MPs argued that he had received special and favourable treatment because of the people he knew – these included the penal reform campaigner Lord Longford.

Unusually, since legal aid was only given for one instead of two counsel – the usual practice in a murder case – the barristers instructed to appear for the youths were not King's Counsel. The urbane, if eccentric, Frank Cassels, son of Mr Justice Cassels and whose brother was, among other things, a popular if not technically brilliant concert pianist, appeared for Bentley, while the young, abrasive John Parris, who had a practice in the north of England, was instructed on behalf of Craig. This would be Parris's first appearance at the Old Bailey. Initially, he thought he would be junior counsel to Derek Curtis-Bennett, but without a certificate for two counsel he had to appear on his own.

Things moved swiftly in criminal trials in the 1950s. The pair were committed for trial on 17 November and the case was fixed to begin on 4 December. A brief to defence counsel would normally include the depositions taken at the magistrates' court, photographs and a plan of the place of the incident and copies of statements from any more witnesses whom the prosecution had decided to call. It would also include a statement from the defendant and any witnesses who might be called on his behalf, along with comments by the instructing solicitor on the strengths and weaknesses of the prosecution's case. According to Parris, his brief delivered to him in Leeds on 2 December comprised only the depositions and the terse sentence, 'Counsel will obtain all the information he needs from the depositions enclosed herewith and conference with his client.'

No statements, nothing else. Parris, who was involved in a case in Leeds, chartered a plane and flew to London to ask for an adjournment. The trial judge, Lord Chief Justice Rayner Goddard, told him he could return the brief, saying there were plenty of counsel in London who could take the case. Parris showed him the papers and pointed out that whoever took the case could not possibly be prepared to begin on the Thursday. Goddard then told Parris his client had no defence to a charge of murder and again he refused to grant an adjournment. Parris responded by saying he would make an application in open court setting out the facts. Goddard then reluctantly agreed to begin the case on the following Tuesday.

Parris recalled that when he first met Cassels he had remarked, 'I think both the fuckers ought to swing.' It was a story Parris repeated to the author David Yallop many years later. It is perhaps unfortunate that Cassels did say this and that Parris repeated it, because over the years there have been unkind and inaccurate suggestions that Cassels did not try his hardest for his client.

That weekend Parris, with the solicitor's elderly secretary, went to see Craig in Brixton Prison. There, Craig told him that early in the rooftop drama Fairfax had sent Bentley to get the gun from him and he had got within six feet before he had told his friend, 'Fuck off, otherwise I'll shoot you too.' This could not, of course, help Parris in his defence of Craig who was claiming that he was only firing to frighten off the officers, but it could have been of enormous help to Bentley. The incident had, he said, taken place well before Miles had arrived on the scene. Craig agreed that Parris could be allowed to tell Cassels about it and that if he was cross-examined on the point he would agree.

One problem for Cassels was that Bentley continually denied he had ever said 'Let him have it, Chris.' There also was the question of joint enterprise. His statement clearly showed he intended to break into the butcher's and then go warehouse-breaking, so here was an agreement to commit a felony. Each, in law, was responsible for the other's actions while the joint enterprise continued. When did it end? Unfortunately Bentley also denied that he was under arrest at the time Craig fired the shot that killed PC Miles, which meant it would be argued that the joint enterprise was continuing. Since Bentley had not told him about going across the roof to get the gun, under the arcane rules of professional conduct for a barrister at the time, nor could Cassels cross-examine either Craig or Fairfax about this crucial piece of evidence.

The tone of the trial was set from the beginning on 9 December when Goddard, after Craig and Bentley had pleaded not guilty, allowed Craig, still on crutches, to sit down. Bentley was made to stand throughout the trial.

Apart from police photographers and plan drawers, the first witness called for the prosecution was Craig's father, who told the jury in cross-examination that the only books his son knew about were the stories of Enid Blyton, and that was only because he got other people to read them for him. Until approximately two years previously he had been a regular attendant at a bible class. He had given up because he was embarrassed by being unable to read a lesson. He had left his job in an engineering firm because he was being ridiculed by other staff over his illiteracy. He had been convicted of having a gun without a licence when he was found on Brighton beach. He had apparently been intending to go over to France.

The next witness was Fairfax who said Craig had fired only

three shots but distinctly heard Bentley call out 'Let him have it, Chris.' He was followed by PC McDonald, who at first resolutely refused to identify Bentley as the one who said, 'Let him have it, Chris.' He was helped out by Goddard who quickly established there were only three people on the roof at the time, Fairfax, Craig and Bentley. Craig had not been talking to himself, Fairfax did not know who the men were, so it could only have been Bentley. When McDonald said it was minutes between the remark 'Let him have it, Chris' and the shot, Goddard intervened again to persuade the officer it was only a matter of seconds.

As for the statement Bentley made in the police station, this, said two officers, was absolutely his own and neither of them had asked him any questions. When Parris, in an effort to show the bullet that hit Fairfax was a ricochet, questioned the forensic expert over the accuracy of the gun, Goddard again intervened to say that however accurate or inaccurate the gunfire, this line of defence was no defence at all.

When Craig came to give evidence he said he had not heard the words, 'Let him have it, Chris.' Goddard was not at all impressed with him. Asked if he had ever apologized, Craig replied he had not until he was in prison. Goddard pressed the matter and the time he was in hospital:

G: You saw plenty of policemen because they were watching you at your bedside.
A: I was not conscious. I was hardly conscious half the time.
G: Hardly conscious! Don't talk such nonsense.

Bentley was appalling in the witness box. Any decent counsel can often make even a totally honest witness look bad and Bentley could never get it across to the jury that he had no idea that gun fanatic Craig had gone out armed that evening. Nor was he helped by the knuckleduster with a spike that Craig had given him, and which Goddard seized on as a lethal weapon in itself. 'A dreadful weapon,' his Lordship commented.

'Not only was Bentley a moron,' wrote Parris, albeit

politically incorrectly, 'but he was a lying moron.' Nothing was brought out in his defence about his low IQ.

Now Goddard told Parris he would not let the jury bring in a verdict of manslaughter, something that, in itself, would have saved Bentley from the gallows. It was murder or nothing. Parris argued that if it was an 'accidental' injury it could be manslaughter. Goddard was firm, 'The question is what is accidental? I cannot say an injury is accidental when a man is firing even if he says, "I did not intend to fire at the man but in another direction." He is doing a deliberate act.'

Nevertheless at that stage he changed his mind, telling Parris he would allow him to argue that the shooting was manslaughter. However, during Parris' closing address to the jury he changed his mind again, interrupting him to say he would not allow it. As for Bentley, the summing-up of his defence amounted to thirty-three words compared with five pages of detailing the case for the prosecution. 'I didn't know he had a gun and I deny that I said, "Let him have it, Chris." I never knew he was going to shoot, and I didn't think he would.'

When one of the jury asked to see Fairfax's coat, an indication that he, at least, might be thinking the shot had been accidental, Goddard was furious. He picked up the knuckleduster he had been showing to the jury, and smashed it into the bench saying, 'You will remember you are not considering the wounding of Sergeant Fairfax. You are considering the murder of a police officer.' In the transcript of the summing-up this was amended to 'You are considering the death of PC Miles.' One barrister who watched the trial later told author David Yallop, 'Lord Goddard lost control of himself.'

The jury returned a verdict of guilty for both youths, adding a recommendation of mercy in the case of Bentley. Goddard sentenced Bentley to death and, sentencing Craig, who was too young to be hanged, to be detained at Her Majesty's pleasure, his Lordship told him, 'I shall tell the Secretary of State when forwarding the recommendation of the jury in Bentley's case that in my opinion you are one of the most dangerous young criminals who has ever stood in that dock.'

The Court of Criminal Appeal dismissed Bentley's appeal

in quick time. The summing-up had been perfectly adequate. Craig did not appeal, and so began a campaign for a reprieve for Bentley. The fickle public, appalled by the death of Miles, were now appalled by the prospect of the death of Bentley for a 'murder he did not commit'. Some writers have described it as the biggest campaign in British penal history, but whether it was *pro rata* as big as that for Mrs Maybrick (the American convicted of murdering her husband in the late nineteenth century) is doubtful. In any event letters poured in by the thousands to the Bentley home. The GPO put in a telephone and the family received 500 supporting calls a day. Cars had windscreen stickers favouring his reprieve.

On 27 January when Sidney Silverman tried to raise the question of a reprieve in Parliament the members behaved with their usual schoolboy enthusiasm. Silverman said he had received more than 200 telegrams, all but one in support of Bentley. That one told him he expected the Home Secretary would tell him to mind his own business, at which there were cheers from the benches. The Speaker refused Silverman's motion, saying there was ample precedent for Parliament not to discuss a case while a capital charge was pending. The House then considered increased meat supplies from Argentina.

It was all to no end. When it was announced there would be no reprieve the police asked Bentley's father to speak to the crowds to try to calm them down.

Bentley was hanged by Albert Pierrepoint at Wandsworth Prison on 28 January 1953. Three of the officers were awarded the George Cross and a fourth the British Empire Medal. Miles was given a posthumous award of the King's Police Medal. His widow was awarded a pension of £2.16 a week, the rough equivalent of £70 today.

Craig was released in May 1963 after serving ten and a half years. He never returned to crime. Two years earlier he had donated to charity damages awarded in an action he brought against the *Daily Sketch*. The paper had quite wrongly said that while Craig was working on the hostel system he had been found taking and driving away a motor vehicle and his release from prison had been put back. As with his brother, questions were asked in Parliament why he had been given parole while an Irishman convicted of a raid on a military unit in Berkshire had not. The reply was that the Home Secretary had taken into account his age and character, his development in prison and the need to protect the public.

Parris, canvassing as a Labour candidate after the trial, criticized Lord Goddard for interfering in the parliamentary process over the death penalty and as a result was suspended for six months. He was later disbarred because he had been a director in a commercial enterprise, something wholly unbefitting a barrister, and became a successful author and businessman. He died in 1996.

Goddard died in 1971. He had been sitting in the Court of Appeal into his eighties. The previous August he had told writer David Yallop that he was unhappy that Bentley should have hanged. He thought Craig the more guilty of the two.

Yallop wrote, 'We can never bring Bentley back from the grave but we can acknowledge that he should never have been put there.' In his analysis of the case he thought that Miles might have accidentally been killed by a bullet fired by a police officer. The bullet that killed Miles was never found.

In 1971 Yallop wrote in his book *To Encourage the Others* that there was probably a third youth on the roof, and that a pathologist had agreed that the bullet which killed Miles was a .45, which could not have been fired by Craig's gun. A Phillip Lee also wrote that he had seen a very different version of events from that described at the trial. Unfortunately he had a number of criminal convictions to his name. Nevertheless an internal investigation was started. Now witnesses who appeared to have supported Yallop's account backtracked and others were interviewed who categorically denied Lee's account.

On 30 December 1985 Croydon magistrates refused an application by freelance writer Philip Huxley, in fact Lee under another name, for four summonses for unlawful arrest against officers involved in the case – Fairfax, McDonald, Harrison and Leslie John Smith. He was told to apply to Bow Street magistrates' court. In turn he said he would go to the Court of Appeal, by which he probably meant the Divisional Court, but he does not seem to have done either.

In 1991 John Parris published *Scapegoat*, his emotive account of the case, in which he castigated Goddard over his conduct of the trial. On 30 July 1998, the case again went before the Court of Appeal. Now the court, headed by Lord Justice Bingham, granted a posthumous acquittal to Derek Bentley on the basis of Goddard's misdirection to the jury. Bingham thought it 'must . . . have driven the jury to conclude that they had little choice but to convict,' adding:

> It is with genuine diffidence that the members of this court direct criticism towards a trial judge widely recognized as one of the outstanding criminal judges of this century. But we cannot escape the duty of decision. In our judgement the summing up in this case was such as to deny the appellant that fair trial which is the birthright of every British citizen.

Whether those who appeared before Goddard, either as lawyers or defendants, would necessarily accept that he deserved the encomium of 'outstanding' is a matter for debate. He was reputed to bring a spare pair of trousers to court because he ejaculated when ordering a flogging or passing the death sentence – something denied by his family. Among the criminal fraternity, it was said an appeal was lost when he began picking his nose, something that often happened in the first few minutes of the hearing.

Why was Bentley hanged? Probably the answer is that the Home Secretary and his advisers took the view that if he was reprieved it would open the way for an adult to take a juvenile along with him to do the dirty work on any criminal enterprise that went wrong, safe in the knowledge that the boy would receive a relatively light sentence. Seventy years later it is a tactic employed by drug gangs in America, who use young boys to carry drugs and weapons who, if caught and convicted, will only receive a spell in a juvenile detention centre before they are back on the streets.

The best that can be said about this whole, sorry affair is that it was one of the first steps on the road to the final abolition of capital punishment in Britain.

Ruth Ellis

Sometimes miscarriages of justice occur because of the state of the law at the time – the persecution of gay people over the centuries is a good example – and whether the case of Ruth Ellis was really a miscarriage of justice has long been debated. That her case contributed substantially to a change in the law and the abolition of hanging is indisputable.

Around 9 p.m. on Easter Sunday, 10 April 1955, drinking-club manageress Ruth Ellis went to the Magdala Tavern, a public house in Hampstead, north London, and waited until her lover, small-time racing driver David Blakely, came out. She then shot him twice with a .38 Smith and Wesson. He tried to run away and she shot him three more times, the last at almost point-blank range. She then tried to shoot herself but, when the gun initially failed to fire, Ellis pulled the trigger again and this time the bullet ricocheted off the pavement and hit a passer-by, Gladys Yule, in the hand. The sound of gunfire brought Alan Thompson, an off-duty policeman, out of the pub. Ellis said to him, 'Please take this gun and arrest me.' She had had a miscarriage a fortnight earlier, possibly brought on by a beating from Blakely.

In his book *Reprieve*, lawyer and author Fenton Bresler wrote derisively of her, 'There was little to commend her, an ex-call girl and drinking-club manageress . . .' He was none too keen on her narcissistic victim either, describing him as 'even more unpleasant'.

The pair came from contrasting backgrounds. Ruth Neilson

was born on 9 October 1926 in Rhyl, North Wales. Arthur Neilson, her father, had been a violinist playing on liners and in cinemas in the days of silent films. Her mother Berthe was a Belgian refugee. With the advent of talkies Arthur and the family faced a slide into genteel poverty and they moved south where Arthur took a job as a chauffeur. Ruth was educated at Fairfield Secondary Girls School at Basingstoke, leaving at the age of fourteen.

Obsessed with an idea to better herself, the next year she began work as a machinist at the Oxo factory in London. In March 1942 she contracted rheumatic fever and was off work for nearly a year. As part of her remedial exercises she was told to take up dancing, and at seventeen she became a photographer's assistant at the Lyceum ballroom off the Strand, one of the smartest and most popular dancehalls around London. It was at one of these she met a French-Canadian soldier, Clare. She became pregnant and he proposed marriage. There was only one impediment, as Mrs Neilson discovered when she wrote to his commanding officer: he was already married. Their son, Clare Andria Neilson, was born in September 1942 and the father continued to visit and pay maintenance until he returned to Canada at the end of the war. Afterwards she would say her son's father had been an American pilot killed in action.

After the war she left her sister looking after her son and became a model at the Camera Club in Soho where middle-aged men in mackintoshes took photographs of young women, or at least pretended to. She was nineteen when she met Morris Conley, a successor to the Messina Brothers who had controlled prostitution in central London for over twenty years, and it was he who introduced her to the delights of the drinking clubs' dinner-jacketed world. Hostesses could earn £20 a week and there was also the opportunity of after-hours prostitution to provide extra income, from which Conley took a cut. She worked at first at the Court Club in Duke Street, near Marble Arch, and it was there she met the alcoholic and divorced dentist, forty-one-year-old George Johnston Ellis. Here was a chance of stability and respectability.

They married in November 1950 and their daughter Georgina was born in October 1951. For a time George obtained work in Southampton but he continued his destructive drinking and in turn she became obsessively jealous. He filed for divorce and she returned to work for Conley at Carroll's, the Court Club under a new name. Andria came with her and arrangements were made for the adoption of Georgina. On her birthday in 1953 Conley promoted her to manageress of the Little Club in Brompton Road, Knightsbridge. With the job went a two-bedroom rent-free flat. It was there she met both the middle-aged Desmond Cussen and David Blakely. For the next two years she conducted a *ménage a trois* with the men.

Before the Second World War Blakely's Glasgow-born father, John, was a popular GP in Sheffield. His clientele was mostly impoverished and he accepted payment for his fees at 6d (two-and-a-half pence) a week. In February 1934 he had been charged with the murder of Phyllis Staton, an unemployed waitress with whom he had been having an affair for some two years. She had died after taking the drug Pituitrin, used at the time in obstetrics. The only evidence against him appears to have been their relationship and that she collapsed and died shortly after he took her to her parents' home and drove away. On 22 February the magistrate refused to commit him for trial, saying the evidence was so weak that he did not think any jury would convict him. His marriage broke up and his wife Annie left him for a racing driver, Humphrey Cook, taking David with her.

Educated at Shrewsbury School, Blakely developed his stepfather's enthusiasm for motor-car racing. A good-looking ne'er-do-well, he was sent to London to work as a trainee hotel manager but spent much of his time acting as a gigolo to bored middle-aged women in the capital without their husbands. The upmarket drinking clubs were the playgrounds of the motor racing world and Blakely, then engaged to a north country textile heiress, tagged on to the Grand Prix driver Mike Hawthorn who frequented them.

Desmond Cussen would seem to have been the ideal

husband for Ellis; a wealthy unattached bachelor who was in love with her and who would have provided a home for her son. Unfortunately she was in love with Blakely who moved into her flat within two weeks of their meeting. Their relationship was stormy, with frequent assaults on each other followed by immediate reconciliations. Blakely had an allowance of £7,000 a year but he sponged off Ellis, paying no rent, borrowing money and drinking for free in the club. He hated Cussen and her clients and she hated his womanizing. His affairs included one with the wife of his friend Ant Findlater, who worked as a mechanic on his racing car 'The Emperor'.

Eventually his behaviour in the club annoyed Conley, who was losing customers. Ellis was sacked and she and Andria moved to Devonshire Place where Cussen had a flat. Except for the fact they were not married, he was an ideal *mari complaisant*. He paid for French lessons and a modelling course for her. He chauffeured her around day and night and allowed her to sleep with Blakely at the flat. This continued until Christmas 1954, during which Blakely broke off his engagement to the north country heiress. Now Cussen paid for a service flat for her in Egerton Gardens in Kensington, but she still thought Blakely would marry her.

In March 1955 she told him she was pregnant again and in yet another quarrel he beat her, punching her in the stomach. She had a miscarriage but they continued to live together until, on Good Friday, 7 April, he left the flat after promising to take her to friends of his, the now reconciled Findlaters, later that evening. He never reappeared. A furious Ellis bombarded the house with telephone calls and the Findlaters, whom she regarded as trying to wean him from her, told her Blakely was not there, hung up on her, and finally did not answer the telephone. Eventually she went over to their home and pushed in the windows of Blakely's van. The Findlaters called the police. It was two days later that she shot and killed her lover.

At Hampstead police station she made a fairly detailed statement about her relationship with Blakely. Of Cussen there was no mention. The statement concluded:

I then took a gun which I had hidden and put it in my handbag. This gun was given to me about three years ago in a
club by a man whose name I do not remember. It was security for money but I accepted it as a curiosity. I did not know
it was loaded when it was given to me but I knew next
morning when I looked at it. When I put the gun in my bag
I intended to find David and shoot him.

Leading for the Crown was Christmas Humphreys, senior
Treasury Counsel and a man who could divorce his day job
from his Buddhist beliefs. With him was Mervyn Griffiths-
Jones, later the Common Sergeant, who on another occasion
told a jury that wives and maidservants should not be
allowed to read *Lady Chatterley's Lover*. Jean Southworth
was their junior.

Ruth Ellis was defended by the autocratic and austere
Melford Stevenson, a man with a substantial divorce practice
but no great experience in criminal cases. It was a curious
choice given that with him was the rather more charismatic
Sebag Shaw and the good-looking, charming ex-guards officer
Peter Rawlinson, who three years earlier had made a name for
himself in the case of Alfred Whiteway, convicted of the
Towpath Murders, although not before Rawlinson had savaged
the prosecution evidence.

The trial generated so much interest that it required the
press and public to apply for seating passes. One man Alfred
Ellis wrote saying he was seventy-seven and suffered a disability. Could he possibly have preferential seating? Enquiries
were made and he was found to be no relation. He was told to
take his chance in the public gallery.

In a criminal trial the appearance of the defendant is often
crucial. In the case of Bentley and Craig they were persuaded
to abandon their Teddy Boy appearance in the hope they
would present a better picture to the jury. There was no question of Ruth Ellis taking advice on the subject. She appeared at
her trial with hair freshly dyed platinum blonde and wearing a
well-cut black suit with astrakhan collar and cuffs; the very
model of the popular image of a nightclub hostess.

The prosecution went swiftly. Stevenson asked few questions, and when he did he did not get the right answers. Cussen, called by the prosecution, said the last time he had seen her was around 7.30 p.m. on the Easter Sunday when he had taken her back to Egerton Gardens and left her there. Cross-examined by Stevenson he would not admit he was very much in love with her. 'I was terribly fond of her' was the best Stevenson could extract. Cussen did say he had seen her badly bruised and on one occasion had taken her to the Middlesex Hospital. Nor did Stevenson make progress with Findlater who would not agree that over the Easter weekend she had been 'in a desperate state of emotion'.

A: No.
Q: What?
A: I said no.

The prosecution case was over almost before it had begun and Stevenson called Ellis to give her account of the affair and the weekend. But between them they could never dispel the impression of a grasping self-controlled young woman. As for the violence, she did not help herself:

Q: How did the violence manifest itself?
A: He only used to hit me with his fists and hands but I bruise very easily . . .

And when Christmas Humphreys asked her, 'When you fired that revolver at close range into the body of David Blakely, what did you intend to do?' she sealed her fate with her cool response, 'It is obvious that when I shot him I intended to kill him.'

A great advocate such as Marshall Hall would have introduced some sort of emotion into the case, but Stevenson was no Marshall Hall. In his opening speech Stevenson told the jury he was going to call a 'very eminent psychologist' who would explain '. . . that the effect of jealousy upon that feminine mind can work so as to unseat the reason and can operate to a degree in which a male mind is quite incapable of operating.'

Unfortunately in the 1950s, to a British jury and judge a psychologist meant a man with a beard and a middle-European accent rather like the actor Peter Lorre and it did not help when his witness, Dr Duncan Whittaker, began talking about Jung and men under stress. 'I thought we were talking about women,' commented Mr Justice Havers. The best Stevenson could do was to have Whittaker agree that 'an emotionally mature woman' would have thought of her children. 'I asked her if she thought about her children. She said she did not think of them at all.'

In cross-examination Humphreys cut the ground from under Stevenson's feet and the psychologist down to size. Whittaker thought Ellis was an hysteric but not even a 'gross hysteric'.

> Q: In your view was she at the time, within the meaning of the English law, sane or insane?
> A: Sane.

Stevenson had wanted to argue provocation as a defence. In his arid manner he told the jury that she had been 'driven to a frenzy which for the time being unseated her understanding'. If that had succeeded, she would have been found guilty of manslaughter and spared the gallows. However, Havers was not happy with allowing such a defence.

Stevenson did the best he could to argue that her mental state excluded malice and so could reduce the verdict to manslaughter. Initially Mr Justice Havers remarked, 'But that is new law' before agreeing to consider the submission overnight. The next day he ruled it out:

'There is not sufficient material, even on a view of the evidence most favourable to the accused, for a reasonable jury to form the view that a reasonable person so provoked, could be driven, through transport of passion and loss of self-control, to the degree and method and continuance of violence which produces death.'

As a result Stevenson capitulated and made no closing speech to the jury. He did not even try to urge a recommendation of mercy. 'I cannot now with propriety address the jury at all.' Christmas Humphreys also declined to make a closing speech. On 20 June the jurors returned a verdict of guilty in fourteen minutes and the death sentence was a formality.

Not that this troubled Ruth Ellis who did not want an appeal to be lodged. Nor, until right at the end of the three-week period before she was due to be hanged, did she take any part in the campaign for her reprieve.

From Holloway prison she wrote to Blakely's mother:

The two people I blame for David's death, and my own, are the Findlayters [*sic*]. No dought [*sic*] you will not understand this, but perhaps before I hang you will know what I mean. Please excuse my writing, but the pen is shocking.

I implore you to try to forgive David for living with me, but we were very much in love with one and other [*sic*]. Unfortunately, David was not satisfied with one woman in his life. I have forgiven David, I only wish I could have found it in my heart to have forgiven when he was alive.

Once again, I say I am very sorry to have caused you this misery and heartache. I shall die loving your son. And you should feel content that his death has been repaid.

Goodbye. Ruth Ellis.

It was her relatives who encouraged her solicitor John Bickford to write a seven-page foolscap appeal to the Home Secretary setting out the grounds for appeal. Finally it was the MP George Rogers who obtained her permission to appeal to the Home Secretary Gwilym Lloyd-George, later Lord Tenby. Ruth's father, Arthur Neilson, also wrote:

I respectfully beg of you to use your great influence to spare my poor daughter's life (Ruth Ellis). This terrible tragedy has been a terrible shock to me. I was injured in the Blitz of May 10th 1941. I received a blow on the head which paralysed me down the left side of my body and Sir you will understand my nerves have gone to pieces under the strain.

My daughter I would have thought to be the last person to become involved in such a crime, as a child she was shy and reserved and never gave me any cause for anxiety and later on she was a devoted mother to her two children. I blame the whole sequence of events to the fact of such an unhappy experience of three bad men, the details of which you will know.

I ask you as a distraught father to show her mercy.

Yours respectfully . . .

Refusing the appeals for clemency Lloyd-George noted on a plain sheet of A4 paper:

Our law takes no account of the so-called *crime passionel*, and I am not prepared to differentiate between the sexes on the grounds that one sex is more susceptible to jealousy than the other.

In the present circumstance, the woman was as unfaithful to her lover as he was to her. If a reprieve were to be granted in this case, I think that we should have seriously to consider whether capital punishment should be retained as a penalty.

After it was announced there would be no reprieve Ellis seems to have turned against her hard-working solicitor John Bickford and looked to the firm of the socialist Victor Mishcon to redraw her will. On the day before her execution he and his clerk Leon Simmons asked Bickford if there was anything that he knew which might be used to help her, even at this stage. Bickford told them to ask her where she got the gun.

The answer, when it came, was she had got it from Cussen. They had been drinking together all weekend and on Easter Sunday she had said, 'If I was near David now I'd shoot him.' 'Well, I've got a gun,' said Cussen. He took out an old gun, oiled it and off they went with Andria to Epping Forest to give the myopic Ellis some target practice. In the evening when

Andria was in bed, Cussen had driven her to where the Findlaters lived, given her the gun, said, 'Go and shoot him,' and driven off.

Quite how Mishcon thought this story would help her is something of a mystery. Any thought that the shooting was an impulsive action on her part was gone. Here was a carefully planned campaign, at least on the part of Cussen, to kill his rival. The best the story would have done was to make a case against Cussen as an accessory before the fact, something which itself would carry the death penalty. Now with great reluctance she agreed that, armed with the information, Mishcon should go to see Sir Frank Newson at the Home Office. He was at Ascot races but agreed to return to London at once and instructed Richard Jackson, head of the CID, to check out the story. In the early hours of the morning a Home Office official telephoned to tell Mishcon that the execution would take place.

In fact, the police had already interviewed Cussen about the gun. On 9 July he had made a short statement at Hampstead police station reiterating that he had dropped her and her son at around 7.30 p.m. from the taxi he drove. He had not discussed a gun with her and denied he drove her to Hampstead. Acting DC Supt Davies thought Cussen was telling the truth and had not supplied the gun. However, Ellis's friend Jackie Dyer, a hostess at the club, told the police she did not know who else could have supplied it. The police thought that, as a Frenchwoman, Dyer did not want Ellis to take sole responsibility for the crime.

Two hours before the execution Ruth Ellis added a postscript to a letter she had written to Mishcon's clerk. 'This . . . is to console my family with the thought that I did not change my way of thinking at the last moment.' She was hanged at 9 a.m. on 13 July 1955. She was the last woman to be hanged in Britain.

Two years later the Homicide Act 1957 relaxed the stringent requirements of the law and introduced the concept of diminished responsibility.

Andria Ellis eventually went to live with his grandmother

Berthe who, in 1969, was found unconscious in a gas-filled room in her flat in Hemel Hempstead. She never fully recovered and did not speak coherently ever again. His stepfather, George Johnston Ellis, descended once more into alcoholism and hanged himself in 1958. Andria, who was ten at the time of his mother's execution, suffered irreparable psychological damage. Continually taunted about his mother, he eventually destroyed the marker on her grave at St Mary's Cemetery, Amersham in Buckinghamshire. It has never been replaced.

Andria committed suicide in a bedsit in Hampstead in 1982. It is said that the trial judge, Sir Cecil Havers, sent money every year for his education and that Christmas Humphreys, the prosecuting counsel, paid for his funeral. Georgina was finally adopted when her father hanged himself. She died of cancer aged fifty. Desmond Cussen emigrated and died in Perth, Australia in 1991. He also had become an alcoholic.

In 1964 a rumour began that Ruth Ellis's prison records had been stolen from Holloway. An extensive search was made but they were never found. The theft was not investigated properly until 1967 when a serving prisoner alleged that a man among prisoners from nearby Pentonville sent to work at Holloway had stolen the file. It was correct that prisoners had been sent to work there and moreover that no records were kept of who they were. Their names were chalked on a blackboard in the morning and wiped off when they returned in the evening. It was thought that the records had come into the possession of a club owner in Hammersmith who was trying to sell them through an intermediary to an American magazine. Both he and his associate had their premises searched but nothing was found. There the inquiry lapsed.

Over the years Ellis's sister Muriel Jakubait campaigned resolutely for a pardon and there seemed to be a window of opportunity when the Criminal Cases Review Commission referred her case to the Court of Appeal in 2003. However, Lord Justice Kay, dismissing the appeal, had some strong words to say about bringing it in the first place:

We have to question whether this exercise of considering an appeal so long after the event when Mrs Ellis herself had consciously and deliberately chosen not to appeal at the time is a sensible use of the limited resources of the Court of Appeal.

'On any view, Mrs Ellis had committed a serious criminal offence. This case is, therefore, quite different from a case like *Hanratty* [2002] 2 Cr. App. R. 30 where the issue was whether a wholly innocent person had been convicted of murder. A wrong on that scale, if it had occurred, might even today be a matter for general public concern, but in this case there was no question that Mrs Ellis was other than the killer and the only issue was the precise crime of which she was guilty.

'If we had not been obliged to consider her case we would perhaps in the time available have dealt with eight to twelve other cases, the majority of which would have involved people who were said to be wrongly in custody. The Court of Appeal's workload is an ever-increasing one and recent legislation will add substantially to that load. Parliament may wish to consider whether going back many years into history to re-examine a case of this kind is a use that ought to be made of the limited resources that are available.

Whether the story she told Mishcon on the day before her death was true has been a matter for speculation and the Director of Public Prosecution's file, now in the National Archives, contains a statement from her French teacher that when she went to the flat to give Ruth a lesson there in a drawer was a gun. Her son Andria showed it to the woman saying she should not be worried as it was not loaded.

CHAPTER 12

Expert Evidence?

Charles Stielow; Sacco and Vanzetti; Stephen Witherell; William Lancaster; Manny Strewl

Bill Dillon; Juan Ramos

Charles Stielow; Sacco and Vanzetti; Stephen Witherell; William Lancaster; Manny Strewl

In 1908 the druggist Albert Hamilton, who styled himself 'That man from Auburn', began his career as one of the great forensic charlatans of the first half of the twentieth century. That year he published a brochure describing himself as an expert in chemistry, microscopy, handwriting, ink analysis, typewriting identification, photography, fingerprints and forensic toxicology. He also claimed expertise in twenty-six forensic subjects, including gunshot wounds, bullet identification, guns, nitroglycerine, gunpowder, bloodstains, causes of death, anatomy and embalming. As many others have done before and after him, he awarded himself a medical degree and now Dr Hamilton was available for hire to whoever could pay him. Over the next quarter of a century he gave inaccurate and often deceitful evidence in more than 160 cases.

Born in December 1859, he claimed he graduated from New York City College in 1885 and ran a drugstore for the next twenty-five years, during which time he produced Hamilton's Remedies, patent medicines such as 'Cleopatra's Secret', which he sold as 'an excellent remedy for female weaknesses'. He then sold the store and studied chemistry before he embarked on his new and highly profitable career as an expert witness.

By the time he appeared for New York State in 1909 in the case of Georgia Sampson, on trial for the murder of her husband Harry, he claimed he had already appeared in forty murder cases. The prosecution alleged she had shot her husband while he was eating a piece of cheese following a quarrel over a love letter he had discovered. She claimed he had committed suicide. Hamilton gave evidence that Sampson could not have committed suicide as his forensic examination showed he had been shot at a distance. On this occasion he had been correct, but the jury nevertheless acquitted her in one hour and fifty-five seconds. Hamilton may not have known much about ballistics and science in general but he did know that juries liked enlarged photographs. At a daily fee of $50 plus expenses he provided them in the case of German-speaking immigrant Charles Stielow, accused of the murder of ninety-year-old Charles Phelps, a farmer from West Shelby, New York, and his housekeeper Margaret Wolcott. Their bodies were found around 6 a.m. on 22 March 1915 by Stielow who lived opposite. He ran to neighbours who in turn reported the matter to the local sheriff. Both Phelps and his housekeeper had been shot with .22 bullets. Robbery was clearly the motive as the drawers in Phelps' room had been emptied and his money taken.

Both Stielow and his brother-in-law Nelson Green, with whom he lived, denied they owned firearms but, after repeated questioning, Green admitted that Stielow did own a .22 revolver, a rifle and a shotgun.

Hamilton was called in and, after examining the four bullets taken from the two victims as well as the .22 calibre revolver but without test-firing it, gave his opinion that it had fired the bullets that had killed Phelps and his housekeeper. On 23 April, while being questioned in the county jail by George Newton, a private investigator hired by the sheriff, and three police officers, Stielow, whose English was imperfect, was said to have confessed to the murders in return for the opportunity to see his wife. He refused, however, to sign a written version of his confession.

Dictograph recordings were secretly made to record the conversations of Stielow with Green and with his counsel.

Sparacino, an agent from the Newton Detective Agency, spent nineteen days posing as a prisoner and finally admitted that Stielow had consistently denied his guilt.

Nevertheless Stielow was indicted with first-degree murder and his trial began before Justice Cuthbert W. Pound of Buffalo on 11 July 1915. Hamilton swore that he had found nine bumps inside the muzzle end of the barrel of Stielow's revolver. These 'projections', he proclaimed, had made nine corresponding scratches on the four bullets taken from the bodies. Hamilton told the jury that no other gun could have fired them. The prosecutor asked Hamilton if the jury members could see these scratches for themselves, to which he replied, 'No, I can tell because I am a highly technical man. I can see what the jury cannot see.' Over the years Hamilton would be one of many so-called experts to say he alone could see evidence invisible to lesser mortals.

It was unfortunate that Stielow's lawyer was both inexperienced and without the necessary funds to find a real expert to challenge Hamilton. Stielow was convicted and sentenced to death on 23 July. Nelson Green received a life sentence. Stielow's conviction was upheld in the New York Supreme Court the next year. 'From an examination of the record, it is inconceivable that the jury could have rendered any other verdict.'

It was then that Stielow's luck took a turn for the better. While in Sing Sing he impressed Spencer Miller, one of the crusading wardens of the time, who referred the case to the Humanitarian Cult, founded by copper merchant Mischa Applebaum. In turn they instructed lawyers, who convinced Governor Whitman to grant a stay of execution. Whitman later commuted Stielow's sentence to life imprisonment and asked a former district attorney George H. Bond to examine the case. Bond duly instructed gunsmith Charles E. Waite to analyze the firearm evidence. Waite concluded that because of the amount of rust on it Stielow's gun had not been fired for two or three years. When the gun was fired it literally went up in flames when a piece of paper placed over it caught fire. Nor could Max Poser, a specialist in applied optics, find any of the scratches evidenced by Hamilton.

Meanwhile two drifters, Erwin King and Clarence O'Connell, had confessed to the killings and then retracted their confessions claiming they had been beaten into making them. They were never charged. Stielow and his brother-in-law Green were pardoned and released in May 1918 but given no compensation for their ordeal. Stielow died in August 1942 from heart problems. Waite would go on to found the Bureau of Forensic Ballistics. Hamilton would go on to give false and misleading evidence in a series of high-profile cases over the next two decades.

In 1923 Hamilton was called by the defence team of two anarchists, Nicola Sacco and Bartolomeo Vanzetti. Two years earlier the pair had been convicted of the murder of Frederick Parmenter and his guard Alessandro Berardelli in a payroll robbery in South Braintree, Massachusetts, on 15 April 1920. The evidence against Sacco came from firearms experts who said that it was a bullet from Sacco's .32 gun which had killed the guard and that Vanzetti had the guard's gun in his possession.

It might have been better for the duo to have based their defence on a case of mistaken identity but, instead, their supporters used the trial as an opportunity to 'unmask the criminal nature of the American government'. Fred H. Moore, a radical lawyer, who had acted in many labour trials on behalf of the IWW, was brought from California to defend them. He was a good choice as in 1912 he had obtained an acquittal in the Ettor–Giovannitti case arising from the textile strike trial in Lawrence, Massachusetts, in which a picketer was killed.

The comparison microscope had still to be invented and the prosecution's witnesses before Judge Thayer were unpromising. Captain William Proctor of the Massachusetts State Police claimed the bullet marked III had come from Sacco's Colt. In tests he had tried to push a bullet through the pistol and when he failed said it was not necessary. The second expert Charles Van Amburgh from the Springfield armoury said he was inclined to believe that bullet III had come from the Colt. Neither could distinguish between types of weapons and Proctor had no experience with even the simplest kind of microscope work. Two defence witnesses, James Burns, who had worked for the US Cartridge Company for thirty years and J. Henry Fitzgerald who had been in the arms business for nearly as long, had serious credentials as experts. Burns was adamant that the bullet had not been fired from Sacco's pistol. 'In my opinion no. It doesn't compare at all.'

Despite this and faced with a hostile judge both men were convicted on 14 July 1921 and sentenced to death. Now Moore began the long and tortuous appeals process, which, many claim, bedevils the American justice system. In 1923 he lost two motions for a retrial and it was then Albert Hamilton appeared as a defence witness. He had boasted to a reporter from the *Boston Globe* that had he given evidence at the trial the result would have been different. The reporter passed the information to Moore and as a result Hamilton joined the team, with disastrous results. The case with its attendant publicity was meat and drink to Hamilton. He examined the firearm evidence and told Moore that the fatal bullet had not been fired from Sacco's gun, and the weapon in Vanzetti's possession was not the gun that had belonged to the body-guard. During the hearing for a new trial, Hamilton conducted an in-court demonstration involving two Colts and Sacco's gun. The new .32 calibre handguns belonged to Hamilton. In front of the judge and the lawyers for both sides, Hamilton disassembled all three pistols and placed their parts in three piles on the table. He then explained the functions of each part and, rather like how a three-card trickster shuffles cards, demonstrated how they were interchangeable. After reassembling the handguns, Hamilton placed the two new weapons back into his pocket and handed Sacco's Colt to the court clerk. A version of the story, spread by Van Amburgh in an article in *True Detective Mysteries,* goes that Hamilton tried to walk out of court with the guns but, before he left the court-room, Judge Thayer ordered him to leave the new guns behind.

Certainly in February 1924 when Judge Thayer asked Van

Amburgh to re-inspect Sacco's gun the expert discovered that the barrel of it was brand new. Following an inquiry held by Thayer in private, Hamilton admitted that the new barrel on Sacco's Colt had come from one of his pistols. Although it was obvious to everyone that Hamilton had made the switch, presumably with a mistrial in mind, very sensibly he denied it. Brazening it out, he suggested the switch must have been made by a member of the prosecution's staff. He continued his association with the Sacco–Vanzetti defence, but he no longer played an important role in the case.

Unsurprisingly, given Hamilton's chicanery, Thayer denied the motion for a new trial. Sacco and Vanzetti were executed on 23 August 1927, and it is now generally thought that the bullet did come from Sacco's gun. However, in 1977 both men were posthumously pardoned.

Hamilton, whom many wrongly thought had been adequately discredited in the aftermath of the Sacco–Vanzetti trial, was still around in the 1930s, proving that the public has a short memory. By now describing himself as a 'Micro-Chemical Engineer', he featured in three major cases of the era.

In 1932 he was hindering things when thirty-two-year-old Stephen Witherell from Hopkinton, New York, was charged with the murder of his father Charles, who had been taunting him about his inability to find a job. When Stephen announced he was going to get married his father scoffed at him, saying no woman in her right mind would have him. That night his father was shot with a deer rifle as he slept. Young Witherell, the jury was told, took $100 after shooting his father, went to New York City, married the young woman and returned to Hopkinton, where he 'found' the body. The police were called and Stephen was arrested shortly afterwards. Questioned, he made a confession and, after he was charged with murder, Hamilton was called as an expert witness for the defence.

By the time of the trial Stephen Witherell had recanted his confession. He gave evidence on his own behalf and denied shooting anyone. In fact, he denied the body in question was even that of his father – decomposition and the massive gunshot wound to the victim's head had made the corpse unrecognizable. Hamilton gave evidence that there were two gunshot wounds on the body; the head wound caused by a rifle, and another wound on the victim's hand, made by a handgun. In fact there was no hand wound at all; Witherell's father had lost two fingers in an industrial accident years earlier.

Hamilton's theory as advanced to the jury was that there had been two gunmen, that Charles had been shot in the hand with a revolver from one side of the bed and from the other side by an exploding bullet from a .250-3000 Savage rifle. Only a rifle of that calibre could have caused the damage and not a .30 Remington, which the prosecution alleged had been the murder weapon. He also claimed someone had switched the bullet that had killed Charles. 'This is not the same bullet, and the fragments are different from the exhibit I examined in the courtroom some weeks ago,' he told the jury. After the Sacco–Vanzetti fiasco who better to know?

The prosecution spent little time cross-examining Hamilton on his theory and a great deal on his past and qualifications. Hamilton cheerfully explained away the Sacco–Vanzetti troubles but admitted he had been arrested in Quebec and detained until a case in which he was a witness was finished. He did, however, deny that the book which described him as 'a mystery solver with the secret power of a Sherlock Holmes' was self-published. He also denied that he had ever advertised any of Hamilton's Remedies as a cure, but claimed he compounded remedies for everything from a turned whisker to something 'soothing for the blues'. As for Cleopatra's Secret, 'It was an excellent remedy for female weaknesses. You understand what that is?' he pried coyly. 'I've never had it,' replied the district attorney. Convicted, Witherell was electrocuted at Sing Sing on 17 August 1933.

The same year Hamilton fared rather better when he was called by the defence as an expert witness in the case of English-born William Lancaster, accused of the murder in Florida of young American writer Haden Clarke, who had become the other lover of Lancaster's girlfriend Jessie Maude 'Chubbie' Miller. It was, Hamilton said, his 296th murder case. In 1927 the West Australian Miller, financing and flying in the *Red Rose* with Lancaster as co-pilot, had become the first woman to complete the England to Australia flight, taking 159 days.

In 1928, on the unfulfilled promise of a Hollywood film, Lancaster and Miller moved to America where he made a living selling engines. Four years later, when Lancaster went to Mexico in search of work, Miller became involved with Haden Clarke, who was helping her write her autobiography, and he convinced her to leave Lancaster. When she told Lancaster this he promptly returned to Florida and, on 20 April, Clarke died from a gunshot wound to the head. It was generally accepted that Lancaster was trying to put a stop to the marriage. The gun used to belong to Lancaster, who agreed, 'I must have been in the room with him' and admitted forging two suicide notes apparently written by Clarke.

At first there was a small hiccup in Hamilton's evidence. Holding Clarke's skull in his hand, he announced that his death was 'definitely homicide'.

'Homicide?' queried James Carson, Lancaster's lawyer.

'I mean suicide,' Hamilton replied unashamed, adding, 'I was thinking of something else.' He was soon back in his stride. He had examined the body and the bullet wound and his opinion, no, not his opinion, his finding was:

'Absolutely suicide. There is not a scintilla of evidence to support a theory of homicide or murder . . . I found nothing to support anything but suicide. I say this not as an opinion, but actual knowledge.'

This time no real attack was made upon his credentials except for a mild question by the prosecuting attorney, N. Vernon Hawthorne, about his entitlement to be called 'Dr'. Hamilton modestly replied that he had no medical qualifications but that lawyers had credited him with the title.

Miller, who allowed herself to be portrayed as a faithless scarlet woman, gave evidence for her surviving boyfriend and Clarke was presented as a depressive drug addict who was suffering from a venereal disease and was in serious financial trouble. The judge summed up for an acquittal and, after a retirement of nearly five hours, the jury followed his directions to thunderous applause.

Once the trial was over Miller and Lancaster returned to England. The next year Lancaster, flying the *Southern Cross Miner*, took part in an attempt to break the London to Cape Town record set by Amy Johnson. Short of sleep after spending thirty hours in the air, he crashed two hours after taking off from Reggane in the Sahara. He died eight days later. Lancaster's mummified body, the remains of the plane and a diary he kept – in which he recorded his final days – were not discovered until 1962. Chubbie Miller died in London in 1972.

Hamilton also tried to insert himself in the Lindbergh baby kidnapping case by identifying a man named Manny Strewl as the writer of the ransom letters. That Hamilton was not a qualified questioned-document expert, mattered not one iota. Now describing himself as 'Chemical and Microscopic Investigations, Auburn', on 29 August 1933 he requested specimens of the handwriting of suspects and months later submitted a report saying he had compared the writing on the ransom notes with specimens taken from a racketeer 'Manning Strawl' and, 'The person who wrote the request writings and then signed the name Manning Strawl to same was the person who wrote all the "kidnap" letters and envelopes. This finding cannot be modified by any other standard. Albert H. Hamilton.'

In fact the writer of the extortion notes turned out to be Bruno Richard Hauptmann. A carpenter from the Bronx, and an illegal alien from Germany with a criminal history in his home country, Hauptmann was executed in 1936 for the murder of the Lindbergh baby.

Hamilton was nothing if not equal handed because he next gave evidence on behalf of Manny Strewl – his surname was Strewl, not Strawl – accused of kidnapping John J. O'Connell, nephew of Democratic leaders Ed and Des O'Connell. John O'Connell was twenty-three when, on 30 July 1933, he was abducted at 1 a.m. in front of his uncle's house. He was held for twenty-three days in Hoboken, New Jersey, as ransom negotiations took place.

Respected in criminal circles, Strewl, a friend of the O'Connells, had volunteered to act as an intermediary between them and the kidnappers, and a week after the kidnapping, he and Des O'Connell arranged a meeting in Washington Park. After ransom demands were discussed, Strewl left, saying he would consult with the kidnappers. Three or four meetings later, a deal was completed, and the O'Connells gave Strewl $42,500 to hand over. The kidnappers had first demanded $250,000. The money was never recovered and rumours were that it was buried in Washington Park.

After John O'Connell was released, Strewl was charged with masterminding the scheme and writing at least three of the five ransom notes. One ransom note read, in large block letters: 'What you offered is really an insult. What kind of people do you think you're dealing with? What we want is action. One way or the other if you want John alive kick in two hundred and fifty Gs.'

Hamilton gave evidence that the documents allegedly written by Strewl were not in the same handwriting as those in the ransom messages. Unfortunately, on cross-examination, it became clear he had earlier given a wholly different opinion to the prosecutor. Asked if he wanted the jury to believe he had deceived the prosecutor, he said he did not care.

Two years later the New York Appeal Court was scathing about his evidence, saying he had been 'entirely destroyed on cross-examination'. Hamilton was 'Confronted with a letter which he had written to the district attorney wherein he expressed the opinion that the defendant wrote the ransom notes. His testimony to the contrary has little value.' Convicted of the kidnapping, Strewl received a fifty-year sentence but, although Hamilton avoided a prosecution, he was at last effectively retired from the witness box. He died at his Auburn home on 1 July 1938.

Bill Dillon; Juan Ramos

The English barrister Patrick Back QC, who specialized in criminal defence work, used to say that if he could somehow introduce a dog into the evidence he was halfway to an acquittal. His favourite story, which he used to show the errors in rushing to judgement, was of the nobleman who came home from hunting and found both his baby and his guard dog covered in blood. He immediately presumed the dog had attacked the child and he killed it. Later he found a dead wolf in the room. The dog had been defending the child.

Unfortunately, in the 1970s the Florida state prosecutors regularly introduced dogs and their handlers into their cases to secure a conviction. The southern states tended to allow dog-tracking evidence whereas others, such as Ohio, did not. In many of the Floridian cases the handler was John Preston and the dogs were Harrass and Harrass II, which he claimed were 'infallible' German Shepherds who could track criminals. Their evidence led to over a hundred convictions nationwide.

One of the worst examples was the case of twenty-one-year-old Bill Dillon who, in 1981, days before he was supposed to try out as a pitching prospect for the Major League baseball side the Detroit Tigers, was arrested and charged with the murder of a vagrant, James Dvorak. In the early morning hours of 17 August, Dvorak's naked body was found in a wooded area near Canova Beach, in Brevard County not far from Cocoa on Florida's east coast. He had been beaten to death. Law enforcement officers collected the victim's discarded clothing and other items from the crime scene.

Later the same day, a truck driver saw a news story about the murder and called police to tell them about a hitchhiker he had picked up near the beach. The man had been wearing a bloody yellow T-shirt bearing the words 'Surf It' and blood was also smeared on his legs and shorts. He agreed to drive the hitchhiker to a tavern three miles away. On the way he stopped the truck and performed oral sex on the man, who he said was around six feet tall. He then dropped him at the tavern. Later that morning, the driver had found that the man had left the bloody T-shirt in his truck and he threw it in a trash can near a grocery store from where the police recovered it. They also collected other forensic evidence from the driver's truck.

The police included Dillon in their investigation because, five days after the murder, he and his brother showed up at the beach where Dvorak's body was found and appeared to know facts about the murder. This was hardly surprising since the case had been reported extensively in the local papers. Dillon was taken to the local police station and questioned further. As part of the investigation, authorities hired John Preston, a purported expert in handling scent-tracking dogs. He claimed his dogs could smell human traces months or even years after a suspect walked over the ground or in heavily trafficked streets even after a hurricane.

Eight days after the crime Preston, with his dog Harrass II, conducted two tests which he said linked the T-shirt to the crime scene and Dillon to the T-shirt. In the second test – a 'paper line-up' – Preston allowed his dog to sniff the T-shirt and then pieces of paper, including one that Dillon had touched. Preston said the dog selected Dillon's paper. He was arrested and charged with the murder.

Apart from Preston, the evidence against Dillon was a mishmash. There was some identification. The truck driver who picked up the hitchhiker was legally blind in one eye, but said he was able to see the man by his truck's interior light, and identified Dillon. A prison informer gave the obligatory evidence against him and so did his former girlfriend, who said she had seen him standing over the body on the night of the murder wearing the yellow T-shirt. But best of all there was Preston's evidence that his dog had connected Dillon with the crime scene and the T-shirt worn by the perpetrator.

Dillon went into the witness box in his own defence and gave evidence that he had been miles away from the beach on the night of the crime. Witnesses corroborated his alibi, but, after a five-day trial, he was convicted of first-degree murder and sentenced to life in prison. His appeal was rejected.

In fact, quite apart from Preston's canine capers, the evidence was flawed. In his first statement to the police the truck driver had said the hitchhiker was six feet tall and had a moustache. Dillon was six foot four and physically unable to grow a moustache. Other aspects of his description also did not match Dillon.

The former girlfriend's evidence in the witness box had been confused and two weeks after the trial she said she had been threatened with twenty-five years as an accessory if she did not give evidence against him. It also turned out she had had a brief affair with the senior detective in the case, who was promptly suspended and later resigned.

As for the prison informer, his evidence was contradictory and although other prisoners had been in the prison's dining room and were well able to hear Dillon, none came forward to support the snitch. The man had received his due reward. After giving evidence against Dillon, rape charges against him were dropped.

Three months after Dillon was sentenced, another Brevard County man – Wilton Dedge – was convicted of murder, again based on an unreliable identification, a jailhouse snitch and the testimony of the dog handler John Preston. Dedge, who became an Innocence Project of Florida client, was exonerated by DNA testing in 2004 after serving twenty-two years in prison.

Dillon filed several appeals in the five years following his conviction; all were denied. In 1996, he began to seek access to biological evidence for DNA testing, but these requests were also denied. In 2007, with the help of public defenders and lawyers at the Innocence Project, Dillon again requested DNA testing. This time, officials claimed that most of the evidence from the investigation – including fingernail scrapings from the victim and blood and hair from the crime scene – had been lost or destroyed. The yellow T-shirt, however, had been saved and a judge ordered testing on the remaining evidence.

Two years after Dillon's conviction, questions had begun to be raised around the country about Preston's qualifications. He had first been used by the Assistant State Attorney John Dean Moxley when, on 3 May 1981, Mark Wayne Jones was charged with the murders of two Titusville teenagers. Both had been sexually assaulted. Harrass II had sniffed paper towels with Jones' scent and had dug holes around the crime scene. Moxley told the jury that the dog had 'alerted on the scent' that belonged to Jones. It also picked out Jones' car from a line-up of five as containing the scent of one of the girls. In fact the evidence was never tested. In a plea bargain to avoid the death penalty Jones pleaded guilty to killing the girls 'in self-defence'. From then on Preston and Harrass II's career was onwards and upwards.

Over the years defence attempts to exclude Preston's evidence regularly failed. In 1982 in the case of Eugene Wiley, accused of drowning a student, Assistant State Attorney Moxley, qualifying Preston to give evidence, told the judge that the Eighteenth Circuit had accepted him as an expert tracker and that Brevard prosecutors had won ten cases, five of them murders, using his evidence. The motion to suppress his evidence was denied. Now, as an expert witness, Preston was paid $300 a day. His salary as a Pennsylvania State Trooper had been $20,000 a year. One of the reasons for Harrass II's success rate was, it seems, that Preston knew what results were required when he had advance knowledge before the animal was put to work.

By the time Preston was unmasked in 1984, he and his dogs had participated in hundreds of cases and his testimony helped lead to countless convictions. His downfall came when Brevard County's Judge Gilbert Goshorn conducted tests during the trial of five men for the murder of eighty-nine-year-old Irene

Allen of Titusville. Preston claimed his dog had found Elton Kimborough's scent as well as that of Kenneth Burch on a washcloth that had been stuffed down the victim's throat. However, Harrass II failed to track a scent much simpler, fresher and shorter in length than those it supposedly tracked in other cases. Goshorn offered Preston another chance at the test the next day, but he and Harrass II left town instead. He never returned to Brevard to testify again. Even so Moxley continued to champion Preston. In 1983 after Harrass II had sniffed a shirt belonging to Nicholas Lennear he found the man's scent in a rape victim's house. When in 1986 the case came before the Circuit Court, Moxley, by then a circuit court judge himself, gave evidence in support of Preston who had been accused of lying about his credentials.

In a 2008 affidavit, Judge Goshorn swore:

> It is my belief that the only way Preston could achieve the results he achieved in numerous other cases was having obtained information about the case prior to the scent tracking so that Preston could lead the dog to the suspect or evidence in question. I believe that Preston was regularly retained to confirm the state's preconceived notions about a case.

Sam Bardwell, a former prosecutor in Brevard County in the 1980s who had used Preston as a witness in a rape case, later said, 'John Preston was a total fraud, and everyone knew it.' But Karen Brandon, who worked in the same office at the same time, denied that anyone knew this. In another case, this time before the Arizona Supreme Court, a judge called him a 'charlatan'. Dillon's attorneys have alleged that prosecutors had doubts about the reliability of Preston's evidence before their man's trial but did not share these doubts with his lawyers at the time.

The results of DNA testing showed that the yellow T-shirt was conclusively tied to the killer and had not been worn by Dillon. Blood on the T-shirt matched the DNA profile of the victim. Biological material of another man was discovered on the collar and armpit of the T-shirt, indicating sweat or skin cells from the man who wore the shirt. The DNA profile developed from these areas of the shirt excluded both the victim and William Dillon.

Based on the results of these DNA tests, Dillon was released from prison on 18 November 2008, and his exoneration became official when prosecutors dropped all charges against him on 10 December. In 2009, J. Preston Silvernail, chief judge of Florida's Eighteenth Judicial Circuit, declined to call a Grand Jury to investigate how the Florida State Attorney's Offices had come to hire Preston. The Innocence Project of Florida believes that as many as sixty people may have been convicted based partially or solely upon Preston's evidence.

Florida Today found fifteen cases in the state in which Preston testified and, across the country, Preston's testimony led at least in part to more than a hundred criminal convictions. Preston, who was never charged with any crime, died in the same year that Dillon was released after serving twenty-seven years.

On 23 April 1982, the year after Dillon's arrest, Juan Ramos was arrested for the rape and murder of Mary Sue Cobb in Cocoa. She had been stabbed seventeen times and Ramos had been watching her sunbathe through binoculars. Harrass II tracked a scent on a white rope found near the victim to a garage apartment where Ramos lived. Using a cigarette pack thrown away by Ramos he picked out a shirt that had belonged to Mary Cobb as well as the knife with which she had been stabbed. Defence counsel filed a motion to suppress any evidence regarding dog scent discrimination line-ups on the grounds that the state could not show a proper predicate for its admission, in that no reliable controls were placed on the tests. Counsel also asked that the dog be subjected to testing to ensure accuracy. At the hearing of the motion Preston said that he did not feel it was necessary to have his dog tested for accuracy and skill by any of the national organizations such as the United States Police Canine Association, the American Kennel Club or Schutzhund USA. The motion to exclude the evidence was overruled. Ramos was found guilty and the judge, overriding the jury's recommendation of life imprisonment without parole, sentenced him to death.

However, Ramos was fortunate. In 1983 the Florida Supreme Court vacated his sentence after deciding that the Harrass II evidence was questionable:

> In attempting to qualify the dog, Preston testified that Harrass's tests have been affirmed by appellate courts all over the country. However it has recently come to light that in several cases in which Harrass II was used to secure criminal convictions, the dog is being proven wrong. The July 26, 1983 *Daytona Beach Morning Journal* newspaper carried an Associated Press wire story wherein it was noted that the reliability of Harrass II as well as the testimony of John Preston has been seriously attacked. It noted that in Cleveland, Dale Sutton was released from prison after serving two years of a 25-year sentence for armed mail robbery. He had been convicted after Harrass II's identification of a scent from a bedsheet placed by Sutton at the scene. However, Sutton was cleared when another person confessed to committing the offence. Similarly, the reliability of Harrass II has been attacked in New York and Virginia.

Juan Ramos was acquitted at a retrial.

The nearest the unfortunate Dillon came to pitching in a major league game was when shortly after his release he was invited to sing the National Anthem before a Tampa Bay Rays game. He was however awarded $1.25 million compensation. In the longer term, however, he has been more successful than many wrongly convicted men and women. He has made a career in the music industry and serves on the board of directors for the Innocence Project of Florida.

CHAPTER 13

False Forensics?

Lindy Chamberlain

James Hooten; Darwin Haselhuhn; Donald Lee
Shirley; Eddie Browning; Glen Woodall;
Jeffrey Todd Pierce; David Gibson;
Randall Dale Adams

Ray Krone; Levon Brooks and Kennedy Brewer;
William Richards

David Wayne Kunze; Mark Dallagher

The Narborough Murders; Kirk Bloodsworth;
John Kogut, Dennis Halstead and John Restivo;
John Schneeberger

Lindy Chamberlain

In his essay 'Miscarriages of Justice in Serious Cases in Australia' Paul Wilson gives six reasons why the Lindy Chamberlain case resulted in a miscarriage of justice. They run the gamut from overzealous police conduct through partisan expert evidence, inconclusive expert evidence, circumstantial evidence and media pressure, to media stereotyping and prejudice.

On 16 August 1980 Lindy Chamberlain and her husband Michael, a minister of the Seventh Day Adventist church, camped near Uluru, then known as Ayers Rock, on their motoring holiday in central Australia. With them were their two sons – Aidan, aged six years and ten months and Reagan, aged four years and four months – and their two-month-old baby daughter, Azaria. The Chamberlains pitched their tent in a camping area where a number of other people, strangers to them, were also camped. The Chamberlains' tent was some twenty to thirty metres to the east of a barbecue area, and the entrance to the tent faced the barbecue. The Chamberlains' Torana car was parked on the southern side of the tent, close to it, and also facing towards the barbecue area. At about eight o'clock on the evening of the seventeenth the Chamberlains, Aidan and Azaria were at the barbecue having their evening meal. Reagan was in bed in the tent, apparently asleep. According to witnesses, Mrs Chamberlain was nursing Azaria and seemed happy and cheerful. Two other campers, Greg and Sally Lowe, were also at the barbecue area, and both saw Azaria. At the subsequent trial of Lindy Chamberlain for the murder of her daughter it was common ground that the baby was then alive.

Lindy Chamberlain, carrying Azaria and followed by Aidan, left the barbecue area and walked towards the tent intending, she said, to put both children to bed. Her evidence as to what then occurred was that she placed the baby, who was asleep, in a bassinet in the tent and tucked her under the blankets. Aidan told his mother that he was still hungry, so she went to the car, got a tin of baked beans, went back to the tent and then, with Aidan, returned to the barbecue area, leaving Azaria and Reagan in the tent. There is no doubt that she did return to the barbecue area, accompanied by Aidan and carrying the tin of beans and a tin opener, about five or ten minutes after she had left. She seemed normal and quite composed. No one saw any blood on her or her clothes. That, said the Crown, was pure good luck.

The Crown case was that during this short absence from the barbecue area, Mrs Chamberlain took Azaria, dressed in a baby's jumpsuit, to the car, sat in the front passenger seat and cut the baby's throat. According to the Crown, the baby's dead body was probably left in the car (possibly in a camera bag) and was later that evening buried in the vicinity by Mr and Mrs Chamberlain. Lindy Chamberlain claimed that Azaria must have been snatched by one of a number of dingoes in the area. Azaria's jumpsuit was found a few days later.

She was not helped at the first inquest by the evidence of Dr Kenneth Brown, a forensic odontologist who had been trained in England by Professor James 'Taffy' Cameron, himself the pupil of Francis Camps, who in his later career became something of an expert for sale. Brown told the December 1980 inquest that holes made in Azaria's jumpsuit were cuts made by scissors or a knife rather than a dingo's teeth. An experiment had been conducted at Adelaide Zoo when meat wrapped in a similar jumpsuit had been thrown into the dingoes' den and the animals left teeth marks that did not resemble those on Azaria's clothing.

On the other hand the investigation had been marred by serious mismanagement at the crime scene. The photographs taken were of little help, evidence had been handled without protective gloves and there had been no serious forensic testing. Using phrases such as 'national disgrace' and 'the most malicious gossip ever witnessed in this country', the coroner Denis Barritt exonerated the Chamberlains.

After the public scourging, Brown flew to England bringing with him Azaria's clothing to seek vindication by his former teacher who, since Camps' retirement in 1972, had held the prestigious post of Professor of Forensic Medicine at the University of London. Cameron and his team backed Brown's findings, as did Joy Kuhl, a forensic biologist with the Health Commission in Sydney, who examined the Chamberlains' car, which a year after the disappearance of Azaria had been sent down to Sydney. Unfortunately it had spent most of the time in the sun and insufficient allowance had been made as to the effect of the heat on samples taken from it.

Now the Cameron–Kuhl findings were sufficient to obtain an order from the Northern Territory Supreme Court quashing the coroner's verdict and ordering a second inquest.

The second inquest began on 14 December 1981 with Cameron winging his way across the world to say that there was blood on Azaria's jumpsuit and that the blood all came from the neck and not from separate areas as might be expected from a dog attack. His most sensational piece of evidence, however, was at the end of his stint in the witness box. In the underarm region of the jumpsuit he could see what appeared to be the bloodstained handprint of a young adult. No matter that neither counsel for the Chamberlains nor the coroner could make it out. Their eyes were untrained in this sort of matter. What was clear to the expert often baffled the layman. It would, in the distant future, be seen as a classic example of *merda taurorum animas conturbuit*, or bullshit baffles brains. Cameron's cross-examination was directed to his mistaken evidence in the Confait case, over which he had been criticized in a subsequent Royal Commisision.

Then came Professor Malcolm Chaikin from the University of New South Wales who thought that cuts in the jumpsuit were caused by scissors, and when he tried to reconstruct the attack by a dingo using a mounted tooth he found that the dingo would tear but not cut.

Part of Cameron's success, and indeed that of all the doctors and scientists who appeared for the prosecution, was his ability to explain things in a simple way. None more so than Joyce Kuhl who found blood all over the front of the car, on brackets and the carpet, on a pair of nail scissors between the front seats and traces on the zipper of Michael Chamberlain's camera bag, which detectives thought had been used to take Azaria's body away. Kuhl said that the blood was definitely fetal and from a child under the age of six. Dingoes, however talented, cannot open car doors.

The Chamberlains were committed for trial, she charged with murder, he as an accessory. Although there was no evidence on the question of motive it was assumed Lindy Chamberlain had killed the child while suffering from post-natal depression.

The trial was something of an anticlimax and a foregone conclusion. The star witness for the defence, the spiky Professor Plueckhahn of Melbourne University was abrasive, challenging Cameron's findings at every possible opportunity. As to the handprint on the jumper, he joined the ranks of the layman, saying 'With due respect to Professor Cameron . . . I cannot in the wildest imagination . . . see the imprint of a hand.' He thought the staining had been caused by irregular blood flow.

Dr Dan Cornell, who had introduced the crossover electro-phoresis screening test used by Kuhl to detect fetal blood, thought she 'didn't know what she was doing'.

It was to no avail. The defence experts lacked the charisma of Cameron and his colleagues. Juries, and for that matter judges, become conditioned to the international expert as opposed to home-grown ones. As Colin Evans pointed out in his book *A Question of Evidence*, 'For some reason, when a witness has flown across a continent – or in this case, halfway around the world – to deliver his or her testimony, it invariably carries more weight than if the same testimony had emanated from a local lab.'

Despite heavy betting by journalists and spectators on an acquittal and a summing-up by the judge that favoured her, Lindy Chamberlain was convicted on 29 October 1982. She received a life sentence and her husband a modest eighteen months suspended, coupled with an A$500 good behaviour bond.

At that point a campaign by her supporters took off, led by Les Smith who had a diploma in applied science and who was supported by microbiologist Dr Roland Bernett and chemist Ken Chapman as well as journalist Malcolm Brown. With the scientists as observers, Smith began a series of experiments using meat wrapped in towelling and fed to his collie Susie. Sometimes she tore the wrapping, sometimes she bit through it. It took until September 1984 before he was allowed access to Azaria's jumpsuit, and when he compared it with Susie's attacks on wrapped meat the marks were similar. Hans Brunner of the Department of Conservation in Victoria and co-author of *Identification of Mammalian Hair* examined the hairs on the jumpsuit and found six canid hairs, which he identified as belonging to a dingo.

There still remained the blood. Kuhl had apparently found sand in the blood spray and Smith thought it might have been inherent in the manufacturing of the vehicle. He examined forty cars of the same type as that of the Chamberlains and found five had an almost identical spray pattern on the roof of the footwell.

On 2 February 1986 the baby's missing matinee jacket was discovered a few metres from where Azaria's clothing had been found. It had been partially buried near a dingo lair. Lindy Chamberlain, who had insisted all the time the child had been wearing it, was released within a week.

In 1987 a Royal Commission under Justice Morling was followed by an acquittal in the Supreme Court the next year which found, 'The alleged "baby blood" found in the Chamberlains' car, upon which the prosecution so heavily relied, could have been any substance, but was likely to be that of a sound-deadening compound from a manufacturing overspray.'

There was a sop to Cerebus. The court also noted that as

DNA testing was not advanced in the early 1980s, the expert testimony given by the prosecution at the trial and relied on by the jurors was reasonable evidence at the time, even though it was ultimately found to be wrong.

With their marriage under strain from the case the Chamberlains were divorced in 1991. The next year she married an American publisher, Rick Creighton.

The Chamberlains' hopes for a full vindication remained unfulfilled. A third inquest took place in 1995, with the coroner's report stating that it was a 'paper inquest' rather than a full inquest since there was little new evidence and the second inquest had never been fully completed. The coroner considered the Morling Royal Commission's report enquiring into the correctness of the convictions against Lindy Chamberlain along with submissions made on behalf of the Chamberlains, and returned an open verdict in Azaria's cause of death, or, 'insufficient evidence by the prosecution that failed to meet the required standard of proof for conviction'. Specifically, he wrote, 'After examining all the evidence I am unable to be satisfied on the balance of probabilities that Azaria Chamberlain died at the hands of Alice Lynne Chamberlain. It automatically follows that I am also unable to be satisfied on the balance of probabilities that Michael Leigh Chamberlain had any involvement in the death.' He also wrote that because the evidence for the death-by-dingo hypothesis was never fully developed, 'I am unable to be reasonably satisfied that Azaria Chamberlain died accidentally as a result of being taken by a dingo.'

Later it transpired that Uluru chief ranger Derek Roff had written to the government at least two years before Azaria's disappearance warning that dingoes in the area were becoming increasingly fearless, and were approaching and sometimes biting people. He had called for a dingo cull and warned of a possible human tragedy.

A final inquest began in February 2012 and new figures on dingo attacks on Fraser Island had been collated by the Queensland Government's Department of Environment and Resource Management (DERM). They showed ninety-eight 'dangerous dingo attacks' had been recorded since 2002 and there had been two high-profile attacks before that year. In 1997, a five-year-old boy was badly attacked by two dingoes and in 2001 nine-year-old Clinton Gage had been mauled to death.

The coroner ruled that it had, after all, been the dingo that did it.

James Hooten; Darwin Haselhuhn; Donald Lee Shirley; Eddie Browning; Glen Woodall; Jeffery Todd Pierce; David Gibson; Randall Dale Adams

If anyone thought that by the end of the twentieth century charlatans such as Albert Hamilton had been eliminated from the criminal justice system, they thought wrongly.

If the evidence given by false experts in criminal trials was not so damaging, their claims would be laughable. What is even more worrying is how the prosecutors and the judges have thought that in any way these witnesses resembled experts. The second trial in Mississippi of James L. Hooten for murder is a great example. The first trial itself is a good example of prosecutorial misconduct.

Reuben Wood, who lived in a mobile home on Narcissus Street, Gautier in Jackson County, Mississippi, was shot and killed there on the night of 3 November 1977. Hooten, a resident of Savannah, Georgia, was indicted for the murder by a Jackson County Grand Jury on 25 August 1978. His trial began on 20 August 1980.

The state's case was that around 2.20 p.m on 3 November 1977, Hooten arrived in Mobile, Alabama, on a commercial flight. According to a witness from National Car Rental Systems, he then rented a car that was to be returned the following day. The vehicle was delivered back to the rental office at 6.08 a.m. on the morning of 4 November. It was the state's case that Hooten drove to Gautier in the rental car, a distance of 44.6 miles from Mobile, shot Wood some time that night, returned to Mobile and caught a flight back to Georgia.

The state called eighteen witnesses and one of the most crucial was Charlotte Acheson, the manager of a convenience store in Gautier. She gave evidence that on the afternoon of 3 November, a man whom she identified as Hooten had come into the store and asked for directions to Narcissus Street. She drew him a map on a piece of paper and explained to him how to get there. She said she was sure it happened on the afternoon of 3 November but told the court, 'I don't know what time.' She said she normally finished work at 2 p.m. but about half the time, as manager, she was still in the store after two o'clock.

Prior to the trial, on 5 April 1980 the defence had filed a 'Motion to Compel Discovery of All Material and Tangible Evidence', and on 19 August the court ordered that the state disclose essentially everything requested in the motion, including, 'The statements of all persons, . . . if said statements are exculpatory,' and 'copy of all exculpatory material concerning the defendant'. At no time before the conclusion of Charlotte Acheson's evidence was any information or material sent to Hooten's lawyers regarding prior written statements by her.

It all went wrong when, during the examination of the state's final witness, it became clear that Acheson had made a prior statement on 9 November 1977, which had not been disclosed. In it she said at the time that the car the man was driving when she drew him the map had a Georgia licence plate. The car rental witness said the hired car had been one with a Mississippi plate. Acheson was also sure that the man came into the store before 2 p.m. She did not go back to the store on the day in question after that time because she had to stay home and babysit for her two grandchildren. She made the positive statement, 'I know I left at two o'clock or thereabouts.' Hooten had not rented a car until 2.20 p.m. – and from a rental outlet that was forty miles away.

Unfortunately there had been yet another statement that also had not been disclosed. This time it was by Juana Robinson and was made six days after the shooting. She had attempted to identify Hooten as the man she saw at her beverage store in Gautier on 3 November, stating positively that he was at the store between 11 a.m. and noon that day. In theory this completely wrecked the state's case since Hooten had arrived on an afternoon flight.

In practice he was found guilty and the Mississippi Supreme Court quashed the verdict, ordered a new trial and recommended that there should be a change of venue. And at the September 1983 retrial it all went wrong again.

Part of the state's case now was that a legal writing pad with some of Hooten's writing on it was found near Wood's body. Unlike the practice in England when anyone can appear as an expert, in America the trial judge has the right to exclude the evidence of an expert witness if he or she is not shown to have the relevant qualifications and expertise.

The state called a special agent from the document section of the FBI to give evidence that the handwriting was that of Hooten. Robert B. Hallett had received a Bachelor of Arts degree from New Jersey State College in Trenton, and for the next ten years was an elementary school teacher and high school coach. During this time he taught students penmanship.

He had been an agent with the FBI for fifteen years. For his first five years he was a field agent, after which he was sent to the Federal Bureau of Investigation Laboratory in Washington. He received three years' training in the discipline of examining questioned documents. This consisted of attending regular classes, reading prescribed books, articles and pamphlets, and taking regular tests. At the time of the trial he was on a Master's programme in forensic science at Georgetown University. He had testified in more than one hundred cases in forty different states and was a member of the Mid-Atlantic Association of Forensic Scientists and the Document Examiners' Association in Washington, D.C.

Now the defence tried to call an expert witness to show the writing was not Hooten's. And the expert witness they called was Marie B. Hill who said she had given evidence in around 300 cases in Mississippi. The judge ruled she was not sufficiently qualified in the subject. Hooten was again found guilty and the defence appealed.

Marie B. Hill's formal education had gone no further than high school. She had done some secretarial work in a chancery clerk and law office. While a housewife, and going to school at night studying typing, bookkeeping and secretarial work, she also took a correspondence course with the 'International Graph-Analysis Society Institute' in Chicago, which taught entirely by correspondence courses. She told the court, 'I had a sister that was married to a doctor in Pennsylvania. And got a hold of it from somewhere and introduced it to me. And I thought I would love it.'

She was evidently a good student because she had finished an eighteen-month course of twenty lessons in approximately nine months to a year, she said. Hill was not quite sure whether or not the answers to all the examination questions were given at the end of her course book. She had also obtained a 'Master's Degree' from this same institution by taking further correspondence courses, the length of which she did not state.

When she finished her course, for a fee they permitted her to go to a graduation ceremony in Chicago, wear a cap and gown and attend all the festivities. There she met her 'Professor' for the first time.

Questioned about other accredited experts, she knew nothing about Ardway Hilton, the author of *The Scientific Examination of Questioned Documents*; nothing about *Conway on Evidential Documents*; nothing about Wilson R. Harrison, the author of *Suspect Documents*.

She thought she knew Albert S. Osborn who had written *Questioned Documents* and *The Problems of Proof*. Indeed she believed he had gone to the grapho-analysis school just as she had, and written a book about it that made him rich. But, she added, 'I don't know if he knows any more about it than I do.' Osborn had died in 1946.

She was frank about her limitations:

Q: Did you study Graphology or Grapho-Analysis?
A: I don't know anything about Graphology. I don't even

know the definition of it really. I just know that it is not Grapho-Analysis.

Asked if she was keeping up to date with literature and developments in her field, she replied: 'I don't intend to. I feel like what I know is sufficient for the amount that I intend to do. I don't intend to overstep my bounds in the examination. When it gets past what I can do, then I will turn it over to somebody with a higher education.'

At least she was in touch with the people. She was asked about county fairs, malls and shopping centres where there are 'handwriting computers' that take specimens of handwriting and instantly render statements concerning the personality of the writer:

Q: Do you know those program computers they have out at the fair?
A: Yes.
Q: One where you stick a card in there and it . . .
A: . . . I used one of them.
Q: You used one. They analyze your handwriting, don't they?
A: It's pretty good, too.

On 7 May 1986, by a two to one majority, the appeal court decided she should have been allowed to give evidence in which she would have been subject to cross-examination of her expertise. Once again they overturned Hooten's conviction and now ordered a third trial. However the presiding (and dissenting) Judge Hawkins thought the circuit judge had been right in refusing to allow Hill into the witness box: 'If this witness has indeed testified over 300 times as an expert on discovering spurious handwriting as she claimed, it is an astonishing indictment on the gullibility of lawyers and judges.'
Hawkins concluded:

Indeed, it takes remarkable ignorance or gall, one or the other, for any lawyer to *offer* her as an *expert* on the subject.

One lawyer did his homework and exposed her short-comings. The circuit judge upheld his motion to exclude her testimony as an expert. They both reflected credit on the administration of justice.

It was not only handwriting experts who came under scrutiny in 1983. That year there was also the vexed subject of hypnotized witnesses and the expertise of those who hypnotized them.

In Wyoming in *Gee v. State* even the prosecutor had difficulty stating his expert's qualifications. However, the Supreme Court overcame this hurdle on his behalf ruling that the expert did not need any. The dissenting Justice Brown wrote:

It follows, therefore, that a hobo passing through town or a derelict in the county jail could hypnotize a potential witness, and the witness's testimony would be admissible at trial . . . There is a man in Oakland, California, who is the dean and lone 'professor' at 'Croaker College.' For the sum of $150 each, this man trains frogs to jump . . . As part of his rigid training curriculum, the 'professor' claims that he hypnotizes the frog; while they are in their hypnotic trance, he plays an attitude-improvement tape to them. Under our present standards the Dean of 'Croaker College' would be over-qualified as a hypnotist.

In 1986, still in Wyoming in a subsequent case, the majority of the Appeal Court described the hypnotist as a 'non-professional with meagre training in hypnotic techniques'. On 21 April 1984, the Safeway Store in Green River had been robbed by two men, one armed with what appeared to be a sawn-off shotgun and the other armed with a knife. Two of the staff were tied up and after hypnosis were able to give details of the men. Their hypnotist was a maintenance man at Pacific Power and Light Company who had undertaken a thirty-three-hour course in the discipline. The conviction of Darwin Haselhuhn was upheld by the majority of the Wyoming Supreme Court, but the dissenting judge, Justice Urbigkit, thought:

This is a perfect example which merits application of Justice Brown's advice in his specially concurring opinion to his own majority opinion in Pote v. State, Wyo., 695 P.2d 617, 632 (1985), that 'People who do not know what they are doing ought not to "monkey around" with hypnotism lest they jeopardize an important case and cost the state a lot of money.'

From 1975 to 1987, 300 police were trained in the technique in California. In 1982 the Californian Supreme Court had ruled in *People v Shirley* on a six to one majority that evidence acquired from a witness who had undergone hypnosis could not be admitted in court. The decision was in line with rulings in Michigan, Minnesota, Arizona, Maryland and Pennsylvania.

In the Shirley case, the complainant Catherine C. was not really the best possible witness. On her own account, before the alleged rape occurred she had been drinking all evening to which she had added anti-psychotic drug Mellaril. She told a variety of stories about how she and Donald Lee Shirley came to have sex before, after undergoing hypnosis, she claimed she had been raped. Justice Kaus thought, 'there is a good possibility that she had no clear memory to be refreshed by hypnosis'. On the other hand Shirley was a man of good character, well thought of by his officers in the marines.

A psychiatrist called by the defence gave evidence:

Q: Person can stand here in this room and lie while not under hypnosis just as easily as they do while under hypnosis?
A: They might even do it easier under hypnosis because the hypnosis would put the responsibility on the shoulders of the hypnotist as the patient would see it or the subject would see it.

Shirley's conviction was quashed. It is interesting to speculate that now, in a British court at least, Shirley might be convicted on the ground that Catherine C. had been too drunk to give proper consent.

Of course it is not only in the United States that questions
have been raised about the value of evidence obtained by
hypnosis and the qualifications of the hypnotist. The battle
over the use or misuse of hypnotized witnesses began in
earnest in the 1980s in many parts of the world. In Britain
hypnosis had been used over the years without the prosecution
telling the defence that witnesses had been hypnotized, and no
statistics were kept to show how often it had been used and
whether it had produced correct results. In 1987 the Home
Office issued guidelines to the effect that there must be an
uninterrupted videotape of the session and that a witness who
may be called to give evidence on material matters should not
normally be hypnotized. But the guidelines were never made
mandatory. Then in June that year in *R v Coster*, a trial at
Maidstone Crown Court, the judge stopped the case against
the defendants after hearing that the hypnotist used by the
police was self-taught and had learned his technique by reading books borrowed from his local public library.

Unfortunately that was not the end of the hypnotized
witness however, and the case of Eddie Browning had much
more serious consequences. On 18 June 1988 the car of
twenty-two-year-old and seven months' pregnant Marie Wilks
broke down on the M50 motorway near Bristol. She left her
ten-year-old sister and her one-year-old baby in the car while
she walked to the nearest emergency telephone. While she was
talking to the police operator she was attacked, stabbed in the
neck and abducted. She was driven for two miles down the
road before her killer threw her over the motorway embankment where she bled to death.

Under hypnosis Peter Clarke, an off-duty police inspector,
said he had seen the car into which Mrs Wilks was bundled,
adding there was no clear maker's mark on the back of the car,
but that it was not a hatchback. He believed it to be a silver-
grey Renault with chrome bumpers and a registration plate
C856HPK or C856HFK.

Eddie Browning, a former Welsh guardsman with a conviction for violence, was arrested after a colleague, who had seen
an identikit picture of the killer and knew detectives were

looking for the driver of a silver Renault, contacted police. The evidence against him was thin. As a motive it was suggested he had rowed with his also pregnant wife and had taken his anger out on Mrs Wilks. He said that on the evening of the murder he had driven to Scotland but it was alleged his car was seen on the M50, not the shortest way, and he had therefore lied. There were no traces of blood in his car despite the fact Mrs Wilks must have bled profusely. On 8 November 1989 he was sentenced to life with a minimum of twenty-five years.

The videotape of the hypnosis of Peter Clarke, which was made before Browning's arrest and retained by West Mercia police, had never been mentioned to either the prosecution lawyers or the defence. Years later it was finally handed to Browning's solicitor.

Browning's silver hatchback Renault 25 had the registration C754VAD, plastic bumpers and the maker's logo clearly on the back. The police had also failed to disclose two messages provided by Inspector Clarke and another witness of what they had seen on the M50. Neither message mentioned a C registration, although both witnesses later gave evidence referring to this letter. In 1994 the Court of Appeal ruled that this was sufficient to make the conviction unsafe. Browning was awarded around £600,000 compensation for his years in prison, but it was suggested that £18 per week should be deducted for his board and lodging. After the case Dr H. B. Gibson, President of the British Society of Experimental and Clinical Hypnosis, wrote to *The Times*, calling for the Home Secretary to make it 'mandatory for police forces totally to eschew the use of hypnosis'. In the United Kingdom hypnosis now appears to have fallen into disuse as a tool for forensic investigation.

In 1987, back in America the trial judge refused to allow the 'experimental new' DNA evidence in the case of Glen Woodall, accused of two rapes in West Virginia. After he received two life sentences, an early DNA test proved inconclusive. Later, using the newly developed polymerase chain reaction (PCR) technique to amplify a single or a few copies of a piece of DNA on spermatozoa from the rapes, the samples matched but they excluded Woodall. It also emerged that one of the investigating officers and one of the victims had been in a relationship, and both the victims had been hypnotized without this being disclosed to the defence. The case against Woodall was dismissed in April 1992.

This was the first case in which a defendant had been convicted on the evidence of the later disgraced police officer Fred Salem Zain who ran the West Virginia state laboratory. Zain had used flawed blood-typing methods in tying the semen to Woodall. He had also initially found a piece of hair to be unidentifiable pubic hair, but later changed his identification to hair from Woodall's beard. In 1993 the West Virginia Supreme Court ruled: 'Any evidence offered by Zain at any time in any criminal prosecution should be deemed invalid, unreliable and inadmissible in determining whether to award a new trial in any *habeus corpus* proceeding.'

Thought to be very pro-prosecution, as early as 1985 there had been concerns over Zain's conduct but these had been ignored by his supervisors. After the Woodall case a special judge and a panel of lawyers and scientists was appointed to investigate West Virginia's serology department. On 4 November 1993, Senior Circuit Court Judge James Holliday reported that Zain had misstated evidence, falsified lab results and reported scientifically implausible results that might have resulted in as many as 134 people being wrongfully convicted. He also found serious deficiencies in the serology division's quality-control procedures. The Supreme Court unanimously accepted Holliday's report, on 12 November calling Zain's actions 'egregious violations of the right of a defendant to a fair trial' and a 'corruption of our legal system'.

Indeed Zain's whole career was based on lies. To become a Trooper he had claimed to have graduated with a major in biology. In fact he had failed most of the chemistry examinations he had taken and had only a degree in English. After graduation he had failed an FBI course in forensic science. Zain was never prosecuted and died in 2002.

Zain was not the only scientist accused of falsifying the evidence. In Oklahoma City Joyce Gilchrist was dubbed

'Black Magic' by her colleagues because of her ability to find matches other examiners could not. Whether Gilchrist was even qualified to conduct such tests became a topic in a lawsuit brought by David Bryson, wrongly convicted on her evidence. Records of Gilchrist's college transcript and early training at FBI labs show the chemist had difficulty with some of her science classes. According to her transcripts from the University of Oklahoma (UO) and University of Central Oklahoma (UCO), Gilchrist was placed on academic probation more than once, as well as academic suspension. At UO, she received a grade of D in general chemistry. At UCO, her grades did not improve and she was given C and D grades in chemistry courses such as general physics and quantitative analysis.

Very much a protégé of District Attorney Bob Macy, she was dismissed in September 2001 over claims of flawed casework analysis and laboratory mismanagement. Concerns about her actions were first raised when a landscaper, Jeffrey Todd Pierce, was convicted of rape in 1986 largely based on Gilchrist's evidence despite a clean criminal record and good alibi.

After Pierce had been wrongly picked out on a police line-up, voluntarily giving hair and blood samples in an attempt to clear his name, he was arrested and charged with the rape. Gilchrist claimed his hair samples were 'microscopically consistent' with the hairs found at the crime scene. Pierce was cleared in 2001 after DNA evidence was re-examined, and he was released after fifteen years in prison. He subsequently received compensation of $4 million in 2007. Gilchrist had given evidence in more than 3,000 cases, in which eleven defendants were executed. In turn she filed a suit claiming her dismissal was as a result of her alleging sexual harassment by her supervisor.

In another case in 1983 David Gibson was convicted of kidnapping and rape and served seventeen years before his conviction was vacated based on exculpatory DNA test results, but it took another three and a half years before the charges against him were finally dismissed. A subsequent analysis of the blood and hair evidence that was tested before his criminal

conviction showed that, even without the benefit of DNA testing, Gilchrist should have excluded him as the criminal.
Indeed, her own lab results indicated Gibson could not have
been the donor of the semen found at the scene, contrary to
the evidence she gave at his trial. After his release he sued her
and the City of Oklahoma as her employer and obtained $16
million damages against her, but it was a pyrrhic victory. Of
course, she did not have the money to pay and the courts ruled
that the city was not liable.

In 1991 it was found that the Texas pathologist Ralph
Erdmann had not carried out autopsies as he claimed. He
was unmasked after he said that during one autopsy he had
weighed the spleen of a victim. The family pointed out the
spleen had been removed years earlier and when the body
was exhumed there was no evidence of any autopsy at all.
Erdmann had also kept blood samples in his refrigerator
along with his condiments. The next year he received concurrent ten-year sentences.

Meanwhile, across America, psychiatrist James Grigson
was causing havoc. Following in the tradition of Albert
Hamilton, towards the end of the twentieth century Grigson,
known as Dr Death because of his willingness to give evidence
against defendants, some of whom he had not seen, became
one of the country's most dangerous forensic psychiatrists.
His specialty was giving evidence in the death penalty phase
of trials, usually labelling the defendants as psychopaths who
would not hesitate to kill again. In Texas, a jury may
recommend capital punishment only if it believes there is a
probability that the defendant will commit further criminal
acts of violence and be a continuing threat to society. In 1981
in *Estelle v Smith* the US Supreme Court ruled that defendants
could not be examined by a psychiatrist without their
permission, and the information could not be used in court
unless they had been warned of the possibility.

Part of the problem with Grigson, who dressed and looked
like a cowboy rather than the stereotypical suspect Viennese
psychiatrist, was that like Hamilton and many others he was
too good a communicator. He could explain things to a jury in

words of one syllable and they loved him for telling them what they really believed anyway. He also claimed 100 per cent accuracy in his predictions and in effect crossed the line between independence and joining the prosecutorial team. In an eighteen-year period he gave evidence in 111 capital cases; in all but eight the defendant was sentenced to death. As a result defence lawyers took to paying him a retainer so that he could not appear for the prosecution and over time prosecutors took to paying him a retainer for the same reason.

The nadir of his career came in 1976 in the case of Randall Dale Adams, convicted of the murder of Robert Wood, a Dallas police officer. Grigson labelled Adams, a man with no previous convictions, as an extreme sociopath who would kill again whether he was in or out of prison. Adams was later freed after David Harris, then on death row himself and who had earlier given evidence against him, confessed that he had lied and that he was the killer. Fortunately, Adams, who spent twelve years on death row, had been reprieved earlier because of faults in the jury selection. His conviction was finally overturned on the grounds of prosecutorial misconduct by the District Attorney. Adams died of a brain tumour in 2010. He had never been reconvicted.

Grigson's comeuppance came in 1988 when he came under fire from the Supreme Court in the case of *Satterwhite v Texas*, which expanded on *Estelle v Smith*. Kenneth Leron Satterwhite, who had convictions ranging from aggravated assault to armed robbery, had been assessed by Grigson as having 'a severe antisocial personality disorder' and 'is extremely dangerous and will commit further acts of violence'. Ruling that the use of Grigson's evidence, based on a psychiatric examination that took place without the knowledge of the defendant's lawyer, could not be considered harmless, the court held that the death penalty that had been imposed could not stand. Following the decision the American Civil Liberties Union lawyers called Grigson 'a menace' and officials of the American Psychiatric Association began to question his professional ethics.

One judge sitting on the Texas Court of Criminal Appeals wrote:

When Dr Grigson speaks to a lay jury about a person who he characterizes as a 'severe' sociopath the defendant should stop what he is doing and commence writing out his last will and testament – because he will in all probability soon be ordered by the trial judge to suffer a premature death. When Dr Grigson is shown to have testified in a capital murder case in which the defendant challenges his conviction and sentence of death, the captions of those cases in which relief was granted, read almost like the following: 'THIS IS ANOTHER DR GRIGSON CASE.' The number of these cases is so great that I will simply refer the reader to either Westlaw or Lexis and not cite them.

Grigson was later expelled by the Texas Association of Psychiatric Physicians (TAPP) for making statements in evidence on defendants he had not examined. TAPP said his expulsion was due not only because of his replies to hypothetical questions but also for predicting dangerousness with 100 per cent certainty. Grigson died in 2004. He had been suffering from lung cancer.

Another charismatic and therefore thoroughly dangerous expert was Dr Louise Robbins, Professor of Anthropology at the University of North Carolina, who took the science of footprint identification a step too far. Generally, as what might be called a rule of toe, shoe prints left at a crime scene are first photographed against a reference ruler. They are then peeled off the surface in the same way as a fingerprint is lifted. Footwear impressions are often preserved with plaster casts of the depressions. Shoes and their crime scene prints and impressions can then be compared side by side, or through the use of transparent overlays. Professor Robbins did not need these techniques and did not need to look at the prints made at crime scenes. She claimed that no two people walked the same way and that after looking at a crime scene she could identify the wearer of the shoes that had made the mark without the trouble of matching the print with the shoe. Again this was an example of *ipse dixit* (I myself said it) and in effect the jury had to take her word that she was correct.

As an anthropologist, she claimed to have identified a footprint in Africa three and a half million years old as made by a-five-and-a-half months pregnant woman, something Timothy White, Professor of Anthropology at the University of California at Berkeley, described as pure nonsense. And she carried on from there. Before she died in 1987 at the age of fifty-eight, suffering from brain cancer, her conclusions had been reviewed by a panel of 135 anthropologists, lawyers and forensic scientists, one of whom described her theories as 'pure hogwash'. Unfortunately for defendants, by then she had appeared in courtrooms all over the United States and in Canada for the previous twelve years.

Ray Krone; Levon Brooks and Kennedy Brewer; William Richards

In 2002 Ray Krone had the doubtful distinction of being the one-hundredth person on death row to have his conviction quashed through DNA evidence. In 1992, Krone, who was dubbed 'the snaggle-toothed killer', had been convicted of killing bartender Kim Ancona in the men's lavatory of the CBS lounge, a bar in Phoenix, Arizona where he played darts. She had been stabbed to death. The killer had left behind little physical evidence. There were no fingerprints; the blood at the scene matched the victim's type; and saliva on her naked body came from someone with the most common blood type. There was no semen, and no DNA tests were performed. The prosecution's case was based in a large part on the evidence of a forensic dentist, Raymond Rawson, who said he had matched an impression of Krone's jagged teeth on a Styrofoam cup to the bitemarks on Ancona's breast and neck. In evidence Rawson said that he had 'the highest order of confidence that no other person caused the bitemark injuries'. Despite the fact that Krone had an alibi and his shoe size of ten and a half did not match the size nine-and-a-half shoe print left at the murder scene, he was convicted and sentenced to death.

That conviction was reversed due to a technicality and now nine other forensic odontologists reviewed the evidence and concluded that Krone was not the biter. In 1996 Rawson gave evidence again at Krone's second trial, sticking by his original analysis, and Krone was again convicted. Before the second trial Noel Levy, the prosecuting attorney, had been personally told by two of the country's most respected dental forensic experts that there was 'no way' the teeth marks on Ancona's body were made by Krone. They said Rawson was absolutely wrong to identify Krone as the source of the bitemarks. Not only did the prosecutor not inform the defence of this exculpatory information but, convinced of Krone's guilt, he proceeded to seek the death penalty a second time. He believed Krone and Ancona were dating. 'The ways of the human heart are mysterious,' he said, but when asked why he thought Krone killed her, replied, 'I can't address that.'

Krone spent three years on Arizona's death row and a total of ten years in prison. In 2002, belated DNA testing of blood found on the victim proved that Rawson had been wrong all along; the evidence exonerated Krone and identified a convicted sex offender as the real killer.

Overruled experts are often unwilling to back down and, even after the DNA exonerated Krone, following the standard of never apologizing for mistakes set nearly a century earlier by England's Sir Bernard Spilsbury, Rawson commented, 'The bitemark evidence was solid.' Krone was awarded $4.4 million compensation. In August 2006 Kenneth Phillips, then serving a sentence for rape, pleaded guilty to Ancona's murder and was sentenced to fifty-three years to life.

Overall, bitemark evidence has had an unfortunate history in criminal law. The appellate courts in the United States had accepted bitemark analysis from the Texan case of *Doyle* back in 1954 and, while the Arizona case of *Marx* determined that the methodology of bitemark analysis was not novel and that the use of dental models and photography was well established, the following year bitemark analysis took something of a buffeting in Illinois in the case of Richard Milone, convicted by a judge sitting alone in DuPage County. He had been accused of the September 1972 murder of fourteen-year-old Sally Kandel who was found apparently bludgeoned to death in a cornfield. A human bitemark, thought to have been inflicted some time after death, was found on the inside of her right thigh. Of eleven experts who gave evidence, six believed Milone made the bitemark; five did not. It was rather like Haig in the First World War who believed that since there were more British soldiers than Germans they must eventually triumph. Found guilty and sentenced to 90 to 175 years, Milone was paroled after serving twenty. Lengthy and repeated appeals against the forensic evidence failed. But forensic odontologist Dr Mary A. Bush has pointed out, rather than setting a precedent of acceptance, the difference of expert opinion in the Milone case should have sounded an alarm that the technique was based on opinion, not science.

Bitemark analysis is particularly troubling because of the almost complete absence of validated rules, regulations or processes for accreditation that establish standards for experts or the evidence they provide. In America, unlike other areas of forensic analysis, forensic dentists are generally self-employed rather than employees of an accredited laboratory, and as such have no opportunity for peer discussion and supervision.

There are approximately a hundred forensic odontologists in America who have been certified by boards controlled by other odontologists – generally speaking, their friends and colleagues – but not accredited by an entity that applies scientific rigour. Much forensic odontology work involves comparing dental records with well-preserved teeth of people who have died in fires or other accidents and is relatively simple. The technique dates back to the identification of the body of Major General Joseph Warren, killed in the Battle of Bunker Hill, from false teeth made for him by Paul Revere.

In contrast the comparison of a suspect's teeth with marks on the body of a dead victim is far more subjective and, since it is often done through photographs, is far more error prone.

As noted in *Modern Scientific Evidence*, 'The rate of error in bitemark identification, particularly the rate of false positive errors, appears to be quite high.' In fact, only three studies have examined the reliability of bitemark analysis. All three show serious problems. One showed an error rate – a rate of false identifications – as high as 91 per cent. Another (conducted by the American Board of Forensic Odontology) found a 63.5 per cent rate of false identifications, and the third showed an error rate of 11.9 to 22 per cent of false identifications among forensic odontologists. It noted that the 'poor performance' is cause for concern because it has 'very serious implications for the accused, the discipline, and society'.

Others who have suffered through fallible odontological identification include Levon Brooks and Kennedy Brewer, separately convicted principally on the evidence of Dr Michael West of Hattiesburg.

Late at night on 15 September 1990, three-year-old Courtney Smith was abducted from her Brooksville, Mississippi home where she shared a bedroom with her two sisters, aged six and one. Her twenty-six-year-old uncle was asleep in the next room when she disappeared. Her body was found two days later in a pond about eighty yards from her house. She had been sexually assaulted and murdered. As an ex-boyfriend of Courtney's mother, Brooks came under suspicion. After the coroner Steven Hayne said he found bitemarks on the girl, initially West took impressions of bitemarks from twelve men not including Brooks but including a Justin Albert Johnson, who had a history of rape. Johnson's ex-wife and son lived next door to Courtney. Ten days later the six-year-old sister identified Brooks as the man she saw take Courtney from the room. On 25 September West took a sample of Brooks's teeth at the local jail. Giving evidence at the subsequent trial he told the jury he had compared Brooks' sample with the marks on the victim's body and found that the marks of Brooks's two top front teeth 'matched' the marks on the child's body. Brooks was charged with capital murder and West gave evidence that 'it could be no one but Levon Brooks that bit this girl's arm'.

Brooks called an alibi to the effect that that he was working in a club on the night of the murder and the defence challenged both West's forensic credentials and findings but, after deliberating for about nine hours, the jury convicted Brooks of capital murder. He was sentenced to life in prison.

Three years after the kidnapping of Courtney and four months after Brooks was sentenced, another three-year-old girl from Brooksville, Christine Jackson, was abducted from her home at night, raped and killed. The facts were startlingly similar. Again the body was found in water, this time a creek.

Now the police focused on Kennedy Brewer, boyfriend of the child's mother. Again the coroner Dr Steven Hayne conducted the autopsy and said he found bitemarks on Christine's body. West, once more called to analyze the bitemarks, confirmed that the marks were from a human, and said that they were made by Brewer. Based on this evidence, Brewer was convicted in 1995 and he was sentenced to death.

Brewer's conviction was quashed in 2001 while he awaited execution after DNA testing organized by his lawyers, and the Innocence Project excluded him as the man who had left semen on the child's body. Nevertheless he was kept in prison until 2008 because the prosecutor said he wished to retry him. He was the first person in Mississippi to be exonerated through post-conviction DNA testing. Brooks was also released that year.

The DNA testing in both cases had matched Albert Johnson, who admitted abducting and killing both girls but denied biting them. He pleaded guilty and was sentenced to life in prison. Further investigation showed the bitemarks on both girls were more likely to have been made by crawfish and insects after their bodies were dumped in water.

When the recriminations began, West said that he never told jurors that Brooks and Brewer were the killers, only that they bit the children, and that he was not responsible for juries who found them guilty. He said that DNA had made bitemark analysis almost obsolete and that he no longer practised it. Coroner Hayne had been acting as a *de facto* chief medical examiner from the late 1980s because he was not board-qualified to take a permanent position. He said he had been performing between 1,200 and 1,800 autopsies a year for the state. After the conviction of Johnson, the State of Mississippi ceased to use him.

But the most egregious case of the dangers of odontology must be that of William Richards of San Bernadino, convicted of the murder of his wife Pamela, strangled and beaten with rocks on 10 August 1993. They appeared to be a perfectly happy couple and were building a home on their property, in the meantime living in a motorhome running their power from a generator. On the day of his wife's death Richards worked his usual night shift and he said when he returned home he found the generator was not working and the power was off. On his way to the generator he found his wife's half-naked body; she had been beaten to death with two stones. He telephoned the police and when they did not arrive immediately, telephoned twice more. Unfortunately in the dark the crime scene was not secured and dogs scuffed up the ground, spoiling footprints and blood evidence. No tests were carried out to determine how long Pamela Richards had been dead.

On the basis of a bitemark on her body Richards was charged with his wife's murder. He had no defensive injuries and made no confession. Two top forensic dentists Norman Sperber and Gregory Golden, certified by the American Board of Forensic Odontology, gave evidence during the trial. Sperber, who gave evidence for the prosecution, said that a suspected crescent-shaped bitemark on Pam Richards' body was consistent with a rare abnormality in her husband's teeth and that only about 2 per cent of the population had such teeth. Golden, giving evidence for Richards, said that he thought the bitemark evidence was inconclusive and should be disregarded. After two hung juries a third convicted him based on the bitemark. He was sentenced to life in prison.

Earlier, in a 1988 adulatory piece in the *Los Angeles Times*, Sperber was pointed up as being, 'A pioneer in bite-mark evidence, testifying in 56 felony cases since 1975. In the 48 cases in which Sperber testified for the prosecution, 46 ended in conviction. "I don't think I've made any mistakes," Sperber said.'

In 2001, the California Innocence Project filed a post-conviction DNA testing motion on Richards' behalf. The items to be tested included the murder weapons, several items at the house that were covered in blood, and the hairs found under Pamela's fingernails. The testing revealed that the DNA on the murder weapons and the hairs under Pamela's finger-nails belonged to neither of the Richardses. A blue fibre, which had been found at the autopsy under Pamela's fingernail, supposedly matching the shirt Richards was wearing that night, had supported Sperber's evidence. Now it was shown to be missing from photographs of her fingers before police moved her body from the crime scene to the morgue, leading to the possibility that the fibre was either planted there or the body had been contaminated.

As a result San Bernardino Superior Court Judge Brian McCarville granted Richards an evidentiary hearing beginning in January of 2009, at which the California Innocence Project challenged the state's evidence presented against him at his 1997 trial. The hearing took place over several days in the spring and summer months of that year. At the hearing Sperber accepted he had been wrong and that current bitemark science excluded Richards from making the mark. The Project also presented evidence that male DNA found on the two rocks used to beat Pam Richards did not match that of her husband.

Judge McCarville ruled that the totality of the evidence required the quashing of Richards' conviction:

> Taking the evidence as to the tuft fiber ... and the DNA and the bite mark evidence, the Court finds that the entire prosecution case has been undermined, and that [Richards] has established his burden of proof to show that the evidence before me points unerringly to innocence. Not only does the bite mark evidence appear to be questionable, it puts [Richards] as being excluded. And ... the DNA evidence establishes that someone other than [Richards] and the victim was at the crime scene.

Any celebration of the McCarville decision was short-lived. The district attorney appealed and the California Court of Appeal reversed the reversal. Next up was the California Supreme Court.

In December 2012 by a majority of five to four the Supreme Court upheld the conviction. The majority said that forensic evidence, even if later recanted, may be deemed false only in narrow circumstances. 'The falsity of the trial evidence must be proved,' Justice Joyce L. Kennard wrote on behalf of the majority of the judges. 'Otherwise, every criminal case becomes a never-ending battle of experts over subjective assertions that can never be conclusively determined one way or the other.'

The majority said Richards had failed to prove the original bitemark evidence was false because 'experts still could not definitively rule out petitioner's teeth as a possible source of the mark' during the 2009 hearing.

Justice Goodwin Liu disagreed. In a dissenting judgement she noted that three of four dental experts who testified at the 2009 hearing ruled out Richards as the source of the mark, and the fourth refused to give an opinion. As for the DNA on the stone, the genetic traces could have resulted from contamination during handling in the courtroom, said the majority of the judges.

This has left Richards with only the chance of a federal hearing. At the 2009 hearing he had been offered a plea bargain and had declined. However in March 2015 the justices of the high court unanimously decided to hear a new challenge by Richards.

According to the Innocence Project and the Associated Press, by 2013 at least twenty-four men convicted or arrested based largely on bitemark evidence have been exonerated by DNA testing, had charges dropped or otherwise been shown to be not guilty.

David Wayne Kunze; Mark Dallagher

The first time the vexed question of earprint evidence arose was in the mid-1960s when marks made by ears were used to solve a string of burglary cases in Switzerland. The chief proponent was Fritz Hirschi, a fingerprint expert, who maintained that the ear as a means of establishing the identity of its owner had been well known since the beginning of the century. Indeed Alphonse Bertillon, the French forensic scientist, had considered the ear to be the most distinctive part of the body. In identifying a suspect whose earmark was found on the entry door of a flat, Hirschi had undertaken some basic research comparing the mark with earprints taken from about fifty individuals. He found that no marks from these people were found to match both the mark and the print from the suspect.

Cornelis van der Lugt, a Dutch policeman without any scientific training, began his study of earprints in the late 1980s and by the end of the 1990s more police forces were taking note of the new quasi-science. In Britain, the National Training Centre for Scientific Support to Crime Investigation had collected 1,200 ear images on its database in County Durham and there was interest throughout Europe and in America.

In 1997 van der Lugt, by now an instructor at the Dutch National Police College in criminal investigations, was a prosecution witness in the first murder trial in which earprint evidence featured. Real estate appraiser David Wayne Kunze was tried for the murder of his ex-wife's fiancé, James W. McCann, beaten to death – his skull was smashed into twenty-six pieces – in his sleep at his Vancouver home in December 1994. McCann's twelve-year-old son, Tyler, was bound with duct tape and also severely beaten. He managed to crawl to the street where a passer-by found him.

Questioned at the hospital, Tyler told the police he had not had a good look at the attacker, but he described him as twenty-five to thirty-five years old, dark complexioned, about six feet tall, and of medium build.

Although he had red hair and did not fit Tyler's description of the killer, the police suspected Kunze, the forty-five-year-old former husband of the woman James McCann was about to marry. Kunze had already been arrested in a domestic violence incident when he was alleged to have smashed his ex-wife's car with a baseball bat.

When Kunze had learned of the forthcoming marriage four days before the murder, he had become upset and the detectives' theory was that he had attacked McCann and his son out of jealousy and rage. The intruder had stolen McCann's television set, VCR, stereo speakers and wallet, but the detectives thought this was the sign of a staged burglary by Kunze to throw them off the scent.

A Seattle Police Department criminal profiler told local authorities that whoever killed McCann had displayed a 'high level of emotion' in the crime and the killing was motivated by 'something personal'. In interviews with police shortly after the murder, Kunze denied any involvement, saying, 'I still have emotions for Diana, but I certainly wouldn't kill someone.'

In another example of a refusal to look for exculpatory evidence when the police believe they have the right man, and convinced that the scene had been staged to look like a burglary, no attempt was made to identify an intruder through the missing property. Kunze agreed to a search of his truck, boat, storage locker and safety deposit box but the police found nothing that connected him to the break-in and murder.

On 8 September 1995, a boater on the Columbia River discovered a packet of James McCann's credit cards half-buried on an island beach under the Interstate 205 bridge. Again, so far as the police were concerned this was another diversionary tactic by Kunze.

In the days after the murder, detectives had questioned Kunze for a total of twelve hours during which he accepted he was jealous of McCann. He also agreed that he had paid a private investigator $25 to trace the licence plate of McCann's truck to obtain his address and in the week of the murder had gone to the McCann home and peered into the garage. The reason, he said, was that he thought McCann was stalking him.

Kunze told officers he was alone on the night of the murder, painting in his garage, spending some time looking for his father in Vancouver-area motels and later buying cigarettes at a store near his home.

However, George Miller, a fingerprint examiner with the Washington State Crime Laboratory, had lifted a latent earprint from the surface of James McCann's bedroom door. The theory was that the killer had pressed his head against the door listening for signs of activity before entering the room. Miller examined the house for fingerprints as well but there were none that related to Kunze.

Now the police called in van der Lugt who claimed to have been involved in 600 earprint cases. He said the ear has fifteen distinct features, and no two ears are alike. He was 'a hundred per cent certain' that the earprint left on McCann's bedroom door belonged to Kunze. Backed by another earologist this was sufficient for an arrest for McCann's murder.

At the trial the defence argued that the earprint evidence should be excluded under the rule in the 1923 *Frye* case. In that case the court decided that a technique – in this instance of fingerprinting – had to be sufficiently scientifically accepted to be admitted in evidence.

Now the defence argued that earprinting was not sufficiently recognized. Alfred Iannarelli, former campus police chief at two Californian universities, describing himself as the world's only 'earologist', accepted in cross-examination that his twelve-point system for identifying individual ears, developed over his forty-year career, was unsanctioned by any law-enforcement or professional body. He had, however, written a book *Ear Identification*, published in California. It contained no bibliography and no scientific verification.

He was backed up by Michael Grubb, manager of the Washington State Patrol Laboratory in Seattle, who said he had examined between twenty-five and thirty people who might have been in McCann's home and another 100 prints taken randomly. Kunze's earprint was the only one that appeared to match the one on the door. Comparing an earmark to a known earprint was not unlike other forms of impression identification. A criminalist who specialized in bullet patterns and tool-mark identification, Grubb took the view that if patterns made by tyres, shoes, fingers, gun barrels and tools could be analyzed, it was just as possible to give an opinion on the source of an earmark.

For the defence Andre Moenssens, a former fingerprint expert in Belgium, now a law professor at the University of Missouri at Kansas City and the author of articles and law school texts on forensic science, gave evidence that:

> ... forensic sciences ... do not recognize, as a separate discipline, the identification of ear impressions. There are people in the forensic science community, the broader forensic science community, who feel that it can be done. But if we are talking about a general acceptance by scientists, there is no such general acceptance. To my knowledge, there has been no investigation in the possible rate of error that comparisons between known and unknown ear samples might produce.

Ten other forensic scientists also gave evidence that they did not regard earprinting as a true science. Nevertheless, to considerable surprise, the trial judge Robert Harris admitted the evidence. When it came to it the prosecution did not call Iannarelli and, for some reason, which has never been explained, the defence did not call the anti-earologists either.

Kunze was convicted and sentenced to life imprisonment

without parole. He hired a new attorney, John Henry Browne, who appealed the verdict and the state Court of Appeals rejected the argument that earprints are conclusive identifiers like fingerprints, remitting the case to Clark County Superior Court for a new trial. In overturning Kunze's conviction, the Appeals Court noted that the FBI did not use earprint identification, which it would 'surely do' if the practice was accepted as forensic science. It ruled that Harris should have restricted the earprint evidence to the fact that Kunze 'could not have been excluded as the maker' of the print.

The court also disagreed with Grubb's claim that earprint comparison was accepted in the scientific community: 'We reject his premise that latent ear prints automatically have the same degree of acceptance and reliability as fingerprints, tool marks, ballistics, handwriting and other diverse forms of impression evidence.'

In addition to the earprint evidence there had been the obligatory evidence from a jail snitch, Lawrence, that Kunze had confessed to him. Harris had restricted his cross-examination, refusing to allow the defence to ask Lawrence in detail about two Class A felonies – each of which was a first-degree child molestation – that he had lied under oath on welfare applications and lied, although not under oath, on several employment and rental applications. He had also lied to his wife about the child molestations. In 1990 Lawrence had also informed on another man accused of murder. Now he wanted to be enrolled in the Twin Rivers treatment program and to have supervised visits with his children. In response to the state's motion to limit cross-examination, Harris had ruled that Kunze could not show the exact nature of Lawrence's offences (the first-degree child molestation) or the unsworn lies. However, the Court of Appeal was not prepared to say the trial judge had erred in allowing only this limited cross-examination.

Preparing for the retrial of the case, John Henry Browne interviewed Lawrence under oath and discovered he had received several hundred dollars in witness fees for his evidence, but the prosecution had failed to disclose the payments to the defence as was required.

In May 2001 at the retrial Grubb was allowed to give evidence as to his comparison of Kunze's ear to the latent print, but was not allowed to give an opinion on whether there was a match.

Lawrence again testified that Kunze had confessed to him. However, ten days into the hearing, things got dirty when Browne called Dennis Hunter, one of the prosecutors at Kunze's first trial, to question him about the witness fees paid to Lawrence and to show that the payments had not been disclosed prior to the first trial. In an angry exchange with Browne, Hunter said in front of the jury that Browne had represented Kunze on appeal – showing the jury that Kunze had previously been convicted. The trial judge immediately declared a mistrial because of the improper comment and ordered another trial to begin almost at once.

After several jurors said that, had the case gone to them, they would have acquitted the defendant, the prosecution announced they would not seek a third trial. Kunze was released.

Meanwhile in England in 1999, in the first successful British prosecution of a defendant on the basis of an earprint, Mark Dallagher was convicted of murdering ninety-four-year-old Dorothy Wood in Huddersfield in May three years earlier. The prosecution had convinced the jury that earprints on a newly washed window on the transom above a door could only have been left by him as he listened for signs of movement inside the house. Imported from Holland for the trial, van der Lugt told the court he was 'absolutely convinced' that the prints were of Dallagher's ears. He was given some support by Professor Peter Vanezis, Regius Professor of Forensic Medicine and Science at the University of Glasgow. Both experts were satisfied that the earprints found at the scene matched the control prints provided by Dallagher, who lived not far away and who had committed a number of dwelling house burglaries, often effecting entry by means of a transom window.

Once again there was evidence from a prison snitch. In August 1996 Dallagher had been sentenced to imprisonment for burglary and shared a cell with prisoner X. According to X, Dallagher then told him about the killing, and in particular about the use of a pillow to suffocate Dorothy Wood, information that had not been made public. It was therefore the case for the prosecution that the earprint identification was supported by Dallagher's *modus operandi* and by what he revealed to X. When interviewed about the killing on 20 August 1996 he denied any involvement and said that he had been with his girlfriend Deborah Booth when the murder was committed, but that because she was asleep and on medication she would not be able to support his account.

Dallagher's counsel, David Hatton QC, had not tried to exclude the evidence of the prosecution experts, but he did submit, unsuccessfully, that the evidence of other burglaries should not be admitted. The experts were cross-examined, not on the basis that they had made any mistake in making their comparisons, but because such comparisons are necessarily imprecise, and cannot point with any certainty to an individual who has provided a control print as being the person responsible for a print found at the scene of a crime. No expert evidence was called on Dallagher's behalf. He received life imprisonment and Norman Sarsfield, of the Wakefield Crown Prosecution Service, described it as 'a great step forward for forensic science'.

The next month John Kennerley, Chief Fingerprint Officer with Lancashire police and the detective pioneering this new science, told the BBC, 'Essentially they're like fingerprints. Although they don't have the ridges, the cartilage and contours of every ear give it a unique shape.' He believed that police had detected about a hundred earprints in the past two years and hundreds more went unnoticed because officers, unaware of their importance, were not looking for them. Now van der Lugt became a witness on the international circuit.

By 2001 the tide had turned against earprint evidence after Professor Peter von Coppen, of Leiden University in Holland, published a paper saying, 'There has been no research done in which you can say, for instance, what the national distribution of lobes is, so you don't know if the earprint is one which would match 80 per cent of everyone else's or whether it has unique characteristics.'

Further research showed that, contrary to earlier belief, earprints are not unique to individuals as are fingerprints, and that an ear changes shape depending on the temperature or how hard it is being pressed to a surface. Sceptical non-scientists might have thought the latter to be self-evident.

Earprint evidence may now have been discredited both in Holland and America where the Kunze conviction had been overturned, but it was not until January 2004 that Mark Dallagher was freed in England. His appeal against his conviction was allowed in 2002 and after ten days of his retrial in June 2003 he was released on bail while the Crown Prosecution Service reviewed the evidence. On 22 January 2004 they accepted that a DNA profile showed the print belonged to another man. Sir Stephen Mitchell, the judge, said, 'this most unfortunate saga' was now at an end, adding, 'It was the most terrible killing and the centrepoint of the evidence was the earprint – scrutiny and examination of earprints was then in its infancy.'

But earprint evidence is not completely finished. In 2006 Cornelis van der Lugt published another article on the subject, and in May 2012 the German magazine *Der Spiegel* reported a case in which a burglar had been convicted of nearly 100 burglaries when he had pressed his ear on front doors. However, on this occasion there was also fingerprint and DNA evidence to back it up.

The Narborough Murders; Kirk Bloodsworth; John Kogut, Dennis Halstead and John Restivo; John Schneeberger

Even before DNA testing was used to convict anyone of murder or reverse a wrongful conviction it had prevented another potential miscarriage of justice.

It was in November 1984 that Sir Alec Jeffreys, the British geneticist, first publicly discussed the discovery of the genetic fingerprint and DNA profiling. In March the next year he published an article in which he claimed that the chances of two people having the same genetic print were for all practical purposes nil. But what was a genetic fingerprint?

Every human is made up of a vast number of different types of living cells. Inside the nucleus of every cell there is a string of coded information in the form of a ribbon-like molecule of deoxyribonucleic acid (DNA), which contains a genetic blueprint of that particular person's make-up. The amount of information contained in the codes is enormous. Each human cell contains a string of twenty-three pairs of chromosomes, each of which contains almost 100,000 genes and DNA chains. The complete human genetic code involves three billion base pairs controlling everything from height and build to the colour of the hair and eyes.

Humans share many basic characteristics and large sections of the genetic code are common to all individuals. But because everyone's DNA – except for twins – is unique, the coded information is as individual as a perfect set of fingerprints. Jeffreys claimed his DNA test could be used with any bodily fluid – semen, blood, saliva and even hair roots.

On 21 November 1984 a fifteen-year-old girl had left her home in The Coppice, Enderby, a small village in Leicestershire, to visit a friend. She did not return home that night, and around 7 a.m. the next morning a hospital porter discovered her body on a pathway in Narborough, two and a half miles away near the Carlton Hayes psychiatric hospital. There were traces of semen in her pubic hair and tests showed a high sperm count indicating that the killer was probably a young man. Results from the post-mortem two days later showed the offender was an A-group secretor, the same as 80 per cent of the population.

On 22 January 1985 a police officer, checking local sex offenders, called on the home of a young man who, with his wife and young child, had moved into the village some months earlier. The reason for the visit was that the man had had two convictions for indecent exposure before his marriage in 1981. At the time psychiatrists had said he would 'grow out of it' and there was no thought he might become violent. He told the police officer that on the night of the murder he had taken his wife to her evening class in sociology – she was hoping to become a probation officer – with their baby in a carrycot. He had returned home and had then gone out again to collect her. Although this was not a cast-iron alibi he was eliminated from the inquiry and by the summer of 1985 there were no really positive leads. A list of thirty possible suspects had been reduced to eight.

In October that year a sixteen-year-old hairdresser was attacked and forced to fellate a man in Narborough. The subsequent investigation came to nothing. Then on 31 July 1986 another girl left her local newsagents in Enderby, where she had a part-time job, to visit friends also in Narborough. The quickest route was along Ten Pound Lane near the M1 motorway. Her friends were out and she was last seen walking back towards the lane. At 9.30 that evening her parents telephoned the police to say she was missing. Two days later her body was found nearby. She had been raped and she also had semen in her pubic hair. It now seemed almost certain a local man was involved in all three attacks.

One of the men seen in the area was a kitchen porter who fitted a psychological profile of the killer. Better still, from the prosecution's point of view, he had a history of sexual disturbance and liked to talk about deviant sex. A former girlfriend said he was keen on rough and anal sex and that he spoke in disparaging terms about women generally. Arrested, he made a written confession showing some detailed knowledge of the second killing but it was wrong in other aspects. He said he had 'probably gone mad'. He was charged and remanded in custody.

When Alec Jeffreys was invited to test material from the youth and the semen samples found on the bodies of the girls, he said unequivocally that they did not match. Three months after his arrest the youth was released when no evidence was offered.

The young man with convictions for indecent exposure was Colin Pitchfork and when all young men in the town were invited to give DNA samples he had a friend tested in his name. The deception was discovered when the friend was overheard bragging about the test in a restaurant. Pitchfork was arrested for the two murders and received life imprisonment. His was the first murder conviction based on DNA evidence.

In America the judiciary was by no means convinced of the infallibility of DNA testing and in 1987 the trial judge refused to allow the 'experimental new' exculpatory DNA evidence in the case of Glen Woodall, charged with two rapes in West Virginia when two girls were abducted, raped and robbed. Their attacker wore a ski mask but both girls were able to say that, despite being forced to close their eyes, the man was uncircumcised, and they were able to give some information regarding his clothing. The prosecution's evidence included a partial identification by one of the victims, an identification of clothing taken from Woodall's house and an identification of a smell common to the perpetrator and Woodall's workplace. Additionally, conventional serology and hair comparisons could not exclude Woodall.

After his conviction, with the help of the Innocence Project, he continued to press for DNA testing in his appeals and finally spermatozoa found in the rape kits was tested. The samples matched each other, but excluded Woodall. The results were duplicated by another laboratory with the same results. Based on these results, Woodall was granted a new hearing and his conviction was vacated. He was placed on electronic monitoring while yet further advanced DNA tests were performed. The results eliminated both Woodall and three others, disproving the prosecution's theory that the samples could have been deposited by consensual partners. Finally the state then repeated the tests, with the same results. It then moved to dismiss the case, which the court granted in May 1992.

As the years have gone by more and more people have had their convictions overturned following improved taking and testing of DNA samples. One particularly egregious case is that of Kirk Bloodsworth.

On 25 July 1984 the body of nine-year-old Dawn Hamilton was found naked from the waist down in woodland near her Maryland home. She had been raped, beaten and killed. Two boys fishing in the area that morning told police they had seen her walking with a strange man. After a composite picture was publicized, a caller, ringing the police hotline, suggested that police check out former marine and discus champion Kirk Bloodsworth, who had recently moved up from Cambridge in an effort to save his failing marriage.

He was arrested and, at the trial in March 1985, the prosecution's case was based on first, the anonymous caller, while another witness identified Bloodsworth from a police sketch compiled by five witnesses who gave evidence that they had seen Bloodsworth with the little girl. Bloodsworth had also told acquaintances he had done something 'terrible' that day that would affect his marriage. In his first police interrogation, he mentioned a 'bloody rock', though no weapons were known of at the time. Evidence was given that an impression found near the victim's body was made by a shoe that matched Bloodsworth's size.

Convicted and sentenced to death, Bloodsworth appealed on the grounds that he mentioned the bloody rock because the police had one on the table next to him while they questioned him; the terrible thing mentioned to friends was that he had failed to buy his wife a taco salad as he had promised, so further endangering their already fragile relationship; and the police had withheld information relating to the possibility of another suspect. His sentence was overturned in 1987 and a retrial was ordered. At the retrial he was convicted again and this time was given two life sentences without parole. His appeal was dismissed.

Bloodsworth's lawyer now pressed to have the evidence released for more sophisticated testing than had been available at the time of trial. Initially, the available evidence in the case – traces of semen in the victim's underwear – was thought to have been destroyed. However it was eventually located in a paper bag in the judge's chambers. The prosecution agreed, and in April 1992 the victim's pants and shorts together with a stick found near the murder scene, reference blood samples from Bloodsworth and the victim, and an autopsy slide were sent to Forensic Science Associates (FSA) for polymerase chain reaction (PCR) testing.

The testers in the FSA report of 17 May 1993 found that semen on the autopsy slide was insufficient for testing but that a small semen stain had been found on the underwear. They concluded that Bloodsworth's DNA did not match any of the evidence received for testing but asked for a fresh sample of Bloodsworth's blood for retesting because of doubts about proper labelling on the original sample. On 3 June the FSA issued a second report that Bloodsworth could not be responsible for the stain on the victim's underwear.

On 25 June the FBI conducted its own test of the evidence, which produced the same results as those of the FSA. In Maryland, new evidence can be presented no later than one year after the final appeal so the prosecution joined a petition with Bloodsworth's attorneys to grant him a pardon. He was released from prison on 28 June and Maryland's governor pardoned him in December 1993. He had served almost nine years including two years on death row. His was the first DNA exoneration in America of someone who had been on death row.

On 28 August, nineteen years to the day after Kimberley Shay Ruffner was arrested after trying to rape a young woman in the Fells Point area of Baltimore, state police reported that they had found a positive match for Dawn Hamilton's killer. A month after her 1984 murder, Ruffner had been sentenced to forty-five years for the unrelated burglary, attempted rape and assault with intent to murder, and had, coincidentally, been in the same prison one floor below Bloodsworth's cell.

On 5 September 2003 Ruffner was formally charged with Dawn's murder. He pleaded guilty and in May 2004 was sentenced to life imprisonment. According to court records, Ruffner had been acquitted of rape twelve days before Dawn's death. In prison the two men had lifted weights together and Bloodsworth delivered books to Ruffner's cell in his job as a prison librarian. He has subsequently said Ruffner knew about his case, his attempts to win a new trial and his claims of innocence.

The State of Maryland later paid Bloodsworth $300,000 compensation, which worked out at $92.39 for each day of his wrongful imprisonment. It was in sharp contrast to the $21 million a Chicago jury awarded Juan Johnson, a former Spanish Cobras gang member who had been wrongly convicted of murdering a Latin Eagle in a fight at North and Western Avenue, Chicago.

At 9.45 p.m. on 10 November 1984, sixteen-year-old Theresa Fusco left her part-time job at Hot Skates, a Lynbrook, Long Island roller-skating rink. She was never seen alive again and on 10 December her naked body was found, buried under leaves in a wooded area near the rink.

She had died as a result of ligature strangulation. Vaginal swabs showed semen and spermatozoa were present but serology tests necessary to determine the semen donor's blood type were never performed.

The murder of a young girl brings additional pressure to a police investigation and it was no different for the Nassau

County Police Department, which was under enormous pressure to solve this crime, particularly since there had been several disappearances of other young girls in the area in recent years. Fifteen-year-old Kelly Morrissey, a friend of Theresa's, had disappeared in June 1984, when she was last seen heading for a video game arcade, and in March 1985 nineteen-year-old Jacqueline Martarella, whose body was later found, disappeared in Oceanside. Neither case has been solved. John Kogut, Dennis Halstead and John Restivo were all initially interrogated as part of an investigation into the disappearance of Kelly Morrissey, before the police changed their focus to Theresa Fusco's rape and murder. John Kogut had occasionally dated Kelly and all the men knew each other, working from time to time for Halstead's father. Kelly and her friends would visit Halstead's flat.

After three polygraph examinations, detectives began to focus on Kogut as a suspect for Theresa's murder but even after he was told he failed the polygraph test, he continued to maintain his innocence. After nearly eighteen hours of interrogation, however, the police produced a confession from him. It was handwritten by the interrogating officer for Kogut's signature, allegedly after five other versions of the confession that were never transcribed. Kogut was then taken to the crime scene. He could not point out to the police any evidence missing from the crime scene such as the victim's clothes and he was not in possession of any of Theresa's jewellery The next day, the confession was recorded on videotape. It contained no details that were not previously known by the detectives. According to it, they were all in Restivo's van when they offered the girl a lift. When she asked to be let out of the van, she was stripped, and raped by Halstead and Restivo. They drove to a cemetery, where she was taken out of the van and Halstead and Restivo persuaded Kogut to strangle her with a piece of rope. Her body was then rolled into a blanket and dumped near the roller rink. Based on Kogut's alleged confession, Restivo's van was searched, and several hairs were recovered and tested forensically. Despite Kogut's immediate retraction of his confession, all three men were charged with rape and murder.

Kogut was tried first, and Restivo and Halstead tried together after him. At Kogut's trial, the prosecution argued that the hairs found in Restivo's van provided corroboration of the alleged confession. There was also evidence from jailhouse snitches to say the trio had told them all about the killing.

It was the analysis of the hairs that counted against them. Despite the fact that hair sample matching is no longer regarded as an exact science, the prosecution's expert witness gave evidence that two hairs found in the front passenger seat were microscopically similar to those of the victim, telling the jury, 'In this particular instance the questioned hair could have originated from the scalp of Theresa Fusco, with a high degree of probability.'

All three men denied having anything to do with the crime and offered separate alibi defences. Kogut was convicted in May 1986 and sentenced to thirty one and a half years to life. Restivo and Halstead were convicted in November that year and sentenced to thirty-three and a third years to life.

After the men's appeals were dismissed in the early 1990s they contacted the Centurion Ministries in Princeton, New Jersey, which represents people wrongly convicted of crimes, and they took on the case. In turn the Innocence Project became involved.

DNA tests were conducted, comparing semen taken from Theresa's body and preserved on a slide, with the DNA of the three men. Two of the tests eliminated all three men as sources of the semen but one test did not exclude all three, so a judge ruled that the results could not be trusted.

Then in the early years of this century the slide was analyzed once more, this time using a more advanced DNA technique known as Short Tandem Repeat. That test indicated that the DNA belonged to a man other than the three in prison. In 2003 their lawyers made a crucial discovery, that of a previously untested vaginal swab, which the defence had not known to exist. The swab showed a DNA profile identical to the one lifted from the slide.

The charges against Halstead and Restivo were dismissed in 2005. Kogut was again put on trial and was discharged when, in a bench trial, the judge dismissed the case against him, finding that much of the confession was contradicted by DNA and other forensic evidence, and that the hairs in Restivo's van were not Theresa's.

Restivo and Halstead began civil actions against Nassau County and in April 2014 in a federal civil rights lawsuit they were each awarded $18 million, the equivalent of $1 million for every year they had spent in prison. The verdict followed a four-week trial and the jury found that the lead detective in the police investigation, Joseph Volpe, who had died in the meantime, had both planted hair evidence and hidden other evidence from prosecutors.

Nick Brustin, one of the lawyers representing Restivo and Halstead, said the jury's verdict showed his clients were the victims of intentional misconduct by Nassau County detectives:

> When a promising initial lead reached a dead end, Volpe, desperate to solve this high profile crime, planted hairs from the victim's head in John Restivo's van, and deliberately hid evidence that proved their innocence . . . Today a jury finally acknowledged what the County never has – that its own officers' intentional misconduct robbed these innocent men of eighteen years of their lives.

The plus side of DNA testing is incalculable, but it was not long before someone discovered a way to get round a test, and who better than a doctor? South African Dr John Schneeberger successfully defeated DNA testing for some years after he had drugged and raped a patient while working in Kipling, Saskatchewan, where he practised at the medical centre. The well-liked and respected Schneeberger was born in Zambia and trained at Stellenbosch University in South Africa before moving to Canada in 1987. He married the divorced Lisa Dillman and had two daughters with her. In 1993 he acquired Canadian citizenship.

On the night of 31 October 1992, using Versed, which has a strong amnesic effect, Schneeberger sedated a twenty-three-year-old patient, Candice, and raped her. The girl was, however, still able to remember the rape and reported the attack to the police.

On testing, Schneeberger's blood sample was found not to match the samples of the rapist's semen and he was cleared of suspicion. A repeat test the following year again proved negative and so far as the prosecution was concerned the case was closed.

Candice, still convinced that her recollections were true, hired Larry O'Brien, a private detective, to investigate the case. He broke into Schneeberger's car and obtained another sample for DNA testing, which this time matched the semen on Candice's underwear. As a result, a third official test was organized. Now, however, the sample from the underwear was found to be too small and of too poor quality to be useful for analysis.

In 1997, Schneeberger's wife discovered that her husband had repeatedly drugged and raped her fifteen-year-old daughter from her first marriage. She reported the matter to the police and when a fourth DNA test was made, this time multiple samples were taken from Schneeberger – blood, mouth swab and hair follicle. All three matched Candice's rapist's semen.

Schneeberger's method of defeating the earlier tests had been very simple and not dissimilar from the way in which athletes can defeat a drugs test. He had inserted a soft rubber tube, filled with blood stolen from a patient and anticoagulants, in his arm and persuaded the laboratory technician to take the blood sample from the place where the tube was planted. In 1999 he was found guilty of sexual assault, of administering a noxious substance and of obstruction of justice. He was sentenced to six years.

While in prison, Schneeberger demanded visiting rights with his two daughters and, when his wife refused, he obtained a court order in his favour. When she again refused to comply she was fined $2,000. She appealed the decision to a higher court, but lost again in 2001 when the judge told her she must take her daughters to the prison, saying there was no proof that the girls would be harmed by the visits.

Lisa Schneeberger duly took her two sobbing, hysterical girls to the prison where a court-appointed social worker intervened and allowed her to take them home. Schneeberger finally stopped demanding to see them. In 2003 he was released on parole after serving four years in prison and deported to South Africa.

CHAPTER 14

The Future

How can miscarriages of justice be eliminated? The simple answer is that, like war and corruption, they cannot be. All that can be done is to limit the damage as far as possible.

And how can that be achieved? Identification evidence will always be suspect. Time and again it has been shown that when the police fasten on a suspect they become blind to the possibility that they may have the wrong person. Exculpatory evidence will be ignored and, in the worst scenario, evidence will be planted, confessions fabricated and members of the public induced to give false evidence. To eliminate this, prosecutors, judges and magistrates will have to adopt a stricter view towards police evidence. Given the American system of elected district attorneys and judges this is likely to prove particularly difficult in the United States.

A failure to check credentials of forensic experts both in and out of court has been around a long, long time and in England one man who railed against the expert for hire was the highly respected Zakaria Erzinçlioglu, known as Dr Zak. In 1984, as an employee of the Field Studies Council, he moved to Cambridge University where he worked in the zoology department. He was then funded by the Home Office to undertake research in forensic entomology. In 1993 the House of Lords select committee on science and technology said that a new and independent forensic science research centre was needed. One was duly established at Durham University with Dr Zak installed as its first director. It lasted six months before lack of funds forced its closure. He returned to Cambridge as an affiliated researcher at the department of zoology, continuing to do case work for the police.

In 1997, however, he announced that, in future, he would only carry out forensic work if paid by the judiciary. Explaining his decision in an article in *Nature* in 1998, Erzinçlioglu claimed that incompetent and dishonest forensic scientists were undermining Britain's criminal justice system. The government's decision to make the forensic science service an agency of the Home Office, he argued, had led to the development of an unregulated market in which lawyers acting for one side or the other in criminal trials could effectively buy the evidence most favourable to their cause. 'The scientific specialist is not looked upon kindly if his findings fail to satisfy the preconceived notions of those who consult him.'

Erzinçlioglu recommended that a fully staffed statutory body should be set up, answerable solely to the judiciary and not dependent on the 'goodwill' of its customers.

In Britain and also Australia there has been a disturbing increase in conducting criminal trials with suppression orders in force to prevent the press from reporting names of witnesses, defendants and even the results of the trial. In Australia these suppression orders may run literally for years on end. All too often the phrase, 'who cannot be named for legal reasons' appears in the newspapers. In London in November 2014 the jury in a terror trial was discharged after four days of deliberations without returning a verdict. A suppression order prevents the public from knowing why or what evidence was heard. At one time it had been intended to hold the whole trial in camera, but after applications by the press two-thirds of it was heard in secret and, of the other one-third, the ten journalists allowed into court were banned from reporting what they had heard. One safeguard against miscarriages of justice is that it is seen and heard by public and press alike, but all too often this is now no longer the case.

Those who watch crime documentaries and serials on television may be forgiven for thinking that DNA testing has effectively eliminated the potential for miscarriages of justice.

Sadly, they are wrong. Certainly DNA more than anything else has been responsible for correcting miscarriages, but with every silver lining there is a cloud and, as DNA testing has become more and more sophisticated and results can be obtained from the most minute of samples, one such cloud hovers over this forensic paradise. In the spring of 2014 the English scientist Professor Peter Gill said that the courts were being given subjective summaries of complex DNA evidence rather than direct access to solid statistics. These, he said, presented a 'significant risk' of juries being misled as to the actual strength of the prosecution case.

As with police misconduct there is a tendency to say of miscarriages of justice, 'But that was in another country, and besides, the wench is dead.'

Shortly before Christmas 2014 a South Carolina court overturned the conviction of the black boy George Stinney Jnr who, in 1944, had been electrocuted for the murder of two young white girls. Stinney, then fourteen, was arrested, convicted and executed in a three-month period after the bodies of the girls were found in a ditch behind a church in the small mill town of Alcolu. They had been battered to death with an iron spike.

At five foot one and weighing only 90 lbs Stinney, who was interviewed without a lawyer, was too small for the electric chair and had to sit on a telephone directory – other reports say a bible – to enable his electrocution to take place.

However, Circuit Court Judge Carmen T. Mullen did not deal with the question of Stinney's guilt or innocence, but whether the case could be reversed according to the rarely used legal principle of *oram nobis*, employed to correct judicial errors 'of the most fundamental character' when 'no other remedy' is available.

She found that Stinney's attorney had done 'little or nothing' in his defence. The entire case consisted of a confession, obtained by the police, which a psychiatrist who examined it thought was 'coerced, compliant, false'. There was supposedly supporting evidence from a cellmate; no physical evidence linked the boy to the crime. A man from a wealthy white family later made a confession.

Sixty years after Stinney's death, shortly before Christmas 2014, ten-year-old Tristen Kurilla was being detained in an adult prison in Pennsylvania. He has been accused of the killing of a ninety-year-old woman at his grandfather's Honesdale, Pennsylvania home on 11 October. As was the case with Stinney, much of the evidence against him is his own 'confession', made to a state trooper after the boy allegedly waived his right to an attorney.

Perhaps a more apposite person to quote is George Santayana who wrote, 'Those who cannot remember the past are condemned to repeat it.'

Select Bibliography

Introduction

John Mortimer, *Famous Trials*, Penguin, Harmondsworth, 1984.

Paul Wilson, 'Miscarriages of Justice in Serious Cases in Australia' in Kerry Carrington (ed), *Travesty! Miscarriages of Justice*, Pluto Press, Sydney, 1991.

1. No Bodies

Nat Arch: Assi 84/170; 94/48; *R v Onufrejczyk*.

Edwin M Borchard, *Convicting The Innocent : SIXTY-FIVE ACTUAL ERRORS OF CRIMINAL JUSTICE*, Garden City Publishing Company, Inc. New York, 1932.

Paula Doneman, *Things a Killer Would Know: The True Story of Leonard Fraser*, Allen & Unwin, Crow's Nest, NSW, 2006.

Victor Hervé, *Justice pour Seznec*, Editions Hervé, Paris, 1933.

Gerald M. McFarland, *The Counterfeit Man/The True Story of the Boorn–Colvin Murder Case*, University of Massachusetts Press, Mass., 1990.

Sherman R. Moulton, *The Boorn Mystery/An Episode from the Judicial Annals of Vermont*, Vermont Historical Society, Vermont, 1937.

Sir Thomas Overbury, 'A true and perfect account of the examination, trial, condemnation and execution of Joan Perry and her two sons, John and Richard Perry, for the supposed murder of Will. Harrison gent', *Hereford Times*, 1963.

Linda Stratman, *Gloucestershire Murders*, The History Press, Stroud, 2013.

John Spargo, *The Return of Russell Colvin*, Historical Museum and Art Gallery of Bennington, Vermont, 1945.

2. Folk Devils and Moral Panics

Damien Wayne Echols and Charles Jason Baldwin v. State of Arkansas 326 Ark. 917, 936 S.W.2d 509.

North Carolina v. Alford, 400 U.S. 25 (1970).

Aleaume Cachemarée, *Registre Criminel du Châtelet de Paris du 6 September 1389 au 18 Mai 1392*, Societé des Bibliophiles Français, Paris, 1861.

Anne Commire (ed), *Women in World History, a Biographical Encyclopaedia*, Yorkin Pub., Detroit, 2002.

Malcolm Gaskill, *Hellish Nell: Last of Britain's Witches*, Fourth Estate, 2001.

Charles Mackay, *Memoirs of Extraordinary Popular Delusions and the Madness of Crowds*, Office of the National Illustrated Library, London, 1848.

Mara Leveritt, *Devil's Knot: The True Story of the West Memphis Three*, Atria Books, New York, 2002.

Brian McConnell, *The Possessed*, Headline, London, 1995.

Helena Normanton, *The Trial of Mrs Duncan*, Jarrolds, London, 1945.

Robert Rapley, *A Case of Witchcraft: The Trial of Urbain Grandier*, McGill-Queen's University Press, Montreal, 1998.

Bryan H. Ward, 'A Plea Best Not Taken: Why Criminal Defendants Should Avoid the Alford Plea', *Missouri Law Review* 68: 913, 2003.

3. The Road to the Court of Appeal

Nat Arch: HO 144/23/60198 [Habron]; HO 144/985/112737-51 to 130. [Edalji].

[Anon] *Did Peace Commit the Whalley Range Murder?* Manchester, 1879.

Arthur Conan Doyle, (eds Richard and Molly Whittington-Egan) *The Story of Mr George Edalji*, Grey House, London, 1985.

Peter Costello, *Conan Doyle, Detective*, Constable & Robinson, London, 2006.

Sir John Hall (Ed), *The trial of Adelaide Bartlett*, William Hodge, Edinburgh, 1927.

Edward Hancock, *William Habron's Doom of the Gallows*, W. Sutton, London, 1879.

Brian Lane, *The Murder Club Guide to North-West England*, Harrap, London, 1988.

Roger Oldfield, *Outrage: The Edalji Five and the Shadow of Sherlock Holmes*, Vanguard Press, Cambridge, 2010.

Bernard Ryan, *The Poisoned Life of Florence Maybrick*, Penguin Books, Harmondsworth, Middlesex, 1977.

Derek Walker-Smith, *The Life of Sir Edward Clarke*, Thornton Butterworth, London, 1939.

Katherine D. Watson, *Poisoned Lives, English Poisoners and Their Victims*, Hambledon Continuum, London, 2004.
Gordon Weaver, *Conan Doyle and the Parson's Son*, Vanguard Press, Cambridge, 2006.

4. Poison Pen

MEP0 3/380; HO 144/2452 [Gooding].
Douglas Browne, *Sir Travers Humphreys*, Harrap & Co, London, 1960.
G L DuCann, *Miscarriages of Justice*, Frederick Muller, London, 1960.

5. Mistaken Identity

Nat.Arch. PCom 7/181 [Beck].
State v. Conforti, 53 N.J. 239 (1969).
Rubin Carter and John Artis v. John J. Rafferty, Superintendent, Rahway State Prison and others, (and linked cases). 826 F.2d 1299 (1987).
Joseph Beltrami, *A Deadly Innocence: the Meehan File*, Mainstream, Edinburgh, 1989.
Henry Cecil, *The Trial of Walter Rowland*, David & Charles, Devon, 1975.
Sam Chaiton and Terry Swinton, *Lazarus and the Hurricane*, St Martin's Griffin, New York, 2000.
Tim Coates, *The Strange Case of Adolf Beck*, Stationery Office, London, 1999.
Rubin Carter, *Eye of the Hurricane: My Path from Darkness to Freedom*, Lawrence Hill Books, Chicago, 2011.
James S. Hirsch, *Hurricane*, Fourth Estate, London, 2000.
Brian Lane, *The Murder Club Guide to North-West England*, Harrap, London, 1988.
R. T. Paget and S. Silverman, *Hanged – and Innocent?*, Gollancz, London, 1953.
The Revd Jevon Perry, *The Edlingham Burglary, or Circumstantial Evidence*, Sampson Low, London, 1889.
Jurgen Thorwald, *The Marks of Cain*, Thames and Hudson, London, 1965.
Eric R. Watson, *The Trial of Adolf Beck*, Notable British Trials series, William Hodge and Company, Edinburgh, 1924.
Bob Woffinden, *Miscarriages of Justice*, Hodder & Stoughton. London, 1987.

6. Race Hate

Brown v Mississippi, 287 US 56 (1932).
Powell v. State, 1932, 141 So. 201, 209.

R. C. Cortner, *A 'Scottsboro' Case in Mississippi: The Supreme Court and Brown v. Mississippi*, University of Mississippi Press, Jackson, 1986.

James Goodman, *Stories of Scottsboro*, Pantheon Books, New York, 1994.

Neil R. McMillen, *Dark Journey: Black Mississippians in the Age of Jim Crow*, University of Illinois Press, Champaign, 1990.

Quentin Reynolds, *Courtroom*, Victor Gollancz, London, 1951.

7. Incompetent Lawyers

Boodran v. The State (Trinidad and Tobago) [2001] UKPC 20.

James Morton, *Gangland: The Lawyers*, Virgin, London, 2001.

8. The Power of the Press

People v. Majczek, 360 Ill. 261 (1935).

Scotti Cohn, *It Happened in Chicago*, Globe Pequot, Chicago, 2009.

Rob Warden, *JOSEPH M. MAJCZEK*, Northwestern Law, Bluhm Legal Clinic Center on Wrongful Convictions.

Cynthia Cooper, Samuel Reese Sheppard, *Mockery of Justice*, Northeastern University Press, Chicago, 1995.

James Neff, *The Wrong Man*, Random House, New York, 2001.

9. Three Who Got Away

J. D. Casswell, *A Lance for Liberty*, Harrap, London, 1961.

Sandra Hempel, *The Inheritor's Powder: A Cautionary Tale of Poison, Betrayal and Greed*, Weidenfeld & Nicolson, London, 2013.

James Marsh, 'Account of a method of separating small quantities of arsenic from substances with which it may be mixed', *Edinburgh New Philosophical Journal 21*, 1836.

Andrew Rose, *Lethal Witness*, Sutton, Stroud, 2007.

Keith Simpson, *Forty Years of Murder*, Panther Books, London, 1980.

10. Fit-ups and False Confessions

William Adler, *The Man Who Never Died: The Life, Times and Legacy of Joe Hill, American Labor Icon*, Bloomsbury Publishing, New York, 2012.

Denis Bon, *L'Affaire Dreyfus*, Grand Procès Poche, Paris, 2006.

Chris Birt, *The Final Chapter*, Stentorian Publishing, Taupo, 2012.

T. C. Brennan, *The Gun Alley Tragedy*, Gordon & Gotch, Melbourne, 1923.

Frederick Brown, *Zola, A Life*, Macmillan, London, 1996.

Antonio Buti, *Brothers: Justice, Corruption and the Mickelbergs*, Fremantle Press, Fremantle, 2011.

Steven Chernack and Frankie M. Bailey (eds), *Crimes and Trials of the Century*, Greenwood, London, 2007.

Alan Downer, *Crime Chemist: The Life Story of Charles Anthony Taylor, Scientist for the Crown*, John Long, London, 1965.

Curt Gentry, *Frame-up: The Incredible Case of Tom Mooney and Warren Billings*, W. W. Norton & Co., New York, 1967.

David P. H. Jones, QC, 'Report by Independent Counsel appointed to oversee review by New Zealand Police into the Crewe Homicides', 30 July 2014.

Avon Lovell, *The Mickelberg Stitch*, Creative Research, Perth, 1985.

Michael Meeropol, *The Rosenberg Letters*, Garland, New York, 1994.

Kevin Morgan, *Gun Alley*, Hardie Grant, Melbourne, 2012.

National Mooney-Billings Committee, *The Story of Mooney and Billings*, San Francisco, 1929.

New Zealand Police, *Crewe Homicide Investigation Review*, July 2014.

Maurice Paleologue, *My Secret Diary of the Dreyfus Case*, Secker and Warburg, London, 1957.

John C. Ralston, *Fremont Older and the 1916 San Francisco Bombing. A Tireless Crusade for Justice*, The History Press, Charleston, 2013.

Patrick Renshaw, *The Wobblies*, Eyre & Spottiswood, London, 1967.

Jonathan Root, *The Betrayers*, Secker & Warburg, London, 1964.

Satish Sekar, *Fitted In: The Cardiff 3 and the Lynette White Inquiry*, The Fitted In Project, London, 1997.

—*The Cardiff Five: Innocent Beyond Any Doubt*, Waterside Press, Hook, 2012.

Francis Wellman, *The Art of Cross-Examination*, Macmillan, New York, 1928.

John Williams, *Bloody Valentine*, HarperCollins, London 1994.

11. The Road to Abolition

Robert Hancock, *Ruth Ellis*, Arthur Barker, London, 1963.

John Parris, *Most of My Murders*, Frederick Muller, London, 1960.

—*Scapegoat*, Duckworth, London, 1991.

David Yallop, *To Encourage the Others*, Constable, London, 2014.

12/13. Expert Evidence?/False Forensics?

Randall Adams with ors, *Adams v Texas*, St Martins Press, New York, 1991.

Michael Baden and Marion Roach, *Dead Reckoning*, Arrow Books, London, 2002.

Colin Evans, *A Question of Evidence: Great Forensic Controversies from Napoleon to O.J.*, John Wiley, London, 2003.

——*Murder Two, The Second Casebook of Forensic Detection*, John Wiley & Sons, Hoboken, NJ, 2004.

Zac Erzinçlioglu, *Every Contact Leaves a Trace*, London, Carlton Books, 2000.

——*Maggots, Murders and Men*, St Martin's Press, New York, 2000.

Jim Fisher, *Forensics Under Fire: Are Bad Science and Duelling Experts Corrupting Criminal Justice?*, Rutgers University Press, New Jersey, 2008.

Felix Frankfurter, *The Case of Sacco and Vanzetti: A Critical Analysis for Lawyers and Laymen*, Little Brown, Boston, 1927.

Michael Heap in M. Nash and A. Barnier (eds), *Oxford Handbook of Hypnosis*, OUP, Oxford, 2008.

——*Hypnosis: Current Clinical, Experimental and Forensic Practices*, Croom Helm, London, 1988.

Amanda Lee Myers, 'Men wrongly convicted or arrested on bite evidence', *Associated Press*, 16 June 2013.

Jim Rix, *Jingle Jangle The Perfect Crime Turned Inside Out*, Broken Bench Press, 2007.

James E. Starrs, 'Once More Unto the Breech: The Firearms Evidence in the Sacco and Vanzetti Case Revisited,' *Journal of Forensic Sciences* (April 1986): 630-654; (July 1986): 1050–1078.

William A. Woodruff, J. D., 'The Admissibility of Expert Testimony in North Carolina After Howerton: Reconciling the Ruling with the Rules of Evidence,' *Campbell Law Review, Volume 28*, Fall 2005, Number 1.